Treasured Memories of a Sandhills Girl

Memories of my life from the Sandhills of Nebraska to Southern Africa

By Grace Eva Cheney-Reeves

Grace Eva Cheney-Reeves

Treasured Memories of a Sandhills Girl

© 2017 by Grace Eva Cheney-Reeves

ISBN-13:
978-1548406158

ISBN-10:
1548406155

TABLE OF CONTENTS

Chapter Fourteen
Closing Chapter Ending With Third Trip To Africa

My Testimony

All the way through my life God has been my Saviour and Lord, and my Help and Strength. I have never been sorry I chose to follow Jesus. He has been my Guide through Joy and Sorrow and given me a peace in my heart that nothing in this world can give. I praise God with all my heart and soul and give to Him the honor and Glory forever.

YOU TOO CAN HAVE THIS KIND OF TESTIMONY:
If you do not have this kind of relationship with God, you too can know Him personally. You can know that you are ready to meet God and be with Him in heaven for eternity. Remember God loved you so much that He sent Jesus to die on the cross for your sins and to take the punishment you deserved.
This is what you need to do:
1. God – God is Holy. He cannot look on sin but He wants to save you from eternal death. John 3: 16 says: "For God so Loved the world (that includes you) that He gave His one and only Son, Jesus , that whoever believes in Him should not perish but have everlasting life."
2. You—Recognize that you are a sinner—Romans 3:23 "For all have sinned and come short of the Glory of God." Acknowledge that you are a sinner and make this confession to God. Romans 10:9"If you will confess with your mouth the Lord Jesus and believe in your heart that God has raised Him from the dead, you will be saved."
3. Jesus Christ—Believe in Jesus who died for our sins on the cross, He took our punishment. Acts 16:31 "... Believe on the Lord Jesus Christ, and you shall be saved..."
4. Faith—You need to have Faith and believe in Jesus. Ephesians 2:8-9 "For by grace you are saved through faith and that not of yourselves: it is the gift of God. Not of works lest any man should boast". And so we must believe in what Jesus has done for us. We cannot do anything in ourselves to earn our way to heaven. It is only by believing in what Jesus did for us on the cross.
5. Works—But God does want us to do good works even though we aren't saved by good works. James 2:18-26

Never forget God Loves you and has a special place just for you to fill. If you are unsure how to pray you can pray these words and if you really mean them in your heart God will make you His child and give you eternal life forever.
Prayer: "Jesus Christ, thank you for dying on the cross for my sins. I confess those things in my life that are not right and do not please you. I ask you to

forgive me and make my life clean. In the best way I know how, I open up my life before you for I know you see all things even the hidden things in my life. I trust you by faith as my Saviour and Lord. Please control my life. Change me from the inside and outside. Help me to be the type of person you want me to be. Thank you for coming into my life as I believe and have faith in Jesus. I pray this all in the name of Jesus Christ, now the Saviour and Lord of my life. Amen"

Now to help you live for God and do what is right, read the Bible everyday and pray to Jesus. He's your friend and Saviour now, so talk to Him often. He hears you when you call on him. And God talks to you through His Word the Bible. Start with reading the Gospel of St. John in the New Testament. Ask Jesus to open up your understanding of the Bible.

Chapter One
Early Years 1936 – 1969

My life journey begins May 12th about 8:30 on Thursday evening in 1936. Earlier in the day my mother and dad were at Grandpa and Grandma French's in the sandhills about five miles north of Racket, Nebraska. It was a beautiful spring and sunny day. Dad was doing some mechanical work on the car. My mother had started labor earlier in the day. About 4:00 p.m. Grandma Alice French came out of the house and told my dad, "We have to go now." So Grandma, Mom and Dad headed for Lewellen to meet Dr. Blackstone.

I guess I decided to come quicker than they expected and when they realized they weren't going to make it to Lewellen, they stopped at the Mennonite Brethren in Christ Church where Orpha Reader, the pastor, was living in the parsonage in the church basement. I was born in the northwest bedroom with my grandmother, Alice French, attending the birth. She did do quite a few births in the area. I guess you would say she was a midwife of that day. I seemed to be a healthy baby and all went well. I was told they took me to church the first time when I was eight days old. (The pastor that married Mom and Dad the year before on May 19, 1935 was Clayton Severn. He and Orpha Reader married in August, 1936.)

Sometime later Aunt Chrystal told me my dad very solemnly stopped by the school where she taught(I think it was the Box A School south of Racket) and told her that he had a baby daughter and that they had named me Grace Eva. Dad told me he took Mom a bouquet of lilacs. They were in full bloom that year. Maybe that is why I love lilacs so much.

Mother told me that the first year I was a baby was quite difficult. But, she also said Daddy, she and their baby daughter were very healthy, although they mainly had only potatoes and tomatoes to eat. This was coming to the end of the depression years and people were getting back on their feet from the 1929Depression. Everyone was facing hard times even several years later.

Going to Church as a Baby/ My Dedication

Rebecca Mecham, my mother's cousin that was raised with her, told me this, "It was hard times and your mother and daddy didn't have a lot. However, they tried their best to go to the Racket church every Sunday." It was probably around eight miles west and north of the Thornton place where they lived. Rebecca said they rode horse back to this church. I'm sure it was during the summer time or fall. So as a tiny baby I found out what it was like to ride on a horse. No wonder I enjoyed riding horseback as I got older.

Mother told me about my dedication. I think it may have been the

District Superintendent or the presiding elder who came for this occasion. Mother said as she and Daddy stood before the altar with their tiny baby girl, God's presence was very close. She couldn't express how wonderful this time was but she felt God had something special for this child to do. How could they have known that I would one day be a pastor's wife and then a missionary to Africa? They didn't know but they promised before the Lord to bring me up, their baby daughter, in the ways of the Lord. To my own children and grandchildren I remind you of what God's word says: "Train up your children in the ways they should go and when they are older they will not depart from the right way."

First Memories

My memories sort of began with two things in my mind. First, I remember a crib that Grandma Alice had put me in to sleep and I remember her either putting a diaper on me or taking one off. Another memory is of a Christmas tree in Grandpa and Grandma French's living room. It stood in a corner of the room and seems to me there was a round tub of Christmas gifts under the tree.

My most vivid memory came at 3 years of age when I got a baby sister. Again, my mother didn't make it to Lewellen. Esther was born at some friends, the Brenaman place, about five miles north of Lewellen, August 17th, 1939. She shared this birthday with Charles E. Cheney who would later become my brother-in-law as well as, two years later, a cousin, James French who was also born on the 17th of August. My memory so clearly sees Mother in bed on the west side of the room with baby Esther in a nearby basket that had legs. I must have been short enough that I could not see into it. Daddy lifted me up and then I saw my new baby sister for the first time. What I remember most is that she had lots of dark hair.

I'm sure that after Esther was born there were times when I felt left out. I remember my Uncle Jewel (this was my mother's oldest brother) telling me that one time he was walking past our outside toilet and he heard me in there crying my little heart out. He called out "What's the matter in there?" And I said tearfully "Nobody loves me." It could have been that I had done something I should not have done. But whatever it was I'm sure it passed.

Mother used to dress Esther and me in dresses with long sleeves and long stockings. I think she felt under bondage to one of her aunts who thought you were not Christian if you didn't wear long sleeves and long stockings. I really don't think it was a conviction of mother's but she struggled over what others thought. Daddy got Mother a very nice sewing machine and she used it to make all our dresses out of flour sacks, or at least many of them. You see, when I was little Mothers made their own bread and the flour came in great big sacks which probably would be a yard of colorful flowered material.

One time, probably when Esther was about two and I would have been five, I can remember visiting in the Earl Miller home. I'm not sure what the occasion was. Esther and I wandered out amongst the machinery. There, by one of the rakes or mowers, was a tin full of oil. Mother had just gotten Esther some new shoes. So here we were and Esther proceeded to step into that can of oil. As I remember the shoes were white and after the oil bath they turned rather black or gray color. Needless to say Mom was not at all pleased. I can't remember what she did for punishment or how she managed to clean those shoes. I was not always a good girl and sometimes I wonder if I convinced my little sister to step into that can of oil.

We liked to visit Grandpa and Grandma Devasher who lived some fifteen or twenty miles north of us. Grandpa Devasher was the only grandpa we knew on Dad's side because our real grandpa, John Wesley Thornton, died in 1929. Two years later Grandma married a wealthy rancher. My dad was 16 or 17 years old. Anyway, our step-grandpa was really nice to us. I can remember when we went to Racket (there was a little store and post office in this Sandhill community) that Grandpa Devasher would buy us this horehound candy. We seldom got candy so it was a real treat for Esther and me.

It seemed to me like our step Grandpa and Grandma lived in a mansion. The house was big. It had an upstairs and downstairs and a real bathroom with running water. My Mom and Dad had to carry water into our house from a windmill that was about 150 feet from the house. In Grandma's house you could turn on a tap and water would come out. Instead of an outhouse they had a toilet in the 'bathroom' as well as a tub and sink. In the big sitting room Grandpa had a big radio that stood at least 3 or 4 feet tall. I remember hearing voices in that big box with knobs on it. I thought there were actually little people in there talking and running around. You see, at our house we didn't have a radio.

One of those times when we girls visited our grandparents, we stayed with them. Later they brought us home to our parents. Our grandpa had a brand new 1940 Buick. Esther and I were riding in the back seat with Grandma with Grandpa in front. I must have gotten car sick because as we were pulling through the cattle gate on the hill above our house, I puked all over the floor between the front and back seat. I felt really bad that I had made such a mess in Grandpa's new car.

Then came the day I was to start to school. We had neighbors, the Dar Delatour family who lived about two miles west of our home. For my first year of grade school, I went to Dist. 74. It was also called Prairie Belle Country School. The school was a mile and a quarter from our house. This was the same school my dad and his siblings attended years before. The

Delatour family had twins, a girl and a boy, named Geraldine and Gerald, and an older sister. Gerald and Geraldine were about my age and so we were in the same grade. That year we started school, it seems, in May and went to school the whole year. This way we had our kindergarten and first grade in one year. Our teacher's name was Marie Baird. She later married Don Keenan and they lived in the sandhills north of Racket where my mother's parents lived when Mom was growing up.

I don't remember a lot in that first year. However, I do remember a cold winter morning when Mother was taking me to school on the horse. On the way up the hill she remembered something she had forgotten so back down the hill we went. She gave me the reigns to hold. I probably wasn't more than six years old. Well, that silly horse wasn't going to stand still for me. He decided to go right into the barn with me on his back. Fortunately, I bent over as he entered the barn door. He didn't knock me off. Mother found us inside the barn with me still clinging to the saddle all bent down. Mother brought him out of the barn and climbed into the saddle with me. On our way we went to school through some deep snow!!!

When I was around seven or eight I had appendicitis attacks. The pain in my side would get so bad I would almost double over. I don't remember this but Mother told me they called their pastor, Rev. Christiansen, to come and pray for me. Mom said God healed me and I never had any more attacks.

I really don't like to say this but sometimes I could be a bad girl. Our teacher decided she wanted us to stop saying "ain't". It was not proper English and not in the dictionary in my day. So Miss Baird gave each of us brown paper to make clown faces. She hung our clown faces on the wall. Then she told us that if we said the word "ain't" we would have to put a freckle on our clown face. Well, one day I let the word slip out and I had to put a freckle on my clown face. Of course, the idea was to not get freckles but I decided if I had one freckle, I just as well have lots of them. So I stood there and said the "ain't" word many times. I soon had freckles all over my clown. What a naughty girl I was!

For my second grade year at Prairie Belle School, I had a man teacher by the name of John Gordon. I wasn't impressed with him but the Delatour children and I made it through 2nd grade.

Walking a mile and a quarter to school gave me time to pretend and play… that is if there weren't cows in my path. I used to be afraid when there were too many cows. I would walk along the road next to the meadow fence so I could duck underneath if the cows headed my direction. That's where I pretended to have a young girl playmate named Elsie. Her front door was between two soap weeds. I would stop and visit at her 'house' quite often.

Funny enough, when I became a young lady of college age, I did have a very special friend named Elsie Schendel.

For our third year of school we had a lady teacher by the name of Twila Livingston. She was married to Claude Livingston. Twila was a sandhills girl. Her parents were Woody and Agnes Hisel and they lived on a ranch north and east of Racket. I really liked Twila as a teacher and sometimes she would let Esther and me stay with her. During the week she lived at the schoolhouse and on week-ends went to her home. She was amazing. One week-end she took us to her home at the ranch. Something happened that really made an impression on me. Her folks kept hogs at their ranch as well as chickens and probably cows. One evening the chickens were running around the pig pen and I remember one of them flew right into the hog pen. The old sow didn't like that and chased it, catching it in her mouth and chomping down on the poor thing, she killed it. My parents didn't have pigs at that time of my life so this made quite an impression on me.

The next year at Prairie Belle School the school board could not find a teacher so we joined up with Box A School south of Racket. My parents and the Delatours decided to take turns transporting us, four Delatours and two Thorntons. Mrs. Rhoda Brennaman was our teacher. Vernon Delatour and my younger sister, Esther, were just starting school. One week my parents would take us and the following week the Delatours drove us.

Once when it was the week for the Delatours to drive us, Mr. Delatour let us off at school and then went on into town. That afternoon when school got out Mr. Delatour was not there to pick us up. The teacher didn't know what to do with us. Finally she decided to take us to the place where she stayed, the Earl Miller home. The sun had long ago set in the western sky and it was very dark outside. After a while we saw lights coming around the hill. It was Mr. Delatour but unfortunately he had been drinking. My little sister and I were scared but we all got into his car and headed for our homes. It was a scary ride but the older daughter kept hollering at her dad to keep on the road. It is a good thing the road was just trail road without much traffic. There were two scared little girls in that car that night.

About two miles from our house we saw the car lights of Daddy's car. He was coming to see why we were not home yet. We were so happy to see our daddy and so relieved. We weren't use to being around drunken people. We scrambled out of the car and ran to our own car to be with Daddy. Probably there was never a time when I was gladder to see my father. Our dad never drank and he protected us. I am so glad he was a good example for his girls.

That year our teacher, Mrs. Brenaman, had to leave after about two and a half months because her daughter was very sick. The school board looked for another teacher but could not find one. So that year of school was lost and we had to take the same grades over again. This always made us a little older than other kids in our grades.

In 1946, my fourth grade year of school, Miss Alma Graham came to be our teacher. Miss Graham, as we always called her, was a great teacher. Her nephew, Robert Lynn Guy, lost his mother and so he joined his Aunt Alma and became a student along with us in January of 1948. Then we had seven students in our school.

Mother's Surprise

It was September, 1946. One afternoon after we had walked home from school, our mother called us into the kitchen and said, "I have something special to tell you."We couldn't imagine what she would want to talk to us about. She said, "We are going to get a baby." You cannot imagine how excited and delighted I was. For a long while I had wanted my mom to have a baby for us. I was ten years old and I thought it would be wonderful to have a tiny baby at our house. I use to imagine having baby bottles, blankets and diapers around the house like some of our friends and relatives had. In fact, the Delatour family had a baby that was about a year old. So I thought, "Why can't we have a baby, too?" Finally it was going to be. There was no happier news than this surprise that mother had for us.

Then it was Christmas vacation and Daddy decided to take us girls with him to Julesburg. If I remember correctly, we were going to see Santa Claus and do some Christmas shopping and probably buy a few groceries. Mother was getting close to her delivery time and decided she wouldn't go with us. We didn't know at the time but this was a God thing. On the way home from Julesburg, riding in our Model A Ford, we came down through Ash Hollow at about dusk. As we came to the intersection of highways 92 and 26, a lady coming from the opposite direction turned in front of us and we crashed right there. Fortunately the vehicles didn't turn over but the crash caused the doors to fly open and the glass to shatter. Esther and I fell out onto the ground. Blood was coming from my sister's mouth and my eye was bleeding. Someone took us to the doctor at Lewellen. He checked us over for broken bones. Dad seemed to be alright but Esther had a split tongue in which they had to put stitches. Then my eyes had to have two or three stitches in the eye lid. We were grateful it wasn't as serious as it could have been. We were so thankful that Mother wasn't along as it could have been really serious since she was carrying our new baby. Truly God was with all of us.

After our wreck we had Christmas with Grandpa and Grandma French and probably some of our aunts, uncles and cousins. It was a few days later that baby decided to arrive. Very early on December 28th, 1946, about 3:30 or 4:00 in the morning, Mom came into our bedroom to awaken us. It was cold, oh so cold!! But Mom said, "We have to hurry because I need to go to the hospital." We piled into the old 1929 Plymouth and off we went. I'm sure Daddy was driving extra fast, probably remembering that Mom didn't make it to the hospital with her other two little girls. This time he wanted to get her there in time. They stopped to let Esther and me off at our Uncle Jewel's and Aunt Annie's before going on eight more miles to Lewellen. I was told Mother was only in the hospital ten minutes before our baby sister, Elaine Ruth, arrived. I don't think the doctor got there in time either so the nurse and my dad were the only ones present when she was born.

Later that morning Dad came back to Uncle Jewel's to break the news to us that we had a baby sister. Esther and I could hardly wait for the time when we could go to see her. I'm not sure what took place the rest of the day but I assume our dad had to go back home and do some chores. He may have left us with Uncle Jewel and Aunt Annie. One Sunday, December 29th, Daddy took us to the hospital and we got to see Mother and our baby sister. She was in the upstairs nursery and Mother was off in one of the side rooms. Oh, what a joy to see that wee baby girl in a little bassinet. We just thought we couldn't wait to hold her. I don't remember how long Mother was in the hospital with baby Elaine but it was a great day when they got home. Now I had a little baby sister to help care for.

Mother was home with us about three weeks after our sister's birth when her leg started swelling and hurting her. So we had to take her and the baby back to the hospital. It seems she had what they called "milk leg" which I think was a blood clot in her leg. She had to stay in the hospital for a few days.

When Dad went to town to check on Mother and Baby Elaine, our teacher, Alma Graham, stayed with Esther and me so we wouldn't miss school. One evening Miss Graham said she didn't feel well so she went to the kitchen door to get some fresh air. When she turned to come back, she actually fainted, flat out, right in the door way. Esther and I were so scared. We didn't know if our teacher had died and we didn't know what to do.

Remember we didn't have phones in those days! I think I prayed that God would help us. If I remember correctly, Esther said she was so scared that she ran and crawled up in Mom and Dad's bed. It was only a minute or so before Miss Graham came to and got up off the floor. Then she asked, "Oh, where are my glasses?" We looked and looked because we knew our teacher couldn't see well without her thick glasses. Esther and I began to search all around the kitchen floor. Finally we found them behind the kitchen range and, believe it or not, they were unbroken! That was cause to give praise to the Lord. Esther and I were so thankful our teacher was alive and going to be ok. I think this was our first experience with someone fainting.

Playtime for Two Sisters

Our Mother taught us to work but she also gave us time to play. We found many things to do so I want to give you an idea of what playtime was like.

Daddy fixed a rope swing for us with board seats. Esther and I spent a lot of time during our summers swinging under the American Elm Tree. In fact after a wonderful meal at noon, mother would say, "Now I want you to do the dishes before you go out to play." However, my sister and I would slip out to swing. Often we would take crackers with butter on them so we could have a snack out under the cool shade of the Elm tree. When we decided to go back into the house, guess what was waiting for us?? The dirty dishes would still be sitting on the table. Our fun came to an abrupt end!

Another summertime activity that we loved to do was to play church. We had a number of different dollies of various sizes. We would take our dollies to the chicken coup. Of course the chickens were out in the summer sun somewhere getting bugs and sunning themselves so the coup was empty. We placed our dollies on the roosts which we called church pews. One of us would lead the singing and prayer and the other one would preach the sermon. It was surprising how many times our dollies got saved!

Speaking of dolls, one Christmas our daddy made us a little doll bed and an ironing board. Daddy even made kites for us and they really could be flown. What fun it was to see those paper bag kites fly high in the air.

Another playtime event was dressing our pet kitty cat. We had a little doll buggy for our dolls. We decided to put our cat, dressed in doll clothes, into the buggy. He didn't seem to mind as we drove him all over the yard. Kitty was very patient with us.

As we grew older, especially during the summer, it became Esther's and my job to bring in the cows and milk them. To do this we rode Lucky, our saddle horse. I would go out into the pasture to catch the horse with the bridle and a pan of oats. Then I would lead him up to a big sand bank and crawl onto his back. I really loved horseback riding, although I did fall off a number of times.

I especially remember one time when my little sister fell off the horse. Elaine was only four or five years old but because our horse was very docile we let her hold the reigns and lead him, or even ride him around the yard. Dad had an electric fence around the garden. Wouldn't you know that horse didn't realize it was a hot wire? As he reached over the fence for a juicy bit of green grass, he touched it. Well, you can guess what happened. Lucky gave a big jump and our little sister came off his back so quick we barely saw it happen. Poor Elaine, she ended up with a broken arm.

Several summers our cousins, Dale, Dixie and Alan, came to spend a few weeks with us. It was such fun to have them at our ranch. We played in sand blowouts and rode horses. One time we were riding and I let Dixie sit in the saddle. I was on behind her trying to hold onto the reigns and guide the horse. Well, the horse decided he wanted to get to the barn. When he began trotting down the path at a quick pace, I couldn't hold on. I fell off and then as the horse broke into a gallop, Dixie also fell off. Fortunately neither one of us was hurt seriously. Esther tells me that she fell off once and was knocked out for a few seconds. I don't remember that time but I'm sure there were many times during our childhood days this could have happened.

One year Mom and Dad got a snow sled for us girls for Christmas. Seems like we use to get more snow in those days when we were small than we do now days. With so many tall hills around, it was such fun to pull on our snow pants, coats, mittens and hats and traipse up those long hills. Oh, what fun it was to jump on the sled and go whizzing down to the bottom.

During the summer Esther and I would play house with our tea sets. We would put dog weed beans in small bottles and pretend that we were canning them for green beans to serve in our play dishes. Of course we didn't eat them. Another plant we liked to play with was what we called the star plant with sticky leaves. With the leaves we would form words or patterns on our shirts or dresses. We really had fun decorating our clothes. I'm not sure Mom appreciated those sticky leaves on our clothes when it came time to wash them.

My favorite meal during the summer was Mom's fried chicken, mashed potatoes with milk gravy and cut up lettuce from the garden with Mom's special dressing. Yummm. That was so delicious!

Mother and Daddy always raised chickens. They would get baby chicks in the spring and raise some for frying and some for laying eggs. We always seemed to have plenty of eggs and, of course, milk. Several years my parents raised turkeys, too. They butchered and then sold them at Thanksgiving and Christmas time.

In all my childhood days I never remember going hungry. We always seemed to have plenty of food. I guess that was the wonderful thing about being raised in the sandhills of Nebraska. In fact, my parents would sell eggs and cream to get spending money for groceries we couldn't raise: flour, baking powder, yeast and other essentials. I don't think there ever was a dull moment around our house. We always found something to do. When we had to stay inside, many times our activity would consist of playing with the Montgomery Ward or Sears Catalogs. We would use these catalogs to set up doll houses. It was such fun to cut out from the old catalogs, a father, a mother and several children. Each of us girls would have a family. Then we would look for the furniture for our paper doll homes. At other times, we would get a gift book of paper dolls or maybe buy a book of paper dolls. Usually our toys or books were gifts for birthdays or Christmas.

One of my favorite memories was coming home from school and being so hungry. Remember we walked home from school a mile and a quarter. I would get a slice of Mother's homemade bread, put either plums or apple sauce over it and then pour thick sweet cream over it. Oh, how delicious that was!!!

Mother always had a big garden and beans had to be canned for the winter, as well as corn and tomatoes. It was such a busy time. Esther and I helped as much as possible. We tipped the green beans so mother could cut them and put them into jars to can.

One of the high lights in the month of August was camp meeting at Weeping Water, Nebraska. This was a yearly event. I will always remember those fun times and I looked forward to playing with friends and cousins and attending the children's meetings where we learned about the Bible. We had to work hard in order to get ready. It seems like we almost worked night and day to be ready to go. Each year Mother sewed new dresses that we could wear for camp as well as for the coming school year.

It was August, 1945 and I was nine years old. That year we were going to camp meeting with Uncle Homer and Aunt Grace and cousins Ardis and Neal. They had a pretty new car, well maybe about five years old. Cars in those days did not have air conditioners. Instead, they had a water cooler on the window that cooled you down as you traveled. We thought this was really living.

My Grandpa Devasher always furnished beef for the camp. They put it in the lockers in Lewellen so it would be frozen solid. When we got to Lewellen I remember how happy everyone was and so excited because finally World War II was over. We loaded the meat in the trunk of Uncle Homer's car and made our way to Highway 30 and on to Lincoln, Nebraska and then on to Weeping Water. Only Mother, Esther and I were with them. My dad had to care for things at home. Sometimes, too, Dad carried mail from Racket to Bingham, Nebraska. It could be he had to stay home to do that.

After we got a little older, like ten or twelve, Daddy bought a number of dairy calves. When these calves grew up and had babies, their calves were not allowed to suck their mothers after the first week or so. Instead, we milked the cows by hand. They produced many gallons of milk and Daddy got a machine called a "separator" to separate the cream from the milk. The cream went into big cream cans and was shipped to some company in eastern Nebraska where it was made into butter. We fed the "skim" milk to the bucket calves. They were called bucket calves because we had special buckets that had nipples on them and the calves sucked the milk out of the bucket as we held it for them.

Asking Jesus into My Heart

As a child growing up, I remember there would be two revivals at our church. One would be in the spring and another in the fall. After the Racket church closed, my folks drove twenty miles south to the Mennonite church which was eight miles north of Lewellen. I'm not sure when Rev. Tschetter came to hold a revival at the church. At this revival meeting, I remember my mother went to the altar. For the first time in my life, I realized that I needed to invite Jesus into my heart. I probably was about 8 or 9 years old at the time. So after this conviction hit me, I walked up to join my mother. That night I invited Jesus into my heart. I didn't quite understand everything and didn't have any particular feeling. However, I do remember some things began to change. I would never pray at family devotions before this time. Now, the very next morning after Mother and Daddy prayed, I prayed. That was the beginning of my walk with the Lord.

Our Amazing Parents
Teaching Us about Tithing

We three girls had truly amazing parents. They taught us so much, not only by the way they lived their Christian lives, but also in the way they were willing to sacrifice so that we could experience different things. They not only saw that we were in church, they went with us and they saw that we had opportunities to attend Church related events.

Dad told us girls that we could earn money by pulling what we called Texas tacks or goat heads. Daddy really wanted to get rid of those weed pests! He told us if we would pull them by the root and stack them in piles of ten, for every pile he would give us one penny. Well, there were hundreds of these stickers and so it was easy to get many piles.

Another way Mom and Dad let us earn money was by milking cows. Of course this was when we were older. In those days we didn't have milking machines, at least not on our ranch, so all the cows had to be milked by hand. Some cows were easy to milk and others were harder. You had to learn how to squeeze very hard. In our kitchen we had a chart to keep track of the cows that we milked. At the end of the week we would get paid five cents for every cow we milked. Now remember, this was back in the early 1949-1955 and money was worth more then.

Mother explained tithing to us this way. Say we milked 10 cows in one week. That would be fifty cents. Then if we had pulled enough Texas tacks to make twenty piles that would be twenty more cents. So that week we would have seventy cents. Then Mother said that ten percent of seventy cents would be seven cents. She told us that is what belongs to God and we would give this in the offering on Sunday. I feel so privileged to have had parents that taught us tithing. It has never been hard for me to give the tithe to God and my church. Some people find it hard to give and think they will wait until they have more money. Let me tell you that will never work. Start giving to God before you have enough. Giving to God first always makes what is left go farther than you ever expected. Somehow God just increases what is left.

Another memory, not quite so wonderful, was the time I milked eleven cows by myself. I was probably 13 or 14 by that time. It was during the summer. I had stayed home to work on some correspondence school work. (I took my first year of high school through correspondence from the High School Dept. of the University of Nebraska.) Mother and Daddy and my two sisters had gone to town. When they didn't return home by the time we usually milked the cows, I decided I better start the milking. Well, that evening I milked every one of those eleven cows before they got home. I can assure you I was pretty tired that night!

Raising Turkeys

At this point I would like to go back to the times we raised turkeys. One year Daddy built a great big Quonset building to keep the turkeys in. He also decided that it would be easier to bring the turkeys into our ranch by plane. So that year I think there were about 500 turkeys that had a plane ride. Afterwards, Daddy asked the pilot to take us up in the airplane so that we could see what our place looked like from the air. That was our first experience with plane rides.

Our Arizona Trip

One thing I appreciated about my parents was the fact they took us on trips to different parts of our state and our nation. It was a great learning time for us girls. Even though our parents were not plush with money they were so good to take us to places of interest. So the Arizona trip to visit our grandparents was a very special time.

It was December, 1948 and our parents discussed the possibility of going to Arizona to Grandpa and Grandma Devasher's for Christmas. This was our dad's mom and step-dad that lived in Phoenix, Arizona. They had moved to Arizona because of Grandpa's health in 1943 or '44. Of course, we could not leave the ranch without someone to care for our cattle, horses and chickens so my mom's Uncle Caleb Mecham was approached to see if it would be possible for him to stay at the ranch while we were away. He agreed to come and take care of everything.

We didn't have a very good car for this trip so my Uncle Jewel allowed us to borrow one of his newer cars. Our grade school teacher, Miss Alma Graham, also went with us on this trip making a total of six people. My little sister, Elaine, was almost 2 years old. She was just learning to talk and said the cutest things. As we were coming down out of the mountains and looking down on the valley below she said, "Whee! Way high"! It really was an amazing view.

We had begun our trip around Dec.23, 1948 hoping to reach our grandparents for Christmas but it was too far and we traveled on into Christmas night before getting there. In fact we had to travel very slowly over the mountain pass because the fog was so thick. My dad could barely see the white lines down the middle of the road.

Since Elaine had a birthday on the 28th of December, she turned two years old while we were in Arizona. If I remember correctly Grandma made her a birthday cake. We had a lot of new experiences with Grandpa and Grandma. We had never experienced a warm Christmas before. Also seeing oranges, grapefruit and lemons growing on trees in a warm country was a new thing to us as well as seeing date palm trees lining the streets. Our time came to a close all too quickly.

Although it was time to head for our home in Nebraska, we visited some places on the way back. At Carlsbad Caverns in New Mexico, a wonderful cave, we learned about stalactites coming down from the top of the cave and stalagmites that form on the floor of the cave. The lights made the formations so beautiful. As we crossed Oklahoma and into Kansas we saw many oil wells that we had never seen before. In Sawyer, Kansas we visited a couple of Daddy's aunts and their families, my dad's father's sisters. From there we traveled to Plainsville, Kansas where we visited some people who used to live close to our dad's family in the sandhills. Their name was Hendrin.

When it was Sunday Daddy thought we should travel on to Lewellen and get back to our home in the sandhills before the weather changed. We drove up to our church just in time for the Sunday evening service. After church Daddy thought we should travel on to the hills but everyone said, "It's dark and cold, just stay the night and go in the morning." So that is what we did.

The '49 Blizzard

The next morning, January 2, 1949, we awoke to a full blown blizzard, the worst I had ever experienced. Alma Graham, Esther and I stayed with our pastors, Rev. and Mrs. John P Tschetter. Mom, Dad and Elaine stayed with Uncle Jewel and Aunt Annie. The winds blew hard and the drifts mounted many feet high. This storm lasted for three days and finally began clearing by Thursday. Uncle Jewel and Dad were able to drive to Oshkosh that day or maybe it was Friday. Dad asked for a small plane to take them to our ranch to make sure that Uncle Caleb was ok. They didn't land, of course, but Uncle Caleb came out and saw them as they threw out a small package of matches and a note saying they would try to come to the ranch on Saturday. It looked like he had cared well for the cattle and other livestock and everything was ok.

They came back to Uncle Jewel's and we prepared to leave for home on Saturday. There were many huge drifts of snow, 12 feet high or even more. How my dad ever wound around on the hills, missing the huge drifts, is amazing to me. But we did finally make it. It took until spring to melt all those enormous drifts, but while they lasted we made snow caves and snow forts and had a great time sledding.

Backtracking a Bit about My Schooling

Alma Graham was our teacher through 8th grade. The Delatour family decided to move to Oshkosh, Nebraska, in the summer of 1948. This left our school with only three students, the teacher's nephew, Robert Lynn Guy, Esther and me. It was decided that the school building should be moved to the meadow near our place. At that time Alma Graham built a little cabin to live in rather than staying in the school house. A short time later another nephew, LeRoy Morrell, moved in with his aunt and then there were four students.

During my seventh and eighth grades I did not do as well in my studies. I think many young teenagers have a difficult time. They sometimes aren't sure if they want to play as a child or act like a grown up, often daydreaming, kind of acting like they are out in space! Well, my dad noticed this and challenged me. He said, "You are going to fail and will have to take this grade over." I decided in my mind, "I'm going to prove my dad wrong!"
Toward the end of my 8th Grade year I came down with whooping cough. I was so sick I couldn't keep any food down. In fact, I missed my 8th grade graduation because of this illness. It took most of the summer for me to get over the effects of the disease. They sent my 8th grade diploma to me and I was passed to enter high school.

Daddy and Mother did not want to send me to Oshkosh for high school at my young age. After discussing it, a decision was made to have me take my freshman year of high school by correspondence through the University of Nebraska High School division. Sometimes to be motivated in my studies was difficult. Alma Graham was a great counselor for me. However, I drug this freshman year into the summer months. I did finish it off by the time school started in the fall. I'm very happy that I did schooling in this way because years later it helped with my own children having to do home schooling. This was the course we chose in Africa for our oldest son Allen years later.

Daddy and Mother were acquainted with an older couple living in Oshkosh. They approached them about boarding me during my sophomore year of high school. Mr. and Mrs. George Peterson took me in and gave me an upstairs bedroom in which to stay.

When I started my sophomore year of school I got straight A's the first quarter. I studied hard at Garden County High School and was often on the honor roll. I was named a member of the National Honor Society. In fact, in my senior year I was not required to take the finals because I had high marks.

I had some good friends in High School. Three were the grandchildren of George and Anna Peterson: Laurene, Norman, and Marilyn Peterson. I even went to their farm northeast of Oshkosh and spent time with them. They and their parents attended the Pilgrim Holiness Church in Oshkosh. Then there was Kathy Cheney, Cliff Cheney and Charles Cheney— not in my grade—but young people who attended the Lewellen Pilgrim Holiness Church. There were special youth events that we could attend and be a part of, such as ice skating and Youth Rallies.

Kathy Cheney had an older brother, Robert, who graduated from Garden County High School in 1952. I always considered him to be much older than me but I do remember him coming to the high school to visit when a Ministerial Convention was going on at Oshkosh. He was attending Colorado Spring Bible College at the time.

The Mennonite Brethren in Christ Church, my home church, became "The United Missionary Church". I joined this church as a young teenager of about the age 14. Later, I was baptized at our camp in Weeping Water, Nebraska.

Rev. and Mrs. John Tschetter were pastors at the Missionary Church. They had two daughters, Rhoda and Sylvia, and two sons, Walter and Gerald. The two daughters and one son were older than me. The youngest son, Gerald was about my age. Being a young teen-ager, I had a crush on the younger son.

However, the older son was the one who wanted to go out with me. One evening after church he followed me into the parsonage and asked me for a date. I was sixteen at the time and mother had talked with me about going out with this boy. I really didn't like him at all. So I didn't see any reason to go out with him. I just told him, "No, I don't think I want to go out with you." That didn't mean he stopped trying but I never gave in. Sometimes it is just better if you don't go out with certain boys!

I did not mix in all of the activities of my classmates. I remember we had an accordion band with several of us girls playing. Also I had a part in the junior play. There were dances (they did drinking, etc.) but I did not participate in these. I remember one young man (a football player) asked to go out with me—in fact several wanted to do this but I didn't agree to it. I am very thankful that I didn't!!! This young man so urgently wanted to be with me that he took a class that I knew he really was not interested in. It was a class called "Music Appreciation". I think he only did it to be where I was. Maybe he thought somehow he could convince me! It didn't work!

One time in the fall when I was a junior, I had to stay home a few days from school because I had the flu. One day I decided to see if I had a fever. I got out the thermometer and was shaking it down. I happened to hit the end of my middle finger on the left hand and it broke the thermometer. I didn't think much about it although it cut my finger. As the days passed this cut would not heal up. I recovered from the flu but this finger was so sore and the cut would not heal. Finally Daddy and Mother decided I had better see Dr. Albee. The doctor took an x-ray of my finger. Guess what he saw next to the bone??? MERCURY from the thermometer! It was a miracle that it didn't get into my blood stream giving mercury poisoning or into my heart and kill me. So they took me into the hospital operating room and Dr. Albee fished all that mercury out of my finger. I believe God wasn't ready to have me leave this earth. He performed a miracle just for me!!!

During the last half of my junior year I rented a basement room from Mrs. Malhman. One afternoon I went to my bedroom and kneeled by my bedside and prayed for the Lord's guidance. I truly wanted God's plan for my life and I prayed, "Lord, I want to have a Christian home and if I can't have that then I don't want to be married." My prayer was earnest because I had become interested in a young man from Brule, Nebraska. We were going out some. I have always felt that God knew my heart was consecrated to him and that He would give me the desire of my heart. Not long afterwards, the boyfriend broke my heart by dating other girls. Now, I can look back and see God's hand at work in my life.

Summer Jobs during School Years

During the summer of 1954, I worked for Claude and Twila Livingston on their farm south of Lewellen on the table land. They had three children at the time, Jerry, Clinton and Cherri Jo. Jerry was probably about 6 or 7 years old, Clinton about 4 or 5 and Cherri Jo, a year to 18 months. That summer I took care of the three children and did chores such as getting in the cows and caring for chickens. Twila even taught me how to cut up a frying chicken so that there were more meaty pieces. For this I will ever thank her.

During my high school years I had a baby sitting job taking care of three boys. Mr. Graham, our music teacher and his wife lived close to the high school. I don't remember if his wife was a teacher but after school there were two or three hours when they would need someone to care for their three boys. I really liked Mr. Graham and I sang in our high school choir. This may have been the time that I took part in an accordion band.

High School Graduation

May, 1955 arrived quickly and graduation rolled around. It was an exciting time. I attended the Junior- Senior banquet but I didn't stay for the dance. Mom made me a special graduation dress, light blue trimmed with lace with black ribbon highlights. Our class colors were white and blue and my graduation gown was white. I received a scholarship to Scottsbluff nursing school. However, I didn't take it because I wanted to get a Bachelor of Science degree in Nursing from our church college in Mishawaka, Indiana.

The summer after my graduation from high school, I again worked for the Livingstons. This time Twila was pregnant with twins. Since Claude was attending summer school to upgrade his teaching certificate and needed a substitute mail carrier for his Sandhills route they ask me to be his substitute. This was quite an experience for19 year old girl just out of high school and headed for college. My parents were on this mail route.

One day I had a flat tire on the pickup. I had never in my life changed a flat tire. I hoped that someone would come along this sandhill trail road and help me out. That didn't happen!!! I got the jack out and started to work on it. I jacked up the pickup and then realized I should have loosened the lug bolts first .So, after letting it down, I took off the bolts, jacked it up again and pulled the tire off. Then I got the spare out and put it on the wheel. I put on the lug bolts but knew I didn't have them tight enough. Since my uncle, Bill Thornton, lived a couple miles from where I had the flat, I decided to drive up to their house and have my uncle tighten the bolts. He wasn't home but his hired man, Loren Dykes, did it for me. So this was my first flat tire experience.

During those days the mailman not only carried mail but also cans of cream that were to be taken to the train depot in Lewellen. I don't really know how I managed to lift those heavy cans of cream but I did. So the summer of 1955 passed quickly and before I knew it college days had arrived.

College Days

After working for the Livingston's during the summer of 1955, I
made preparation to go to Mishawaka, Indiana to attend Bethel College. My
aunt, Chrystal French, also decided to go there for a semester. She was
preparing to return to Nigeria for her third or fourth term as a missionary. We
said our good byes to family and boarded a Greyhound bus for Indiana. I was
thankful that I didn't have to travel alone. In fact, leaving my home territory
even with my aunt, made me feel a little tinge of home sickness.

We traveled through a number of bigger cities, like Omaha,
DesMoines and Chicago. I can't remember how many hours we spent on the
bus but I'm sure some of the journey was overnight. Chicago seemed very big
to me and the bus seemed to go fast as we neared South Bend. Mishawaka and
South Bend are only divided by a street so you don't realize when you go from
one to the other.

Finally we arrived at Bethel College. Aunt Chrystal roomed at one of
the professor's homes. I was assigned to one of the small house dorms and my
roommate was Joyce Hayward. Eight girls were placed in each of these small
house dorms. I remember that Ethel and Elaine were two of the girls. There
were four rooms with bunk beds and each room housed two girls, eight girls
in all.

At Bethel I could study my main first year subjects and then transfer
to a nursing college to receive my R.N. I planned to attend Bethel for my
degree in nursing in order to be able to teach nursing. Strange to say but this
dream of mine never materialized. I allowed a boyfriend to get me off track.
What I want to insert here is to tell girls, "Don't let boyfriends lead you astray.
Just follow God's plan for your life."

I really enjoyed my college days after getting acquainted and settled
into classes. My best girlfriend was Joann Goodman. She was the niece of the
president of the college, Dr. Woodrow Goodman. She also had a boyfriend but
he was not at Bethel. We seemed to hit it off well. In fact we were assigned to
a little Free Methodist Church to help them with their services.

To help pay for my college expenses I had to a job in the kitchen and
cafeteria. I also was available to baby sit around the city. People liked to have
kids from the college care for their children. In fact, I did have a fairly steady
job for sitting for one couple. This was a great help to me. At the end of the
year I was able to pay college expenses for the whole year.

One particular class I really loved was "The Book of Acts" taught by

Rev. S. I. Emery. He made the class so interesting. One of the other classes I took was "Methods of Sunday School Teaching". Years later I realized how beneficial this class was during our pastoring and missionary careers. Other classes were Christian Philosophy, English, Speech, music and a science class. I enjoyed being in chorus and particularly in the Hallelujah Chorus that we sang in South Bend United Missionary Church around Christmas time.

During this time, our first semester, I was faithful to my boyfriend and did not go out with other boys. I thought we were going to get married someday and I wanted to be true. It wasn't because no boys ask. I could easily have gone out with other boys but as I look back on this situation I do feel God used it to help prepare me for the right one that God had for me in my home area.

Thanksgiving holidays came and Aunt Chrystal and I were invited to her and mom's cousin Rebecca's home in Michigan. Rebecca was raised with my mother and Aunt Chrystal because she had lost her mother when she was not quite two years old. Grandma and Grandpa French took Rebecca and Ruth, her sister, to raise. So really these two, Ruth and Rebecca, seemed like my aunts. Wayne and Rebecca and their three children, Ken, Chrystal, and Joyce, lived very close to the home of one of our professors, Rev. S. I. Emery. The Emerys planned to go to Michigan and said that we could ride along with them to Wayne and Rebecca's. We had a wonderful Thanksgiving at their house and enjoyed sledding with their kids. They had lots of snow, as I remember. The weekend went fast and soon it was time to travel back to school.

There were some really neat experiences that I had while in Bethel College. One time a bus load of us students traveled to Chicago. First we visited the Museum of Science and Industry. I was so glad to see where Moody Bible Institute was located. In the evening we visited Pacific Garden Mission. As a child at home we use to listen to the radio (my last few years at home we did have a radio), stories told of people whose lives were changed. It was so neat to visit their headquarters and even participate in the service and share a meal with these street people. Many of their lives had taken on a real transformation.

I was able to go home for the Christmas holidays. Aunt Chrystal was going to leave in January but she was with us for Christmas. She went back to Bethel College with me after the holidays.

One Saturday weekend in January, I felt really down. We took my aunt to Fort Wayne where she caught the train to New York. There she would board a ship for Nigeria and start a new term as missionary in that country. When I arrived back at the college I just went to bed and I'm sure I cried myself to sleep. I wouldn't even go to the dining room to eat. This soon passed and Joann and I did things together.

On Easter weekend Joann said she would like for me to come home with her. So I agreed and she found a ride for us with a young man who also lived in Ohio. We had a great time in Cincinnati. Joann's boyfriend took us various places. One place was God's Bible School. I had heard of this school a numbers of times and what a privilege it was to see the place.

Bob and Joann also took me to a beautiful flower conservatory. What a lovely place with flowers and more flowers and plants---all kinds of orchids and birds---just unusual plants and gorgeous flowers. I loved it!!! Then they took me to an unusual train station. It very big but one could whisper across that vast expanse and a person clear across on the other side of the station could hear what was said.

That Sunday morning we attended Joann's home church and then headed back for college after Sunday dinner. It truly was a delightful weekend.

The end of the school year was coming up. Lots of studying took place for finals and before we knew it our first year had ended and I was heading home to Nebraska. We rode as far as eastern Nebraska with an older married student, another missionary named Dorothy Hall. She had worked with Aunt Chrystal and had agreed to come as speaker for our Missions Convention at the United Missionary Church.

It was nice to be home but now I wondered what I would do for the summer. My step-grandpa, Jeff Devasher, was sick. He had cancer. Dad and Uncle Bill thought it would be a good idea for me to go and help Grandma take care of Grandpa in Prescott, Arizona, where my grandparents lived at this time. Sometime during June, Dad, Uncle Bill and I went to Arizona. I'm not sure if anyone else went with us. Perhaps Mother and the girls also came but when they left to go back to Nebraska, I stayed. Grandpa Devasher died in the first part of August of 1956. Uncle Bill and my folks came down for the funeral. I'm glad I was able to spend six or seven weeks with my Grandma but now as I look back on it, I wish I had talked more to her and questioned her about her life in Minnesota. Young people never seem to think of these things when they are young. So this is one of the reasons I'm writing my life story. I want my children, grandchildren and great-grandchildren to know about my life.

Living in Colorado Springs

When I first got to Colorado Springs I stayed with my mom's Aunt Hazel and her cousin, Audrey. I first took an entrance test at one of the hospitals to continue nurses training but then was discouraged by my boyfriend so I looked for a job. I tried out at a restaurant but that was not my kind of work so I looked around some more and found a job at a laundry where they did washing for motels and hotels.

In the meantime my girlfriend, Elsie, encouraged me to put in an application at Shepherd Citations where she worked. This was a firm that made law reference books. After working August and September at the laundry I was accepted to start working at Shepherd Citations.

While working in Colorado Springs I had a lot of contact with students at Colorado Springs Bible College. Many of these young people attended the First Pilgrim Holiness church like I did. I joined the church choir, led by Ernie Lewis and his wife Carolyn. There were various Youth activities that we attended making it easy for me to get acquainted with many of the students at the college. My boyfriend kept in touch and we would go out pretty often. His family lived in Colorado Springs.

It was sometime in January or February that he came to take me out on a date, or so I thought. However, that was the night he told me we should break up. I was broken hearted. When he took me back to Aunt Hazel's, I cried about all night and hardly slept a wink. Later Elsie told me that she talked to Willis because he was going out with other girls and I didn't know it. She told him he needed to let me know about this. I thought we were planning to get married sometime in the future. I will ever be thankful to him for breaking us up, because I didn't have enough sense to realize it wasn't right for either of us. But, that left me a "foot loose and free" twenty year old!

Sometime in February, I was staying with the Leland Swan family for a few days. During this time I heard something about Bob Cheney which really made my ears perk up! I had always admired this young man from my home area in Nebraska. He was preparing to be a pastor. When I heard him pray I had a great admiration for him and his testimonies touched my heart. This young man was a very strong Christian. I heard that he had broken off a relationship with a girl at the college. When I heard this, a sudden thought struck me! "I really would like to go out with this young man sometime!" In fact I was pretty good friends with Kathy, his sister, who also was in college. One time we were riding the bus to a Youth Rally at Castle Rock and I sat by Kathy. I ask her so many questions about her brother that she probably wondered what I had in mind.

Several weeks went by and one day shortly before Easter, I got a phone call from Bob Cheney. He asked me if I would type a paper for him for one of his classes. Of course he would pay me. It was Easter weekend and I had decided to go home for this holiday. I told Bob my plans and said I was sorry I wouldn't be able to type the paper. He assured me that he could probably find someone else to do it. I hoped that I hadn't missed an opportunity to get better acquainted with this fine young man.

Graduation was taking place the first part of May at First Church and Bob was one of the graduates. I remember well shaking his hand as we congratulated the graduates.

Memorial week-end was coming up and I had invited Elsie to come home with me. We were planning to ride the bus but then I heard Bob and his sister would be going back to Lewellen and I wondered if he might have room for Elsie and me. I finally got brave enough to call Bob on the phone. He told me he would have room for us and that Marilyn Peterson and, maybe, Kathy would also ride.

I looked forward to this week-end with much anticipation. It was a long holiday weekend. Elsie and I had exciting plans. There was a Youth Convention taking place at my home church. The trip to Nebraska was via Denver where Bob's oldest sister and family lived with their two little girls. Some other family members were also visiting and Kathy decided to stay there.

We continued our journey, Bob, Elsie Schendel, Marilyn Peterson and myself. It was sort of an all-night trip because in those days there were no interstates, just two lane highways. As we traveled over into Nebraska I remember striking up conversation with Bob as he drove. For some reason I did not feel sleepy. Then because of the lateness most gas stations were closed and the gas gage was getting low. Bob finally decided he would have to travel over to Lodgepole to ask the pastors of the Pilgrim Holiness church, the Oliver Browns, for some gas to get us on to Oshkosh and Lewellen. We did find some gas there and were able to continue on our journey.

Then Bob drove Marilyn out to her home northeast of Oshkosh. Although it had rained, Bob thought he could take a short cut and take Elsie and me clear to my Uncle Jewel French's where my folks would then pick us up. I tried to give Bob some travel money but he would not accept it. Bob, knowing there was to be a Convention at our church, indicated that some of the Lewellen youth would try to attend our Youth Rally, at least some of the meetings.

Mom and Dad came for Elsie and me later that morning and Elsie actually visited my sandhill home 28 miles north of Lewellen and saw the place where I grew up. That week-end we attended the Youth Meetings and saw many of my relatives and friends.

Sunday afternoon the big Rally took place. A number of youth came from Lewellen Pilgrim Holiness Church, including Bob Cheney and several of his siblings. I don't remember much about the services but I surely remember what happened afterwards before Elsie and I caught a ride back to Colorado Springs. Bob came over to me by the steps of the church and ask me if I'd like to correspond through the summer. Well, this just thrilled me and I said "Yes, I would like to do that." I told him I'd drop him a note about our return trip. This was so exciting to me that I remember grabbing my sister Esther and running up the steps into the church to tell her. I could hardly contain myself. I said, "Guess what? Bob ask about writing to me this summer." I don't think it impressed her that much!

The Beginning of Our Courtship

After getting back to Colorado Springs I wrote my first letter to Bob Cheney. It was pretty general just telling about our trip back and going to work. I'm sure I thanked him again for the ride home. You see, I didn't want things to go too fast and have my heart broken again. You could say I tried to play a little hard to get. It was about a week or more before I received a very nice letter from Bob telling about his jobs on the farm and helping his father. So the letters started flowing back and forth.

With the second letter from Bob, I knew I better start praying hard about my future and what God had in mind for this relationship. I knew that more than anything else in the world I wanted God's plan for my life. Reading somewhat between the lines I realized Bob was serious about our relationship. I needed to pray through on this before it went too far.

So the next couple or three weeks I spent much time in prayer. I knew Bob felt called to preach. Did God want me to be a pastor's wife? I had thought at one time during our camp meeting that God maybe wanted me to go to China as a missionary.

Later Bob told me about hearing God's voice saying, "I want you to preach." He was in the field cultivating corn. Bob said he was so shy he wasn't sure how he could do it. Then he thought, "Well, maybe I can preach at a church for two years and then go to Africa and preach to the Africans. Little did we know that this would actually happen. (Preaching for two years was what was required before going as missionaries.)

The Colorado-Nebraska Camp Meeting and District Conference were held the last ten days of June in Colorado Springs. Bob wrote that he would be coming out for the last week-end, bringing his mom who was the Lewellen delegate for the conference.

I attended the camp services each night. One of those nights I felt convicted to go forward and pray through before that last weekend. As I knelt at that altar I poured out my heart to the Lord. Before I got up from my knees I felt God's presence and his forgiveness. In my heart I could say I had the witness of His Spirit with mine that all was now well with my soul. What a peace and joy swept over my soul! I knew without a doubt that I was right with the Lord.

The last week-end arrived. Bob arranged to pick me up on Sunday morning from Mrs. Quinn's where I now stayed. Together we went to the morning camp service. That day was such a delightful day. Somehow I knew Bob was the right person to share my life with. It was after the evening service that Bob took me for a drive to view the skyline of Colorado Springs. On a high hill up above the college and camp grounds he stopped so we could get a great view. Then he began talking. He said, "You know I'm really ready to settle down in my life. Are you willing to be my wife?" Needless to say I had not anticipated this quite so soon. I had to catch my breath before answering, "Yes, Bob, if it is the Lord's will." Then he gave me that wonderful kiss to seal the agreement. I was on cloud nine!!!

Of course I had to work the next day but in the evening Bob took me out for dinner along with his mom. When we told her we had gotten engaged, she seemed very delighted, glad that I would become her daughter-in-law.

Since Bob was working with his father on their farm near Lewellen, we did not see each other a lot. During the 4th of July week, Elsie and I had vacation. I decided to ride the Greyhound bus home and my folks met me at Big Springs on Highway 30. Dad and Mother took me around by the Cheney's farm and there I saw Bob in his work clothes and with several days of whiskers on his face. I wasn't feeling real great because my jaw was aching and I thought it might be a wisdom tooth. But, we made plans to see each other soon.

When Bob came to my home in the sandhills, a short ways from our house he got stuck in the sand. My dad went to help him get out. After we had a meal together, he asked my dad for my hand in marriage. Dad and Mom were very pleased that I would become the wife of Robert Alfred Cheney.

What I thought was my tooth giving trouble turned out to be a good case of the mumps. Since I hadn't had them as a child, now I had a royal case so I had to call my work and take two weeks leave, one week of which was without pay. During that time Bob came again to see me. I figured if he loved me enough to make that trip to the sand hills and see me with big fat jaws then he really must love me.

After the episode of mumps I went back to Colorado Springs for work. We did talk about a wedding date. Some of our friends, Kenneth Jantz and Barbara Curry, had their wedding in Oshkosh in August. Bob and I attended their wedding and had a chance to be together for that weekend. We talked about Bob's schooling and a wedding date. Bob wanted to continue his education and get a degree in Secondary Education and he was debating between Friends University in Wichita, Kansas and a Free Methodist school in Indiana. Since his sister Wilma was attending school in Wichita, as well as several other friends Bob knew, he decided to go to Friends University. Before he left home we agreed he should come via Colorado Springs so we could have a few days together.

When I got off work for the Labor Day holiday, Bob was there to pick me up. We went up Manitou Incline and spent some time walking around at the head of the Incline. Then we rode the lift back down. Another place of interest we enjoyed was Garden of the Gods. It was a very special weekend. Before we knew it the time had come for Bob to continue on his journey to Wichita, Kansas and I would go back to work at Shepherd Citations. As we were discussing our plans for our wedding we had thought of getting married the next year around May or June. As time elapsed, we finally decided a December wedding would be nice. Bob found out when the semester ended and we came up with the 22nd of December. So plans began to form for our wedding. Almost every day we would write letters or talk by phone.

It seemed like such a long time that we would not be seeing each other. My friend Elsie knew other friends in Wichita so we made a plan to go together by bus on a weekend in late October, about Halloween time. There were other friends, the Virgil Laws, Barbara and Kenny Jantz, Bob's sister Wilma and Wauneta Bourquin, all people we could visit. In fact, Virgil Law invited Bob and me to a Halloween Party that the youth had planned. In those days celebrating Halloween didn't mean what it does today. It was really fun.

That weekend Bob and I got to be together a lot. I remember fixing Tuna salad sandwiches for us at Wilma's apartment. Then, on Sunday evening our bus was to leave at 9:30 p.m. for Colorado Springs. But Elsie and I had forgotten to change our watches to central time. When we got to the bus station we found it had left an hour before. Oh, dear, now what do we do??? Well, friends put us up for the night and we made reservations for the next day. Both Elsie and I would miss a day's work but—Oh well—just a bit more time to spend with Bob.

Again we decided our wedding date for sure would be December 22. We talked about our wedding party, bridesmaids and groomsmen, the minister and singers and all that goes with planning a big wedding. I got material so Mother could make my wedding dress and my sisters' gowns. If I remember correctly Wilma was able to make the other girls' gowns. I chose silver and blue as my colors. My sister, Esther, and Bob's sisters, Wilma and Kathy, were the maid of honor and bridesmaids. Bob had Cliff and Charles, his brothers, Ken Harvey, his brother-in-law, stand with him. My flower girl was Bob's niece, Susan.

One thing I'd like to mention is about the church where we would be married. I didn't feel my home church north of Lewellen would work for our wedding because we had quite a number of people to invite. So we decided to get married in Bob's home church, the Pilgrim Holiness Church in Lewellen. However, the church needed some repair. Harold Swan, one of the members of the church, suggested that if we would get married there, the men would get together and make it like new!! That is exactly what they did.

My next few weeks were filled with plans and shopping. I had big lists that had to be cared for. One of the highlights was a bridal shower that Mrs. Quinn, my landlady, had for me. It was rather funny about the refreshments for the shower. Mrs. Quinn had the ladies bring cakes and I think she ended up with 20 some cakes. I would say she had enough cake to feed over 200 people. Anyway 15 or 20 ladies attended the shower and I received many nice gifts.

It was around November 11th Bob had a chance to come to Colorado Springs with his friends, Gene Gorley and Ray and Emma Jean Snook from Wichita. It was so nice to see him again. This would be our last time together before getting married.

I continued working at Shepherd Citations until Dec. 11th. I had eleven more days to prepare for our wedding. Mom and Dad again picked me up from the bus on Hwy 30 at Big Springs Junction. There was the wedding cake to see about and the flowers to order. Since our wedding was so close to Christmas the bouquets the bridesmaids held were white bells with red geraniums in side and a silver ball for the ding dong. They were such beautiful arrangements for the girls to hold. I chose an arch for the front of the church with candles around. This was so I could use my little sister Elaine, and Bob's little sisters, Linda and Vivian as candle lighters. Elaine would light candles on the arch and Linda and Vivian the candles on the two candelabras at the side. Since I belonged to the United Missionary Church, it would be my pastor, Sherman Mills, who would perform our marriage ceremony. Elsie Schendel, my girlfriend, would play the music and her father would give a marriage message. Rev. Don Spieker, the pastor at Lewellen offered the prayer. Georgia Rittenhouse and Dorothy Matthews sang "Jesus Like a Shepherd Lead Us" and Rev. Duane Keirnarim sang "God Gave Me You" and the "Wedding Prayer."

On Friday the 20th of December, Bob was to arrive in the afternoon. He was coming from Wichita with his sister Wilma. He did arrive late Friday night. I was quite concerned because we had to get our marriage license at Garden County Court House. Fortunately the Court House opened on Saturday mornings so Bob came to my Uncle Jewel and Aunt Ann's place to pick me up. We headed for the Court House and by 11:00 a.m. we had our license. Saturday evening everyone gathered for the rehearsal. As I remember everything went smoothly. At this point I was pretty excited and not responsible for anything. I went home with my family for the night; realizing things would be forever changed. No longer would I be Grace Eva Thornton, I would be Grace Eva Cheney. I'm not sure how well I slept that night, but I am sure my sister Esther was there with me sleeping our last night at home.

Our Wedding

December 22, 1957—Sunday morning arrived and we prepared everything I'd need for the wedding. After church that morning we had lunch at Uncle Jewel's before heading for Lewellen Pilgrim Holiness Church. They had pulled in a small trailer where I could dress for our 4:00 wedding.. Many people came and the seats filled up fast. The church looked beautiful with all the flowers and candles and the great looking wedding party. It was time for my Dad to walk me down the aisle and give me away. At this time our churches didn't feel the wedding rings were necessary for the Christians. Our marriage was to be built on Christ and His Word. So Bob gave me a white Bible to carry with my flowers. After singing the message and prayer, Pastor Mills conducted the ceremony. We said, "I do" to each other and repeated the vows. Then Pastor Mills pronounced us husband and wife and presented us as Mr. and Mrs. Robert Cheney. This was our special moment blessed by God.

The reception was held at the Lewellen Hall on Main Street. There was a table full of gifts and a table with a beautiful wedding cake and punch, nuts and mints. Many well wishes came to us and after opening our gifts we changed into our going away outfits. Bob had hidden our car so no one had a chance at decorating and messing it up. Cliff took us to the hiding place and we headed out to our Motel in Ogallala. The weather was not real cold but a little windy.

The next morning we decided to have our wedding pictures taken at a photo shop in Ogallala. Then we drove to Lake McConaughy and up to Hill Top Inn lookout. It was there, as we looked out over the lake that I realized, "I'm no longer Grace Eva Thornton. I'm really married to Robert Alfred Cheney and I am Mrs. Robert A. Cheney!!!

So I close this part of my life story at the age of 21 years, married to Bob, age 23 years. We now looked forward to our future together with God at the helm.

Chapter Two
Our New Life Begins

On our second night, December 23, we were in North Platte. I guess we did sort of a strange thing. Bob and I decided to visit a Catholic Church where they were doing Christmas Mass. I really can't remember but I think this may have been my first time in a Catholic Church. For Bob, I would say, probably it wasn't since his oldest sister and husband were Catholics.

Since we wanted to spend Christmas with our parents we cut our honeymoon short and drove back to Bob's parents for Christmas Eve. His mother always made the traditional stroganoff for the evening and we all had a nice Christmas Eve.

On Christmas Day we drove to my Grandpa and Grandma French's to have Christmas dinner with my parents, grandparents and my mother's two brothers and their families. My cousin, James French, decided he wasn't letting us get away without our car being decorated and perfumed. Remember Bob hid our car so that no one could decorate it after our wedding. Well, he perfumed it up alright with onion and horrible limburger cheese. Oh how awful! We should have had someone guard our car.

The next few days were spent getting a U-Haul trailer and packing up our wedding and shower gifts and other belongings for travel to Wichita, Kansas, our first home. Bob had rented an upstairs furnished apartment on Sedgwick Street not far from the university. Bob got back into the school schedule and I set up our home with wedding gifts and what we had brought back from our Nebraska homes. While working in Colorado Springs I had gotten a set of Nobility Ware china. It was a very nice and an unusual design. I loved it. Also, I got a good set of Cutco knives. I still have most of that set today. With all our gifts of towels, linens and blankets, our first home was well furnished.

Bob had been attending a church called People's Mission pastored by Rev. and Mrs. Dean Michener. It wasn't long until I was involved in teaching a Sunday school class of young primary children.

After our arrival in Wichita I got a babysitting job from a young mother who attended Friends University. The daughter lived with her mother. She needed a babysitter since her mother was also taking classes. The little girl was about a year old.

Although we had also gotten some wedding money, my babysitting job brought in a little money for bills, food and rent. Then, in the spring, Bob got a job at a lawn mowing shop and also was able to pick up some yard work.

One incident which I want to tell about was a Saturday night when our friends Ray and Emma Jean invited us to go to a Youth for Christ meeting. They had called and said they would be picking us up, not given us a lot of time to get ready. I hurriedly got out the cheese and bread, planning to make toasted cheese sandwiches to eat before our friends arrived. In my hurry I took one of my Cutco knives to slice the cheese and in cutting through the block of cheese I also cut through to my left hand down the long finger and into the palm of my hand. Needless to say there was blood all over! I held it over the sink while the blood gushed out. Bob was at a loss as to know what he should do. We didn't have money to go to an emergency room for stitches and we had no first aid stuff in our apartment. He decided he would run to a drug store and get some medical things like Band-Aids, gauze, tape, and disinfectant. He also had to quickly call our friends to tell them we had an emergency. Finally the bleeding stopped and we got my hand bandaged. Today I still carry this scare in my left hand.

There are always adjustments with a new marriage. This was really impressed upon my mind when I had asked Bob to pick up a few groceries for me. I hate to even tell this because it reflects on how thoughtless I was. I had made a list of the few things that we needed. One was gelatin of a certain brand that was on special. Well, Bob came bringing Jello that was not on sale. I really said things I should never have said. I felt we needed to save every penny we could and he didn't save by buying the wrong one. When we got back to the apartment Bob disappeared into the bathroom. When I found him, he was almost crying and feeling so bad for what he had done in not paying attention to my list. I was crushed when I realized that I had hurt my husband in this way. Why hadn't I been more caring and understanding in the way I talked to him? Was saving a few cents worth hurting my dear husband by the way I told him off? I ask his forgiveness and we made up but I had really learned a lesson in confronting in a more loving way. I would like to admonish my readers to be more aware of your tone of voice and to be more loving when you confront. It can make a great difference in your marriage.

Then came the day when every time I ate, I started feeling sick and even vomiting. That was our first indication that our first baby was coming. By the close of the school year, I began feeling more and more sick. Eventually the sickness caused me to lose down to 108 pounds. There was just no way I could keep down food.

We finally found a Christian doctor, Dr. Lindley, and he started giving me shots to help with the sickness and he said we would be having our first new baby on January 25, 1959.He was close with his prediction because Roxane was born on January 24th.

By the end of July I began to feel better. In the middle of August we attended the yearly Beulah Park Holiness Camp in Wichita. One afternoon as we were sitting in the service, I had a fluttery feeling in my stomach area, something I had never experienced before. When I realized I was experiencing our baby's life inside me, I was so excited I had to lean over and whisper the news in Bob's ear.

The next two or three weeks passed uneventfully. Then, on September 1ˢᵗ we got a call from Grandpa Cheney that no one likes to get. We were told that Clifford, Bob's brother, had drowned out in Colorado. It was such a shock that Bob felt numb. Wilma was living with us at the time so the three of us headed for Nebraska to attend the funeral. By the time we returned to Wichita, my clothing was becoming tight. I was feeling great but I had to make myself some maternity clothes.

In November my parents and French grandparents made a trip to Arizona. On their way back to Nebraska they came by to visit us for a day or two. It was great to see them. At the time I did not realize it would be the last time I would see my Grandpa French. He died of a heart attack around the 20ᵗʰ of December, 1958. We couldn't go to the funeral because it was too close to my delivery date. That year Thanksgiving and Christmas were pretty much spent by ourselves.

Roxie, Our Baby Girl

On January 23ʳᵈ, Brother and Sister Henderson, a couple from our church, came for supper with us. I fixed chili that night. Everything was going fine and I felt pretty good. Early the next morning I was awakened by some cramping and realized it was labor pains.

"Bob," I said, "you better get a girl's name picked out because I think I'm going into labor." We were going to pick R.A. initials for all our children and I had already chosen Robert Allen if our first baby was a boy. Well, he began looking through name books and chose the name Roxane Annette. Soon after that we drove out to St. Joseph's Hospital. In those days no husband could be with his wife during labor and delivery so he spent the day in the waiting room.

Things were getting hard. I overheard a nurse say something about a breech birth and I wondered. Around 5:00 they gave me a shot that really put me out. That's when I dreamed I went to heaven. As I was waking up I was thinking I had died. I told the doctor to tell Bob that I still loved him. Roxy was born at 7:13 p.m. on January 24, 1959.

Bob came in after they got our baby cleaned up. I said to him, "Oh honey, I hope your folks won't mind that we had a girl." He assured me they would be happy. Then I told him my dream. It really touched his heart. He was so thankful he still had us.

I was in the hospital from Saturday until the next Thursday morning. Since Roxane came as a breech baby she really was a beautiful child without that pointed misshaped little head. Her mother, however, suffered with many, many stitches and found it hard to sit. They put heat lamps on and various ways to heal, but to put it bluntly, "I had a very sore sitter." I decided that maybe I didn't want to have any more babies.

When Bob came to take us home, I got pretty uptight. This tiny baby, weighing about eight pounds, seemed to cry all the time. I tried nursing her and that was quite unnerving. As night time came on, Roxane seemed more and more unhappy and I didn't know what to do for her. Bob's mother was to arrive that evening. About midnight Bob drove to the bus depot to pick her up. Was I ever glad to see my Mother-in-Law! Grandma had her quieted down and asleep in a few minutes. What was it about her magic touch? Could it be experience? She had had ten babies of her own so I think this did make the difference.

We didn't have money to cover the hospital cost so Bob's sister Wilma helped us out. The cost of having our baby was around $500. So we always said Wilma had part ownership in this daughter of ours.

Bob Graduates from Friend's University, Pastors Bethel Church in Wichita and Teaches School

Bob had one more semester left before graduation. Along with his studies he had sermons to prepare and a church to look after. Bethel Church decided that they should buy a house closer to the church for a parsonage. They discovered a house on Beebe Street just off West Central. While processing this business with the church, Bob wrote his finals and in June, 1959, graduated from Friend's University with a secondary teaching certificate, a major in history and minor in English. His little daughter was close to five months old and got to go to her daddy's graduation.

With this event behind us, we made the move from our upstairs apartment to the parsonage on Beebe Street. Bob started looking for a teaching position for the fall. He was able to get on at a school in the northern part of Wichita. Things got a bit easier for us financially and I was even able to take music lessons at a downtown music store in Wichita. It was called evangelistic playing dealing more generally with different types of chords on the piano. I really liked this course and took it several months. I've always been grateful for what I learned in this course.

About the middle of March, Bob had a spring break so we decided to make a trip of western Nebraska to show off our baby daughter. It would be Eva's parents first time to see baby Roxane and Grandpa Cheney's first time as well. It was really fun to show off our baby.

We also had been given a little puppy, a Pekinese. We decided it would be a gift to my little sister Elaine. This little dog had some little birth defect just enough that the owners could not sell it.

Before going on I would like to insert here about Bob's sister Wilma. She had finished her degree and obtained a teaching position in one of the Wichita primary schools. She stayed with us at our apartment for several months and shared the rental expense. Then when we moved out to Beebe Street we invited her to continue living with us. We had three bedrooms and so it all worked out for us.

November, 1959, Roxane started walking at 10 months. She was so cute. At Thanksgiving time my Mom and Dad and sister came for a visit. My Grandma Thornton Devasher and her friend Wes and another young boy also came. It was very nice to have relatives come to visit.

For the Christmas holidays Bob and I made a trip to Nebraska. It was fun to have our baby daughter to show to all the relatives and to be able to visit and spend time with family. Before we knew it a new year had rolled around and it was 1960. What would this year old in store? On January 24th, of course, we celebrated Roxy's first birthday. She looked so cute in her little red dress, walking all over the place. She kept mom busy trailing her and keeping her safe.

The end of last year or the first part of 1960 the Leland Swan family moved to Wichita with his aerosol company. They had a son, Samuel, who was about 8 years old and a daughter, Lela, who was about three. It was a blessing to have this family helping out in our church. In fact our church was beginning to grow from the twenties in number attending to now in the forties and fifties. We were reaching out into our community touching the lives of children and adults.

Later in the Spring I began having problems with my digestion. Oh dear –was it morning sickness again???? Then in July I began hemorrhaging. We contacted the doctor immediately and he ordered me to bed with no getting up for three weeks. He told us he didn't feel giving me something to keep the baby was the thing to do. But he told us, "If God wants you to have this baby, you will have it."Hopefully going to bed would heal the process and our baby would grow normally. The doctor gave us the date of January 18th for baby's arrival. To help us cope with the house hold duties and caring for Roxane, my young sister, Elaine, came to help us a few weeks. She was about 14 years old and helped a lot in caring for Roxane. Bob and I really appreciated her assistance. Within about three weeks I was able to be on my feet again and everything seemed to indicate a normal pregnancy.

Finally after the bleeding stopped, things settled down to a pretty normal pregnancy. Sometimes I would have twinges of labor pains but nothing serious. I got to the point that I really didn't pay much attention to the light pains. I remember that in November we had hoped to go to Kansas City to visit my old college friend but then we called it off because of these pains.

During August our District Conference and camp was held at Hutchison, Kansas. This town was not far from Wichita so we drove back and forth for services. One of the highlights of this conference was Bob's ordination with Reverend R.G. Flexon praying over him. Before this Bob just carried a district license to preach; now he was an ordained minister. So he could give more time to his ministry, Bob decided he would do substitute teaching rather than full time teaching for the 1960-1961 school year. We pastored the Bethel Pilgrim Holiness Church from August, 1959 to August of 1963.

In December, 1960, we got word that Grandpa George Cheney, who had gone back to Northern Ireland, had died. They planned to have the funeral in December, around the 19th or 20th. Since I was nearing my delivery date of January 18, we decided that I should stay with Leland and Joeretta Swan. So Bob and Wilma went to Nebraska for the funeral without me. I believe Wilma stayed for the remainder of the Christmas holidays but Bob came back to spend Christmas with Roxie and me.

Robert Allen Cheney

On Tuesday, December 27[th]there was an all-day holiness meeting at the Salvation Army Church in Wichita. We decided to go although the labor pains came on lightly. In fact, I got to the point of just ignoring them and going on with whatever was taking place. We were close to a shopping center in East Wichita and I wanted to do some shopping over the noon hour. Pains continued but we went back for the afternoon service. I noticed my pains were getting stronger and it seemed Roxy was really irritable so I leaned over to Bob and whispered, "I'll be waiting in the car with Roxane."

Well, before the service ended, I was wishing Bob had come out with me. The pains were getting stronger and stronger and I knew the baby was ready to come. When Bob came from the meeting, I said, "We better head home quick and call the doctor's office." We did and they said come to the office immediately. I took my little case with a few things. We left Roxy with the Greys, members of the church, and headed for the doctor's office. After being checked, they found I was really dilated and sent me straight to the maternity ward at St. Joseph's Hospital.

By then it was after 5:00 p.m. and in about an hour and a half we had a 7 pound, 2 ounce baby boy. December 27th was a medium mild winter day and our boy was three weeks early but he seemed to be very normal. I had chosen Robert Allen because I wanted our boy to be named after Bob. But, when we asked Roxy if she wanted to call her brother Robbie or Allen, she said, "Allen." That's why he ended up being called by his middle name. When I went home from the hospital, we had visitors. Grandpa and Grandma Thornton came, as well as Grandpa Alfred Cheney. Grandma stayed to help me when the Grandpas went back home to Nebraska.

Continuation of Life in Wichita

It was about the beginning of March that Allen, our two month old baby, got a very serious chest cold. In fact he coughed a lot and his lungs sounded like he had pneumonia. We took off to the doctor for a check-up. Our doctor said he needed to be hospitalized right away so we took him to St. Joseph Hospital. There they put him under an oxygen tent and within two or three days he was well enough to come home. When babies this small get lung infections one has to be so careful.

The next two years were filled with church ministry and youth activities, teaching school for Bob and for me, being a busy mother of a little girl and a baby boy. We did have Bob's sister with us during the school year and many times she helped us out by babysitting our children while we took care of church matters. Wilma was a great blessing to us.

In the summer of 1962 we decided to take a vacation. We went on a trip with Mother and Daddy Thornton to visit my Grandmother Devasher in Arizona. This was the first time we got to see Grand Canyon in Arizona. We also drove to Los Angles, California to visit my sister Esther and husband Nathan and their baby Sharon. During our travels my immune system didn't work well and I got a bad cold that went into my lungs. It hurt so badly when I coughed that my sister insisted I go to her doctor.

Sure enough it was the beginning of pneumonia. He prescribed an antibiotic and told me to go to bed. Well, I didn't want to do that because I would miss out on too much. There was the visit to the art center, a visit to Sea World and to Mt. Wilson Observatory and the beautiful Capistrano Mission. Do you see why I didn't want to go to bed? I guess I paid for it because for most of the summer I was still getting back on my feet.

On that trip my dad went deep sea fishing with my cousin Dixie's husband, Earle. What I remember about this was how pale my Dad and Earle looked, kind of green looking around the gills, when they got back from fishing, a little sea sickness from being out there on the ocean, I would say!!!

Dec. 27, 1962 our little boy Allen was 2 years old and January 24, 1963 Roxane turned four. Now we began thinking of returning to the Rocky Mountain District. Bob decided to give his resignation to the Bethel Pilgrim Holiness Church and allow his name to come up for call in Nebraska and Colorado.

That spring, around Easter time, I remember not feeling well, having a fever and red spots coming all over my skin. I had contacted red measles, really a serious case. Not only did I have them, I gave them to our little daughter and son. So Bob became nurse to all of us. What would I have done without this dear husband of mine! It didn't seem as hard on the children as it was on me. Evidently Bob had contacted this kind of measles in his younger life. At least he didn't get them from us.

Going to Stratton

After pastoring the Bethel Church in Wichita for five years, Bob received a call to pastor the Stratton Church in Nebraska. The Stratton Church was located about 35 miles west of McCook, Nebraska on Highway 6. A young couple by the name Don and Fredora Harrison came with their truck to move our household stuff and in August, 1963 we were settled in the parsonage just next door to Stratton Pilgrim Holiness Church. In order to supplement the church salary Bob got a job driving the school bus.

Some of the people who attended this church were Eva Carpenter and husband, Dolly Angermier, a blind lady, the Harrisons and their children, the Cobbs and their children, Mildred and Clifford Swale (she was Ron's nurse when he was born) and two other older couples. It was a small but very friendly church.

We were really kept busy in the church. Bob's sister, Carolyn Cheney, had graduated from University of Nebraska at Lincoln and applied for a job at Culbertson High School as a Home Economics teacher. Many weekends she would come to Stratton and help out in the church. During the fall a young man by the name of Leon Wyatt who worked in oil drilling started attending our church. We learned that he had become a believer under the ministry of Virgil and Ruth Hogarth. He seemed very nice and it didn't take long for him and Carolyn to form a friendship. In the next few months we saw quite a lot of this couple and by Easter they were engaged to be married.

By the end of September, 1963 morning sickness let me know I was pregnant again. In October, we decided to visit Grandpa and Grandma Cheney. Because of Teachers' Convention Bob didn't have to drive the school bus for three days and we had a five day weekend. It was nice to have a break and a chance to visit the grandparents.

A revival was going on at the Oshkosh church while we were there and we decided to attend. As I was sitting in the evening service, I suddenly felt this gush. I quickly got up and headed for the downstairs bathroom. I realized I was hemorrhaging again like I did with Allen and so, after cleaning up as best as I could, I made my way out to the car. There I waited until Bob came out of the church with Roxy and Allen. When I told Bob, we headed to his parents' home. My dear mother-in-law told me to go to bed and stay there. I had a good rest the next couple days.

By the third day the bleeding had quit and we went back to Stratton. I did try to take it easy and it seemed that everything was going to be ok. The doctor thought the baby would arrive around the last of June. When the morning sickness got really bad, I would go to the Stratton Hospital for a shot that really helped.

It was November 22, 1963 and, because I was feeling terrible, Bob took me to the hospital. I will always remember that date because the news coming over the speakers in the entrance was that our President, John F. Kennedy, had just been shot. He was down in Texas in a parade in an open limousine with his wife, Jackie, and some other government officials. What a shock it was that our President was killed that day by a gun shot. We were all in a daze. So this was quite a historical event in U.S. history about six and a half months before Ronald was born.

Tragedy Hits

It was May, 1964 and Vivian Cheney, Bob's youngest sister, was graduating from Garden County High School. Bob and I felt it was too much for me to go but Carolyn wanted to go to her sister's graduation. She wanted to take Roxy and Allen with her so we let her use our car. If I remember correctly, it was Monday afternoon after the graduation that she came back with our two children. When I saw her, I was shocked to see how pale she looked. She told me she had terrible pain in her side. Probably what made things worse was the car wasn't working well and every so often she had to get out and tap on something to get it going again. Anyway, the first thing I thought of was her appendix and I said, "Carolyn, you have to go to the doctor."

I was able to get her an appointment with Doctor Harris. Her white count wasn't especially high but the doctor thought he should go ahead and do an appendectomy. We took her to the hospital and Bob and I waited for the results. The doctor thought the operation would take about an hour but it seemed like the doctor never would come out.

About three hours later when he came to talk with us, Dr. Harris looked like one sick doctor. He said, "Your sister had a large tumor on her ovary, probably ovarian cancer." He showed us what he had taken out of her and it really looked terrible. As I remember, the tumor lay in a 9" square pan, but it had broken as they removed it allowing some of the fluid to get into her abdominal cavity. He told us he would send it off for testing so we could know if it was cancer but the prognosis was not looking good. He advised that she should stay in the hospital until the incision healed. As it turned out, Carolyn's tumor was cancerous. Of course, this was very troubling to us and it fell to us to tell Leon and the rest of the family. Leon and Carolyn had planned to be married. Well, they decided go ahead with their wedding as soon as she recovered from her operation and before she started her cancer treatment, setting their date as June 12, 1964.

With our baby coming in June, it seemed too many things were happening at once!!! However, the next few weeks went pretty smoothly. My doctor had predicted June 25th as my due date but since Allen had come about three weeks early, it was possible that this baby would too. As time drew closer to delivery I called to see if Dr. Harris would allow me to go to the wedding of Leon and Carolyn. Well, guess what??? Dr. Harris was on a fishing trip.

I thought, "If he's not here, how can he deliver my baby anyway?" and I decided to attend the wedding. We arrived for the rehearsal and I watched as they practiced. In fact, Bob was the one who was performing the ceremony. Of course, a lot of family had come for this important event. I told Grandma Cheney we would stay with my cousins, James and Joyce French who lived east of Lewellen on highway 92.

The next morning around 4:00 I woke up to another gush that I couldn't do anything about. This time it wasn't blood. It was water! My membranes had ruptured! It was the first time this had ever happened to me. I was so embarrassed but Joyce was kind and told me not to worry about it. We decided I should be checked by Dr. Albee. We knew that once the membranes ruptured the baby had to appear even though I wasn't having any contractions. At the hospital in Oshkosh Dr. Albee said, "Well, since you haven't dilated much, I'm pretty sure you can make it to Stratton. If things get serious, there's a hospital in Ogallala, one in Grant and another in Imperial.

Ronald Alfred Cheney

We arrived at the parsonage about noon. I felt I needed a quick shower which took more time. At about 1:00 p.m. we entered the hospital. Dr. Harris took me right in for examination. I still was not contracting that much. He said to Bob, "Well, do you want to get back for that wedding? I can give her something to hurry up the birth."

Bob said, "I don't want you to give her something that would harm her or the baby."

"Oh no," Dr. Harris said, "It will only help baby to come quicker."

So I got a shot that really began the contractions in a hurry. It seemed my back hurt so bad. Bob was right there by my head giving encouragement and holding my hand. Since this was a small hospital Dr. Harris allowed Bob to see Ronald A. Cheney arrive, June 12, 1964 about 4:45pm central time. As soon as Bob saw we were o.k. he rushed out and began his trip back to Lewellen to perform Carolyn's and Leon's wedding ceremony.

So Ronald and I missed the wedding but on Sunday we had a number of visitors at the hospital. One of them said our baby had the hands of a farmer. Who would have known then that those were the hands of a surgeon?

While we were at the hospital there was a baby girl in the nursery who had been there since March. She was born pre-mature at around a pound and a half. So when people looked at our baby and this baby girl, they thought ours was the older.

In keeping with our plan to name our children with the initials R. A. we named our baby Ronald Alfred. While we were in Wichita at the beginning of our marriage I taught the cutest little blond haired boy named Ronald in the children's Sunday school class. Since I really liked the name Ronald, we decided to put it with Alfred for Grandpa Alfred Cheney. Alfred was also Bob's middle name. Ronald Alfred weighed 7 pounds 15 ½ ounces. The nurse, Mildred Swale, said she was tempted to place her finger on the scale and make it an even 8 pounds. (Mildred and her husband, Clifford, attended our church in Stratton.)

1964 saw us very busy with three young children as well as with the church work. In September Bob's older sister, Wilma, decided to go to Zambia as a missionary teacher. I remember her coming to say goodbye to us and being able to see our little baby boy, Ronald, who was nearly three months old by then.

That year we celebrated Thanksgiving at home with Carolyn and Leon. Carolyn was going through cancer treatment that made her really sick and we moved in a hospital bed and took care of her along with her husband. As we passed Christmas and into January, Bob's oldest sister, Elaine, ask if she could help us out by caring for the baby. Kathy, another of the Cheney sisters, took Ronald to Denver so Elaine could care for him. Ronald was about 7 or 8 months old. I really missed him but under the circumstances it gave me more time to help Carolyn. For a three week period I was without my baby. I missed him so very much and so did daddy and his big sister and brother.

Carolyn went to be with the Lord on February 20th, 1965. The day of her funeral was very cold. I felt so sorry for Leon. They had been married for only eight months. But God just didn't see fit to heal Carolyn. So now there were only eight Cheney children left for Alfie and Ella Cheney.

I think it was either during the fall of 1964 or perhaps the spring of 1965 when my Grandmother Thornton Devasher came to visit us at Stratton. She came in her new 1964 Buick Sky Lark. She had to see her three great grandchildren, especially the new baby Ronald. I was so glad for my grandmothers and grandpas but I wished I had spent more time with them and asked them more about their young lives. The stories of their past can teach us a lot of lessons. So, grandchildren, take time to ask questions from your grandparents. You won't be sorry you did this!

On September 15th, 1965, I got word that Grandma Devasher had died. She was 72 years old. Bob and I decided that Roxane would stay with her daddy since she was in Kindergarten at Stratton Public Schools and I would take Allen and Ron and ride with my folks to Prescott Arizona where the funeral was held. Grandma would be buried by Grandpa Devasher in the Prescott, Arizona cemetery. I remember all Grandma's children were present and many of her grandchildren. She had fifteen grandchildren and several great grandchildren including Bob's and my three children.

The children divided up Grandma's stuff and my dad got her 1964 Buick Sky Lark car. They drove it many miles after this. Another thing was Grandma's special Chinese Pug dog named Soogie. Allen our oldest son just fell in love with this dear dog and the love seemed to be mutual, so Soogie became our dog.

A Busy Time in Stratton

Stratton was a small town in a farming community and as usual in small towns, the neighbors knew one another and were friendly. Our son Allen found a young boy his age that had a bicycle. One day he came inside the parsonage and said, "Mom, come and see."So Mom and Dad go outside and see him get on his friends bike and ride down the street. He was only four years old but here he was riding a bicycle without us knowing. It didn't have training wheels either! Of course this meant Mom and Dad would have to get some money together and buy him a bike so he would have his own.

When Ronald was six or eight months old we asked our District Superintendent Rev. Schendel to have a dedication service for him. Our two older children had been dedicated at Bethel Church in Wichita, Kansas. Bob and I always wanted to do this with each of our children because we knew God had given these children to us and we wanted to give them back to God. Of course we knew that each of the children would later need to make their own decision to follow Christ.

Between Bob's school duties and caring for our congregation we kept very busy. In the summer there were youth camps, family camps and conferences. In 1965 we took several of our youth to Maranatha, a camp near North Platte, Nebraska. Our three children stayed with Claude and Twila Livingston on their farm north of Wauneta so we could work in the camp. It was very rewarding for me to be a counselor for some of the girls. The campers had many activities, one of which was a hunter safety course offered by a trained NRA teacher. I took it and earned my hunter safety card in August of 1965.

Roxane began school at Stratton Nebraska. I very much wanted her to get started with music lessons. There was a lady north of town, Mrs. Eggle, who gave music lessons. I got Roxy enrolled but we felt we should also get her a piano to practice on. We headed for McCook Nebraska. There they had a pretty good music store that sold pianos and organs and various other instruments. I remember sitting down to various brands of pianos to try them out. I'm not sure how many pianos I tried playing that day but I always came back to the Baldwin Acrosonic. It seemed to have the best sound and touch and I thought it would make a great piano for our daughter. We bought it for over $900.00. These many years later I'm still playing it. I think it was the spring of 1966 that Roxy had her first recital. Her Grandpa and Grandma Cheney came for that occasion.

After school ended in May of 1965 we decided to make a trip to Oregon. At this time my sister Esther and husband Nathan lived at Selma Oregon. Nathan was a school teacher in that area. My parents decided to make this trip too so that it could be an Earl Thornton family reunion. We started out about the first of June. It really was a neat time for all three of us girls to be together. Esther and Nathan had only little Sharon. Elaine was still young and single and, of course, Bob and I had three children, Roxane age 6, Allen age 4 and Ronald almost one year. It was nice for Mom and Dad to be with their girls, their husbands and the four little grandchildren.

One of the events I remember happening on that trip was an airplane ride for Bob, our two older children and me. One of Esther and Nathan's friends had a small plane. He took us for a ride and showed us the city of Grants Pass so we could see the layout of the land. I remember our four year old Allen was so impressed. He loved airplanes anyway and I think this just increased his desire to fly in a plane. As we were finishing our sightseeing and landing the plane on the air strip he looked over at me and said, "Mommy, do we have to put it away?" He wanted to keep on flying and to this day he has always wanted to build his own plane and fly. Well, somehow that dream of flying ended up in the medical field and that makes his family very proud.

Another sightseeing trip was down along the Northern coast of California. Esther and Nathan took us to see the "Trees of Mystery". Oh, what an awesome sight that was! We had never seen the giant Red Woods before. I think those trees are one of God's great wonders. They are such tall trees reaching up into the heavens and with their trunks so big that you could have cut a tunnel and driven a car through. Although we didn't get to see it, in California there is a tree where they have done this very thing. Truly these trees are an amazing creation of God!

On our way home we drove south through Redding and Sacramento, California so we could go home by way of Salt Lake City. This is a great Mormon city where the Mormon Temple and tabernacle are located. When we got there, we got a motel for the night since we wanted to see the Mormon facilities. They would not allow us to go inside the temple. Only true Mormons can enjoy that sacred place. However they told us that we were welcome to go in and listen to the Mormon choir practicing in the Tabernacle. My, what a big place and so many people singing! The singing was beautiful.

The next day we were on our way to Denver, Colorado where Elaine, Ken and their three girls, Susan, Karen and Carol Jean lived. I don't remember if the day we arrived was Ron's birthday or if it was the next day. I do remember that Elaine decided he needed a birthday cake. She went out and bought him a small round cake and one great big candle that she put right in the center of the cake. Baby Ronald was now one year old.

Blind-sided by a Blizzard

One spring-like morning in March, 1966 Bob found that the school was closing for the day because a bad storm was predicted. In those days we didn't get weather reports as much as now. So Bob and I figured the sun was up and it seemed like there wouldn't be a storm very soon. It was fairly nice that morning. We decided it would be a good time to head for McCook and do some shopping.

Well, on the way home, soon after passing Culbertson it began to snow. It kept coming harder and harder and we realized we should have stayed home because this was a real blizzard. We kept inching along slowly and were getting closer and closer to Stratton. But suddenly our Studebaker Lark slid off the road and we could go no further.

Praise the Lord, there was a farm house right across the road from us. God had provided for us. We all walked over to the house and knocked on the door but no one answered. We knew someone lived there so we just opened the door and walked in. Finally the owner arrived. He told us we could stay the night because he had enough room for our whole family. The next morning the sun came out and the roads were opened so we traveled on to Stratton, only about six miles from where we got stuck.

While in Stratton, Bob was able to acquire a teaching /principal's job at a small school in Parks, Nebraska. It kept him really busy but financially helped us with family expenses. During our three plus years at Stratton we always attended family camps and conferences at the old Colorado Springs Bible College Campus. I loved this setting for these camps.

As I recall, we attended the summer camp of 1966 with our three children, Roxane, Allen and Ronald. At this camp our boys made their decision to follow Jesus. I can still see these two little boys dressed in red suit jackets bowing at the camp altar where I had bowed some nine years before. God truly is so faithful to speak even to the young hearts of our children.

As for Roxane, while we were still in Wichita, she gave her heart to Jesus after I had explained to her the Bible story of Jesus' death on the cross and explained why He died. She told me, "Mommy, I want to pray and ask Jesus in my heart." She was about three or four years old when this happened. One thing Bob and I always tried to do was teach our children about the Bible. We read many, many Bible stories over and over.

To my Children and grandchildren I say, "It is never wasted time to read the Bible stories and discuss them with your children." Take the time to do it!

During the time we lived at Stratton my Aunt Chrystal French came to visit. She was my mom's sister and had spent many years as a missionary in Nigeria, Africa. She was one of my favorite aunts, although I had a number of favorites. I don't remember the length of her visit but one of the days she came to me and said she felt really sick and feverish. I got a doctor's appointment for her and took her in. I suppose he prescribed some medication and did the usual check over. We went back to the house and things did not get better. Finally she said to me, "I know what is wrong now. I have a reoccurrence of malaria. Please just get me back home to Lewellen so I can get my special malaria medication."

So I made some quick phone calls and we arranged for my sister Elaine to meet us at Enders and take her on home to Lewellen. When people get this disease caused by mosquitoes, it can reoccur if the immune system is weak. I've seen what can happen to people with malaria and it is not a pleasant sight. They get to shaking so bad with fever that all the blankets in the world cannot make them stop.

Elaine was pretty worried but she got her back to Grandma's where she lived and was able to start her malaria medicine. She soon recovered. Doctors in the U.S. don't have much of this disease to contend with and so it is hard for them to diagnosis. I guess you could say it is more of an African disease. I am so glad to report that our family did not get malaria at any time during the period of 25 years that we were back and forth in the African countries.

Moving to Imperial, Nebraska

During the early spring of 1966 we learned that the pastor of Imperial Pilgrim Holiness Church was moving to another church and we were given a call to pastor the somewhat bigger church at Imperial. After praying and seeking God's plan for us we felt this was of God. Bob checked around seeing what possibilities there might be of obtaining a teaching position. There was a Junior High position open in Wauneta, a small town ten or twelve miles from Imperial on the road leading to McCook Nebraska. Bob applied for this position and was accepted.

Some of the families attending the Imperial church were: the Andersons, the Dinnel families, the Fergusons, Hixons, Johnsons and several others. There were really greater possibilities for outreach in Imperial. In fact it wasn't long after moving there that the church decided to start a building fund. After all these years, seeing what has taken place in this Wesleyan Church and the outreach it has had really gives me a sense of praise and thanksgiving.

When we moved, Allen started school and Roxy began 2nd grade. Ron was only two years old and quite a live wire. We moved after our camp at Colorado Springs, August of 1966. The Verlon Dinnels from Stratton helped move our things with their truck. We truly appreciated this church family. They had four girls, some in high school and others in grade school. They were a big help with our children.

In the spring of 1967 we received word from my folks that my mom's uncle, Caleb Mecham, had passed away. The funeral service would be held in Oregon. Mother and Daddy and Mom's brother, Jewel, were driving out and wondered if I would like to go along. Since Bob was teaching and Roxy and Allen were in school, they could not go but it would be a good chance for me to see my sister Esther and her family. This was March of 1967. Fortunately the weather was not too bad.

The service was held at Klamath Falls and "Uncle Cabbie" as we called him was buried beside his wife who had died back in the 1920's from the bad flu epidemic. Their two daughters, Ruth and Rebecca lived with my grandparents after their mother's death so they seemed more like aunts than cousins. Ruth was at the service but not Rebecca. After the funeral we drove to Selma, Oregon, where Esther, Nathan and family lived and we visited a few days before returning to Nebraska. Ronald did pretty well at traveling but he had some ear infection. I'm sure traveling over mountains didn't help this situation but we made it. We were glad to meet Bob in Ogallala along with Roxy and Allen and head to our home in Imperial.

We attended our last camp in Colorado Springs toward the end of June. From that time on we were with the Nebraska District.

The 1968 Merger of
The Pilgrim Holiness Church and the Wesleyan Methodist Church

In June of 1968 a conference was held in Anderson, Indiana. It was a historical occasion, the joining of two big church denominations, the Pilgrim Holiness Church and Wesleyan Methodist churches. We wanted to experience this event and, since Bob and I had just gotten a new 1968 Ford Fair lane car, we could go. My mother was willing to stay with our three children. We asked Phil Nettleton, the pastor of our Lincoln, Nebraska church, to go with us. It was nice having a new car to travel in. I think this was the first new car we ever had.

The conference was quite impressive. With two General Superindents from each denomination, the newly formed denomination had four Generals and a new name: 'The Wesleyan Church. It truly was an historical point in our church's history. It was a great experience for us and, because we had witnessed the event, we were better able to explain the merger to our congregations. Afterwards we returned to Nebraska, leaving Phil Nettleton at Lincoln and going on to Lewellen to pick up our kids.

There were some other important events taking place that summer. My mom's sister, Chrystal French met the right man, Ken Hunt. They set their wedding date as August 3rd and were married in the Methodist Church in Lewellen, Nebraska. Aunt Chrystal always was a very special aunt to me. She spent about five terms in the country of Nigeria, Africa. I believe this was a big influence on my life of becoming a missionary. This was the first wedding we attended that summer.

My youngest sister, Elaine, met the man of her life while she attended a Bible college in Red Deer, Alberta, Canada. She and Steve chose August 5th as their wedding date. They were married at the Oshkosh Wesleyan church. Her matrons of honor were my sister, Esther and me. My husband, Bob performed the ceremony. Our youngest son Ronald was the ring bearer and Jackie French was the little miniature bride and flower girl. Seems like little kids do cute things at weddings or maybe some not so cute. Ronald decided during the ceremony that he was tired so he laid down on the steps to rest. I don't know what little Jackie thought. Ron was just four years old and, of course, you never know what a little four year old will do!

Now our Mom and Dad had seen all three daughters married. This last daughter would live in Canada because she had married a Canadian. He really is a great brother-in-law and ministers for the Lord. I call him my brother.

School began after Labor Day, 1968; Roxy was in third grade. Allen started first grade. That year I helped count votes at the court house after Election Day. It seems like we had many varied experiences at Imperial and a nice congregation at our Imperial Wesleyan church. I know the older children had a number of friends, especially the Hixon girls who lived down the alley. They had a TV that was very enticing to our kids since we didn't own a television. The Hixon family attended our church and they were good people. In fact, Mr. Guy Hixon owned the music store in Imperial. Allen took some guitar lessons from Mr. Hixon and Roxy got her new tenor saxophone from him. She played in the school band and it went with us to Africa in our first term in Swaziland.

Rylan Arthur Cheney

This is the story of Rylan A. Cheney's birth on July 19, 1969. We planned for his birth five years after our third child. Let me explain why there were five years between, Rylan and Ronald.

In 1967 when Ron was two years and 2 or 3 months old, I became pregnant. Things seemed to be going quite well. In fact, I wasn't really sick like usual and we were looking forward to having a new baby. Then, about 8 or 10 weeks later, I started having cramps. We talked with Doctor Shoppe and he said I should go to bed but within a few days I lost the baby. It was hard going through it but Bob and I felt God knew what was best. I often wondered if this child would have been a little sister for Roxanne. I wondered, too, if something would have been wrong with this child and God chose to take this one to His Kingdom. Afterward, the doctor said I should take birth control pills for a while. I didn't want to but did it because the doctor said I should not get pregnant for a few months.

Between our church and Bob's teaching we were kept busy. We had a nice youth group to work with and took a big part in getting young people to Youth Camps. Then, in 1968 I got pregnant again and I even took chiropractor treatments at Atwood, Kansas in Dr. Warta's Clinic to help me feel better during the first few months of pregnancy. But I did have a craving for dill pickles and tomato juice. This was to be my last pregnancy so I made several nice new dresses for myself. But as spring of 1969 came on, and especially the beginning of summer, it became very hot. We thought that maybe baby would come around the first part of July because I was getting bigger and bigger.

Bob had to take young people to a youth camp out in the Rockies but he didn't want me to stay by myself. So the children and I went to one of our church families—the Verlon Dinnel family that lived near Enders. They had a wonderful large cool farm house with a full basement. During the really hot days of July it felt so good to be in there nice comfortable basement. In fact, I think one of the days we were there the temperature was 108 degrees.

Bob was gone the whole week, enjoying the cool of the mountains while the children and I were at the Dinnel farm. After the week was over we went back to Imperial as Bob was now home again from the youth camp. But Oh HOW HOT IT WAS! We didn't have fans and, for sure, the parsonage didn't have an air conditioner. It was too hot to sleep. Already I was over my due date at least by a week. One night, around midnight, I got a cup of ice from 'frig' to chomp on to cool down.

On Wednesday, July 16, I went to the doctor's office because I was beginning to feel a few cramps. However, they sent me home and nothing much happened until Friday the 18th. Early that morning I went to the hospital for the nurse to check me to see if dilation was taking place. They decided I should do a lot of walking. That evening Bob and I started walking the halls of the hospital.

What started out at 6:00 a.m. on the 18th continued into the evening and night. Finally the doctor decided to break the membrane. That was not fun! However, it wasn't long until the pushing started. It was so hard because baby was big. Finally, about 2 or 3 minutes past midnight, the 19th of July, our Rylan Arthur Cheney arrived safe and sound, all 9 pounds, 10 and 1/2 oz. of him. What a cutie! He was so filled out that he didn't really look like a new born. His sister and two brothers came with Daddy to see their new baby brother but they had to look through the hospital window with Mother holding him up.

One thing about Rylan's birthday is that the astronauts landed on the moon on the 20th of July, 1969, just the day after he was born. I was holding our new baby and watching TV when I saw Neil Armstrong walk on the moon. All the church members were happy with the safe arrival of our new son and soon organized a baby shower that was held at the Dinnel farm.

After we got out of the hospital we made arrangements for Mother, baby and the three older kids to travel up to Grandpa and Grandma Thornton's ranch. We stayed about a week and Grandpa and Grandma enjoyed their grandchildren, especially their new grandson. Then, when he was about 2 or 3 weeks old Rylan had his first trip to the Wesleyan Family Camp at Atkinson, Nebraska. He was such a good baby!

So, God blessed our family with our one daughter and three sons.

We wanted to dedicate Rylan to the Lord so in September, 1969 we asked our District Superintendent Reverend Winnie Brown to come and hold this service at our Imperial Wesleyan Church. Grandma and Grandpa Thornton and Great Grandma French came for this special service. This wonderful little son that the Lord had given us we now dedicated to God to use in His Kingdom building. I truly praise God as I see him and his family serving the Lord.

At this point I would like to bring this section of my life story to a close and begin with our Africa Adventures. We had spent twelve years pastoring churches in Kansas and Nebraska. In November of 1969 we received a telephone call that would change our lives forever. May God receive all the glory for the wondrous things He has done!

The Telephone Call

One frosty November morning in 1969 at Imperial, Nebraska, Bob was just getting ready to go out the door on his way to teach school when the telephone rang. I called him to the phone, not recognizing the voice on the other end. As they talked, I listened. "I'm Rev. Jones, Mission Director over Zambia, Africa and I have had some recommendations that you folks would be good missionary teachers. We are in need of a missionary teacher here in Zambia and wondered if you would be interested?" Bob explained that we would have to do some praying about this matter before giving them an answer. Rev. Jones said that he would call back later.

There was a thrill of excitement going through my bones as I thought of our family being missionaries in Africa. We had pastored three different churches during the past eleven years and the thought of being anything else had not really occurred to us. Although, as a young person I had felt that God might be calling me to go to China as a missionary, this did not happen. The doors of China were closed at that time. But being a missionary in Africa— how thrilling…and that is exactly what I hoped we could do. I began to dream about it, thinking of all that it would mean. I could hardly wait to tell the children that evening to see what their reaction might be. When I broke the news to them that we might go to Africa as missionaries, they too became very excited.

Several weeks passed and it seemed like we would never get another call from Rev. Jones. Would we ever hear from him again? It was getting to the point that I really needed to pray through about this matter of being a missionary. I was ready to go, but was I ready to stay? This was the big question. I remember going to our bedroom and getting down on my knees. There I cried my heart out to the Lord and finally I was able to say, "Yes, Lord, I am willing to stay if that is what you want. Truly, I want your will for our lives." From then on I knew the Lord had a plan for our family and that He would work everything out even if it meant we didn't go to Africa.

Bob told me that when the Lord called him to preach he was so shy that the thought occurred to him, "If the Lord will just help me get through two years of preaching here in the States (that was what was required before couples could go overseas as missionaries) then he would go preach to the African people. Little did he realize that this would one day come true. Nevertheless, after eleven years of preaching the shyness had worn off. Teaching school along with pastoring had brought about that change. We kept waiting for that call but it never came. Christmas was drawing closer. Just after Christmas there was a Conference on Evangelism that we really wanted to attend. The Richard Longs who pastored the Oshkosh, Nebraska Wesleyan Church ask us if we would like to ride back to Cincinnati, Ohio for that conference the end of December, 1969. We were delighted to ride with them and share expenses. They had been missionaries in Zambia for several years and it gave us a chance to share with them.

Bob's sister, Wilma, who was on furlough from Zambia very willingly offered to take care of our children. We had four children at this time: Roxane who was nearly 11, Allen age 9, Ron age 5, and our baby Rylan who was five months. It would be a big job but Aunt Wilma had lots of experience and was very capable. Everything went well and baby Rylan even cut his first two teeth!

What an experience the Conference on Evangelism was! It touched our hearts and encouraged us to work even harder at soul winning and helping our church to catch a new vision for the lost. At the conference we met the General Secretary of World Missions, Rev. Ermal Wilson. Since we had heard no more from Rev. Jones, we decided to approach Rev. Wilson about the possibility of going as missionaries to Africa. He was very friendly to us and quite delighted that we were willing to offer ourselves as missionary material. He promised that we would be hearing from headquarters in the near future. He was planning to leave soon for Africa. Rev. Wilson promised that some applications would be sent to us along with some psychological test that we were required to take.

On the way home we again felt renewed excitement and joy knowing that God was working out His plan for our lives. The material Rev. Wilson promised would come to us didn't come right away. Bob knew that he was going to have to give resignation for his school teaching very soon and still we did not hear from the mission department. God was teaching us to have patience, I believe. Finally in March, just before the dead line for signing a school contract, our papers came from the mission department. It was then that we knew our lives were going to make a change from pastoring to being missionaries.

Preparing to Go to Africa

Our applications and psychological papers were completed quickly and put into the mail. Bob gave his resignation to the school and we began thinking about things like passports and visas, packing things for the family for four years and many other things.

During their regular board meeting in May, 1970 the General Board appointed us as missionaries. At that time we were told there were two places where missionaries were needed, Zambia and Swaziland. We prayed about this and finally felt the Lord leading us to Swaziland. Bob's sister, Wilma, was serving as a missionary in Zambia, teaching in the school at Jembo Mission and his other sister and husband, Orai and Linda Lehman, were serving in Swaziland.

Our church at Imperial had given us a two year call the year before and therefore we had to ask that they release us from this appointment. They did this with some hesitation for they did not want to give us up. Our spring and summer of 1970 were spent in preparation. People came with gifts and supplies. During July we attended Family Camp at Atkinson, Nebraska. They ask us to speak and tell how the Lord had called us. I remember that one of the verses that God gave us was Revelation 3:18 "Behold I have set before you an open door which no man can shut." We could feel God opening this door before us to go to Africa. At the Mission's service the Women's Missionary Society surprised us with tables of supplies that we knew would be needed. What a great feeling to know that our District was behind us and giving their full support for our going to the mission field.

During August we gave our farewell to Imperial Wesleyan Church and packed up our things to move to Grandpa Cheney's old farm house west of Lewellen. All our furniture and personal belongings were moved into the house. The three older children enrolled in Oshkosh Grade School and Rylan was with us at home. He loved the farm and all the animals. He would stand by the yard fence and look out into the feed yard and say, "tow, tow"! He loved to watch the cows by the hour and enjoyed riding on the tractors with his dad. It was also nice to be close to both sets of grandparents. My mother was able to care for the children while Bob and I attended the Missionary Retreat in Indiana in August.

Now it seemed things were falling into place fast. There were several speaking engagements that we attended. I particularly remember the Mission Convention they called us to in Omaha, Nebraska. There we met Alma Robertson, a former missionary to Sierra Leone. People were very nice to us and they seemed glad when we shared with them what God was doing. It was a good time to meet families of the church. On Sunday afternoon one family invited us over for the evening meal. Our boys enjoyed playing football with their boys until Ronald, our six year old, came in crying that he had hurt his arm. The doctor at Oshkosh confirmed that his collar bone was broken. With a sling on and several weeks of being careful the broken bone repaired itself as good as new and Ronald was back in full swing!

Fall came on and the packing began in earnest. Two very special people gave us encouragement and help. Rev. and Mrs. Richard Long, now pastors but formerly missionaries to Zambia became our source of information when we had questions or didn't know how to do things. One day they came out to the farm to have dinner with us. Rev. Long helped Bob build a great big crate that held the children's bicycles, our stove, and washer, and other big equipment. They packed eleven steel barrels with household equipment, linens and even some of our clothing we would need for later.

There were the physicals that we had to take at the doctor's office in Oshkosh and all those shots---Yellow fever, small pox, polio and typhoid and probably others. This was the painful but necessary part we were told by Headquarters. I even decided that I must learn to ride the bicycle if I was going to be a missionary in Africa. I was sure that every missionary did that! So one evening I got out the bike and began riding it down the lane. What really happened I can't tell for sure but I found myself down on the ground with my back hurting so bad I could hardly walk. That ended my learning to ride the bike!!!

Finally, goodbyes were said to family and friends and our suitcases were packed. The things we were leaving behind were packed into one room of Grandpa Cheney's old house and we moved over to Grandma and Grandpa Cheney's new house with all our bags. My parents, Earl and Beulah Thornton, came down to join us and on November 17th we headed to Denver where we stayed all night with Bob's sister, Elaine, near Stapleton Airport.

On November 18th we headed for the Airport. We arrived several hours early and waited around for our flight to be called. We said goodbyes many times. It was almost noon when our flight was finally called. "Goodbye", "Goodbye, write to us soon!"

Chapter Three
1ˢᵗ Term as Missionaries
November, 1970- December, 1975

It was our first jet airplane ride. We all were excited beyond words. Here we were in the air looking down upon the earth beneath. The stewardesses brought us lunch and passed out games and pins and trinkets to the children. The time seemed so short going from Denver to Chicago. The first thing we knew they were announcing over the intercom to fasten our seat belts that we were arriving in Chicago. The stress was too great for Mom and the first thing she had to do as soon as we got into the airport was make a dive for the ladies room. After that, things went more smoothly.

We had about an hour to wait before boarding our BOAC (British airlines) plane. On this plane we would head for Montreal, Canada and then across the Atlantic Ocean to London. They presented us with a huge evening meal. I didn't sleep too well wondering about how to keep the children all comfortable for the night as we flew in the dark above the clouds. Little Rylan lay down on the floor of the plane under my feet and the other children all had seats. If you have ever tried to sleep sitting up in an airplane seat for the first time it just isn't too comfortable and the children all wanted to stretch out. Eventually the drone of the engines put them to sleep. In a matter of about four hours it was already beginning to get light. I knew we were coming close to England and so I looked out the window and noticed you could actually see the southern tip of Ireland. I mentioned it to Bob and we woke the older children so they could see it. Roxy said, "Sure enough, there it is just like on the map."

Before long they brought out breakfast, juice, rolls, eggs etc. It really was too early for some to eat so much. There were long lines standing, waiting to use the toilets. Then came the announcement, "Fasten your seatbelts. We will be landing in London Heathrow Airport in about 10 minutes."

This was our first time to land and walk in a different country and everything seemed strange. The cars were small and mostly black it seemed. Everyone drove on the left side of the road. Going through doors was really different because they didn't have round knobs but long and straight ones. The toilet flushers were on the opposite side from American ones. The people talked with a different accent. This was the beginning of our learning about different cultures.

Bob took Roxane, Allen and Ronald with him to the South Africa House where we were to obtain our South African visas. Along the way they did some sightseeing. To the children it was like living out their history book about England. As they traveled along their Dad pointed out historical places: as Buckingham Palace, Trafalgar Square, Big Ben and many other things the children had read about. I stayed at our hotel room with little Rylan because I was really exhausted and he seemed tired, too. We crawled into bed and slept. The day passed quickly and that evening we headed for the airport again, this time boarding a Zambian Airways plane for Lusaka, Zambia. Everyone was so tired that we slept a little better.

Our first glimpse of Africa was probably pretty much as we imagined it. As we were coming in for landing we could see many little brown thatch roofed huts and rolling green hills with bush and short trees. Soon we landed for the first time on African soil. The airport was fairly modern but not as big as the airports we had just been in the past two days. It was good to see familiar faces standing and waving at us as we disembarked our plane. Wilma Cheney, Bob's sister who had been a missionary for nearly six years, and friends, Gerald and Elsie Kahre and their two boys were there to meet us. What a happy reunion. We planned to spend ten days with them here in Zambia.

As we were traveling down the narrow highway toward Jembo Mission, Gerald came upon a vehicle and began to pass it. I had such a strange feeling because to me he was passing on the wrong side. I blurted out, "Why are you passing on this side!!"

Gerald replied, "Because this is the side I'm supposed to pass on."

How foolish I felt! It was just part of the many things we would have to get use to in this different culture.

Jembo Mission

Wilma was a school teacher at Jembo Mission and stayed with another single lady missionary, Marion Donaldson. Quite a number of missionaries lived on this mission station because they had a hospital, a primary and secondary school, and a Bible College. The Doctor, Hal Burchel, and his family, and another couple, John and Marge Connor, had just recently come to the station. The Joe Watkins family lived at the Bible College.

I shall never forget how the nurse, Marion Donaldson, and Dr. Burchel invited me down to the hospital to watch an emergency operation where they saw little hope for the man. God miraculously touched and healed him, not only in body, but spiritually.

In a visit to Chabbaboma Mission where the Russell family and Esther Nettleton lived, for the first time, I watched a real live birth at the hospital where Esther worked and ministered. While I was there, the others went out in a boat on Lake Kariba. The American holiday of Thanksgiving was celebrated at the Jembo Mission with all of the missionaries making it seem like we were in a little bit of America right in Africa. What a time of celebration. We laughed like we had never laughed before.

One of our visits after we went over to Choma was with the Twingings and Naomi Swan. Elwood Twinging took us to see the famous Victoria Falls from the Zambian side. At the time we could not cross over to Zimbabwe because of the fighting between the two countries.

All too soon our ten day visit came to an end and it was time for us to fly to South Africa. The Kahres took us to Lusaka where we boarded an Air Malawi Plane. This plane would fly us to Blantyre and there we boarded another plane headed for Johannesburg, South Africa. In Malawi a big rainstorm came up and delayed our flight ten or fifteen minutes. As soon as there was a letup in the rain they hurried us to the plane and then we had to wait for another rain to stop before takeoff. As we became airborne we hit an air pocket that made our plane take a scary drop. But the Lord protected us and soon we landed in Jan Smutts Airport.

We had met the Lehmans at the Merging Conference in 1968 and so we had a small idea of how they looked. Sure enough they were there waiting for us. By this time flying was not nearly as much fun for the kids as at the beginning and mom and dad were also getting pretty tired of popping ears and oozy stomachs. The Lehmans treated us royally for a couple of days. Bro. Lehman (who is the father of Orai D. Lehman our brother-in-law) took the older children and Bob to Pretoria the capital city of South Africa. They had a wonderful day sightseeing. I stayed with baby Rylan so that we could get some rest.

December 2, 1970 dawned as a beautiful summer morning. It really didn't seem like December. It seemed more like June or July. This was another part of missionary life that we were going to have to get used to. Now we were south of the Equator and the seasons are just the opposite of the seasons in the United States. We left where the trees were bare and leafless and the grass was dried and brown coming to a beautiful summer land where trees were gorgeous green and the grass and flowers covered the countryside. This was the day we were to arrive at our new home in Swaziland. The Lehmans saw us off at the airport in Johannesburg and about an hour later we were cruising down the run way at Matsapa Airport in Swaziland. Standing by the fence we saw a small group of people. It was our missionary family in Swaziland who had come to welcome us, Orai and Linda Lehman and their daughter Valarie, Jim and Carol Ramsay and their daughter Shari and nurse Alberta Lemley. What a welcome they gave us!

I'm going to let you read what Roxy wrote about the trip into

Manzini and to the Mission. "We drove from the airport to Manzini. We stopped in Manzini to get my mom and dad's pictures for residence permits. I had to keep hold of Rylan while they were inside and when we went past the vegetable shop the smell was so strong I nearly brought up. I was feeling quite bad."

Our First Christmas in Africa, 1970

It was hard to get into the Christmas Spirit after we arrived in Swaziland. I think one of the main reasons was the summer weather. We were used to having cold Christmases not hot ones. I painted a Christmas picture that had been given to me with Tri-chem. Unfortunately, I hadn't thought to put an imitation tree in our barrels. Trees in Africa were terribly expensive and there were no evergreens to cut. I wanted to buy some red material and make all the children stockings to hang up at the fireplace, thinking it might seem a little more like Christmas. We couldn't afford much but some inexpensive things. We had gotten several Christmas cards and surely appreciated them.

Many times holidays are the times when missionaries feel homesickness. Our first Christmas turned out to be a really fun one. Linda just happened to find a beautiful evergreen long needle tree at a store in Manzini and bought it. We made a star for the top and a few other decorations and then Linda had some decorations to add to it. Also, we drew names and so had packages under the tree and the children did hang their Christmas stockings on the fireplace on Christmas Eve. In fact we played, just for fun, that Bob was Santa. He had a pair of real bright red coveralls and we put a pair of Rylan's red shorts on his head for a cap. He put on shaving cream for a white beard. It looked so funny and we laughed and laughed. This really got us into the Spirit of Christmas!

Christmas morning we all got up and went to the Special Christmas Service they had at the Joy Mission Church. Orai gave the Christmas message. Roxy sang her first special with two of the African girls. They sang in English. This was a nice way to celebrate the birth of our Savior, having a service in honor of Him on Christmas day. It was very different from the way we did it back in America.

We had a delicious Christmas dinner of goose with dressing and the trimmings. I made apple pies too. In the afternoon Linda and I cut out dresses to sew and Orai and Bob played Chess. It rained in the afternoon. For Allen's 10th birthday on the 27th I baked a chocolate cake with chocolate frosting and a green "HAPPY BIRTHDAY" on top with ten big red candles. Since his birthday fell on Sunday we spent the day at Phonjwane church. They had a baptismal service and communion. Bob preached for this service and Orai interpreted. The church was really filled with people.

Various Impressions of Our New Life

One cannot imagine the differences in other cultures until you have experienced living in them. Some of our first impressions had to do with being on the south side of the equator. My directions were not always straight and of course that bothered me some since I came from the Sandhills of Nebraska where directions were very important to knowing your location. In Southern Africa your shadow always falls to the south instead of the north. In winter the sun always was in the northern part of the sky and in summer in the southern part of the sky. Since we arrived it was December it felt more like the 4th of July weather and so to get into the mood of Christmas was a little hard. There was no snow, only rains. On Christmas day right after lunch we had a rain storm and it felt so warm the children went out into the mud holes to play in the water. At first it was hard to even tell that there were seasons because any time of year you could see trees with green leaves and green grass. But as we became use to the change we began to see that during June, July and part of August it was much colder and the grass turned browner. It felt good to have a sweater on in the cold mornings. Sometimes when the wind blew hard a coat felt really good. Probably the temperatures never got much below the 50's.

We soon learned that houses were not centrally heated during the cold days and so sometimes we would build a fire in the fireplace. In fact, it seemed every room in the houses had what was called air brick where cold air could come in at the top of the wall. This did help the houses to be cooler in summer but it made them very cold on windy cold days in winter.

One of the shocking things to me was that you had to go so many places to do your shopping, to the butchery for meat, to the bakery for bread, to the main store for canned goods, flour, coffee etc. Probably the hardest thing for me to get use to was the fact that there were no evening services and no midweek evening prayer meetings.

Getting use to interrupters was something else! If the preacher happened to be speaking English on that Sunday morning it wasn't hard to hear the message but if one of the African pastors spoke, someone interpreted. Often Orai Lehman interpreted for us. New words and sounds were coming to our ears and our thoughts and we wondered, "Will we ever know what they are saying?"

Fortunately we found an African pastor's wife, Mrs. Nzalo, who became our first teacher of Zulu. In those days the Swazi schools were using the Zulu language in school because SiSwati didn't have enough printed books yet.

One time Orai and Bob had to be undertakers. A man asked Orai to get his son who had died at the hospital and take him to their village so they could bury him. They were heathen people and Orai had never been to their village although it was only five miles away. It was quite an experience for both of them. A witch doctor rode out with them and Orai witnessed to her. It is really sad to think of such heathen darkness. This was neither the first time nor the last time that Orai furnished a hearse!

We had many interesting foods to try out. Fresh fruits were so good and even the new ones were not hard to like. We were introduced to litches. Litches grow on big trees in clusters. A litche is a small fruit that looks like a strawberry but has a hard shell which you peel off. After you get it peeled, you have a white, round, sweet, juicy fruit with a brown seed in the middle.

The pineapple we got in Swaziland was really delicious, sweet and juicy. We paid five cents for a pineapple. There were fields and fields of them near the capital city of Mbabane.

In South Africa where Orai's parents lived, there are peach orchards that begin ripening in November and December. They also have grapes, apple trees, a pear tree and fig trees. Another delicious fruit which we learned to like is the pawpaw (papaya). There are definitely plenty of fresh fruits!

One thing the children had to get use to was wearing uniforms to school. This was very different for them. Roxy wore green and white checked dresses with full skirts and belt, white anklets, and black shoes. The boys wore gray shorts, white shirts, brown sandals and gray knee socks. During the winter term the girls wore white blouses and gray jumpers and green sweaters or a green blazer. It really made the children look neat but for us to get three children outfitted became quite an expense.

At Joy Mission we were supplied with water by a windmill pumping water into a tank. Our electricity came from a generator that the men started each night when it got dusk and it ran until 9:00 or 9:30 p.m. This was difficult at times when you wanted to finish something like writing a letter or doing a bit more sewing. What happened many times was that I finished my letter by candle light or whatever I was doing that didn't need electricity.

Cockroaches—I never really had them when I lived in America but we sure did in Swaziland and they grew big!!! I learned about them when I helped Linda clean her cupboards. There were a great many of them and never in my life had I seen such enormous ones. They were at least two inches long and I'm not stretching it either! Of course some were smaller, waiting to grow up! We sprayed all over the cupboard hoping to kill as many as possible.

Snakes—One week Orai shot a green Mamba snake. It was four feet nine inches long. He also killed several snakes in his pigeon cage. We were counting up all the snakes we had killed since we'd been here and it was around six of them. All snakes here are deadly poisonous. One night we heard the dog barking up a storm so looked out and there was a little snake about 10 inches long. Africa is sure no place to walk outside after dark without a flashlight.

Probably the most impressive part of Africa was the people themselves. At first when we went into the church service everyone looked the same to us—black curly hair and brownish black skin. We could not tell one from the other but as time went on we began to see that these people had unique appearances and personalities. They even reminded us of people we knew back home who were white. People like Mfundisi Gamedze and his family, Pastor Andreas Mamba and his family who pastored the Joy Mission church, Lena Manana and Veronica who helped out in the missionary home all became our personal friends.

First impressions could go on and on but as we became use to our new home we realized that God was caring for us and keeping us from harm. God was allowing us to gain many new brothers and sisters in the Lord from this new culture!

Joy Mission

Our house had not been completed before we arrived so we lived with Orai and Linda Lehman for about five months. Orai had three building projects going at once— our house and the secondary High School at Phonjwane as well as the Bible School building at Joy Mission. It was a big job!

Joy Mission was a very interesting place, situated on a hillside where the wind can get a good sweep at it. But what a view! The house that Lehmans shared with us had been built by Rev. Richard Long. It had fairly large rooms: three bedrooms, a bathroom, a large living-dining room area and the kitchen. Out back was a veranda and out the front door another veranda. All floors were cement and the walls were made of cement block. Most houses are made of cement block because of termites. The roof was made of corrugated iron. It was a little cramped with two families living there, but with Lehmans taking one bedroom, Bob and I and baby Rylan taking the second bedroom, the boys in the third bedroom and Roxane the sofa, we were able to manage.

The Chicken Thief

Orai and Linda kept geese and chickens and there were a few cows on the mission which the African boy milked for us. Of course the milk had to be pasteurized in a machine which Linda had. Orai also had pigeons and a large cage for them. Flying pigeons was his hobby.

One week I was awakened several times by the squawking of chickens. When I finally told Orai, he discovered that around twenty of his fifty chickens were missing. This really bothered him and he told me, "When you hear it again, call me." A day or so later, Bob and I both heard it about midnight. The men went dashing out to the chicken yard shining flashlights in all directions but the stealer got away. Orai rigged up his own burglar alarm. He fixed thread in front of the chicken roosts which when the thief breaks would sets off a bell in Orai's and Linda's bedroom. He also had it hooked to a flashlight. One morning at break of day a chicken set it off so we knew it worked! I think the thief was scared off for a few nights.

Sunday night, about 9:30, I heard the chickens squawking again and I hurried to tell Orai. He and Bob ran out and saw a dog. He rushed back after his rifle, then went out to wait. Sure enough the dog came again for a chicken so Orai shot. After the fifth shot, the dog dropped dead by the chicken fence. Orai just left the dog for two days to see if anyone would claim it. No one came so one of the boys buried it. Orai thinks it was a trained chicken thief dog but we aren't sure. We haven't lost any more chickens since the dog was shot!!!"

At the beginning of 1971, I began working at the Nazarene hospital in the accountant office while the children attended classes at Sydney Williams School in Manzini. In April we moved to Phonjawane.

Surprises!

During the month of August, Orai Lehman began feeling sick. He couldn't eat very well and it was hard to get much work done. We really didn't know what his problem was but eventually he decided to go to the doctor in Manzini. After some testing, the doctor diagnosed him as having hepatitis. This could be picked up quite easily by eating out at different places. The doctor's order was for him to go to bed and rest.

This left a load on Linda's shoulders but we tried to assist her as much as we could. We had district conferences going on. Later in September plans were made for a Sunday school teachers' workshop. The children had to get ready for the third term of school.

Before third term school started, we and the missionary family from Ebenezer Mission, the Ramsays, decided to make a quick trip to the Kruger National Game Park in South Africa. This would be our first time to visit the park. It truly was a delightful place to relax. Seeing the wild animals running free in the wild while we drove around in our cars made things very interesting. Some of my favorite animals were giraffes, zebras, impalas and silver monkeys. Roxy could give you an exciting story of her experience with a baboon. This crazy old baboon was hopping around on the cars in the park where we stopped to eat. He was trying to find food. So, when he saw the car window open, he hopped into Jim Ramsay's car where Roxy was reading a book. Jim hollered at Roxy and opened the back door of the car just as Roxy saw the baboon looking at her. She made a very undignified exit from the car. Jim said he wished he would have had his movie camera, taking pictures as the baboon hopped in one side of the car and Roxy rolled out the other side. We had quite a laugh.

So we entered the last term of school for the children. The weather was much hotter in October and November, the spring months in the southern hemisphere, so the children could take swimming lessons. At that time our car was having quite a few problems. And I was glad the last term ended. If we'd had problems earlier I don't know how I would have coped. As it was, I was tired and without energy. I had told Linda about not feeling well and along with lack of energy my stomach felt bad. Since I speculated that I might have hepatitis like Orai, I decided to see the doctor.

Well, the doctor said, "Perhaps we should do a pregnancy test." That was when I learned our 5th child would arrive sometime in July. What a shock! When I wrote to my parents I said, "Before you hear from some other source, I better mention a bit of news, so brace yourselves! I've hardly been able to recover myself since I learned...if all goes well, as predicted by the doctor, you will be Grandpa and Grandma again."

My dear husband assured me we were in this together. What I didn't realize was that God was giving us a very special gift in this child. I'm glad God knows best and I had to learn to trust Him more. I hadn't even brought a maternity dress pattern with me. Now, although I wasn't feeling too awfully sick but I couldn't stand to do much cooking. At the time, Rylan was such a cute little fellow with curly blond hair that was getting so long that it started to curl around his ears and I thought that it would be good for him to have a little brother or sister.

So, as our second Christmas in Africa neared, I began to feel sick. Knowing what was happening to my body made it easier to take. We began praising God because He was sending us an unexpected gift – the gift of a child.

The older Lehman's from South Africa. Eleanor Hunsinger and Wilma, John and Marge and their children came from Zambia. Since our regional conference was to be held at Ebenezer Mission after Christmas and Marge, John and Wilma were helping with it, they had decided to come early and have Christmas with the Swaziland missionaries.

Fortunately, Linda Lehman did most of the cooking. This was fine with me because even the smell of food was making me sick. Even though my husband, Bob, was not a cook, with my coaching and by using recipes, he always helped me out.

End of 1971

At the end of 1971, missionaries came from all over Southern Africa – the Bagleys, Morgans, Sanders, Keirsteds, Haywoods and Gormans to Ebenezer Mission where the secondary school was. Bob and I stayed at the school with our family while the meetings were going on. There was quite a group of us. It was always so nice to be with so many missionaries, but this time I was not enjoying it much; my back was really hurting.

As soon as the conference was over I headed for the doctor. He found I had a kidney infection, on top of morning sickness, hence the reason for not feeling well. With medication I got better and after the conference we headed for the European camp meeting in Brakpan. It was always so nice to be with the white people in services because they spoke in English and it was easier to understand the preacher's messages and people's testimonies. Sometimes they spoke in Afrikaans. Actually, most all white people spoke in English or Afrikaans, depending on their background.

After returning home, Bob prepared for the opening of school. This year I had ordered correspondence courses for Roxy, Allen and Ron and so we did not have to take them back and forth to Sydney Williams School in Manzini. By the end of January and beginning of February I began feeling some better and was able to do homeschooling with the children. Rylan, two and a half, pretty much entertained himself or played with the native children.
An incident that really frightened us was when we were not able to find Rylan anywhere. There were reports of witchcraft happenings in the area, and we had heard that if a witch doctor could obtain the body parts of a white person, his medicine would be more powerful. So when Rylan could not be found around the school area, our thoughts were that he might have been kidnapped.

A search party was formed. We prayed hard that God would protect our little son. Native children and adults, teachers and our family went all over calling Rylan's name. There are a number of native homes around the school and some people began searching at those places. When one of the young secondary students came bringing Rylan by the hand, our hearts beat with joy and thankfulness, praising the Lord. Our son who was lost had been found playing with some of the young children at one of the nearby homes.

The Accident

It was time for the first term break the end of April, beginning of May. At this time the District had a youth camp planned to take place at Phonjawane. The Ramsay's and Lehman's were a part of this camp and came to Phonjawane, as well. In preparing for the camp it turned out that I had to go to Manzini for supplies, including nine dozen eggs, for the next few days of camp. So I departed for town in our little Fiat car to obtain the things Carol Ramsay asked for, as well as items for our family.

On the way back from Manzini, I stopped at Joy Mission to pack up my washing. My sister-in-law, Linda, always tried to help me out and since we did not have running water or electricity she did my laundry for me. I packed up all my clean clothes, washed and folded. I asked if little Michael could go back to Phonjawane with me, but Linda said he had been kind of sick. She didn't think it wise to let him go.

On my way back, about a mile from Phonjawane, I saw two buses coming down a long hill toward me as I rounded the corner. Then I noticed the bus behind began passing the front bus. I was afraid the one bus might not make it around. I pressed hard on my brakes to slow down and give them a chance. I didn't want to meet them head on. In the process of doing this my light car began to slide sideways toward the buses. I cried out, "Lord help me!" Suddenly my car went to the other side of the road, hit the bank and I turned upside down very slowly with my laundry, nine dozen eggs and other groceries. I didn't seem to be hurt but egg was dropping from my hair and clothes. I thanked the Lord I was o.k. and I didn't think baby inside me was hurt either. (I was seven months pregnant.)

The buses stopped and some from the South African tour bus came to my car. I knocked on the window to let them know I was alive. They pushed the door open and I crawled out. When they saw I was pregnant, the men were fearful and asked, "Are you okay?" "Please sit down," they said. "What can we do to help?"

I said, "Please can you go to Phonjawane just up the road and call my husband?" Someone went. In the meantime several of the men turned our car right side up while I sat by the side of the road, dripping with egg. I truly felt the angel of the Lord protected me and our unborn child. We were very thankful to the Lord.

Bob and Orai came down and they pulled the car back to Phonjawane. However, after that, the car smelled of egg and, not surprising, all my laundry had to be re-washed. How thankful I was that little Michael Lehman wasn't with me.

Vacation Time, 1972

After the Youth Camp the Lehman's, along with our family, vacationed at St. Lucia on the South Coast. We took two vehicles, a small camper trailer and a tent. With sleeping bags, we could accommodate ten people. For several days we stayed beside the ocean enjoying the beach.

One day while they were out on the water, a big fish jumped right in the little row boat with the children. It caused quite a bit of excitement. We kept the fish and let Rylan and Valerie hold it up for a picture. It was good sized, enough to feed all of us. This was the season for the "Mullet run" and there were many of these fish in the water. They were swimming up the rivers, inland to spawn.

The last night we were at St. Lucia I had a rather strange dream in which I saw a white Jeep Wagoneer pulling a small trailer driving in front of us on the highway. As we followed, I saw the trailer flip over. Then I awoke from my dream. I'm not one to think much of dreams, but next morning as we ate breakfast I told it to everyone and we just laughed. From there we headed for Altona Mission where the Mission Council members meet at the South African District Offices. Orai stopped to fill up with petrol (gas) at a place called Pongola. After filling the car he got ready to leave. Then my dream came to his mind and he decided he should check the wheels on the trailer. What he reported to us almost seemed unbelievable. The left axle of the trailer was cracked and ready to come off. I feel God used my dream to save us from a catastrophe, though I'm not a believer that all dreams have meaning. It was a great vacation, a time of real refreshment and we were all ready for second term of school to begin.

One day a man came by with a little silver monkey and asked if we would like to buy it. The boys had wanted to have a pet monkey from the time we knew we were coming to Africa as missionaries so we paid the man $3.00 American dollars and the monkey was ours. Of course, a cage had to be built for Jocko. The boys fed him peanuts, bananas and oranges. We had him for about six months. Then one day he escaped from the cage. Someone found him for us the first time he got out, but the second time he was gone for good. We think maybe some dogs killed him.

Randal Anthony Cheney, July 12, 1972

As time drew nearer for the birth of our baby, I became more uncomfortable. Our Rylan kept asking, "When will our baby get here?" The baby was due early in July and all four of our children were at home then, the three older children in homeschooling. When I went to the hospital, Linda was so kind to keep our children because Bob was teaching in the second term of school.

On the 10th of July, early Monday morning, I began having pains and realized I better go into the hospital in Manzini. The doctor checked me, but I wasn't dilating much so they began an IV drip to help things along. By late afternoon I was not doing much so we decided I should stay there with Dr. Paul and Martha Riley. Before Bob went back to Phonjawane, we decided he wouldn't come back until Wednesday the 12th of July unless I went into labor. I slept fine that night at the Riley's house. The next day I didn't have much pain at all. In fact, I helped Martha sew covers for cushions on her chairs. Still nothing seemed to be happening. I was really ready to get this delivery over.

Next morning, Bob came early, by 8:00 a.m. to take me into the hospital and Dr. King decided we should begin the drip again. By noon, things began to happen. Bob stayed right with me. It was such a comfort to have him near. A little before 3:00 p.m. they took me into the delivery room and Bob was right there, seeing me through the hard part.

At 3:55 p.m. our little boy arrived, strong and healthy, although the umbilical cord was wrapped loosely about his neck. It wasn't enough to harm the baby. Praise the Lord! We named our fourth baby boy Randal Anthony Cheney. He was born Wednesday, July 12, 1972 and he weighed 8 pounds, 3.5 ounces.

Twelve seems to be an important date in our family. My birthday is May 12th, our Ronald Alfred's birthday is June 12th and now baby Randal July 12th. I told my mother I was making it easy for her to remember birthdays. I stayed in the Raleigh Fitkins Memorial Hospital, a Nazarene Mission Hospital in Manzini, for several days. We had a lot of visitors including our older children, the Lehman family and a number of Nazarene friends.

When Bob went back to Joy Mission to break the news, the children were all anxious to know what was our baby – a boy or a girl? When they broke the news to Rylan and Valerie, little cousin Valerie began crying so hard. She said, "I wanted a baby girl cousin." Of course, there were mostly boys around and she thought it was time for a little girl. It didn't take much time for her to love her little baby boy cousin, however.

Monday the next week, Martha Riley asked me to come and stay in their home so I could get some rest. On July 19th Bob came to the Riley's to get Randal and me at the Nazarene Mission Station. From there we went to Joy Mission to celebrate Rylan's third birthday.

YES Corp Visit

When baby Randal was about three weeks old a couple from the Denver area brought a YES Corp group of Young People to visit Swaziland. Sue Long was among those youth, as well as Cyril Chitty. They came to encourage the Swazi youth by their singing and social program they had prepared.

Birthday Parties

Birthday parties for the children seemed quite important, especially during our first term. At Ebenezer some European farmers (white English) lived near the Ramsay's. They were two brothers, Ken Keel and his younger brother Woodley. Ken and Jean had three boys and Woodley and Doreen had two girls. One of Ken's boys had a birthday in August and we were invited to the party, the Lehman's and Cheney's as well as the Ramsay's.

I want to insert at this point a concern I had about our three year old son, Rylan. When we talked about loving Jesus he would always say "I don't love Jesus." It began to concern me when he said it a number of times and began really praying for him. I wanted more than anything that all my children would love and serve the Lord.

The Lehman's and I, with all the children, were on our way to the birthday party for Collin Keel; Randal being only a few weeks, Rylan and Valerie, three years old, and Michael, a year and a half. Also, Roxane, Allen and Ronald were with us. As we were driving along toward Siteki, Rylan suddenly turned around in the front seat and, out of the clear blue, said, "Now, Mommy, I love Jesus." What a relief it was for me to hear his words. God had answered my prayers for our little son. Never again did he say, "I don't love Jesus".

We got to the Keel farm and, as usual, Jean had a great party planned. All the children enjoyed it to the fullest.

Conference Time for Swaziland District

Toward the end of August, the Swazi District of the Wesleyan Church held their annual conference. All Wesleyan Pastors and many of the church members rode the bus to Ebenezer for this meeting. It was a great time of fellowship, a time of spiritual filling and even of outreach to the unsaved.

Randal's Dedication and Baptism of Older Children

Often dedication of babies and children took place and also baptisms were performed. Our three older children felt they wanted to be baptized. A small river ran through the Mission and in places formed deep enough pools for baptizing. Rev. Nhleko, from our church, called Mpholenjani in the bushveld was the one who did this honor for our Roxane, Allen and Ronald. They, along with Susan Ramsay and a number of African Christians were baptized in a little river that runs through the mission property. One of our ordained preachers, Rev. Nhleko, did the baptizing and later told us that our children were the first missionary children to be baptized at Ebenezer. That truly was a special time for the Cheney and Ramsay families!

A service of dedication was held at the Ebenezer Church on the Sunday of Conference. At this service we asked that Randal, who was about six weeks old, be dedicated to the Lord. Again, Rev. Nhleko did the honors for us. During this same service Lehman's asked for Michael, their son, to be dedicated. It was a precious time in the presence of the Lord.

At this conference a decision had to be made about Joy Mission. It was time for the Lehman's to go on furlough. The conference decided to move the Ramsay's from Ebenezer to Joy Mission by the beginning of December. Since Bob was in process of training a national headmaster for Phonjawane secondary school, the headmaster in training would be able to take over Phonjawane Secondary School by the next school year beginning at the end of January 1973. This would leave Bob free to take over as headmaster (principal) of Ebenezer School.

During this time I had been writing to my parents and encouraging them to make a trip to Africa. My dad had received an inheritance and it gave them money for traveling. My parents were very interested in and supportive of missions, but I also wanted them to be able to see their newest grandchild while he was a baby, so we were hoping and praying for a visit from them about Christmas time.

Ebenezer Clinic

During the month of October we had visitors coming. Our mission house was in real need of paint. I didn't want our visitors to see the condition our house was in, so I headed for Manzini some 50 miles to the west and spent about $30.00 for paint. In three days we had our house looking presentable. When our visitors arrived Wednesday evening everything looked quite lovely. The Karns arrived with Mrs. Karns' mother, Flora Belle Slater, and Miss Buby. Miss Slater's parents are the ones who started Ebenezer Mission back in the early 1900's. Miss Slater and Miss Buby are retired missionaries. Miss Slater spoke a number of times in services here at the mission.

We had been praying for a full time nurse to come in and take the place of our missionary nurse, Alberta Lemley, who would be returning to the U.S. soon. One Saturday we had a boy come to the clinic asking for the nurse to come quickly, for the Induna was about to die. The Induna is the man under the Chief. I guess you would call him the Chief's right hand man. Anyway, Chrystal came and asked me to go with her. We walked down across the river probably a mile or maybe one and a half miles. When we got there the man seemed to be in a coma. The nurse checked him over and gave him an injection of penicillin, then after listening to what the others told her about his eating, etc., we had prayer. The man isn't a Christian and has several wives. Chrystal then suggested that we call the ambulance from Siteki Hospital. The people agreed. Now the man was in Good Shepherd Hospital but is in very poor condition, and probably wouldn't pull through. This happened so much and it makes me so sad that he didn't know Christ Jesus as his Savior.

One of the other things that involved the clinic was what we called baby clinic day. It was announced to the community that on a certain day parents were to bring their babies and young children. The U.N. had an organization that provided milk for children and babies and our clinic would distribute these products. We would also have a "cheapie sale". This is the time we would sell used clothing to the people at very low cost. This clothing was sent to us by churches in the U.S. Sometimes we did give clothes to our pastors, but more often we would sell it piece by piece at a few cents. It seems people appreciate and take better care of things that cost a bit. So you see, the clinic was a busy place at our mission. During this time it was hard for me to teach the children in homeschooling when visitors came or when clinic work needed attention.

I must tell you about an experience I had when someone came for help from the clinic. This incident took place one afternoon after our clinic closed and the nurses had gone home. Some people came to my door sometime after the clinic closed at 3:00 p.m. They were desperate and asked for help for a man whom they said had been bitten by a Black Mamba snake. Since no one was at the clinic I thought, "What can I do for this man?" He was rolling on the ground and seemed in great pain. I thought to myself, "Oh yes, we do have anti-snake bite serum at the clinic but I'm not sure how to give it." I started to the clinic but then figured I should call the Good Shepherd Hospital in Siteki for directions in administering this anti-snake bite serum. Calling on phones in Swaziland was very frustrating at times. It took me several minutes to get through to the hospital. All this time I was looking at this snake bitten man rolling in pain and expecting him to die on the spot.

The nurse at the hospital asked, "Can you give this man a shot intravenous?" and I said, "I don't really know how to do this." So she said, "Where is the bite?" I said, "It is on the calf of his leg." She replied, "Okay, give the shot in the muscle near the calf.

In the meantime, I sent my two older boys down to the secondary school to have dad come quickly to take the man to the hospital. I ran out the back door toward the clinic, calling to the people to bring this snake bitten man in. I rushed to open the clinic and find our snake bite serum and a clean syringe to give him the shot. I administered the shot just in time to have this fellow ready for my husband to rush him to Siteki.

I tell you, when that ordeal was over my stomach felt in knots! Later I learned that the man actually pulled through. Some people seemed to think the snake had bitten a cow or another animal first and so had used a lot of his venom up by the time he bit the man. Also, the bite was in a part of his leg where not many veins run.

I learned a lot about giving out medication and examining people from Alberta Lemley, the missionary nurse, when she came to our mission clinic, sometimes I would help her. I really loved this type of work and often wished I had become a trained nurse.

There is one more incident I would like to add about another experience I had with clinic work. This actually happened about a year later in late November or early December before we left on furlough in 1974. It was a rainy evening and we had all retired for the night. Not long after midnight we heard this loud knock at our front door. Bob went to the front door, where he found several people standing. One of them was a lady ready to have her baby. Bob asked about taking them into the Good Shepherd Hospital, but they said, "No, she wants to have the baby at the Ebenezer Clinic." Bob came to tell me and we discussed about getting our nurse from across the river where she lived. Bob suggested he would take a couple of the boys with him to fetch the nurse and I could go ahead and take the women to the clinic and prepare her for the delivery.

I got her into our delivery room and got the bassinet and everything ready. I then realized this baby wasn't going to wait for the nurse to arrive. "Oh dear," I thought, "I'm going to do the delivery!"

Fortunately I had helped our missionary nurse several times with deliveries and so was somewhat acquainted with the process. Sure enough, I could see that she was pushing and the little head was emerging.

In a very short time, baby was out. Still the nurse had not arrived so I decided I had to cut the umbilical cord. This I did and then very carefully wrapped the tiny baby girl in a warm blanket and laid her in the bassinet. I had, for the first time, delivered a baby. Our nurse arrived in time to finish up with the mother. What an experience it was, seeing and helping a new little life into our world. God is so good to help us with unexpected events.

Grandpa and Grandma Thornton Come to Visit, January of '73

Our whole family was really looking forward to Grandpa and Grandma Thornton's visit. We had hoped they could come for the Christmas of 1972, but they were unable to meet all their responsibilities in getting ready, so it was the latter part of January when Bob and I made a trip to Johannesburg to pick them up at the airport only to find they were not on that plane. What a disappointment! We checked around and found they had missed their flight in Spain and would be coming on a later flight.

Finally their flight came in and, yes, they were on this one. What a wonderful reunion! It had been just over two years since Mom and Dad Thornton had seen our family, so what a change they saw in the older children and, of course, we now had a baby boy they had not yet seen. We were so happy to show off our Randal. He was now going on seven months. He could crawl and get wherever he wanted to go. In fact, not long after they came, my dad saw him climbing around and said, "It isn't going to be long and that little boy will be walking."

Randal could stand and walk around things at seven months. He even would try climbing out of his playpen. It was one of those net playpens with holes and he would put his little toes in the holes and start coming to the top. I really had to watch him closely. Randal was so active that sometimes I wondered if I had enough energy to care for him.

My folks really enjoyed the children. Of course, the three older children had to continue in their homeschooling so that they would be ready for their next year. Especially Roxy had to keep up because the plan was for her to go stay with our missionaries, the Don Karns family in Dundee Natal so she could attend public school for her first year of high school. She would be in the same year as the Karns' daughter, Sheryl.

We tried to give Mother and Daddy as many experiences as possible. Mother later told me that their time with us actually made missions more alive to them. Mother truly loved to see the clinic work, especially being with our nurse, Chrystal. Perhaps that was because my mother's sister was also named Chrystal. Mother and Daddy also went to some of our Bible studies in nearby villages. They loved seeing the different churches and visiting with our pastors. They saw and witnessed much that they had never experienced before.

One experience I want to relate is going to Kruger National Game Park in eastern Transvaal South Africa. Since Bob was in school we decided that I should be the one to take them. Of course, there wasn't room to take all our children and Mom, Dad and me. Plans were made for Roxy to visit the

Ramsey's and she didn't mind keeping her baby brother. So it seemed our little Fiat car would be able to manage three small boys, my parents and myself.

We planned to be away about three days. We would stay in one of the camps in the park for a couple of nights. Of course, when you visit this game park you want to see as many of the wild animals as possible. One of these animals everyone wants to see is the Lion, "King of Beasts". We saw many zebra, giraffe, elephant, Impala and wild beasts the first day, but no lions. I was so in hopes we would come across a lion kill.

I believe it was the last day as we were heading toward home, driving along a river road, that I looked down the road ahead. Lo and behold there, coming toward us, was a male lion! I stopped the car and we waited and watched breathless as the lion kept walking toward us. My dad, in his excitement, had forgotten to switch off the zoom button on his movie camera. The lion kept moseying toward us. Of course, we had the car windows closed, but I believe if we had opened the window we could have reached out and touched him! What a great experience for my parents and for our boys, coming within three or four feet of a male lion! An incredible experience!

Soon it was time to take Grandma and Grandpa back to Johannesburg. The whole month of February had passed all too quickly. At the end of their visit we decided to go a few days early so that Mother and Daddy could continue their journey on to Zambia where they would visit Mom's cousin, Naomi Swan, Bob's sister, Wilma, and our friends, the Kahrs.

Randal, Our Sick Little Son

Randal was starting to stand just a little by himself. At eight months he could climb on the picnic bench pull himself up onto the top of the table. I couldn't leave him in the playpen without some shoes on his feet. He would stick his toes in the mesh and climb right up and hang halfway out. But, I was concerned. Although he had lots of energy, he also had diarrhea. The medication from nurse Alberta Lemley didn't help so we took him to Manzini to the Nazarene Hospital. I thought he might have an amebic infection

Well, Dr. King didn't think a baby his size would have amebic infection but he thought he should observe him for a while. Bob, too, wasn't feeling too good and had been running fever off and on. He had a tiny bite on his leg which he thought was a little pimple but evidently was from a tick. Dr. Paul Riley gave him some pills to clear up the infection. He also gave us medication for Randal.

Randal has reddish blonde his hair. Allen said he had the temper to go with his hair. Once Randal was really mad at me and didn't want to eat when I made him sit in his high chair. I smacked him and made him sit there until he ate his cereal. He really was a pill. One time he pulled the encyclopedias out of the bookcase. He had his quiet moments though when he was innocent and loveable.

African Weddings

Jim and Carol Ramsey came over from Joy Mission for a teacher's wedding which was to be held at Ebenezer Church. It was to have taken place at 11:00 a.m. but the bride's husband-to-be didn't come and didn't come. Everyone wondered what happened and the poor bride was nearly in tears. Her father called Manzini and learned they had car trouble. Around 1:00 p.m. the groom finally appeared.

After the wedding feast the Ramsay's started back to Joy Mission, taking Roxy and Rylan with them. They only got past the Siteki turnoff on Manzini road when Jim lost the wheel off his car. He had a man call us from Siteki to ask Bob to come and get them and bring Elias to stay with the broken down car.

After several phone calls and traveling muddy roads we all made it back to Ebenezer for the night. It was about 1:30 a.m. the next morning before we got to bed. Bob and Jim went back to fix the wheel Sunday morning and Carol, the kids and I went to church at Ebenezer. Apparently the bolts that hold the brake drum and wheel hub came loose and allowed the wheel to come off.

Well, car break downs seemed to be the stories of our first term, even at special occasions such as weddings.

On September 1st Israel Langa, one of our young preachers, married Victoria Dlamini. It was a thrill to Mrs. Ramsay and me to help prepare for this wedding. I suppose it was the most Americanized Swazi wedding there had been. Mrs. Ramsay baked a beautiful three-tiered wedding cake. Israel asked to have music at the wedding, so the piano in the mission house was moved to the church and I played traditional wedding music. Roxy and Mrs. Ramsay decorated the church with real flowers. The wedding reception and feast were held at the science room with big white bells and blue and white crepe paper. We managed to find enough things to make a veil for the bride and a white runner out of old sheets for the bride to walk on. Victoria made the most beautiful Swazi bride I had ever seen. After the feast we drove to the groom's home and watched their Swazi custom of the bride giving gifts to the groom's family. This was very interesting to us missionaries."

Just one more interesting wedding…this wedding took place while we lived at Joy Mission when Bob's sister, Vivian, came to visit. I guess the main thought I want to get across with the mention of this wedding is the importance of the event to Swazi people. We realized that in the Swazi culture the people are more event oriented, whereas in American culture we seem more time oriented.

Vivian was very excited to think she would get to experience a Swazi wedding. It was to take place at Phonjawane at 10:00 a.m. All of us dressed and prepared for the wedding but Bob and I did not get in a hurry to leave because we knew how these events took place. However, Vivian was very concerned that we were going to be late. We just did not hurry. Finally Vivian said, "We need to go, don't we? I don't want to be late."

"It's okay," I said, "We will get there in time for the wedding."

Finally we left around 10:00 a.m. and drove to the church at Phonjawane. When we arrived, no one was around, not one soul.

Vivian exclaimed, "Where is everyone?"

Bob said we would just drive over to the nearby home. Guess what, the wedding party was still getting ready. Finally, at around noon, the wedding took place. Vivian learned just like we had, Swazis are event oriented, not time oriented!

Subject Close to My Heart

Since I was the District Sunday School leader of Swaziland, my committee and I felt it would be well to hold a workshop for Sunday school teachers and workers. So, on August 20 – 22, we set up classes at Ebenezer. Bob, Mrs. Ramsay and my two faithful zone leaders, Mrs. Nzalo and Samson Ndabandaba, taught the classes. It was a time of real enrichment and learning for our Sunday school workers. We thanked God for the help he gave us in these services.

Fall to Christmas, 1973

Just around this time, we saw Alberta Lemley and the little African boy she adopted off at the airport and headed for furlough in the U.S. Now was a critical time for our Ebenezer Clinic because we no longer had a qualified nurse to work out of our clinic.

While I was helping Miss Lemley get permission to take an African child with her to the States, I was driving through unfamiliar territory. While crossing a cattle guard, a middle part of the gate hit the oil pan, making a hole in it. Alberta and I had to walk in order to get to a phone to call Bob. Bob got the car back in working order but the Ramsay's let us borrow one of their vehicles while ours was out of order.

Trying to keep our old cars and other vehicles running took a big chunk out of our days many times. Sometimes it seemed we almost spend more time in repair work than we did working for the Lord. However, it was a blessing that Bob and Jim Ramsay could usually do the work such as putting in a new clutch plate on the Massey-Ferguson tractor. The tractor was needed for building a new church over in the Ebenezer zone.

Trying to home school my three older children seemed overwhelming at times. Looking back at those years, I sometimes wonder how I ever did it. I know it was only through the strength the Lord gives. As Paul wrote to the Philippians 4:13, "I can do all things through Christ who strengthens me."

When the Jim Ramsay family went on furlough November, 1973 we were left as the only mission family in Swaziland. We looked forward to the Lehman's who would be returning from furlough in a few weeks.

On November 20th we had six guests arrive from Johannesburg. Our Mission Director, Rev. Bill Morgan, brought Rev. and Mrs. Cockrill and Mr. and Mrs. Bell, as well as David Keith from Marion, Indiana. Their purpose for coming was to make a missionary movie film for the churches in the States. This movie used Rev. Sigewane as the main character from childhood to now and our three older children got an education in movie film production.

November and December is the rainy season in Africa. One day of nice sunshine can be followed the rest of the week with rains, mists and fogs. Fortunately, the roads are passable and I was certainly glad for that. We had a big mud hole in the drive and I had one terrible time trying to keep Randal out of it. One day, and just for a few minutes, I let Randal go outside. In that short time when I went to look for him, he was a horrible mess. He sat down in the mud and his bottom and legs were just plastered. I had such a time trying to get people to close the doors. While I would think he was safe in the house, someone would have gone out and left a door open. Just like that Randal would find it open before I did. He thought nothing of going out to play in the mud in his pajamas.

Christmas 1973 was spent with some guests, four people whom we had never met before. We had a nice visit with the Wayne Fisher's and Mike and Verie Bertoglios. They came on the 24th and stayed two nights with us. Mike and Verie were from the state of Washington. They seemed like a lovely young Christian couple. They came to Swaziland as teachers under Peace Corp. The Wayne Fishers were a very nice older couple who came from around Lincoln, Nebraska. He taught at U.B.L.S. in the field of Agriculture. The Fisher's brought a great big turkey for our Christmas dinner. It was the first we had eaten since being in Africa.

Right after Christmas we headed to Joburg so we could meet Orai and Linda, Valerie and Mike, coming back from America. This was such a nice closing out of our third year as missionaries.

Last Year of Term One

What would this year of 1974 hold for us? At the top of the list was the return of the Orai Lehman family. The children were excited to see their cousins again. Bob and I felt rather alone and isolated since the Ramsay family left in November; and Lehman's were on furlough.

The first part of January was a busy one, especially trying to get Roxane ready for her first year of high school. She managed to finish up her year of homeschooling. I also had sewing to do for her so that she would have what she needed to begin high school.

One thing Bob and I talked over before we came to the mission field was the schooling of our children. We determined we would never send them to a public or government boarding school. We also were choosy as to what missionary family we let them board with. This is why the Karns family, the Miller family, Ramsay family and Lehman's became such special people to us. Missionary families become your family on the mission field. I can never thank them enough for taking in our children.

Roxy was going to stay with Don and Elizabeth Karns in Dundee Natal, South Africa for her first year of high school. This was just before Roxy's birthday, January 24th so, after taking her to Dundee Natal, we decided to stick around until we could celebrate her 15th birthday. It was very nice for Roxy to have the Karns' daughter the same age and year of school. They were good for each other. The Karns had another daughter, Brenda, who was in Bible College at that time and then two sons, Donnie and John, at home. After the birthday was celebrated we headed back to Swaziland. I had to get Allen and Ron back to homeschooling. It was a little different without our daughter /sister at home. We really missed her.

Back at Ebenezer Mission we again had a very busy schedule. Bob, teaching at the secondary school and I was busy trying to get our boys through 4th and 7th grade of schooling. I wanted them to be ready for 5th and 8th grade by September so that they would fit in with schooling in the U.S. when we left for furlough in December.

One day Randal pulled the motorcycle over on top of himself before I could catch it (he was just trying to climb up on it). When we got it up and I picked him up, I noticed he couldn't stand on one leg very well. After looking down I saw a great big hole poked into his leg just below the knee. I could see the bone, but it didn't look as though it was broken. I knew we had to get him into the hospital so it could be sewed up. The problem was the Jeep Wagoneer would only go into second gear. (Orai and Linda had taken our car.) Because Bob was helping Israel with his car, he hadn't had time to look at what was troubling the Jeep. Bob said, "We will just have to try making it in second gear."

Thank the Lord we did make it to the Good Shepherd Hospital in Siteki and back again to the mission. The doctor cleaned out the wound really well and sewed it up with about eight stitches in his leg. The foot rest on the motorcycle had the rubber pushed back and was rather sharp. This is what went into his leg when the bike fell on top of him. It pushed past the bone and down into the calf of his leg. We just thank the Lord it was not any worse."

Roxy seemed to be having quite an easy time in school at Dundee. She said that school was quite easy and she had received the highest grades in History and English Composition. She was getting quite anxious to see us as we were to see her. Her first holiday break came near the end of April so she could be with us for Easter." Sheryl Karns came to Ebenezer Mission, our home, for the Easter season. It was so nice to have both girls with us."

There was need for a water pump down at the Little River where we got our water. We had ordered a pump but sometimes people who take your order take their own sweet time in fulfilling the orders! Such was the case for a new pump. In the meantime the way we got our water was to take barrels down to the river, fill them, and bring them back to the mission by tractor. Bob took time to teach Allen how to put the barrels on the tractor and after filling them, to drive the tractor and water back to the mission house. This was quite a chore, but fortunately our oldest son was able to do it. It wasn't until about the second week of May that we got our new water pump.

In the latter part of May we took our tent and Lehman's took their trailer to Mpholenjani Church down at the foot of the Lobamba Mountains. Rev. and Mrs. Nhleko were the pastors there. There was a primary school located there also. They were having a weekend Revival and Sunday school workshop. The Swazis always try to make their best meals when the missionaries come to be with them. This weekend they had killed a goat. Goat meat is really good. Since the Swazi custom is to not waste any part of the goat, Mrs. Nhleko even cooked the liver and the stomach. The liver was delicious, but the stomach... well, as Orai Lehman commented, "Goat stomach didn't have much flavor and it was kind of like eating a piece of old carpet."

We were very careful about drinking the water when we went into the homes of the rural people. There was no knowing where their water came from. Probably most of it was from the ponds or little rivers where cattle drank or people washed their clothes or probably took baths. If they did serve us drinks it was usually hot tea or some kind of cold drink they purchased from a nearby shop.

King Sobuza's Birthday

Swaziland is ruled by a King. When we arrived in the country back in the 1970, Swaziland was ruled by King Sobuza. They do have a parliament. There are different representatives from the various districts in the parliament. The various areas within the districts are represented by a chief.

King Sobuza's birthday was on the 19th of July. The first year we were in Swaziland his birthday was celebrated at Siteki, a small town over on the east side of Swaziland. Many schools and music groups performed and there were speeches from different government officials. Bob was out with our Minolta camera getting pictures. He even was close enough to get good pictures of King Sobuza. Of course, the big event of this celebration was the feast. Many animals were slaughtered for the King's birthday celebration. It was quite impressive!

Miscellaneous Stories

It was late May when we heard that my Grandma Alice French died. She was 96 years old. When we got word from my mother, our oldest son, Allen, said, "Oh, what a shame. It's too bad she couldn't have waited until we got back."

Of course, our three oldest children remembered their Great-Grandma French. I remember her well, too, because she used to tell my sister and me, such interesting stories of when her children were small. Actually, all four of our older children had seen her. However, I doubt that Rylan remembers because he was only 16 months old when we left the states. So I never got to attend either one of Grandpa or Grandma French's funerals. Also, in July that Grandma's sister, Aunt Hazel, passed away.

We had many Nazarene Missionaries as friends. One of these couples was Hilbert and Norma Miller. They had a couple girls and a boy named Danny. Danny and Ronald were nearly the same age with both their birthdays falling in June. Norma Miller and I worked together on a birthday celebration for both Danny and Ronald. Norma would prepare their birthday meal and we would have all the boys come out to our mission and set up tents to stay all night. It was always so nice to have friends that we could share special times with. Here I'd like to mention how nice Norma was in offering to bring us a meal just shortly before we went on furlough. They brought the whole meal and came out from Siteki to share it with us at Ebenezer Mission.

Our mission Council wanted us to go to Port Shepstone after furlough to work in our Bible College. The mission and the Bible College are about 24 miles inland from the city of Port Shepstone. This town is right on the coast of the Indian Ocean and was quite a tourist attraction with many lovely beaches. We, of course, said that we needed to make this a matter of prayer.

At the end of June our Regional Ladies Retreat took place in Altona, our mission in South Africa. The ladies in Swaziland wanted to attend this meeting so I took them even though I wanted to get more things done at the mission. Time was passing quickly and there were many projects we needed to finish. To top off everything, we had a lot of rain which was unusual for that time of year. The roads were so muddy that we only got our vehicle maybe a quarter mile from the mission. My husband and Israel Langa decided they should hitch the tractor to our vehicle and pull us into Siteki.

After reaching Siteki, about eight miles from our mission, the roads became a little better and our vehicles made it to Joy Mission. I really learned how to drive on muddy roads. Fortunately, we did not get stuck and we arrived at Altona Mission that evening. It was a wonderful Women's Retreat. The women that went with us received spiritual food and encouragement. It made us all so glad we had gone to it. I was also able to pick our daughter up for her long July holiday from school at Dundee. We always looked forward to having her at home with us.

I need to tell about our little boys, Rylan and Randal. While I was at Women's Retreat Linda Lehman, my sister-in-law, looked after the boys. Randal started calling Linda mommy and when I returned he called me auntie! Randal was two years old on July 12th and was potty trained very well. Often I would keep Valarie and Michael Lehman too. Linda and I always tried to help each other out.

One night during July, our winter time, we had some thieves come to the mission. We heard one of the cows bawling and carrying on. Bob went down to look in the cattle corral and found no cattle shut in. So then he wondered if the boys who help us had forgotten to shut them in for the night. He jumped in the car and went out around the road, but saw nothing. By doing this we figure the thieves got scared. Early next morning, a woman reported to us she had found a dead calf on the path just outside the mission gate, south of where the African boys live. The cattle were out grazing in the pasture. Bob went to Siteki and brought out the police to make an investigation. I don't know if they ever caught anyone but I did wish our dogs were more like watch dogs to keep the thieves away. Anyway, the Lord helps us in all things.

Also in July we had a tour group come from the States. They were people who came with Rev. Lietzel, one of our men from Mission Headquarters. They stayed at our mission one night. They were coming just to experience what the work was like that we were doing. That night I had to find places for 18 people to sleep. That was counting all our family and Lehman's as well. There were seven people in the group, quite a few extra mouths to feed, I must say. So the busy month of July ended.

Earlier I mentioned the young couple, Israel and Victoria Langa, who had married September 1, of 1973. He called on August 13th 1974 to report the birth of a baby girl. He was a proud papa and we were very proud of this young couple. They named their baby Fakazile. Later I had a shower for the baby.

We had a fine lovely white cat around our house. We kept her inside to catch rats. About every morning I would find a dead one, or maybe even more, under the table or divan. I'm sure she caught two or three a night. They weren't little mice, they were big rats. So she became quite a prized possession.

We had a District Conference at Phonjawane last of August and first of September. One of my jobs was to put our mission books in order. In other words, balance our books. Well, this is not my thing. I really did not like math much in school, but it is something missionaries need to learn to do. Since I had not done the books in several months they had to be balanced before we left on furlough. It meant I worked on them during Conference although I did attend the Sunday school meeting on Tuesday and on Friday.

We all attended the Malihambe Service. This service is the one in which all the churches of the District bring their offerings together. It is especially the work of the women, although many men do give. I wish you could see how this offering is taken in joyful singing and marching to the front of the church, each church carrying their offering. And of course, there is kind of a race between them to see what church gives the most. Our offering at this time was 500 rands approximately $500 in U.S. money, the most it had ever been in the history of this District. We praise God that our Swazis are catching the vision.

It wasn't too long after our Conference in September the brother of Esther Mazibuko, the girl who worked in my house, was killed in a car accident. I remember so well when word was brought to her. She went around our yard screaming and crying out for her brother. This way of outward visible mourning is a Swazi custom. When women lose their husbands they always wear a black dress for a year. At the end of the year, the black can be taken off.

The month of October arrived and we began to feel more and more stress in trying to get everything accomplished. Roxy again came home for her last short school holiday. Orai was able to help get her home from Dundee since he had to go that way.

One day Rylan, our five-year-old, decided to stir up a bee's nest not far from the house. He took a pipe and stuck it in the nest. Of course, they started out in droves. Rylan ran away and didn't get stung, but poor little Randal got stung in a lot of places. Ronald tried to get his little brother away from the swarm. In doing so, he got stung several times. Allen got stung a few times, too. In time they were able to get to a safe place until the bees settled down. It reminds me of when Bob was stung by bees while my mom and dad were visiting in 1973. His face was so swollen one could hardly recognize him.

Our African boys who mowed our grass had to be careful about stirring up the bees, too. I remember them driving the lawn mowers with blankets over their heads, trying to keep the bees away. I guess the bees didn't like the sound of the lawn mowers.

About the 9th of November we received some important visitors. Bob's parents, Alfie and Ella Cheney, came for a visit. They visited with the Lehmans, too. Grandpa Cheney was even able to go with Orai for a short visit over in Mozambique, around the area of Maputo, the capital city. It was so nice to have Grandpa and Grandma Cheney visiting our work in Swaziland.

Something rather funny happened to Grandpa one day. There was a young African man who had recently returned from studying in one of our U.S. Universities came up to our mission to visit a bit with Bob. Grandpa happened to be nearby as Bob and the young man were conversing in English. After he left my father-in-law turned to Bob and asked, "What language was that man speaking?" With a smile Bob answered, "English". You see my father-in-law couldn't detect that it was English because of the accent. The accent does make a big difference.

We had decided that on our way home we would like to visit the Holy Land. We talked with Bob's folks about going with us but Grandpa wanted to go on to Northern Ireland to visit relatives. Grandma really did want to go with us, but decided she better stay with Grandpa.

We had talked to our Nazarene friends and gotten an address of a place that was reasonable to stay in. So arrangements were made. We got our plane tickets ordered. Our route would be to fly from Joburg to Athens and from Athens to Tel Aviv. From there we would take a bus up to Jerusalem.

The last few days of our term were spent packing our bags, all six of them, for overseas travel. In those days there weren't the dangers from bombs that we have today, so size of bottles of liquid didn't matter. We would be leaving on the 9th of December and arriving on Sunday evening, the 10th, in Jerusalem.

One other thing we had to do was prepare the nurse's house near the mission for a young couple coming as YES Corps workers for a year. The Dick Grindstaffs would be coming to teach in the schools. So there was painting and cleaning to do besides our clearing out the mission house for Rev. Sigwanes to move into. Orai and Linda helped us a lot. In fact, the five children went to Joy Mission ahead of us.

Jean Keel knitted jerseys (sweaters) for each of our children, This was so kind of her. She made all five sweaters alike. This made it easier for us to keep track of our children in the airports!

Our First Furlough
And our visit to the Holy Land and Northern Ireland

Our first four years in Swaziland passed very quickly. Before we knew it we were scheduled to take our one year furlough in the U.S. Just three weeks or so before we were going to leave, Bob's parents came to visit us. They had plans to visit in Northern Ireland. They said, "Why don't you come with us on your way back to the States?"

My father-in-law had many relatives in Northern Ireland. He had lived there until he was seven years old when, with his mother, Annie, he made his way to the U.S. to join his Dad in Garden County. After discussing this plan we decided that first we would visit the Holy Land for a couple days and then fly on to London, then to Belfast. Friends from the Imperial Wesleyan Church sent a check to us for our travel expenses. This truly was a help and a blessing.

Packing suitcases for a family of seven is not an easy task. However, we also had to pack up and leave the mission to the National District. Nationals had been trained and missionaries no longer needed to stay at Ebenezer Mission. We were turning it over to them to care for the school, the church and the clinic.

As Bob and I left the Siteki area in the Lobamba Mountains, it felt like a great burden rolled from our shoulders. During these four years Bob had trained two Swazi men to serve in the headmaster positions in the Phonjawane

Secondary School and the Ebenezer Secondary School. Besides this, we worked with the church on weekends. Of course, my time was taken up with being mother to the Sand- pile Tribe and homeschooling our three older children, besides the duties of the home and church.

So we traveled with our baggage to Joburg where we got on a plane that would take us to Israel via Athens. We landed in Tel Aviv, Israel and after going through security we got on a bus taking us up to Jerusalem.

The next couple days were filled with sightseeing and learning where our Bible stories took place. I can't begin to tell how great it was seeing the Garden Tomb, the Eastern Gate, the Mosque on the Temple site, the Mount of Olives, the Garden of Gethsemane, the City of Bethlehem, the Old Wall of the Temple and a Bar Mitzvah Service. This was on the first day we were there. The second day we hired an Arab taxi driver who drove us north of Jerusalem to Jacob's Well, Nazareth and the Sea of Galilee, Cana and Capernaum. Then we followed the Jordan River down to Jericho before driving back to Jerusalem. What a trip! It made our Bibles mean more than ever.

The one thing that meant a great deal to our family was forming a circle and holding hands while we prayed on the shore of the Sea of Galilee. The one thing I felt sorry about was that we didn't let our two little boys, Rylan 5 and Randal 2, ride a camel. It was just too much to cram into two days.

On Wednesday morning we again boarded an Israeli Airlines plane and headed for London. At Heathrow Airport we stored two of our cases that were things we didn't need for the week that we would spend in Northern Ireland. When we landed in London we stayed overnight before taking a flight to Belfast. It was December, but truly this Irish country was a land of green, even in December. The stone fences dividing the green fields looked like a patchwork quilt.

My father-in-law and mother-in-law met us at the Belfast airport along with Allen Cheney, a cousin to my father-in-law. They had a van that could carry all our family as well as three others. The Allen and Mary Cheney's put us up for that night since they lived in Belfast.

The next day our family, including Grandpa and Grandma, drove to Drumquin in county Tyrone, Grandpa Cheney's home area. We visited a number of relatives: the Gordon's, the McCormicks and even Aunt Eva Cheney, Grandpa Cheney's old aunt. Our family stayed with Valarie and Robert Hastings. Valarie is the daughter of Mary and Allen Cheney.

At this time I guess you could say some terrorist activity was going on along the border of Ireland and Northern Ireland. This is where we became acquainted with what they called speed bumps across the roads so one would not want to drive a vehicle fast down this road. It was definitely dangerous! This was to slow down terrorist activity.

Before we knew it, our time in Northern Ireland came to an end and we were back at the Belfast airport. Our flight would take us to London where we would change planes and head for our homeland. For some reason, our plane from Belfast kept delaying and it made us late for our U.S. flight.

Oh my, now what would we do? Two suitcases were stored on the one side of Heathrow airport and we were to leave from the opposite side. It was decided Bob would ride the airport bus to where our two cases were stored and the children and I would wait for him. You know how long time can seem when you are waiting for someone! It occurred to me, perhaps I could see if any other airline would have room for our family to fly to New York, so I began looking around while the children stayed at a certain area, leaving Roxy and Allen in charge of the younger ones.

While both Bob and I were gone and the children were sitting in the area we had designated, Randal suddenly started choking. Fortunately our 15-year-old daughter noticed him turning blue. She grabbed him by the feet and started pounding him on the back. Out popped a hard candy and Randal could again breathe. I know God was looking out for all of us that day. I praise the Lord because our Roxane knew what to do when she saw her little brother choking.

Now, remember, this was just before Christmas, something like December 19th. Well, I did find room on an Air India 747. They would allow us on this plane, although we could not all sit together. Now I needed to see Bob, but where was he and would he be able to find us? I was in a predicament and I'm sure I said some prayers. As I was standing in line, out of the crowd Bob appeared with our two suitcases. What a relief! We got the children and our other carryon luggage to the gate we were loading from. Before long, we were given boarding passes on a huge plane. Now we were all safe and sound and on the last leg of our journey to New York.

After finding seats, I remember getting myself buckled in and having a terrible headache. I'm sure it was the stress of missing our plane to New York, getting the stored luggage and finding another flight for all seven of us. It didn't help that some American young people on the flight refused to obey the rules of buckling up during takeoff. I was embarrassed to think Americans would act like that.

The flight went well and in about five hours we were landing at JFK airport in New York. How exciting it was coming off the plane and setting foot in our home country. It was Christmas and in the huge terminal we saw a huge Santa Claus and snowman inflating and deflating. It really impressed our five children. Our little two-year-old, Randal, was making his first discovery of our homeland, the good old U.S.A.

We made our way to baggage claim to pick up our six bags. We found our two cases, but the four bags could not be found. After inquiring, the baggage people told us the four suitcases had probably been sent on another flight to Denver. So we boarded our final flight of the trip and headed for Denver, Colorado. We were a very tired bunch, but we were too excited to sleep.

Here we met up with family at Elaine Harveys, Bob's oldest sister, and her family. I can't remember who all was there to welcome us home, but it was a delightful reunion. Now we could show off our little two-year-old son for the first time. Bob went to baggage claim again to get our luggage, but the only ones that turned up were the two suitcases retrieved from storage in London.

On my, what a predicament! Where had our four big cases gone? Baggage personnel told us to check back in the morning, so now we were taken to relatives to stay for the night. Our beds were a welcome sight for sure this night. It had been a very long and stressful day.

We had a chance to visit with Elaine and her family. The next morning Bob again checked with the airport for our luggage, but it could not be found. Oh my, what would we do for clothes? The baggage claim personnel took down all the information they needed and told Bob they would send it to the address in Nebraska where we would locate.

Home for Christmas

It was so good to see our parents again, brothers and sisters and other relatives and friends. Orai and Linda and family were there for Christmas as well. We were blessed by some churches that sent gift boxes to us. In fact, it was a double blessing because without our four lost suitcases we were really short of clothes. The ones I had in the two suitcases were mostly summer clothing and we had come straight into winter. The Christmas boxes had a good assortment of winter clothing and really helped us to cope. It wasn't too many days after we arrived that a letter came through from the airlines saying they could not find our bags. We asked people to pray that somehow these cases would show up. We just needed to trust the Lord with this situation.

Bob was planning to attend Asbury Seminary in Wilmore, Kentucky for the semester starting in January, around the 15th. We borrowed a motor home that Grandpa Cheney bought from Orai and Linda. They had used it in Home Ministries as they traveled around with their family. Now they were heading back to Africa, so Grandpa took it off their hands and let us use it.

The time drew closer for our departure to Kentucky and still our suitcases had not shown up. We really made it a matter of prayer because God knew we needed some more clothes. We just had to trust that somehow God was going to take care of our situation.

About two or three days before we were to leave for Kentucky we got a phone call from a gas station in Lewellen. They said, "We have four big suitcases here, dropped off by a trucking company. Do you know anything about them?" Bob said, "Yes, I'll be right down to pick them up."

How those four cases ever got to us was a real mystery. We always thought that one of God's angels must have placed them on the truck, one that was coming to Lewellen. This was how God answered our prayer for the four lost suitcases.

Heading for Kentucky

Our trip to Wilmore, Kentucky went smoothly in the motor home. When we arrived in Wilmore, January of 1975, there was a mission house that was especially made available for missionaries on furlough wanting to go to school at Asbury Seminary. We got Roxane and Allen enrolled at the high school in Nicholasville. They had to ride a bus. Ronald could go to school right in Wilmore and we entered Rylan in a preschool kindergarten held at the Methodist Church in Wilmore. Then Bob got situated for further training at Asbury Seminary.

We found a small church in Wilmore to get involved in, the United Missionary Church. Strange enough, a man who attended Bethel College with me was pastoring this church. We felt more attracted to this smaller church than to the big Methodist Church where Rev. Semonds, one of the professors of Asbury, was the minister.

We met other missionaries who lived near us and made friends with our neighbors. One couple had been missionaries in Japan. Another couple from the Nazarene Church had been missionaries in Korea. Since we had only the motor home as a mode of travel, often these couples helped us out with transport. We truly appreciated their assistance. There was a couple from Michigan living next to us. They had two boys. One of the boys gave us a picture of an owl he had painted, which I still have to this day. I decided to go to one of the classes just to get information and the feel of what it was like to be in a classroom again.

When we arrived back in the States our mission headquarters suggested that I should see a psychologist or psychiatrist. There happened to be a Wesleyan man with whom we could set up appointments. I never really understood why our mission department felt I should see a psychiatrist, but we made appointments with him for a couple of sessions. I truly believe my problem was just being tired from the stress of coming on furlough and I just needed to rest up. I guess after a couple sessions the doctor figured I was normal.

We celebrated Roxy's 16th birthday in January with a special Princess Doll cake that we bought from a lady I had learned about. During Easter vacation we had made arrangements to go visit our friends, Hubert and Irma Hughes, in Nashville, Tennessee. They were pastoring one of our Wesleyan churches there. On our way we paid a visit to the Mammoth Caves in Kentucky. We felt this would be a good experience for our children. In May, on our way back to Nebraska, we stopped in Evansville, Indiana to visit the Karns family. They were on furlough. It was nice to renew connections. Our Rylan graduated from preschool in May. The five months went quickly and before we knew it, school was coming to a close.

During the summer of 1975 we made connections with a number of churches and camp meetings. One event that stands out in my mind was the trip we made to Whitefish, Montana, where my Uncle Jewel and Aunt Annie and Aunt Chrystal and Uncle Ken lived. My sisters and I decided we would all meet at Whitefish and celebrate our parent's 40th wedding anniversary. Esther and Nathan and family came from Oregon and Elaine, Steve and April came from Alberta, Canada. Of course, not as many friends could attend because it was far from Nebraska. We traveled in the motor home with a tent and my folks rode with us. It really was a lot of fun getting together with the whole Earl Thornton family.

When we returned to Oshkosh we found a house to rent near the grade school. Roxane was ready to be a junior and Allen would be a freshman. Ron went into fifth grade and Rylan started kindergarten.

While the children were in school in Oshkosh, I was unable to travel with Bob. He went to a number of churches to share about our mission work in Swaziland. I put together a slide show for children. I called it, "Missionary Mother to the Sand Pile Tribe". It was made to show what missionary kids do on the mission field.

It was really a blessing to be close to both parents and other relatives. In many ways I felt we were giving our children some roots and stability. It is very hard for missionary kids moving around, but having family around us helped so much.

So, as we moved to the close of our first furlough, we celebrated Christmas, packed up and said our goodbyes. We truly had a great first furlough in the U.S.A. but we were ready to settle down in our own home back in Africa.

Chapter Four
Beginning Our Second Term in Africa, 1976

We left very soon after Christmas 1975 and flew with our family to the east coast. I had relatives living in Delaware and Bob's sister, Kathy and husband Jim, lived on the military base in Washington D.C. When we arrived at National Airport, Uncle Homer, Aunt Grace and Jim were there to meet us. We went home with Uncle Homer's and I was able to see all my cousins and their families. Then my Uncle and Aunt brought us back to Jim and Kathy's in D.C. although Jim and Kathy had gone to some of his folks in Pennsylvania for a few days. They let us rest up at their house. It was very nice with four bedrooms and two-and-a-half bathrooms. While we were there I stayed at the house with Rylan and Randal and Bob took the three older children to see the capital, the Washington, Lincoln and Jefferson monuments and the Smithsonian Institute. When Jim & Kathy returned it was good to spend a little time with them and their little son, Douglas before leaving for Dulles Airport.

We got our South African visas Wednesday morning and our plane TWA left at 6:45 p.m. We got into Paris, France at 8:25 a.m. on the 6th of January. Since our next flight didn't leave until 9:55 that night we decided to take a bus into the city and look around. We went to the museum where Napoleon lays in a casket and there are lots of tanks and military stuff sitting around. This got a little boring so we began walking the streets thinking that perhaps we could walk to the Eiffel Tower.

Well this turned out to be much farther than we thought. It was getting to be afternoon, so we caught an airport bus and headed back to catch our flight. I remember being so glad that we were not driving in a car. When we came to the famous archway in Paris, cars and buses and all sorts of vehicles were going in every direction – no lights, no rhyme nor reason to the flow of traffic. That's one time I was happy to be in a big bus.

Finally, as we were driving back to the terminal, the bus took us close to the Eiffel Tower and we were able to get some good pictures. We boarded our Air France flight and headed for South Africa. In Johannesburg we again had to change planes and fly a South African Airways flight to Durban.

Upon arriving in Durban, Carol Ramsay and girls, and Linda Lehman and cousins, Valarie and Mike were there to meet us. Needless to say, we were all very weary after two nights of flying and were ready for a good night's sleep; but, oh how happy we were to be back in our beloved Africa.

When we arrived at Emmanuel Mission the South African field conference was drawing to a close. We did have the privilege of seeing most of the missionaries and many of the African pastors and delegates. For Roxane, Allen, Ron and Rylan, it was back to school uniforms and a regular school schedule on January 21st. However, just before this we were able to go back with the Lehman's to Swaziland. It was like going home for the children, meeting old friends among our Swazi people. While there we picked up some of our household supplies, which we had stored before going on furlough.

We had thought we would be living at Emmanuel Mission and that the Millers would be keeping our four children who were in school; but our mission department had approached us about Bob being the principal of our Bible College. We prayed about this and felt it was the right thing for us to do. At this time the Forrest Grays who lived in the missionary home for the bible school still had six more months of their time to finish. The Naphtali Langa family, also teachers, lived in the mission home, so there was no place for us to live. It was also suggested we take concentrated Zulu language study during the time the Grays were still there. We were happy with this situation and felt God leading in this direction.

The Field Counsel decided to let us look for a place to live near Port Shepstone. There was a resort with rondoval houses (grass thatched round buildings) about three miles out of Port Shepstone. They had one of the larger rondovals in which our family could fit and which we could rent by the month. It was a little tight, but in the end they included another smaller rondoval for our three older children. Even though the living space was small, there was a lot of play area, swimming, golfing and many other things to play with. This was the place we met the Bramsbys. Eva Bramsby was owner and Patti Bramsby, her youngest daughter, was Ron's age. We got to know and love this family.

It was nice to have our children with us. Roxy began her matric or senior year of high school. Allen was in Standard 7, Ron in Standard 4 and Rylan in grade 1. The children were all able to ride the bus to school.

Our little Rylan had kind of a bad experience riding the school bus. I was in town at the Miller's doing my washing and had wanted all the children to come there and ride home with me, but since I didn't write a note to his teacher she put him on the bus. He didn't know where to get off and Bob didn't get to the bus stop in time. So our poor little 1st grader just stayed on the bus and rode around the route back to school. The school let us know that he was there and we went back to school to get him. I was sorry this happened, but tried to build his confidence back up so he wouldn't be so afraid.

One of Bob's and my assignments was to enroll in a Zulu language class and spend time learning this language. We began this class at one of the schools in Port Shepstone on the 29th of January. We had done some private lessons during our first term, but had never had much time for studying. Now during the next five months we wanted to do a more concentrated study.

As we settled into more of a routine we learned more about the mission work of this area. One of the things Bob and I were assigned was churches to visit and work with on the district.

In April, 1976, we were appointed by the district to go to a little church called Shiloh far out into the "boondoos". Bob and I had a really interesting experience. We didn't take the children because of not knowing what we might have to go through. With all the rains we'd been having, the roads were well-washed away in some places. We managed to get through. The last little distance we had to park our car and cross a big flowing river on foot. The river was over 100 feet across and came up pretty high on my thighs and was swirling quite a bit. We walked very carefully so got across without falling.

Then we walked about a quarter mile up the hill to the little church. The people weren't expecting anyone since we arrived about 11:30. We had to ring the bell and wait until 12:30 to start the service. At the close of the service we had around 30 people besides us, our interpreter and another man who was helping. God helped us in our speaking, but, oh how frustrating it was that we couldn't talk to them and understand everything they said. I know we couldn't expect to talk all at once or know a language in a few days. As we crossed the river going back, we got across without falling down. What an interesting experience it can be just to take the Gospel to people in very hard to get to places.

Ronald Sees the Dentist

When Ronald was about four years old, back in the late 60's, we were visiting at Grandpa and Grandma Cheney's. The boys were jumping across cement irrigation ditches. Ron fell and knocked out his two top front teeth. Of course, it was too early for him to lose these teeth so for three or more years he had no front top teeth. When we arrived in Africa he was six and a half, but still had no front teeth. This is when the Africans gave him the nickname "Gumza". When his two front teeth did finally come in, they protruded almost straight out. We didn't want our little boy to have this all his life.

After arriving back in South Africa and getting settled, we decided that our Ronald needed to see an orthodontist in Durban to learn what it was going to take to correct his teeth. The dentist thought we should get started right away by removing two of his teeth. Then they would put bands on the teeth and start pulling his two front teeth in. This would be the treatment for about the first year. The orthodontist said we should get these front teeth in before he gets them knocked out. This could easily happen if he played rugby or soccer. He also gave Ronald a head brace to wear at night which would help pull these teeth back to where they belonged. I really felt so sorry for Ronald when he wore this brace at night because it hurt and ached, but we encouraged him to stick with this regimen because in a couple years his teeth would look normal and straight.

Busy Days

In April the children had school holidays. The Millers had gone on vacation so we told them we would take care of their shop in Port Shepstone. They had a Christian book store selling school books, Christian literature and used clothing as a part of Evangelism Outreach. It really kept them busy and they needed a rest. We stayed in their house during this time. It was nice to live in such a lovely, big house for a change.

On Easter morning our family did something we had never done before. We went to a sunrise service on the beach close to Port Shepstone on the South Coast. They also had Easter weekend services which we attended throughout the District.

Since we were still in school holidays, Orai called us and said they planned to be in Durban. "Would it be possible for you to meet us there for the day?" he asked. We agreed and planned to meet them at the Holiday Inn. We were late but finally found them on the beach front. During school holidays many South Africans take their vacations; the beach front was crowded with hundreds of people. We ate, then let the children go to the Amusement Park to get rides .

In my April 19th letter I said, "Roxy took the younger kids down on the beach so they could swim. They all had a grand time and seemed to enjoy their day. I'm sure they will feel better about starting back to school on Wednesday."

During the latter part of April the Ramsay's and Lehman's came for a visit. Since it was holiday time for the schools we had to have the three older kids move in with us so the Park would have more space for visitors. It was so lovely to have missionary family coming for a visit.

From my May 3rd letter I wrote: "Roxy said she heard Rylan telling some little kids at the park something about his cousins. She questioned him again, but he wouldn't say anymore so she thinks that Rylan feels like Suzan and Sheri are his cousins! I guess it would stand to reason that he'd feel this way, calling Jim and Carol Auntie and Uncle most of his knowing life."

During the Lehman's visit we had such a nice time together. It was so nice that we were in Eden Park. That night Rylan didn't go to sleep like he usually does, so when we got home he was sort of moping around and finally he said, "Why do they have to go?" Then I knew what was troubling him. The four little kids have such good times playing together. Rylan and Valarie, Michael and Randal were not only first cousins, they had become good friends.

The Grays who lived at the mission had 16-year-old twin boys named Lester and Lenard. The boys enjoyed spending time with them. The last day of May, Allen and Ron went fishing with Les and Len down on the beach. They didn't catch anything but had nibbles. They fish with little sardine fish. Allen and Ron decided they wanted to buy the Gray boys' fishing poles when they leave for the States. We brought a big tent from the States and our boys and the Grays have had good times camping out at the mission."We took the Grays to the Airport on the 16th of June and bid them goodbye. They are retiring after they do Home Ministries. However, their boys left on the 11th of June from Durban so they could visit with their married brother and sister before going overseas.

Moving to Emmanuel Mission

Our move to Emmanuel Mission took place on the 18th of June, 1976, after we had done some painting. We traveled inland to the mission about 18 miles. We were all quite anxious to get moved into a house. Randy said to Patti (the little girl at the park whose mother is the park owner) that she is lucky because she has a house. He would be happy to be in a house.

I had been doing my washing at the Miller's while living at Eden Park. They get quite a lot of rain in Port Shepstone area and so often I would need to hang clothes a second time as it would rain or humidity was too high for drying. I truly appreciated that Carolyn Miller allowed me to wash at their house. My last time to wash I hurried back to Eden Park, after hanging it, then we loaded up our car as much as possible and headed for the mission.

Sister Gray wanted to explain some things to me and show me around so that I would know where things for Bible School were located. Since we were out there at lunch time Miss Brown (our single missionary who was teaching at the Bible College) fixed our lunch for us and we all ate with Brother and Sister Gray and Miss Brown. Sister Gray showed Bob about the book work and accounts for the Bible College. Our holiday was over and real responsibility began! Our older children would be boarding at the Miller's during school time from Sunday evening until Friday afternoon. They did well at the Miller's for two weeks before they had a long school holiday in July.

The first week of July, Carolyn and I attended a Women's Conference at Altona Mission. The Rev. Hudson (missionaries in Durban area) let us take their Hi-Ace Van. We took five women from our District and two girls from the Bible College. So there were nine of us total. It was so nice that Carolyn and I could share the driving with one vehicle.

About one week before this meeting the Women's Leader had contacted us and asked us to prepare lessons for the conference. In my July 7th letter I wrote: "Well, this is something else I had to think up while trying to unpack our barrels and get our house situated. But anyway, the Lord really helped and we were able to give good lessons for the ladies." A lady from the States had sent me a book entitled "All Things Are Possible through Prayer" for my birthday. I gave lessons on prayer in the Christian woman's life. Thank the Lord for that special lady in the States who sent this book to me.

In July, a YES Corp group came out to the Bible School for services. I made dinner for the group. It was so nice to see Sharon Long again. We also met the Gene Hudson family who were missionaries in Rhodesia (later called Zimbabwe). Our field felt it might be safer for them to work in South Africa because of fighting in Zimbabwe. There were five children in their family, too. They were looking for a house in Durban. Their two older boys, Kevin and Ronald, were about the ages of Allen and Ronald. They had three girls, Susan, Gillian and the youngest, Ruth, was about Randal's age.

Patti Bramsby from Eden Park came on Tuesday when the YES Corp group came out. And then the Hudson boys had been staying with us at that time while their folks were looking for a house in Durban. As it happened they found a house, but they couldn't move in until the 4th of August. So they asked us to keep the boys a while longer. Really it wasn't too bad. It certainly involved more work but it was great to see all those kids sprawled out in the living room close to the fireplace. Because it was so cold they had started a fire. Roxy was studying in her room with a kerosene heater on. It had rained just a little that morning so that was why it was quite cold, a good time for popping popcorn! Really it was nice to have them all home.

We enjoyed the YES Corp a great deal. It was nice to see Sharon again and Roxy was especially glad to have her spend time here. They gave a service here at the Bible School and also at the church for the Malihambe Service. They gave an example in witnessing for the students. It was really good. I was also amused at the group when they ate with us. I fixed a regular American type meal with mashed potatoes, meat loaf, salad, vegetables and tea. It was quite warm that day, so I made iced tea and they drank it like it was going out of style. In fact, they ate and ate and practically cleaned everything up, commenting how good it was to have some good American food. I sort of felt they might appreciate a meal like this as they had been having African food, Indian Food, etc., and I guess I was right. Only wished I had cooked a bit more, but I believe they were pretty well filled up. That day I fed about 20 people. For dessert I fixed a big cake. Here is the recipe: Take a couple small packages of vanilla wafers and crush them up. Add ¾ pound of butter and 1 pound powdered sugar, add 2 Tbls. cocoa, 2 eggs and 1 tsp vanilla. Method: Roll out wafers until they are broken to bits. Melt butter, add sugar, cocoa and vanilla. Beat eggs well and add to mixture. Add to biscuits and mix thoroughly and press into baking tins. Keep in fridge. It's very rich, but delicious. The group really liked this dessert.

The boys had fun playing together but we had an incident happen that really scared me. The boys had made what they call a 'Foofie Slide'. It was a cable hooked between two trees with a short pipe to grab hold of and slide down to the ground. Of course, the one side was probably over 15 feet high and the cable gradually tapered down to a lower tree where their feet could touch the ground. They had the cable tied to one of the tall trees down toward our house.

After supper our Ronnie and Ronald Hudson decided they were going to try sliding down when it was dark. I really didn't want them to do this and told them so. Anyway, a short while later our Ron came running and yelled, "I think Ronnie's been hurt bad." So we rushed out to find he had fallen about 15 feet. Right away I could see that his pelvis was broken and he couldn't get up. He said his leg hurt. I was really scared. We called the hospital and the Hudsons who were at the Millers. Cheryl Hudson, Ron's mom, who was a nurse, told us how to carry Ronald. So Bob, Allen and Kevin Hudson lifted him very carefully into the car and rushed him to the hospital in Port Shepstone. It was about 8:30 p.m. After taking x-rays they found he had broken his wrist and his pelvic bone in three places. He had to be in hospital for a long time. We thank the Lord that it didn't break his back or kill him. He could also have been paralyzed for life from this. I shudder to think of it.

Before the long July school holiday ended we decided to make a trip to Swaziland to see the Lehman's. We all wanted to make a trip to Kruger National Game Park in Transvaal on North of Swaziland. The Lehmans had a Land Rover big enough to take our family as well as the Lehmans. In this way, we could share expenses and it wouldn't cost so much for each family.

We spent three days in the park. The first day we had a lioness cross right in front of us on the road. We saw one elephant in the distance and many impala, kudu, water buck, monkeys and baboons. The second day on our way to the camp called Skakuza, right in front of us a beautiful leopard ambled across the road. We had never seen a leopard like this one so close. Other animals we saw were African buffalo and two young lions. Of course always there are warthogs, giraffe and zebras. On our last day we had the wonderful privilege of seeing ten lions that had killed a zebra. They were just cleaning up the last bit of the zebra when one of the lions crossed the road in front of us and headed for the water hole on the other side of the road. What a privilege to witness the ways of the wildlife in this famous park.

At the end of the day we headed back to Swaziland to be able to attend Sunday morning service at Ebenezer Mission. We had to be back in South Africa by Monday morning. We weren't sure how it was going to work out about petrol (gas) because on Sundays in South Africa you can't buy. However, in Swaziland you could buy on Sundays, so before leaving Swaziland we filled our car's tank and Bob also got 21 liters of gas in a jerry can. Bob put the gas from the jerry can into our car when we had gone about half way. This got us all the way into Port Shepstone at 5:15 a.m. We thanked the Lord for a great short vacation and for God's journey mercies.

Some of Our Responsibilities as Missionaries

Of course our first responsibility was Bob being Principal of our Bible Training Center. Both Bob and I taught classes. One of my obligations was to see that our students were well fed. The food supply had to be monitored and purchased. One of the supply sources was our garden down the hill and across from the mission house. One week I put 15 bags of peas in the freezer. We picked lots of lettuce. I really liked to fix wilted lettuce with bacon bits, vinegar and onion. Umm, so good! We also had lots of cabbage and spinach tops (these two things are included in African meals probably more than any other vegetables. They also use a lot of onion and tomato).

We had a lot of bananas since we raised banana plants on the mission. I even sold them for a cent each, reasonable but of course, they were small, but, oh so tasty.

We also worked with the district churches. One thing I always enjoyed was organizing Sunday school workshops. One time we had 20 people from the district enroll besides our eight Bible School students. That August, Bob taught a class on Sunday School Administration and I taught a class on Teaching Methods. One of our men taught a class on The Teacher's Responsibilities and one of the girls had a class in singing.

Another project we tried was to put out a monthly school letter to each of the districts. We wanted the home churches to take more interest in the Bible School and in so doing, realize the need of getting more of their young people to hear God's call for service in the churches. Money seemed to be a big god to many of the African youth and all they could think of was to get more education so they could make more money. Already many churches were suffering because they had no pastor.

One of Bob's other tasks was teaching TEE classes in Port Shepstone. TEE is Theological Education by Extension. Instead of students coming to the Bible School we took the classes to where it is more convenient for them to meet one day each week. Another of Bob's tasks was to attend the field council meetings. They were usually held at Altona Mission in Northern Natal. We certainly didn't lack for anything to do! Even without the kids a home, our time was filled up. Also at this time we were still in a class for the purpose of learning the Zulu language.

We praise God that the Don Millers in Port Shepstone were willing to board our children and children adjusted quite well. Randal, however, our four-year-old didn't like it. Can you imagine what it would be like to have three older, noisy brothers and a sister around your entire lifetime and then suddenly they are gone!!??? The quietness just got to be too much for him so one evening he said to his Daddy, "Please, build a fire in the fireplace so it can make some noise, Daddy."

It was important to keep our supporting churches informed about our mission work. In order to do this we decided to write up a script which we transferred to a cassette tape (remember those were the days before DVD's). Then we would organize a slide show to go along with our script. Of course, this too took time but it was necessary to keep our supporting churches informed.

It was always fun to have visitors. Brother and Sister Isaac Lehman, Sr. stopped in to see us while they were on the South Coast visiting relatives. Also, the Robert Smith's from Swaziland stopped in. They were from England but he was teaching at the University of Swaziland. They had two children of their own and a little adopted daughter about Randal's age.

Another Nazarene missionary couple who became good friends our first term in Swaziland, the Millers, came for a visit. This was very nice, especially for Ron because their son, Dan ,and Ron were nearly the same age and they had many good times together while we lived in Swaziland.

So the list of friends could go on, but we did appreciate all our old friends and the new friends we made in South Africa.

Can you believe we only got a dial phone in September of 1976 at our mission? In fact, my parents were considering getting a phone at their Sandhill Ranch. When they did, in 1977, we could actually dial them and talk. Today I can Skype over the internet with my son Randal and his family in Swaziland and see them as we talk together. Times have definitely changed for missionary families as far as communicating with their families in the U.S.

In September Roxy began taking her trial exams and so was in quite a stew. She was studying for all she was worth most of the time. Her real exams didn't start until November. The pressure seemed great for students doing the Matric (or senior year of high school).

One day in September we had rain, rain, rain! I had a house full of kids on a rainy day! You can imagine what our house looked like. The two Hudson boys were down from Durban. I decided to let the two Ronnies be partners and Kevin and Allen partners and had them bake something. The Ronnies baked a pumpkin pie with a green crust! Can't you just see it? Kevin and Allen made a chocolate cake which they cut up and decorated like an airplane. Then the two little ones felt left out so I asked Ronnie Hudson to help them bake peanut butter cookies. Then everyone seemed to be happy.

Well, October arrived with more rain. This meant muddy roads that we had to travel when going to Port Shepstone and I'm not a fan of muddy roads! It also brought us another visitor, Naomi Swan, missionary from Zambia. She was on her way to the U.S. for furlough. She decided to go home by ship that time. She and Miss Brown, one of the teachers as Emanuel Mission, had a good time visiting. Miss Brown didn't get many single missionary visitors and so this was very nice for her.

We took Naomi to Durban where she boarded her ship, The Galileo Passenger Ship in Durban harbor on October 18th. It was quite interesting to watch them load cars and lots of boxes. A number of whites were leaving Rhodesia and going to Australia to live. This ship was an Italian line and carried 1400 passengers. Just Bob, Randal and I went to Durban to take Naomi to her ship. Miss Brown also went along with us. The Hudson's who lived in Durban came to join us in bidding her bon voyage. She would be docking in Melbourne and Sydney, Australia before heading to Acapulco, Mexico. From there she would go by bus or train to the U.S

At the close of October we had a big banquet for the students. I was in charge of fixing all the salads. We served lots of chicken and some beef. All together we fed around forty-eight people. The students always loved the dessert because it was the one time of the year they got cake and ice cream. On Saturday the graduation was held. We had only one graduate, but next year we expected to have four. So we closed the school year for 1976. Our new school year would start February 8, 1977.

For Roxy, November was pretty well taken up with writing exams and studying hard. She won the Rose Bowl trophy for being first in English. They had a very nice class day for those in matric. Bob couldn't come because he had to take Ron to the dentist in Durban. Carolyn Miller went with me to the program.

Roxy had to write three of her exams. She had Afrikaans language to do on Wednesday and on Friday a math paper. The following week she had only history. I think that we arranged to go in and get her so she can be with us the rest of the week. She felt like her geography exam wasn't quite as hard as she had anticipated, but she was glad it's over.

On November 22nd we brought Roxy home with us and Randal was really thrilled about it. He could hardly wait until all the kids came home to stay! They had only two more weeks of school. Ron and Allen were taking exams, too. Ron wanted to go to a camp the week after school was out so he was working hard trying to earn some money for camp. Allen, too, wanted to make some money so he bought two sheep to use for this project. We hoped it would work. He wished James French was there to show him how to shear the sheep.

Roxy got a job at the play center, working with little kids. She had decided to take up special education, working with slow readers and handicapped children or Child Psychology and English. She went to work December 6th and worked until December 22nd when we planned to go to Boksburg to the Senior Lehman's for Christmas.

Before Roxy began working we made a trip to the Transki to visit the Milton Bagleys. Several of our Bible School students had come from the Transkei District so it was good to visit with them, also. While we were there, Bob got sick. At first we thought this might be a reoccurrence from the tick bite fever he had when we lived in Swaziland. He had gotten quite sick with it. When we got to Transki, his fever came back and he started getting chills so he spent quite a bit of the time in bed. Rev. Bagley and several preachers came into his room to anoint and pray for his healing. After this he didn't have such a high fever. He seemed to improve each day but was quite weak. We knew that God had touched him. On Sunday afternoon we returned to Port Shepstone. The Millers invited us to stay the night with them. Even though Bob was better, he wanted to get into the doctor Monday morning to know for sure what had caused his fever.

Usually a youth camp was held at the Bible College after school let out. So it still was a busy time even though school was out for the year and we were in the long holiday time between school years. Bob and I finished up our Zulu class in Uvongo and then we were on our own in learning the language. The youth camp began on Monday and I had lessons to prepare for that. After Ronald's dental appointment December 15th in Durban we stayed overnight with the Hudson's so as to give more time for Christmas shopping.

Christmas, 1976

We left from the South Coast and headed for Grandpa and Grandma

Lehman's in Boksburg Transvaal to celebrate Christmas. Grandpa and Grandma Cheney decided to come from the States. Then they would head on to Australia where Grandpa had some relatives. Also, the Orai Lehman's came from Swaziland. It was always an exciting time for the cousins to see one another.

On Christmas we ate outside, like the 4th of July in the States, very warm. I enjoyed a wonderful treat of watermelon! How special is that! Of course we all enjoyed having Grandpa and Grandma there to celebrate Christmas with us.

The Year 1977

After spending the Christmas Holiday with O.I. Lehman's in Boksburg, our family headed for Dundee Natal. This was where the European camp was held. Bob's parents and his sister, Wilma, went with us so we needed a bigger vehicle. Orai Lehman let us use their Land Rover and we headed for the camp on December 31st.

Maybe I should explain what we mean by European camp. This was the white district which was separate from our African district. At this time there was the apartheid still functioning in some areas. In fact, it used to really bother me that at the post office and at the borders we had to go to the white side and the African people had to go to the black side. We did see this separation merge slowly during our five terms in Africa. Of course, because of this, I always felt more freedom living in Swaziland. While we were at the European camp in Dundee, we had our Missionary Council meeting, so most of the missionaries were there.

So now, back to our camp meeting. We left our smaller car in Boksburg for Orai and Linda to drive, as they were planning to come to our Mission on South Coast. They came on January 3rd, here to our mission at Methlomyama at the Bible College. Wilma then left on January 5th from Durban to fly back to Zambia. Bob's dad decided they would leave for Australia on January 14th from Durban. Bob's mom would just as soon stay in Africa, as she has quite a lot of trouble with asthma.

One day Bob took his dad to see the sugar cane fields and mills. While they were gone my mother-in-law had a bad asthma attack that really scared me. Her face was turning gray. But she was able to tell me to get her purse where she had a little breathing sprayer. She sprayed into her mouth and then she became normal again. I was glad she was prepared for such emergenies.

Roxy passed her matric exams and was working at the daycare in Port Shepstone Wesleyan Church.

Rev. Wright, our General Mission Director, came to visit our mission. He had the noon meal with 17 of us all together, so We ate out in our big yard around a large table. After they showed him around the Bible School, Bob and Orai Lehman took him to Mt. Frere where the Milton Bagley's are stationed. It was really a big day for Bob and Orai as it is 160 miles there. They didn't get back until 11:15 that night. It was always nice to have the head of our World Mission Department come to visit.

School started February 8th for the Bible College. I stayed home on the Friday Bob went in to get the children from school. I had invited Patti Bramsby to come for the weekend with the children. She brought the most beautiful bouquet of roses to me. On Saturday the Hudson's from Durban came down with their whole family. There was a meeting here at the school and also students are arriving to begin their school year. Only seven students returned and there were no new students. It all looks rather dark for the future of our school. We are going to have to re-evaluate our set up and try, by the Lord's help, to come up with some kind of solution to the problem of why young people aren't training for the Lord's work."

One of the nice things about being close to the Indian Ocean is the beautiful beaches. All up and down the south coast from Durban to Port Elizabeth are nice sandy beaches where one can hunt for sea shells or just walk and run in the sand. Of course, one needs to be sure you are in one of the areas marked for swimming. South of Port Shepstone at Uvongo Beach, they have a lovely swimming pool for little children. I took the children there sometimes when we had time to get away. We even had a birthday party on the beach for Randal and Rylan, and the Hudson kids came as well, as did Kathy Miller and Patti Bramsby. They even had canoes that the kids tried out. One of my favorite things to do was to walk up and down the sandy beaches looking for pretty sea shells. It is also neat to just lie in the sun on the beach and listen to the roar of the ocean and see the big waves come sweeping in. The kids loved to make sand castles and then watch these big waves come in and wash it down.

As I stated earlier, there were certain areas designated for swimming. There are strong ocean currents that can pull you out to sea. I'd like to mention an incident in which Bob was pulled by a strong current. The kids and Bob were enjoying a swim at the Umtentweni Beach. Bob didn't notice as he was swimming that a strong current started pulling him out further than he wanted to be. Ron noticed his dad was getting into trouble and he swam out to help him. I'm very thankful that our son knew how to swim against a strong current and he could help his dad get back to shore safe and sound.

I don't want it to sound like missionary life is all play, for it certainly is not. Bob was involved in two TEE classes. One at the Franklin Church on way to the mission and another class in Port Shepstone at the Book Center in the mall. There was teaching in the classroom at the Bible College. Spread throughout the year he would attend Council meetings involving the work of our whole South African region. The church at Shiloh also took time on Sundays.

For me, time seemed too short for accomplishing all the things that needed done. Usually we, as missionaries, hire a lady to help with house cleaning. This gave us more time for working with the churches and the Bible School, as well as taking care of the needs of our family. Roxy and I found ourselves quite involved with sewing. We made a lot of our clothes. Since Roxy would be going overseas in July of 1977, we tried to prepare her wardrobe for college. One of the older ladies the Gray's had working for them also came to work for me. I decided I had to let her go. Then I had all the cooking and cleaning to do myself. It was not easy to keep up, for sure.

March Happenings

There is never a dull moment around a Bible College. The students at the college had a wonderful opportunity to witness at a sugar cane farm. The farmer was a Christian who had about 80 workers whom he said were very ignorant about Christianity and the Bible. He had approached the school about telling the Bible stories and sharing about Jesus and the salvation He provided for everyone on earth. He felt Bible School students could spend time with these workers and teach them the truth that the Bible is true and it's the Word of God.

About the middle of March, Bob, Randal and I traveled to Swaziland with two of our African pastors for a Church Growth Seminar. Since many people were already at the mission, Linda made arrangements for us to stay at Bob and Sheila Smith's home in Manzani. The Smith's had stayed with us the August before in Port Shepstone. I tried to stay out at the mission as much as possible in order to give Linda a hand. She was expecting their 3rd child in May.

Rev. and Mrs. Deal were at this workshop. Our doctor friends, Paul and Martha Riley, came out one evening to hear him. The seminar ended on Thursday evening. Then we began our journey back to Port Shepstone early Friday morning. It was at this time that gas rationing was on in South Africa. One could not buy gas from Friday noon until Monday morning so we had to be at least halfway back to Port Shepstone by noon. It is about 470 miles from Swaziland, so one does not want to be without gas on the way. As we came through Port Shepstone we picked up our four children at Miller's and took them home with us. I think the happiest days of Randal's life were Friday through Sunday. He said to me the other day, "I like my four kids!" He does feel lonely when they are gone. Over the Easter holidays the three older kids will be at Youth Camp but Rylan will be at home to play with Randal.

At the end of March we were back in Durban for Ronald's dental appointment. The dentist told us he was very pleased with his progress in moving his front teeth back. He said the front teeth had moved back 7.7 millimeters. I know Ron will feel so much better about his teeth when this process is over.

During this month we also had a revival at the Bible College. Rev. Gene Hudson, our missionary living in Durban, came to hold this meeting for us. It was such a good meeting, but we all felt it was too short. It was Wednesday through Sunday morning, but our students received a lot of help.

Lots of Excitement in April

April 19th. "While I was walking to one of the teacher's homes with her, we saw people at this house and they were screaming. A man was beating a woman, saying he was going to kill her. I ran back to our house and called the police. We tried to help the police find the people involved, but this is not easy when they have a forest to run into. Anyway, we aren't sure what is going to come of this case."

Today just at lunchtime a big lorry (that's a big truck) turned upside down by the mission church. Bob said that he didn't know if one man would make it or not. Don Miller from Port Shepstone was here at the mission, so he took the people into hospital at Port Shepstone. One of our Bible School teachers said he was walking home from the Bible School when he saw the truck coming very fast down the road. There is a sharp curve in the road down toward the church and the truck driver lost control. The lorry turned upside down right by the Mission church, blocking the road so that no traffic could pass. There were seven people who were hurt badly, some worse than others. One man was nearly scalped.

This afternoon there was a council meeting, or rather a committee meeting with several missionaries, so I fixed supper for eight people. Rev. Morgan was here besides Rev. Bagley from Transki and Gene Hudson from Durban. Gene brought Ruthie with him so Randy had a friend to play with all afternoon and this pleased him greatly. Ruthie is in the same situation as Randy. She has four older brothers and sisters in school and she is lonely at home so it is nice for both of them."

Earlier this month the older children enjoyed the Youth Camp. They came back on Monday and we picked them up at Port Shepstone. From my letter of April 14th I wrote, "Allen had lots to talk about because he got brave enough to ask a girl to sit with him in church. This was quite an accomplishment for Allen, who is so shy and quiet! This girl was the daughter of the man who was the evangelist for the Youth Camp."

This letter also states, "I have canned dill pickles, 24 quarts of guavas and am freezing some. I have canned some juice from Chinese guavas. It is a beautiful red juice and should make a lovely jelly.

Our single missionary who teaches here at the Bible College is booked to leave April 29th. I'm in the process of planning a farewell for her. Several of the missionaries will be coming. Miss Brown's step-father isn't well and neither is her mother so they feel it best for her to come home. I'm sure it isn't going to be easy for her. I've been helping Miss Brown with sorting and packing and getting ready to fly out by the 29th of April. Rev. Bagley is also flying, as well as Kevin Hudson, on the same flight as Miss Brown. The Bagley's son, Bob, is marrying Brenda Karns and the three of them fly to New York together from Johannesburg.

Last weekend the Hudsons came down to spend it with us. Since Kevin was leaving, he wanted to spend one last weekend with Allen. Allen had to stay in Port Shepstone for a Rugby game, so Kevin stayed with Allen at Miller's on Friday and went to watch Allen play. Rugby is a little like football. Allen made four points for his team the first game they played. They also won their game this last Saturday, so Allen is really excited and pleased.

I took over Miss Brown's sewing class when she left. I have sewing class on Monday, Tuesday and Thursday. We are planning to make four single bed quilts. We also bought her chickens so now I'm feeding chickens and gathering eggs. I do think this would be good because we can have fresh fried chicken and have our own eggs. The price of eggs has just gone up. All together there are about 80 chickens and probably a few more, counting the baby chicks.

Busy May

We had a bookkeeping seminar scheduled for two districts of our field. Twenty-eight people attended, counting our eight Bible School students. The people seemed to get a lot of help from it. It is our purpose to teach these people how to keep their church finance records. Our mission director, Rev. Bill Morgan, is teaching this with another African man as his helper. Rev. Morgan also stayed for another week to work on a Zulu church discipline.

For Mother's Day 1977, my dear daughter wrote this poem for me. I want to share it with you.

My Mother by Roxane Cheney

Your Mother's cast of iron, he said.
But how could iron
Have arms so loving;
Hands so tender;
Heart so true?
And all the while I wondered,
Until at last I knew.
By iron he meant
Dependable; steadfast
And sure and always there;
To laugh with;
Cry with, just to be with;
Even more, to share.

But most of all he spoke of strength
That changeless strength of character,
Unbending in each threatening storm,
Capable in every trial,
Revealing love in every tear and smile.

We learned that Carolyn Miller's folks are coming to visit the end of June, so we are planning to send Roxane back to the States with Carolyn's parents so she can attend college at Central Wesleyan College this fall. I really hate to think of her leaving us.

June - A Colder Month

Drinking tea mid-morning really helps to warm one up. So we got into this habit of tea time. Just putting one's cold hands around the warm tea cup felt so good. I would always fix tea for our workers as well.

I had not been feeling well for several weeks, as I had a pain in my side. Finally, I decided I better make a doctor's appointment. After he saw me he said he thought my problem was a spastic colon, caused by nerves. He told me I should learn to blow off steam, but I didn't know how. My nerve problems are of a different sort, needing to trust the Lord about our future. It's probably result of having quite a bit of company along with the matter of thinking about moving again. It seems quite possible that they will be joining the two Bible Colleges into one, probably located in Swaziland. We only want God's will so I don't think I'm actually worrying about moving. It looks quite possible that we will be moved to Joy Mission in Swaziland to take over EWBC, but things aren't settled yet. I suppose one of the hardest things to live with is the uncertainty. After my doctor visit I started to feel better and didn't have as much pain in my side. My doctor ordered some pills to relax the colon. He also took a test to see if I might have an amebic parasite. He advised me to take one day a week to do something I really liked doing. I decided sewing was something I wanted to do. I went to Port Shepstone on Fridays to spend the day at the parsonage where they have a spare room. I was able to set up my machine and sew with no one knocking at my door and no phones ringing – just peace and quiet. When the children got out school Friday afternoon I would pick them up and head back to the Mission.

We planned to attend Patti's mother's memorial service. She owned

Eden Park, the vacation park where we stayed when we came back for our second term. She had cancer. I felt so sorry for Patti, her youngest child, who is 12½, Ronald's age. Now Patti had no mother or father. She really was a sweet girl. She had been boarding at the Miller's with our kids and going to school with them."

School Holidays

Here they call school vacation, school holidays. We decided to make this school holiday very special because it would be the last one that Roxy could be with us for some time. At the Bible College we let out school the 24th of June and our children in Port Shepstone got out July 1st. The children don't have to be back until July 26th for school.

I'm beginning to feel much better since I've taken one day a week for relaxing and doing what I like to do. In my June 20th letter I wrote: "Friday night I gave a lesson to the students on children in the Christian family and our responsibility to these children in teaching them about God, the Bible and prayer. To some of them this was quite new and different and really gave them something to think about. I tried to base it completely on the Bible and show them how important Christ considered children. I believe it got through to them quite well and one of the girls said, "We must have some more of these kinds of lessons." So I want to work up a whole set of lessons on the Christian family and either give them as a seminar or as a class in the Bible College."

On June 19th I took six ladies from our Methlomyama District to Durban for a special Malihambe Service in the townships. White people have to carry permits to get into the townships and since I do not have a permit, Gene Hudson took them into the township where their church was located. Since Gene and Sheryl live in Durban and work with the churches there, they have the necessary permits. I was able to have a nice visit with Sheryl and as my letter stated, "I was even able to take a bath and wash my hair. By saying this you will probably be able to guess we are having water pump troubles at the Mission. Bob is trying to get the pump fixed. I guess no mission is without water pump troubles."

It was about time for vacation when we suddenly realized our visas would expire June 30th and we wouldn't be able to enter Swaziland. We had to travel to Durban to get them extended to July 6th. We applied for new temporary residence permits and got proper papers so we can travel. However, we could only stay in Swaziland to July 6th and have a short visit with the Lehman's and see baby Paul.

While we were at the border gate on our way to the Kruger National Game Park we found that our small pox shots had expired, except for Roxy, so we had to return to a Swazi clinic to get shots before we could pass through the border and back into South Africa. Since we had no room reservations at Crocodile Bridge, we slept in our tent. Our six sleeping bags and winter coats kept us warm enough. Then we slept one night at Skukuza Camp and at Oliphants the next night.

We didn't get to see a lion up close, but saw two cheetahs very close. Of course, there were elephants, zebra, giraffe and impala, kudu and water buck. We really loved driving around and seeing all the wild animals in the park. On Friday we drove out Orpen Gate and went to Casteel Mission where the Amos's are missionaries. We spent the weekend with them. Our kids enjoyed seeing each other. From Casteel Mission we drove to Louis Trichardt where Jim and Carol Ramsay were missionaries. It was so nice to visit missionary families because they were family to us when our blood families were far away.

Roxy was anxious to get back to Port Shepstone for her last two weeks at home. She was leaving with Carolyn Miller's parents on July 29th for the States. In my July 17th letter I write: "It is Sunday evening and we are sitting in the living room enjoying the nice warm fire from the fireplace. Randal is coloring a book he got for his birthday. Roxy is cutting Rylan's hair while Bob is sleeping and Allen is reading in his bedroom. Ronald had stayed in Durban with the Hudsons until Thursday when he had a dental appointment. Some last minute shopping has to be done for Roxy. Also, Bob wants to take her out to eat."

We had a double birthday party for Randal and Rylan on the 19th (Rylan's birthday). Randal's birthday came when we were at the Ramsay's and I made a round cake which he shared with Susan Ramsay. I told him we would make one for him on Rylan's birthday. He was five years old and Rylan turned eight. We invited the Langa children and Ruth Mehlomakhulu's grandson to a party. A lady from the States sent candy, so we had candies, cake, jello and cold drink.

The Day Our Daughter Leaves for U.S.

I remember the morning of the 29th so well. I fixed a nice breakfast of biscuits and gravy and we had our devotions with all of us around the breakfast table. I wrote a special letter to stick in her suitcase and she also left a very special letter for us.

We headed for the Durban airport. The Millers and Hudsons were all there for the send off. Of course, Carolyn Miller's parents were there to go with our daughter. The flight was to leave at 1:20 p.m. and fly to Joburg where they would board a jumbo jet headed for Zurich, Switzerland. They would spend a few days in Switzerland and then board a flight for Amsterdam, Holland on August 2nd.where they would stay until August 6th when they would fly to the States. Here Roxy would fly into Washington, D.C. where Aunt Kathy and Uncle Jim picked her up.

What a difficult day it was for Bob and me to see Roxane get on that plane. It's hard to have your children clear across the ocean, but now she would go to college and prepare for her life's work.

Roxy didn't have to be at Central Wesleyan College until August 20th, so she had a little time to spend with her aunt and uncle. I can't really describe my feelings as I watched that plane flying off into that blue sky toward Joburg. Carolyn and I hugged and cried together because she was saying goodbye to her parents and we were saying goodbye to our daughter.

Back at the Mission, things returned to a normal routine. The three older boys were in school, staying with the Miller's. At first I couldn't figure out why I was feeling down and not as happy as usual on the weekends. Then it occurred to me; oh yes, I'm used to having my Roxy here on weekends, baking and working together in the kitchen together.

Changes Coming for the Bible Schools

In my letter of August 16, 1977 I wrote: "The outcome for our Field Board Meeting was that at the end of this term our Bible school will merge with the one in Swaziland. So we are having our last teaching term here at Methlomyama near Port Shepstone. Orai and Linda have asked to stay on until June 1st so they will go ahead with the Bible College in February. Then we will be moving to Swaziland when they go on furlough. In the meantime, we will be taking care of the district here and the shops in Port Shepstone while Don and Carolyn Miller have their six month's furlough, starting in November.

Since our kids have been staying with the Millers, this arrangement will let them stay put and we can be with them. Also, it will be nice living at Don and Carolyn's Port Shepstone house. Carolyn said she would be glad to leave her things out and let me use them. This way she wouldn't have to pack them. I could go ahead and pack mine to go to Swaziland. I think we will just do this and it will save some work for both of us. We move up to Swaziland at the end of May when Orai and Linda go on furlough and we will take Rylan with us. Then he will go to school in Manzini where our three older children went when we first came to Africa. It will be nice having our two little boys at home with us. When Don and Carolyn return, Allen and Ronald will again be staying on with them and not have to change schools. With this arrangement, we will only have them during the holidays between terms but, since they are used to staying with Millers, I think there will be no problem."

Our Children in School

"Allen had a bad sore throat and croaky voice yesterday so he stayed home in bed but he did go to church with us Sunday evening and we left him with other kids at Miller's so as to be in school Monday morning. Allen had the highest grade in one of his science tests lately. We are so glad for his interest in school.

Then we had word from our daughter in college at Central, South Carolina. She said that in the English placement test which the college gives she placed second highest. I'm sure she is going to like college very much."

September 5th: "This was a long weekend so the children were with us. I did so enjoy it with five kids at home. I had asked Patti Bramsby to spend the weekend with us. It was like having a daughter in our home again. She helped me in preparing for the birthday party we planned for the students at the Bible School. Patti and Ron baked two cakes and decorated them. Then Patti wrapped and signed all the gifts and cards. We had games for the students, their teachers and the families. They seemed to enjoy it all."

On September 11, Ronnie had a Sports Day on Saturday and since he is the captain of his house team, he felt he must be present. He isn't supposed to run since his foot has been troubling him, but he ran anyway because no one was there to do it. The doctor seems to think he has injured his heel some-time in a high jump and this caused bursitis in his heel. When he does a lot of running it irritates it. So he takes some pills and is not to do running for two weeks. He got second place in the 1500 meter run which is pretty good. Probably he could have come in first if his heel hadn't hurt him."

Then on September 27[th,] "Rylan had his Sports Day so we went to see him run. He did very well. In the two races which he ran he came in first. Rylan is really growing up and is a sturdy built child, but not fat. It just seems different to what the two older boys were because they all were so slim. Randy wants you to know that he ran in a race at Rylan's school and came in 4th. Actually Randal could have come in first, but he wasn't paying attention. He didn't have a belt on and he was afraid of losing his pants!"

"This week we are having a Sunday School seminar so I need to be working on a class which they have asked me to teach. I'm not sure yet what I am going to do, but better hurry and make up my mind for the time is short. Oh yes, I must tell you about all our baby chicks. I'm not sure, but think there are about 24 or 25 new baby ones and then we have eight which are over three weeks old. I wished these had hatched last month then they could have had more time to grow up for eating at our banquet the end of October. Got any suggestions for making chickens grow fast??"

October Flurry

October arrived with a flurry of activity. Of course, it is the last month of our Bible College year which means end of year exams, a banquet for students and staff and conference, all mixed in. Besides the revival at Shiloh, answering prayer partner letters for us as well as the children and preparing for graduation, it all made for a busy, busy month. Then there was garden produce to care for and trips to Durban for Ronald's dental work. One thing I've not said much about was making up slide sets with scripts or tapes to send to the many churches that pray for and support us. Sorting out pictures and writing about our work here does take time, but we needed to let those at home in U.S. and Canada know about the work God has given us to do here at the Bible College and in the District.

In my October 20th letter to my mother, I wrote: "Roxy got to go home with Sheryl Karns to Evansville. She isn't quite as homesick, but she said it would be good to get away from school for a change."

"I feel like I'm being rushed to pieces. I have to plan for the banquet coming up. On the 27th we have our Alumni Banquet and I have to do the decorations. At least I'm not on food committee, but have a feeling I'll be helping out. I wish you could see the new mission church here. They are redoing the old building and it looks like new. They hope to have it finished by conference time next week."

"Week before last I worked like mad getting my typing booklet finished up and handed out, then this last Thursday I gave out a three hour exam in typing (remember these are manual typewriters). For some it took about four hours. But one thing I'm thankful for, they all passed. I feel they have done quite good for just one term of typing – that is from August through October. One of my best students got over 25 words per minute in one of the timings."

"The mission church was beginning to fall down and when you walked up the aisle you never knew when you might fall through some of the rotten boards on the floor. One Sunday morning I felt so sorry for a lady who fell through the floor. I'm sure it was terribly embarrassing." In this same letter I tell about Bob taking the Bible School students to Transkei for a promotional service at their conference. The letter goes on with this paragraph: "This has been one of the most beautiful days we have ever seen. We have been having lots of rain but today it cleared off and the air is so clear, the sky is so blue and the grass and trees so green. It was just gorgeous is all I can say."

I mentioned the revival held at Shiloh and want to add some more about it from my October 14th letter: "This week a group from Casteel Mission in the Transvaal came down for a revival at Shiloh Church. Although we had not planned it, I do believe God had His hand in this matter and a real work has been done at our Shiloh Church. Please pray for the people. They are in such darkness, witchcraft and all this, but God's power is greater than these things."

The first of the week we were having school closing, graduation, District Conference, and on Monday and Tuesday there were council meetings. Five students graduated from the Bible School on October 29th. It was our privilege to have this graduation service in the beautiful newly built mission church at Emmanuel Mission.

This is how our three bedroom house gave sleeping room to those who came. Bob and I slept on the living room floor; Orai, Linda and baby Paul slept in Rylan and Randal's room; Jim and Carol Ramsey in our bedroom; Bill Morgan and Gene Hudson in the big boys' room. We had a house full!

Sunday night our big boys decided to stay, so Mark Amos, Allen and Ron slept in sleeping bags on the veranda. I cooked for the whole group except on Sunday. This day they invited us down to the church to have a meal with our African brothers and sisters. It was nice to have a rest from cooking. We enjoyed having all the Lehman's with us. Little Paul is so cute and has grown a lot, of course, since we last saw him. He is five months old now and it won't be long until he is sitting up by himself. They plan to come down to Port Shepstone and spend Christmas with us."

Here I want to report from my form letter about a decision that was made by the council meeting. "A decision was made by our South African Field Council to merge Emmanuel Wesleyan Bible Institute with the Swaziland Bible College, forming one college for our field, calling it Emmanuel Wesleyan Bible College. Plans are to locate this school at Joy Mission near Manzini, Swaziland. Already we are taking new applications for students and progress for the school is beginning to look up. We are encouraged. A whole new line of promotion is now being planned. With the Lord helping us, we plan to have a better school for training laborers for the Kingdom of God."

November, the Month for Packing and Resettling

"This week I'm packing things and sorting out what we need to take into Millers. It has been a month of real change for our family. Our Field Council has asked that we take care of the Christian Literature work here in Port Shepstone while our missionaries, Don and Carolyn Miller have a six-month furlough in the States. At the moment our heads feel in a whirl trying to learn everything about the work before they leave. We will also have oversight of the Nkosinathi District work. However, since the district has now elected their own district leaders we will only need to assist when help is needed by our nationals. We praise God for this progress".

On Monday and Tuesday I got all our personal things packed into drums so that they are ready to go to Swaziland. I'm glad that job is finally done. After all the packing, Mrs. Langa and I fixed 12 chickens for the deep freeze. I felt bad about killing them for they were egg layers. However, we couldn't leave them for someone probably would have stolen them. Anyway, it is nice to have 12 chickens in the deep freeze. It will help on our meat situation.

After finishing the packing, we finally moved into the Miller's house. We feel it a great privilege to be all together with our boys full time instead of just weekends. As you know from previous chapters, our three older boys stayed with the Millers so they could attend the schools in Port Shepstone during the week. "Randal is so happy to be with all his brothers all the time now!"

On the 24th of November we drove to Durban to see the Gene Hudson family off on furlough. Then the 25th I fixed a special Thanksgiving dinner for the Miller's farewell. It also was a surprise birthday dinner for Patti Bramsby. I got a turkey at the butchery, so as to fix it with all the trimmings. It weighed about 4½ kilograms (nearly 10 pounds) and cost R7.39. I didn't think that was too bad.

"Earlier in the month I had told Bob that if I was going to work in the shops in town (the Literature shops where the Millers have a ministry), I wanted a wedding band since here everyone who is married wears rings and I think the people have wondered about it. So, when we were in Durban we did some shopping and found a matching set, one for him and one for me, just plain gold bands. They agreed to do the engraving free. Inside each ring we asked them to put: 'Bob and Eva, Heirs together with God, Dec. 22, 1957.' Anyway, we wanted to tell you this so when you see us next time, you won't be surprised. When I was pregnant with Ron, someone asked if I didn't feel funny without a ring to show I was married. It was never my conviction that wearing a wedding ring was wrong. Our main reason was because of what a lot of others would think it is. I know you know what that is all about."

Christmas for the Missionaries

One of the things our headquarters does for missionaries is to encourage churches in the homeland to send Christmas boxes to a missionary family. Usually in July or even in June the Wesleyan Women's Organization will send requests to the missionaries asking them to list things they need. If it is clothes, they want to know sizes and even colors. Then when churches ask for a certain missionary family's needs, headquarters will send that family's list.

The Christmas of 1977, a church from California asked for the Robert Cheney family. We learned that this church in California was the one Hubert Jenewein, a Nebraskan whom we knew in earlier years, was pastoring. I guess that is why they took a special interest in us. They sent about ten boxes to us. I didn't let the children open them but put them under our tree for opening on Christmas. It is nice of churches in America to do this for their missionaries. We appreciated their support and care.

December 1st we again went to Durban airport and this time we said goodbye to the Millers. Their leaving kind of left the Cheneys to themselves on the South Coast. The next day the children had their last day of school and their long vacation would last until the next year.

We had a letter from Wilma Cheney in Zambia saying she planned to have Christmas with us. She arrived on December 16th and stayed until January 10th. Orai and Linda and family arrived on December 22nd or 23rd. We had a very nice Christmas together. That year we were well blessed with Christmas trees: one at our place, one at the Miller's and one at Grandpa and Grandma Lehman's!

It was a wonderful Christmas with family except we did miss our Roxy so much. She was able to fly into Denver where Grandpa and Grandma Thornton picked her up. She spent Christmas with both sets of grandparents and relatives.

Beginning a New Year, 1978

We are now located in the town of Port Shepstone in Don and Carolyn Miller's house. We are here while Don and Carolyn and daughter Kathy are on a six month furlough, caring for the Christian Literature Book Stores. Bob also oversees the District work for the Church. Living here is so pleasant because there is always running water and electricity 24 hours a day. Another plus for me is that I have a wonderful African girl working full time in our home. Having to keep shops open downtown with someone present all the time, kept Bob and me on our toes. We did have a couple girls helping in the shops but at least one of us needed to be there too. So at home my girl (she was also the girl who worked for Carolyn) kept our house clean, as well as doing cooking for the family. I never worried about dust on the furniture while Beauty worked for me.

Of course there was still work to do at the mission. Bob had to oversee the packing of Bible School furniture, library books and other things that would go to Swaziland for our Bible College there. A big moving truck was hired to take this as well as our teacher family, Rev. and Mrs. Naphtali Langa's furniture and our drums that were packed with our personal belongings. It really was a big job that needed to be finished before Bible College began in Swaziland.

The boys started back to school January 17th. Ronnie and Allen both went to the Senior High and Rylan was in Standard One (third grade) and still at the lower primary school.

In a January 7th letter I wrote about the matter of Roxane coming for a visit. When Roxy left for college we had in mind that she would be able to come back to Africa for one of her summers. So this is what I wrote in this letter: "We got word from headquarters that Roxy can't come for a visit. You see when this new insert for our missionary policy came we read and reread it and thought that the way it was worded that it gave Roxy a chance to come and visit us sometime during our term here. But I guess we misread it for Dr. Lytle said children who are allowed to come must be separated from their parents for four years. So this leaves us out. Thursday I couldn't keep back my tears while I wrote because I knew I must tell Roxy this. It will really hit her hard because you know how much she was planning to come back to Africa to be with her family". This 24th of January Roxy turns 19. I learned later in one of Roxy's letters that some girls baked a birthday cake and gave her a real nice surprise at her dorm.

I'm not meaning to complain but it is so hard for missionary families when separation takes place. But there are some good points too, for in my January 23rd letter I wrote: "Wish you could eat some litches, mangoes and papayas with us now. So delicious!" In this letter I also said the moving van was coming on Wednesday morning to the mission to load up everything. Orai came in the evening to help with everything; then he will be taking the Langa family in the Hi Ace to Swaziland. Bob and I still do not have temporary residence permits so we can't get into Swaziland until they come. I also want to mention that we have another boy in our family. Mark Amos, son of our mission family at Casteel Mission in the Transvaal, is staying with us and going to school with Allen and Ron."

In my February 1st letter I said: "Today Ronald fell down while playing basketball and got a bad cut on his hand. The school sent him to the clinic and he had to have a tetanus shot and stitches in his hand. I'm really praising the Lord for the good health of our family has had this far. I'm sure it's all this fresh sea air and the good fresh fruits and veggies I get at the market are good for them. I try not to give them much candy and heavy desserts.

Another thing I'm wondering as I write my story is how I found time to sew clothes for myself, as well as my daughter. "This makes the third dress I've sewed for myself." Other letters tell about making blouses and skirts and jumpers for Roxane and even a white blouse for Beauty, the girl helping me. I talked about sewing clothes but my mother also sews a lot. In one of her letters she asked me for my dress size and when I read my answer I was rather shocked. In my letter of February 28th 1978, I wrote: "A size 12 is fine except make waist about 27½ inches and enlarge hips if it is a tighter skirt to about 40 inches and bust is 34 inches. One wonders how those pounds creep on over the years! Also, one wonders about all the letters I've written to family, friends and churches that pray for and support us. I've probably written thousands of letters and have many cassette tapes of our visiting and talking so family and churches can hear from us. This is so amazing to me for now in today's world letter writing and cassette tapes are nearly extinct. Now we email, Skype or call on I-phones, etc.

With school beginning the literature shops get busier and busier with school children coming to buy school books, notebooks and other school supplies. In my February 9th letter I say: "Seems like all I get done is count money, work in the shops and try to see that five boys are cared for." But, it seems I was never too busy to have company. We had Pastor Williams and his family from Manaba Beach Church come for supper. Then later the Woodley's came from Swaziland and the Keel's came from Joburg.

Book work and keeping accounts up for the mission as well as the shops was one of Bob's jobs. I'm so glad he did this for bookkeeping is definitely not my thing. Even so, every missionary needs to have training in this area. From one of my February letters, I write: "Yesterday we had a boy steal money from one of the cash registers. It was about $65.00. The girl watching the shop had just left the room to answer the phone and just the tiny bit she was gone he got the cash register open and had taken the money out. Anyway we are just glad he never got any more of it. There was around R225.00 in the register. I think this girl has learned her lesson: do not leave when one of the other girls is not there. The police came and are on the case".

Have you ever heard of head lice and nits that get in your hair? Well, it happened in our family. Rylan was sent home because he had nits, head lice eggs, in his hair. So, I'm treating his hair. I wrote: "Don't know why those teachers never learn not to use one comb on all these kid's hair at school. Anyway, I think they are all dead now and I'll get his medical clearance tomorrow to go back to school. I'm keeping close track that the rest of us don't get them."

Randal was able to get into a preschool here in Port Shepstone. He seems to like it and while the other children are at school he too can be at school in the mornings. It keeps him from being so bored. Since I have to be at the shops in town quite a bit it really helps me out too.

I have a concern for Roxane. On a tape she told us about going to summer school. I wish it weren't so far to Nebraska or so costly to travel. She mentioned about traveling back after school with Uncle Homer. But I don't know how she could get back to summer school by May 29th. She only gets out of school May 24th. She doesn't want to bum off relatives for the summer. I'm glad she feels this way. She sounds homesick though and I'm afraid if she doesn't get away from school for a while, she will feel worse. Anyway, please help us pray. I feel so helpless in trying to help her so far away."

"I think Roxy is with Carolyn and Don for Easter. She said on the tape she plans to go to them for her spring break." Easter came on March 26th. This is the day Bob's youngest brother, Ted and his wife Sue had their first child, a baby daughter named Tara.

Like my dad, I have had back problems. As most chiropractors have told me, it probably stems from old injuries. And what would that be? Well, as a young person I did a lot of horseback riding and a number of times had fallen off the horse. Also, in our youth group we used to do a lot of ice skating, so it very well could be from old injuries.

March 27th: "This day certainly didn't turn out as I had planned. I know the Bible states 'In whatever state we are we should be content.' Well this morning as I was working away in the kitchen (Beauty, my house girl, took off for the Easter holiday). I was filling some bottles with cooking oil. When I bent over to put the bottles on the bottom shelf of the cupboard, excruciating pain in my back caused me to cry out. Bob came to help me and hold me and finally got me into the bedroom. I know that I must have a real badly pinched nerve. I couldn't call the chiropractor because Easter Monday is a holiday, but first thing in the morning I'll call". "Allen did cooking. He made a delicious pizza for lunch. Ronnie helped a great deal with the cleaning and the little boys ran errands. It is really rainy here today. I think the dampness doesn't help my back."

From my April 5th letter to Mom and Dad: "One reason I guess I forgot about getting your letter off is because I typed about 18 letters for Rylan and Randal's prayer partners. It was a big job. Then yesterday I did two more for Randal because he got another letter. And, I have written to Roxy several times since I've been down with my back. However, now I'm feeling much better although I have to be very careful. I'm so glad to be up and around doing things. It just doesn't do for me to be laid up in bed.

I sent letters to Kathy, Bob's sister, and Sis. Henderson for their birthdays on April 1st. It seems like I've been doing quite a bit of correspondence but still have a stack more to do. Our form letter, too, had to be sent off besides going through our address sheets and getting it up to date."

There was a lady whose husband was sick. The doctors said he wouldn't live long but she had the consolation that he had recently found the Lord so he was ready for heaven. We had been meeting with men at a road camp trying to reach them with the gospel. In a letter I asked for prayer: "Please keep praying for this place. There are around 200 here." Reaching out to people who need Jesus is the most important thing we do. It has been the desire of our mission to reach African men; if one can win the men to God there is no question of them winning their families.

The Christian Literature Shops took a lot of our time but this is a real ministry to our African youth. I write in an April letter: "Today I did such a stupid thing. I locked myself out of the shop at about closing time. Bob was at Dundee at a regional board meeting and missionary council meeting for the week, so the boys and I were on our own. With no Bob nearby, how was I going to get back in the shop? Fortunately, a lady who runs a beauty shop in the mall let me call on her phone. Ron came on his bike. He was able to crawl through a high top window which was open and unlock the door.

Some family news to grandparents from April 17th letter: "You might be interested to know that Allen is nearly 6 feet 1 inch tall and Ron is about 5 feet 6 inches tall. Ronald is growing so fast now his clothes hardly fit him. Randal just loves play school. Rylan doesn't want to leave his school here now. Last week Rylan was in a swimming competition and won third place in two of the races. Oh yes, I wanted to mention that the orthodontist has taken prints or forms of Ronald's teeth and is deciding what the second phase of correction should involve for Ron. We are to go back to the dentist in Durban May 2nd."

This was written to my mom on May 14th: "Today at the dinner table we were talking about asking the boy's girlfriends (Mark and Allen both have girlfriends) to come over for a meal and we would fix chicken on the grill. Mark likes it so much this way. Then Randal piped up and said to me, "and you could invite your mom," I replied, 'I do wish I could do that very thing!' Anyway Mother, I want you to know how much I appreciate you. I think the older one grows the more you appreciate your parents. My boys have treated me so nicely today. Ronald, in particular, has been very thoughtful. He baked a German chocolate cake last night and decorated it. For my birthday Allen offered to get the supper which I thought was a very nice birthday present. Mother, did I ever offer to get the supper or dinner for your birthday or any special day? I can't remember doing it, but I hope I did."

Bob left for Swaziland yesterday morning about 6:30. He was going to call but evidently the lines are down. When I tried to call him, I was told the lines were out of order. He's going to come back in about two weeks. He was taking Linda and Orai and family to Joburg to leave on the 18th of May. I have so many things to see about before the Millers return. I want to do some painting and I would like to get most of my letters answered. Being at the shops and head of the house, as well as mother, takes a great deal of time, but I will manage with the Lord's help.

Yesterday I went to watch Ron and Mark play Rugby. Mark got his leg hurt quite badly so he had to go to the hospital and have it x-rayed. That was quite an ordeal but we are thankful his leg wasn't cracked or broken. He will probably be back playing by the weekend. While Bob is in Swaziland he is going to see what can be done about getting Rylan in school at Manzini."

"We just got a letter from Carolyn Miller and they are arriving in Durban on June 2nd. We are getting quite excited, needless to say. It will be so nice to be with them again. Bob is to be back this weekend on Friday. I really miss him, but it's only three more days. He is packing some drums to bring down for Orai and Linda, for shipping from Durban. Today the second term of school at the Bible College begins. So Bob is getting things all lined up in Swaziland before returning here.

It has really been cold here yesterday and today. My hands are freezing cold. However, on Saturday it was a gorgeous day. The sea was beautiful and so smooth and the weather was perfect and sunny. So I took Rylan, Randal and Mark to the beach and we spent a relaxing afternoon. On Saturday Ron and Allen had to go to Durban to play rugby. Since Mark had hurt his ankle the week before he was afraid to play so soon again. His ankle is better though.

Don and Carolyn and Kathy arrived June 2nd at Durban airport. We allowed all the boys to take off from school so that everyone could welcome them home. We were so happy to see them.

Swaziland, Here We Come

It is June 5th and we are on our way to Swaziland. On the way we stopped in Durban as we had a student traveling with us who had to get a smallpox injection before he could enter another country. The little dog of Randal's "Fishane" had to have the state vet sign papers and there was Ronald's passport to see about, as well as school permits for Allen and Ron. All this had to be done in Durban. It tugged at my heart to leave Allen and Ron in Port Shepstone with Don and Carolyn. Ronald had tears in his eyes. It is not easy to leave children behind even though we knew they were in good care. By then I was afraid the border would be closed but, thank the Lord, we had about an hour to spare.

The next three or four days I worked on getting the house at Joy Mission in order. Bob tried to see about getting our residence permits for Swaziland which really took up about two weeks with travel here and there. We found that the principal of the school in Manzini where Rylan would attend had to have a letter for Rylan and finally, last Thursday, Bob was able to obtain that in Mbabne, the capital of Swaziland. While in Mbabane taking care of business he had a little scrape with another car. Because of putting a scratch on another man's car the police had to come. This is when they found Bob had the wrong insurance sticker on our car. So they took the car and Bob had to ride a bus from Mbabne back to Manzeni. There a Nazarene missionary came to his rescue and took Bob back out to our mission.

In the meantime, I had to take Mrs. Langa to the hospital to have her baby. The only vehicle left at the mission that ran was an old Land Rover which I had never driven. It was nighttime but I got it started. However, I could only turn on the park lights. I just could not figure out how to turn on the headlights. It was a bright moonlit night so we managed.

Well, the next problem we faced was that the Land Rover ran out of gas when we were about halfway to the hospital. Believe me, I wasn't very anxious to deliver a baby, especially out on the highway with no facilities. Fortunately, I was able to flag down a Swazi "For Hire" pickup and explained our situation. I begged, "Please, this lady needs to get to the hospital for she's having a baby." He took me and Mrs. Langa to the hospital and she delivered a healthy baby girl in about 40 minutes. The Nazarene missionary who took Bob to our mission came in and started a conversation with me. I didn't know him so I asked his name and he jokingly said, "I'm your guardian angel." Then he told me he had just taken my husband to our mission and then he of-fered to drive me home. Oh my, what a day! Praise the Lord, He saw us through it.

Now how insurance stickers could ever get turned around and put on the wrong vehicles we will never know. It's funny they never caught this mis-take in South Africa. Carolyn is sending out our other sticker which got on their van. When it comes Bob will try to get our car back.

Then we also have windmill problems and leaking tanks, which means no water in our house most of the time we have been here. Our dear friends, the Paul Rileys, have been so kind in letting me do washing at their place and also for providing us with drinking water, filling our big plastic con-tainer.

In a letter to my folks, I said, Guess what? "Bob is growing a beard! I said he just as well since we have a water shortage." It makes him look like Grandpa Moses! Then I continued to write in this June 18th letter: "Really I guess I'm giving you all a rather pessimistic coverage of our situation here so I'll try to go on to happier things. Today was Malihambe here at Joy Mission Church. We had a good offering of $65.00 for two churches.

As I mentioned earlier, Rylan had a letter to get into school so we made plans to take him. Randal got into Shena Shirley's playschool and we were very grateful. The boys seemed content and happy, although it was quite different to be a family of only four."

My Depression

I'm not the type of person to get depressed easily. For this I am thankful. When we first returned to Swaziland, however, a deep depression settled upon me. I felt my prayers were just hitting the ceiling and bouncing back. I wondered why God allowed me to go through this experience when it really wasn't my nature. Looking back now, I believe God allowed it so that I would have more understanding of others going through depression.

My husband, Bob, was very sympathetic and loving at this time. One morning before he went to the Bible College to teach, he put his arms around me and prayed for me. I shall never forget what a wonderful feeling came to me as he prayed and I realized the depression had lifted. I thank God for my faithful, praying husband who stood with me at all times. God is our loving Heavenly Father who takes us through times of joy, as well as trials, but He is always with us, even when there is no feeling.

This is what I wrote to my parents in July: "I realize that you must wonder what is wrong with your oldest daughter because I am not at all keeping up with writing. Actually, I did write but the letter sounded so terrible that I just tore it up and threw it away. Anyway, I'm now over my "culture shock" as Bob called it. We have faced some difficult times but I feel I'm getting on top of everything.

"We are getting a bit more water in the tanks now so it is coming some through the taps in the house. At least the other day I got enough water to do two washers of clothes. We have a gas motor ringer-type machine. What I mean by two washers is, I washed till the water became dirty, then emptied and filled it again with clean water. I washed all the dirty clothes we had collected along with bedding. This made me feel so much better. I hate piles of clothes sitting around. This week I also got curtains made for the dining room at the Bible College and it looks much better. I still have lots of drapes or curtains to make for the boys' dorm, classrooms, girls' dorm, staff room and Bob's office."

"Carolyn Miller and daughter, Kathy, came June 30 from Port Shepstone with Patti Bramsby, Allen and Ronald. It is so nice to all be together again. We are having a real grand time. The boys will have holiday until July

24th. This time we will have to send them back by plane to Durban because our permanent residence permits aren't in yet. Of course, after this we will have to apply for visas for South Africa before we can leave Swaziland. The boys can get cheaper rates because they are students in South Africa. This will probably be cheaper for us in the long run. The boys then will ride the train from Durban to Port Shepstone."

It is July, 1978 so our two younger boys have birthdays this month. I made a cake for Randal on the 12th but it wasn't anything special so I told him I would fix two cakes when I did Rylan's. So now we have a nine year old and a six year old.

We are in the painting mood, or at least I am. The boys are doing it for me while they have their holiday. They have done the sitting room and now are painting the little boys' room. We have a long way to go but eventually we will have quite a nice looking house. Patti stayed with us after Carolyn and Kathy went back to Port Shepstone. Her brother is coming to pick her up around the 17th of July.

Roxane stayed in South Carolina for the summer and lived in a trailer house with two or three other girls. She took some summer school and also had a job at Burger Meister making $70.00 a week. She put it in savings so she could make a trip to see us.

In my July letter I wrote: "What is so exasperating as getting an overseas call from your daughter and not being able to hear much of what she said!!! Yes, you've guessed it, Roxy called us last night and the line was so terrible we could hardly hear. At first, I thought it was Carol Ramsey calling and then discovered it was our daughter. About all I could hear was that she was okay, that she had sent a tape about two weeks ago and that she loves us. Otherwise, we wasted the entire time saying, 'I can't hear you', 'pardon?', 'what did you say?' etc. Anyway it was just good to know she was well. Roxy told us on July 11th she had $500.00 in savings. She's really doing well at saving her money.

The boys really helped me with painting but I still have our room to paint and the doors of the closet and drawers to varnish. I would like to get some tile to put down on the kitchen floor. The linoleum is nearly worn out. Also, I want to paint the guest room.

We began an English speaking service over at Siteki on Sunday evenings. July 23rd we had about 25 folks present including a lovely group of children.. The Keel brothers, Ken and Woodly, and their families come. This outreach is quite enjoyable.

Chasing Donkeys at Midnight

Maybe I should explain that Joy Mission and Emmanuel Wesleyan Bible College are at the same location. More and more buildings are being built around the mission for the Bible College. Upon arriving the first part of June, we found many things needing to be fixed. One of those things was the need for fences. I remember the donkeys coming in at night and eating whatever was in our yard. One night around midnight we heard the crunching and chewing sound by our windows. We grabbed our flashlights and headed out the door. Sure enough there were the donkeys eating away. We chased them down the road and hoped they wouldn't come back. Anyway school vacation was coming up and I wanted to plant a garden, but it would do no good with no fences to keep the donkeys out. Well, the Langa boys began working full time and within another week or two a fence was up and things were looking a little better. The girls planted the flower beds. So, the fences keep the flowers safe and we'll be able to put in a garden.

"You'll never guess what I did this morning! I got up at 6:00 a.m., had a bath and at 6:30 went down to the school kitchen to fry pancakes for the students since we didn't have any bread. They usually have what they call 'soft porridge' with milk and sugar and bread for their breakfast. I need to go into town and buy some bread.

Rylan and Randal are out of school until September 12th for school holiday. One of the things Rylan and Randal like is for Mom to read to them. In fact, we are reading the Lassie books and, of course, they like them very much.

"Oh yes, Bob has sold the Land Rover, as is, for R900.00, so we won't need to spend time working on it. We still need about R1300.00 to finish paying for our ten-seat Datsun for the Bible College. (Remember the Land Rover is the one I tried to take Mrs. N. Langa to hospital to have her baby).

September 5, 1978: "Guess where I am sitting? I am right down by the beach watching the beautiful waves come in. The sun is nice and warm in this sheltered place. We are only about 100 feet or maybe 150 feet from the beach in the Miller's backyard. Rylan and Randal are down playing in the sand. The tide seems to be out pretty much now. The Lord answered our prayers. He saw that we needed a rest and so our visas did come through. We just praise the Lord. We came down on Thursday August 31st and will either go back on Saturday or Monday. School begins September 12th for Rylan and Randal. It is so wonderful to get away and relax, a much needed rest. Don and Carolyn are renting this house and it also has a small apartment, or what we call a 'flat' here. It's big enough for Bob and me and the little boys, very convenient. It's nice to be here with Allen and Ron again. Yesterday we all went down to a river, the border between Natal and Transkei, and had boat rides and a picnic.

Another answer to prayer is that we now have a new 1978 Datsun 10-seat for the Bible College. We drove it down here and got rid of the Chevrolet. The timing was just right because the Chevrolet was due for some work on it very soon. We actually didn't have enough money in savings for a new vehicle but since prices were going up again in September and since we had some money for kitchen and library facilities, we decided to use it for a car. It cost 5900 Emalangeni (Swazi currency) with turning in our Chevrolet. I think Bob said the original price was E6850.00. Vehicles here are really expensive. Anyway, we are glad we have a new vehicle that we aren't afraid will break down. We thought we had sold the Land Rover, but after the man paid for it, he brought it back and said he wanted his money back. This was quite a letdown to us, because that would have been about 1000.00 more toward the new vehicle. Now this means Bob will have to spend time working on the Land Rover and then perhaps we can get more out of it."

We stayed until Monday September 11th. Then we had to rush around some for school, but I feel our boys are important and they need us as much as possible. Allen and Ron will fly back to Swaziland for their ten day break. Bob fixed up their tickets for round trip so when the holiday time is up they can fly back. As I mentioned before, it's cheaper to have them fly than for us to take them by car since they can get student rates.

From my letter of September 19th I tell about finally getting a girl to work in our house. It really helps with keeping things cleaner and gives me more time for studying Zulu and writing letters. I'm getting pretty concerned about the Zulu exam coming up in November.

"Yesterday, September 25th, we went over to Siteki for our regular services. We had a nice group. We showed our pictures of Israel and the people seemed to enjoy it. Some of the Nazarene missionaries want us to come on the 6th of October and show them to their youth group at Siteki. One of the couples invited us to come over for supper that night, very enjoyable.

This morning Bob asked me to speak at chapel, so I did this and then did some posting in his books. He hasn't done any bookwork since we came last June and so it needs to be done. Bob is also hoping to get the motor put in the brown Cortina pickup so we can use it for hauling stuff back and forth to Manzini. This way we don't have to use our new Datsun bus all the time. Allen and Ron will be coming on Friday so we need to pick them up at the airport. Bob is taking students to Mbabane that day, so I guess it will be my job to get them. They come in on the plane at 4:30 p.m."

End of September and October is a beautiful time of year in Swaziland. It's when the Jacaranda trees start coming out. These are the trees that get clusters of big lavender blossoms before their leaves develop. Going down into Manzini the sides of the road are lined with these Jacaranda trees. It is beautiful!

Since fences are in now, to keep out the donkeys and other animals, we are starting our gardens. The students are working on gardens down by the windmill for the school. It helps with providing food for our students. Spring in Swaziland truly is a beautiful time of year!

From October 18th letter I said: "Mother, I believe it was Monday we got your letter. It brought back old memories when you mentioned going on the mail route with Grace Reeves. I think that was such a nice thing for you to do. Please give Grace and Clinton our greetings. It brought back old memories of when I ran this mail route for Claude Livingston in summer of 1955."

"Bob left on Sunday to go to Joburg for a missionary council meeting. He rode up with a Nazarene missionary then flew back yesterday. We have flights every day from Joburg so it's quite easy to travel by air. Bob thinks it is cheaper than he could go by car when he is alone. Before he came back he spoke at the European Bible College for their chapel. Since Bob was gone, the little boys and I went to the Nazarene's English Church in Manzini. Dr. and Mrs. Riley invited us to have dinner then we attended the evening service. Israel and Victoria Langa had taken our Bible School students out for a scheduled service that morning, but were back in time to attend the evening Nazarene service. Rylan, Randal and I rode back to Joy Mission with them. Then, while Bob was still gone, the Rileys invited us to stay in town with them. This was a nice little break for us. On Tuesday we went to airport at 3:30 p.m. to meet Bob.

Zulu Study

Bob and I took a Zulu course from the University of South Africa at Port Shepstone. We didn't pass it at first. So, we took it again in Swaziland. Our problem was that we had so many obligations we didn't have adequate time to study. However, after coming back into Swaziland, we decided to try again. For Bob, it was impossible for him to continue because of his eyesight. I was studying, though, and wanted very much to be ready for the exam to be taken November 13th and 15th. I did get my eight lessons done for the year and so I hoped to pass the course. Later in my November 18th letter I wrote: "I took one Zulu exam on Tuesday and the other one on Thursday. The one on Tuesday was very difficult but the one on Thursday was much easier. In fact, I hope I have passed this year. My only fear is that my Zulu essay isn't very good. Can you guess what subject I chose to write on? It was 'Abazali bami" which means 'My Parents.' I find it takes so much time to put my thoughts in order and my Zulu vocabulary is so limited it is very hard to express thoughts. I found interpretation quite easy from Zulu to English, but the other way around is difficult.

October 26th letter: "I'm really in a big hurry to get back to the mission to study Zulu. (I'm in Manzini after taking boys to school and waiting for post office to open). I'm just about living with my head in the Zulu book these days. Woke up this morning about 3:30 and Bob and I started discussing what might be on our exams. I still have about six more stories to interpret and understand so these next two weeks will be hectic. Anyway, all I can do is my best. I just hope and pray I don't fail or otherwise I'll feel I'm throwing away the Field's money. Our Field Department has paid for this study. The exams are scheduled for November 9th and 13th."

From my November 17th letter: "Bob and I took one three-hour exam the 9th of November and another three-hour exam on the 13th. All I can say is that they were hard exams and I won't even venture to say how we did except we hope we passed. They said we should know our results about the middle of December." My letter continues, "I got pushed from Zulu study right into baking a wedding cake for a couple who will be married at Ebenezer Mission. This wasn't planned because a Nazarene missionary was going to do it, but then they suddenly decided to go home to U.S. I really tried hard to find someone else to do it, but failed, so I ended up with the job. I must say I don't think I'd like this type of work, although it is interesting. It's just not my line. The cake really didn't look too bad for an amateur." In fact, this began my making wedding cakes for a number of African couples.

The rest of the month of November was filled with projects of getting ready for school Christmas party, the Alumni Banquet and school closing. I had many more curtains to make, painting to do and other jobs before Christmas. Randal also had a Christmas program at his preschool on December 5th.

After Randal's program we drove to Port Shepstone to pick up Allen and Ron. They actually got out of school December 1st, but they wanted to attend a youth camp before coming home to Swaziland. We stayed at Millers until the 9th, as we had Christmas shopping to do, as well as other shopping. Well, as if I didn't have enough to do, I offered to crochet eight table place mats for a lady at Margate. I never seem to be able to say "no" to people. I had 160 little motifs to crochet into eight mats, but I got them done when we picked our boys up on December 6th. The lady paid me so I thought this would be a way of getting Bob a watch for Christmas.

The Nazarene missionaries invited us to their annual Thanksgiving dinner this year. They had the usual turkey dinner and we enjoyed it very much. At the big hospital dining room, where they had the dinner, there was a large veiled box sitting up on the table. Of course, everyone was wondering what is under those sheets. When they unveiled it there was old Mr. Tom Turkey, himself! This was quite a sight for some of our children. In fact, it was so cute yesterday when Randal was talking about the way the turkey "sings"! He said, "I like the way the turkey sings!" You know to me a turkey is just a common thing, but to our kids it is a real novelty. What was so funny was that during one of the special songs the turkey just gobbled and gobbled quite to the delight of our kids!

From my letter of December 5th I write: "Our big day at Bible School was Saturday and we felt it was quite successful. A total of 17 alumni were present and one of these was a girl who graduated at our school when we lived at the mission near Port Shepstone. She is still true to the Lord, which was such an encouragement to us. We had a really big feast for all of our students and alumni. I think that our former students were quite impressed and perhaps they are forming a new interest in their school. Our purpose is to promote the school so that others would encourage new students to come. It really takes a lot of hard work but the Lord is helping us."

After getting our two older boys home from Port Shepstone we were involved in a VBS held at the Nazarene mission in Manzini. They asked me to teach one group of kids and Ron helped with the sports. Allen helped his dad with the financial books for the school and mission at Joy. Our two younger boys didn't actually know what VBS was but they just love it. We also take Israel Langa's two children to VBS too. It is from 9:00 to 12:00 noon.

I just couldn't believe when I saw Ronnie, how much the child had grown. Just in the seven to eight weeks they were at Port Shepstone going to school he grew several inches and he hardly has clothes to fit him. He is probably 5 feet 9 inches by now and if he keeps growing at this rate he will pass Allen who is 6 feet 1 inch. Really, Ron needs to be tall to match his feet for he has such big ones. He wears the same size as Allen now.

Ramsays were planning to come and have Christmas with us but their plans were changed and they came the day after Christmas. However, for Christmas Day we were invited into Manzini to Dr. Paul Riley's. We had a great Christmas with Paul and Martha and their three girls and our four boys.

So the year 1978 ends with the older boys interacting with Nazarene missionary kids. In fact, it seems change for schooling for Ron may be going to the Nazarene missionary kid's home in Pietermaritzburg where they have an older couple as parents for missionary children. It will depend if there is space, but it appears it is quite possible. We are asking for prayer in the letter to my parents.

The Year 1979

At the end of 1978 and the beginning of 1979, the Lord provided enough money for us to attend the European Camp in Dundee. Praise God for this spiritual filling station along the way! A former missionary, Rev. N. N. Bonner and Rev. Norman Wilson, preacher on the "Wesleyan Hour" radio program, were our speakers. Being with other missionaries and having the fellowship of Christian South Africans gave us a great start to our New Year.

While at camp, Ron injured the little finger on his right hand. It became more and more swollen so we decided to take him to see Dr. Riley at the Nazarene Hospital in Manzini. The doctor had it x-rayed and found the metacarpal bone was broken, so he put a small cast on it. Silly boy! I guess he was trying to show how strong he was by beating up on an old cupboard, a hard lesson to learn.

Some changes needed to take place in the education of our two older boys. Since Allen would be doing his last year of high school and didn't want the pressure of matric (last year of high school in South Africa) he enrolled in the University of Nebraska High School Department and was able to take correspondence courses he needed to graduate and be ready for college by August.

We were able to get Ron into the Nazarene Missionary Children's Home so he could attend high school in Pietermaritzburg, South Africa. A number of the missionary children from Swaziland also went to school in Pietermaritzburg and stayed at the home. Rev. and Mrs. David Wardlaw, an older couple, were the house parents for all the missionary kids. Besides our son, a couple of kids from Trans World Radio were able to get into the home. Since our mission had a good vehicle, large enough to transport a number of children, it was decided I would take all of the missionary kids from Swaziland to Pietermaritzburg for school. It was an inconvenient time for us. Rev. Norman Wilson came to visit our mission in Swaziland and my absence left Bob with entertaining him, but he managed it okay.

In my letter to Mom and Dad, February 14th, I mentioned about them being snowed in. It seems that the year 1979 was a really bad winter in Nebraska during late January and all February. "I've missed your letters so much and I've been so grateful that you have a telephone. Have you ever before been snowed in like this or for so long? Of course, the 1949 blizzard was bad. I appreciate having Grace Reeves open your letters and read them to you." Much later, Clint told me they took mail to my parents by snowmobile. While Mom and Dad were having a terrible winter we were enjoying a nice summer time.

During the first semester I taught typing and Sunday School Methods at the Bible College. Allen took typing with my class while he was waiting for his courses to come from the States. During that time, Bob had to attend a Regional Board meeting in Dundee. Since we had only one dependable vehicle, he took a plane to Joburg and caught a ride with Rev. Bauer.

Allen enjoyed going to the Nazarene Hospital in Manzini to watch some operations. But he is also interested in becoming a pilot and he wanted to write Missionary Aviation Fellowship.

I want to tell about Rylan's and Randal's schooling in Swaziland. A number of us missionaries were unhappy with the schooling our children were getting at Sidney Williams School where the older children went when we first arrived in Swaziland. So the Wesleyan, Nazarene and TransWorld Radio missionaries decided to meet and discuss doing a correspondence schooling with the Calvert's Course. Calvert is a school in U.S.A. offering correspondence which can be done by grade school children anywhere in the world.

Apparently there was some talk among the Swazi's that we missionaries were prejudiced against the blacks. Of course, this was not at all true. God helped us show our true feelings by providing an African American teacher, Mrs. Williams. There was no way now the Swazis could say we were prejudiced. Our other teacher was a qualified Trans World missionary by the name of Mrs. Kitner. Both she and Mrs. Williams were Rylan's teachers.

Because Swazi children were learning in the English language, their second language, it slowed our children up too much and they became bored. Mrs. Williams was an answer to our prayers. Mothers would take turns coming in to help as we had around 21 students. My days to help were Tuesday and Thursday. Then, Monday, Wednesday and Friday I was teaching at the Bible College. Later on the teacher told me I would only need to come on Thursdays. That was a real help to me.

Randal took preschool at Mrs. Shirley's, and then he stayed there for 1st grade which was a British course. He liked school very much and especially enjoyed two Swedish missionary boys who became his good friends.

"I started a Sunday School teacher training class for the Joy Mission Church on Friday afternoons. Even now, prayers are needed to help Sunday school teachers and workers catch a vision of the importance of this work in the Sunday school. Many people seem to think that Sunday school is not very important so they, especially the teachers, don't worry much if they don't get to Sunday school. I know the Holy Spirit is the only one who can convict them of this."

In March we were getting excited that Roxane, having finished her second year of college at Central Wesleyan in South Carolina, would be coming to Swaziland for a visit from the end of May until August.

Near the end of March we entertained a tour group of 16 people led by Don Bray. I really didn't know where I was going to put everyone but my friend, Martha Riley, offered to keep two couples and Allen. Mrs. Edgerton, another Nazarene missionary friend, kept our two little boys, Rylan and Randal. Bob and I slept on our living room floor and we gave our room to two ladies, Allen's room to two ladies and Rylan's and Randal's room to three ladies. We had an extra room at the boy's dorm for three men and also the trailer where the bus driver and Rev. Paul Bauer stayed.

We always looked forward to groups coming. As I wrote in one of my form letters: "It does help when one can see the work that is happening here but to the many of you who are not able to visit and yet sacrifice your time and giving, I believe Jesus would say 'Blessed are you who have not seen but have believed, worked and labored for Me in the homeland.'

Getting ready for the tour group was a big job. At the same time I also was trying to get my form letters ready to send and retyping updated sheets. I think I typed about 346 addresses and names. Getting them into order was a real job. One of the ladies on the tour was Mrs. Verna Miller from New York State had taken great interest in our family. She was kind enough to take our letter and addresses to the church in New York who would post them. Another of the ladies brought something for us and told us about Roxy. Also, she carried a letter back to Roxy for us.

I got to bed about 2:00 a.m. and on Friday morning I cooked breakfast for 20 people. They all had to leave at 7:30 in the morning. It was a very short time for them but we were happy to have the group!

Allen wanted to get his Swazi driver's license. Israel Langa took it upon himself to help Allen learn what he would probably be tested over. The examiner never passes anyone the first time. Surprise! Thanks to Israel for his great coaching, Allen came home with his driver's license the first time he took the test!   Ron was home for a short ten day holiday from school in Pietermaritzburg. It seemed too short! He did very well in school that first term. However, he was really looking forward to Roxy's visit as we all were.

Not seeing her for nearly two years was just too long! We were already making plans for May 23rd and a wonderful visit.

The Bible School got out for their first term holiday at the end of April. However, on May 2nd, 3rd and 4th we taught classes for the youth campers at Ebenezer Mission, 'Preparation for Marriage'. Bob taught the boys and I taught the girls. Often when I wrote to my mother I would ask for prayer but since I knew she would not receive the request in time, I asked her to pray that the message would be impressed upon these young people and that they would heed and do what we taught. I felt that Bob and I could be living examples to them with our own happy marriage, blessed by God!"

Roxane's Visit

"We are so happy that Roxy will soon be here." Our whole family is getting excited. I was crocheting a tablecloth for Roxy and also making a lavender doily which I planned to sell and give the money into our Women's Malilambi offering. I wanted to show these things to Roxy when she came.

The days before her arrival were very busy. I was getting prepared for our daughter and also for our trip to Port Shepstone and to Pietermaritzburg to see Ron. Roxy left from Atlanta with her friend, Terri, flying to London for a few days. From London they went to Lusaka, Zambia where Terri would meet her family. Roxy then flew Swazi Air from Lusaka, Zambia to Matsapa Airport in Swaziland where she arrived at just after 2:00 p.m. We were so happy to see her and she was delighted to be in Swaziland with Mom and Dad and three of her brothers: Allen, Rylan and Randal.

As soon as we picked her up we headed for Pietermaritzburg to be with Ron The next day we left for Port Shepstone and got a rondoval at Eden Park where we were close to the Millers, the Motleys and others whom Roxy would enjoy seeing again. On Sunday evening we took Ron back to school and stayed the night before heading to Durban so Roxy could do some shopping.

Life settled down after we arrived in Swaziland. Roxy started helping out at the 'correspondence' study hall. I had developed a cough and sinus head cold so it was nice of her to take my place at the school. She began helping out three days a week, giving some of the other mothers a rest and gaining some good experience.

Trying to communicate by phone from Swaziland to the U.S. was almost impossible. By June there was the prospect of having dial phones because poles were up, but it was a very slow process. A lot went on in the U.S. that we missed out on, although my mother tried to keep us informed about the extended family. For instance, one letter mentioned that Karen Muldoon, Bob's niece, had twin boys.

Some of the discussion of what our plans would be after we returned to the States was quite interesting. In fact, some of these ideas I had totally forgotten until I began writing this book. I'm taking this from one of my letters: "If Bob is gone a whole year doing deputation then I want to be close to our parents. But if he decides to get a job or go to school then I suppose there won't be much to do around Oshkosh. There is the possibility of pastoring again. I've been suggesting perhaps Bob take a two year leave to go to school for his Master's degree. Then he could again teach in a Bible College. But he wants me to go into nurse's training, so I don't know what will happen. We are just praying that we will know God's will!"

June 18th letter: "Tonight I'm sitting in a very cold room at the Dundee campgrounds in Dundee. I'm very glad I could come with Bob this time for a seminar for the field on Stewardship and Metro-Move. If you have read any of the Wesleyan literature, Wesleyan World or Advocate, you probably know something about Metro-Move. Anyway, I'm looking forward to hearing some good enthusiastic things to help us catch on fire more for God. We brought four of our Bible School students and Rev. Israel Langa. I may be the only missionary lady. I was hoping Carol Ramsey would come, but they aren't here yet. Rose Motley is here, of course, so I can visit with her. I've also brought along crocheting and letter writing, so I won't lack for anything to do. It's so nice to leave the two little boys with Roxy and Allen and know they will be well taken care of."

Continued from the same letter: "Last night we went into the Nazarene Church in Manzini and after the service, I invited Dr. Paul and Martha Riley for tea. Ann Brauteseth from Joburg was with them and I wanted to meet her. The Brauteseths, Ann's folks, were at Ebenezer for a few months."

As I'm writing this letter I say: "I have just killed three mosquitoes in here! One would think they would be frozen by now, but evidently not! It has really been cold in Swaziland too, lately. So I guess winter has arrived. Of course, it isn't all that cold because it never freezes, but with no heating in our houses it seems terribly cold. Guess I should get some wood to burn in the fireplace. Wood is rather scarce around Joy Mission though. I was telling our students and teacher Israel Langa about gathering cow chips to burn when I was just a little girl. I think they were a bit surprised. I'm telling you, petrol (gas) is expensive around here! It's about $2.50 a gallon. We are trying to cut down on our trips to town and other places. I may have to learn to ride a bicycle yet!"

We had a good seminar at Dundee and I really appreciated getting to go with Bob. Roxy and Allen managed very well. Allen had even taken Israel and Victoria Langa to Mbabane to the U.S. Embassy to take their English comprehensive tests (you see the South African field is getting ready to send this couple under the TOOL program for more education in the U.S.). So Bob doesn't need to see about getting this taken care of now. Really, I don't know how we will manage when Roxy and Allen leave for college. We are depending on them so much right now. Roxy had helped Rylan do his tests on Thursday, so I didn't need to do much with them when I got home. Roxy is really enjoying teaching missionary kids. Allen is making plans to go to the library in Manzini in the mornings to study; then he can pick up the kids and Roxy on his way back. Then we won't have that extra trip. We have just got to cut down our mileage somewhere! The other night some Nazarene friends of ours said that one of their missionaries got his big car filled up and it cost him R44.00. Can you imagine?"

At the end of June Ron got a long break from school. It was wonderful to have all five of our children together again. Also, Patti Bramsby came to spend part of her school holiday with us. In my July 2nd letter I stated: "It is delightful to have two girls in the house."

During the first part of July we made plans for a week of holiday. We wanted to go to Kruger National Game Park and see other missionary friends. One night we stayed in the Game Park in our tent, and then went to the Amos' who live just outside the Park. Mark Amos and our boys were glad to see each other. From there we traveled to the Ramsay's at Louis Trichardt for the weekend. On Monday the Ramsays traveled with us to Rhodesia in our 12 seater E-20 Datsun so we could share travel expenses. We traveled by convoy from the South Africa/Rhodesia border. a safer way of going than on Swaziland roads. We didn't see any terrorists and we drove to the Milton Bagley's house in Bulawayo where they had a great meal prepared for us. From there we drove out to the Matopas where Cecil Rhodes' grave is on top of the high granite rocks in the Park. One morning we got to visit a very interesting museum. The Ramsays knew a 7th Day Adventist dentist in Bulawayo. They were very good friends with them so Roxy was able to get her teeth checked for free.

On the 11th of July we took time to drive down the wide streets of downtown Bulawayo. Then at 1:00 p.m. we caught our convoy back to the South African border. We stayed an extra day at the Ramsays because they wanted the kids to hike in the forest up above Louis Trichardt. It was about a 15 kilometer hike. We arrived back in Swaziland on July 13th.

We celebrated Randal's birthday at Ramsays on the 12th of July with cake and ice cream and Uncle Jim got two movie films to show at home so Randal had a nice 7th birthday. Then we took Patti Bramsby to Matsapa Airport to catch the Royal Swazi plane to Durban. She has been with us for sixteen days and we enjoyed her so much.

Words from my July 26th letter leave me breathless as I read it: "Since coming back from holiday it has been nothing but full speed ahead. The coming days will be so full, clear up to our furlough time, so please pray for us." The letter continues: "Roxy leaves a week from today. She dreads to go back and of course we are dreading it too. We have all had such a great time together. Ron had to go back to school the 23rd of July. Roxy leaves August 2nd and Allen on the 7th. It's going to be terribly lonely, so it is probably a good thing that I have lots of work lined up.

I ask for prayer for Bob in this same letter, "…because he is having such a time with boils. Of all places he has one on the end of his nose. If ever anyone looked like Rudolph the red-nosed reindeer, I suppose it's Bob! He is so miserable. He has had these boils off and on since last November and has been to the doctor many times. He has some powerful expensive medicine now so maybe this will do the trick.

August 6th letter: "It's the night before Allen leaves us and his bags are all packed. We sure had a time getting everything in and keeping within 44 pounds, but I think we have made it. After Allen leaves tomorrow Bob leaves for a board meeting in Dundee. He won't get back until Friday, so Rylan, Randal and I are going to feel lonely. Last night we had such a good service at a large high school at Matsapa. I mentioned about these singers coming from Joburg. They arrived Saturday evening and we had a 'Bri'. There are only seven in the group. I have one couple sleeping in Roxy's room, one couple in the trailer and three men down at the boys' dorm. They are a very nice singing group. One of the men said that there were 95 decisions made at the high school last night.

With a new baby girl named Nonto, born July 19th, Israel and Victoria Langa now had two girls and a boy. We asked for prayer for them about going for further studies in the U.S. We had been trying to get them into college at Bartlesville, but were running into problems with finances. "I believe if God wants them there he will help us see a way through."(Well, he and his family did go and his desires were met. He graduated with a degree and returned to Swaziland to teach in the Bible College.)

Vacation Bible School and Swaziland Conference

We are planning for a Vacation Bible School at Joy Mission Church so this is a very big responsibility I have coming up. This matter of VBS is a rather new concept for the Africans. They feel in their culture children should be seen, but not heard. All this week I have been preparing the teachers and workers and getting all the lessons in order for them. One almost has to teach the lessons to the teachers first before letting them teach it to the children. It seems even Sunday school teachers know so little about the Bible. This is the great advantage of attending Bible College, to learn how to do these things in the Church.

In a later letter: "I want to tell you about our VBS last week. With the prayers of many and the Lord's help we felt it was a great success. We had a total of 105 children enroll, an average daily attendance of 74. Counting teachers and workers our average was over 83 per day. Yesterday at the program Victoria and I counted 149, but I'm sure before the service finished there was 150 or more. The children said their Bible verses so nicely. I think the older people were really amazed and impressed at what the children had learned. I wish I could go around to our various churches and hold Vacation Bible School for the children. It is so rewarding to work with them."

Mid- August: "We have a lady eye doctor here from England. She is staying with us all weekend since her car isn't in good working order. She doesn't want to buy another one, as she is due to go back to England this next month. This lady optometrist checked Bob's eyes and says there has been such a drastic change just since he's gotten his new glasses. She suggests he should have a thorough physical exam by a medical doctor. He is still battling with boils and we wonder if this is affecting his eyesight."

After our VBS at Joy Mission, Swaziland Conference took place at Ebenezer Mission. Wilma arrived in Swaziland for a few days on her way to Zambia. She will again be teaching at Choma Secondary School. Then later in September Bob's youngest sister, Vivian, arrived. Vivian is a registered nurse and will be helping or volunteering at the Nazarene Hospital in Manzini. We are having real spring weather here now. In fact, it has been very wet and rainy today. Everything is looking beautiful and green. I told Vivian she couldn't have come at a better time.

Now I want to go back to the subject of Bob's eyes. From September 24th letter: 'Bob went up to Mbabane this morning and had a specialist check his eyes. The doctor told him his problem is cataracts and that he will need an operation. His eyes seem to be steadily getting worse. We are in a dither to know just what we should do. We have so much to do for these last two or three months that we hardly know where to turn. I told Bob maybe this is just the reason the Lord let Vivian come out because He knew we would need her help. Anyway, we trust the Lord. We can say as Paul said, "We know that all things work together for good for those who love God and those who are called according to His purpose." (Romans 8:28)' Bob talked to Dr. Paul Riley and he says that a patient should not travel for about two months after having this type of eye surgery. So it looks like Bob will be having eye surgery in the States after we come on furlough." He is going into the doctor who sent him up to the specialist to see what he will suggest.

Our Second Furlough,
Dec. '79-Aug 31, 1982

Another four years passed quickly and it was time for our second furlough. This time we had only three of our boys traveling with us. Allen had left in August 1979 for college at Bartlesville Wesleyan College. Roxane, who had taken two years of college at Central Wesleyan College, transferred to Bartlesville Wesleyan to be where her brother was and also to be closer to us while we were home. At that time Ron was about 15 ½ years, Rylan was 10 and Randal was 7.

On our trip home, we stopped in Germany to visit the Blum family who had been missionaries of the Lutheran Church in Swaziland. They had invited us to visit them when we came through on furlough, so we took them up on their offer and made arrangements to visit them.

Before we left Swaziland, arrangements had been made for Israel Langa and his family to fly with us. Israel planned to take four years of training at Bartlesville Wesleyan College in preparation for being a principal of our Bible College in Swaziland. His whole family, wife and three children, were going to America as well. I remember stopping in Mbabane to get papers that Victoria needed in order to go with Israel. The Cheneys and Langas went to Johannesburg and caught their flight to Brussels. It was fun to see the reaction of the two little Langa children as they got on the plane and prepared for flying.

The next morning when we arrived at the Belgium International Airport, we sent the Langa family on to New York. Our family changed planes and flew Lufthansa Air to Frankfurt Germany where Rev. Blum met us. He took us to their home in Frankfurt and we had a great visit with our German friends, Hans and Barbara, and their children. I am not sure how long we stayed but I believe it was three days. It was really interesting to walk around the streets and see beautiful paintings on the buildings. In fact, it was amazing. One of the days Mrs. Blum took us to their Christmas Market in the city. This was quite different – many little booths all along the sidewalks with all sorts of gifts for sale. It was very cold, however, so Barbara said, "I know what will warm us up. Some hot spiced wine." Bob and I didn't quite know what to say, as we weren't accustomed to drinking any type of wine. But we decided this time it probably did not have a lot of alcohol content as it was spiced and heated. We drank the special drink and then proceeded to check out the churches. It did seem, as we walked along, that we were beginning to feel warmer. So our day spent at the Christmas Market in Frankfurt, Germany was a day of fun and learning. We were tired at the end of the day and ready for our beds.

After saying our goodbyes, Rev. Blum took us back to the Frankfurt airport. Our youngest son got really sick as we were flying into London. We didn't know what was wrong because he seemed to have a lot of pain. We wondered if maybe he was having an appendicitis attack. So when we landed the people at the airport said we should take an ambulance to a nearby hospital. So I rode with Randal in the ambulance when they took him to the emergency room. He was checked thoroughly and they decided it wasn't his appendix, so they gave him some pills to dull the pain.

We again boarded an airplane, this time headed for the United States. It was really a long day but we finally arrived at Denver with family to meet us. Before long we were in Nebraska again, just in time for Christmas and New Year's with the Cheneys and Thorntons.

During this time Bob was finding it pretty hard to read anything or to see plainly. Right after Christmas we set up an appointment for him see Dr. Van Newkirk and we got the boys enrolled for second semester in Oshkosh elementary and Garden County high schools.

Dr. Van Newkirk determined that Bob had cataracts. I went with Bob to the hospital in Scottsbluff and stayed while he had the surgery. Dr. Van Newkirk asked, "If the first eye does well would you like for me to do the second one?" Bob decided he just as well get both done and have it over so Dr. Van Newkirk did the second eye. Bob was really very young to even be having cataracts. We wondered if some of his medication taken for other ailments caused the condition but we never really knew.

These medical procedures seemed to have gone well and, about a week later, I took Bob back to Oshkosh to the old farmhouse that became our home for the next 2 ½ years. Since Bob still could not see well, it seemed like a long time for the healing process. They did not put the inner ocular lens in for him, but polished his own lens. This meant he would wear thick glasses but with the hope of eventually wearing contacts.

I'm sure the days seemed long since there was not much Bob could do. He felt a bit depressed at times. However, when he finally was able to be fitted for glasses, things got a better. Our mission department at headquarters was very kind in giving us about 2 ½ months off so that Bob could get his sight back and eventually get back to our home ministry assignments. His eyes finally healed enough for him to get contacts. Oh my, what a process that was trying to learn how to put contacts in and take them out. At times it was very frustrating trying to get them in and then I often helped get the contacts out with a little suction cup. But with time things improved.

Our first assignment was a church in Michigan for home ministries. We tried to encourage some couples to hear a call to Zimbabwe to lead our churches there. I remember on our way home we stopped at Marion and visited with Jim and Carol Ramsay. This was a real blessing to Bob. Jim also wore contacts so he gave Bob some very helpful hints for putting in and taking out contacts. From this time on it was much easier for Bob to deal with his contacts.

Ted, Bob's Brother Has Cancer

It was in August of 1979 that we had learned Bob's youngest brother, Ted, was sick. They told us he had a lot of trouble with his stomach. During that time he and Sue went to Mayo Clinic and that is when they found out for sure he had cancer. We were all so shocked and of course hoping that our furlough time in December would allow us time to get there in the States so that we could see him again. They had one little girl, Tara, about 17 or 18 months old when we arrived in December. Also we learned before we arrived home that Sue, Ted's wife, was expecting again just after Tara turned two in March of 1980. Ted had to take chemo to see if the cancer could be eradicated from his body. He would go to Denver every so often for treatment.

Sue was teaching at the time but would try to be available to go with him on these trips. Of course as the time for their baby's arrival drew nearer she had time off for her delivery and recovery. It was April 20th when the new baby arrived. They named her Kristin Sue and what a cutie she was. A lot of times I would look after the little ones for Sue and also help Ted with meals, etc. I remember one day as I got lunch ready and called Ted and little Tara to come and eat. I had placed baby Kristin on the dining room floor by the table in her little baby seat. As Ted came into the dining room he looked down at Kristin, I will never forget what he said to his baby daughter. He looked down at her and said "You know little one, there is just something really special about you."

The one great thing that was so important about Ted's illness was that he wanted a relationship with the Lord in his life again. He had gotten away from God and was not living the way he knew he should. In fact, it was during the time he was in the Oshkosh Hospital that late one night he called for Pastor Richard Long to come and pray with him. Ted accepted Jesus back into his life and he witnessed to a real change in his heart and life. I know Mother Cheney prayed hard for her son to get back into a relationship with Christ. I often wondered if she might have prayed "Lord, save Ted, my son, at any cost." We never know what it might take to bring people back to God! Ted was a real witness to many of his old friends and many of their hearts were touched.

Because of Ted's illness Bob felt he should help his brother Charles on the farm and with the cattle. Ted and Charles worked together – Ted mostly took care of the cattle and Charles did the farming. So this was the reason Bob and I wanted to extend our furlough. Also, Ron had about two more years of high school left and we felt it was better for him to finish high school in Oshkosh.

Bob had to travel for various meetings and he had to visit various churches. Most of the time, I stayed home with the three boys even though sometimes he was gone for several weeks. I think the longest time he was away was about seven weeks. That seemed too long to me and the boys but we really weren't alone. Charles and Linda and family were nearby. Being close to grandparents also helped. I was able to go with him sometimes and so did the two younger boys, Randal and Rylan.

Fall of 1980, Tornado Hits

It was the fall of this year. Ron began his junior year of high school and I think Rylan was a fifth grader and Randal a second grader. One day when I went to pick the boys up from school the weather was acting very strange. In fact, the day was October 15, 1980. Ted was at the Oshkosh Hospital and Sue was with him, as he was getting into the last stages of his cancer. The sky seemed full of angry clouds and it had been raining and hailing. It was Wednesday evening the day for CYC at church, a Christian club for kids that our church had in Lewellen. I planned to pick up Linda, as she and I both were teaching children. Rylan and Randal were both in this club. I came back to our house on the farm and Linda was there, so she jumped in the car with the boys and me and we headed for Lewellen.

As we started out on the highway I said to Linda, "Oh, look at those haystacks rolling!" Just a bit further down the road I said "Look! See that ball of blue fire on the power line!"

What we didn't realize was that a tornado was passing over us. As we arrived at the church Pastor Paul came to the door of the parsonage and told us that there was a tornado out by Charles and Linda's place and they thought they should get all the children to the parsonage basement so they would be safe if it came toward Lewellen.

Needless to say, we didn't have CYC that night but the children all got home safely. This tornado made a path through Charles and Linda's place and destroyed their barn, chicken house and kitchen and garage part of their house. How thankful we were that no lives were lost. Actually, Grandma Cheney had been staying at Charles and Linda's house but Linda had brought her back to the pink house just before I picked her up for CYC. I'm glad Grandma wasn't at their house where she could have been hurt.

We were scheduled for a weekend mission's conference at Prairie City, South Dakota for November 7th, 8th and 9th. This time Rylan, Randal and I went with Bob. It was nice to be in services with our two younger boys and to meet these wonderful, friendly Wesleyans. It was a really great mission's weekend. After the Sunday service and dinner they served we headed back to Nebraska. It was probably nine or 10 o'clock when we got back, that night on November 9th.

Early the next morning we got a phone call from Sue, "Ted is really bad. Bob could you come to the hospital with me?" Of course Bob was glad to give Sue support as it did look like Ted would not be with us much longer. I stayed with Tara and Kristin while Sue went with Bob to the hospital. Later that morning Ted went to be with the Lord. I'm so glad Bob was there to give Sue support. At that time I wasn't aware of what it was like to lose a spouse. Sue needed all the help and support she could get.

The Year 1981 and Eight Months of 1982

Now that both Bob and I were working it was much easier to make ends meet. It was also very nice to be near both Bob's parents and my parents. This way our boys got to enjoy their grandparents. My parents only lived about 30 miles north of us in the sandhills.

Bob and I decided we should sever from the mission department so that he could help Charles with the farm and the cattle since we no longer had Ted. Bob finished with home ministries at the end of November and then began working for Charles.

I took a course in nurse's aide so I could get a job at the Oshkosh nursing home. I started out working during the day and then later on they put me on the 11 PM to 7 AM shift. I enjoyed this work, helping the older people. I especially felt privileged to care for my mother-in-law, Ella Cheney. When she came into the rest home during August 1981, I remember so well how happy she was to be there. She expressed her happiness by saying, "Now I don't need to worry about cooking or taking my pills. I don't need to clean either. This is just wonderful." Not many coming into the home looked on the positive side like she did. She was a very special mother-in-law.

Since I was not keeping a diary in those days I will only hit highlights of this year. Roxane, our daughter, was a senior and ready to graduate with a BA degree in elementary education from Oklahoma Wesleyan University. At that time it was called Bartlesville Wesleyan College. In the fall of 1980 we were able to attend the college's homecoming. Roxane was chosen as homecoming queen. Bob and I enjoyed attending these events, as well as meeting up with old friends from years before.

After her graduation Roxane applied for a teaching job in the fall of 1981. It was not long until she heard about a country school near Lake McConaughy in Keith County. They needed a teacher for the fall of 1981 through spring of 1982. She filled out her application and very soon learned she was hired. We told her, if she wanted to, that we didn't mind her staying at home with us and driving back and forth to school. This was how it worked out so we had four of our children with us until the next summer.

Our son, Allen, transferred from Bartlesville to Marymount College in Salina, Kansas, so he could get his degree in Biology. That summer he worked for my cousin, Jim French, and I believe that was when we met Allen's girlfriend, Kim Cavaness. Her folks lived at Atkinson, Nebraska and attended the Wesleyan Church there.

Our three younger sons Ron, Rylan and Randal, again entered school in Oshkosh. They were quite involved in sports and Ron was in speech and traveled to different speech contests. He also was king at the homecoming football game. He, with his teammates, set some records for the track team too.

At Christmas vacation time, all the children were home for Christmas. Grandma Cheney wasn't doing too well health wise but I remember one of the days Roxy and Allen went up to play Scrabble with her. Grandma Ella loved the game of Scrabble. She did have a lot of trouble with her asthma. One morning Bob received a call that his mom had to be put in the hospital. He went up to spend a little time with her. During that visit the nurse brought in mom's medication for her to take. Before she could get the pills in her mouth she sort of gasped and lay over as Bob caught her. This is how the Lord took Mom Cheney home. I'm so glad my husband, her son, was right there by her side.

Of course, since her death was during the Christmas vacation, our children were all at home and her funeral was planned for the 2nd of January.

This is how our year 1982 began. Grandma Cheney was 77 years old and had lived a good life. She took a lot of interest in each of her children's lives and was a good mother to them. She definitely had a big impact upon all her children, praying for them and counseling them. She truly was a great mother-in-law, too.

I have to include here a funny incident that happened with my mother-in-law. The home church always had monthly missionary meetings for the women of the church. At one of these meetings the ladies were packing used clothing to send overseas for the missionaries to distribute to the Nationals. As the ladies finished packing and tying up the packages, they then prepared to go home. Since it was cold weather they all started getting their coats on. Grandma Ella began looking for her coat and could not find it anywhere. The other ladies also helped her look. It was nowhere to be found. So where did it go? Oh my, it got put in one of the boxes going overseas to missionaries. I'm not sure what they did but Grandma Ella learned you don't lay your coat down where the used clothing is! It just might be sent overseas!

During the month of March the churches of the district held a ministerial convention at Oshkosh. All pastors and their wives were supposed to attend these meetings. A few months before this we knew that our daughter was going out with one of the Pastor's son's. In fact, it was Ron, son of Duane and Lita Lauber. He was a youth pastor at the North Platte church and he and Roxy would go out now and then. He attended Roxy's country school Christmas program during the Christmas of 1981. At this ministerial convention he and Roxy asked us if we could meet at the place where the Laubers were staying so that we could all visit. So we did meet and enjoyed a time of fellowship with our friends. Then Ron and Roxy made the announcement they had plans to get married. At this time I believe Bob and I had plans to return as missionaries to Zimbabwe. We, of course, gave them our blessing. So we knew our daughter would become a pastor's wife.

I have to tell you this on her. When she was younger, probably in high school, she very emphatically stated, "I am never going to be a pastor's wife!" I have to smile now because this is exactly what she became. So girls, never say I'm never going to do this or be that. It might just be exactly what God wants you to do or be.

So, wedding plans got underway. They wanted to be married before we left for the mission field. That meant they would be getting married sometime in the summer. We also learned that our son Allen had gotten engaged and they were planning a June 12th wedding. It was wonderful that our children had decided to have their weddings before we left for Africa.

It was a busy time. I was working, Roxy was teaching and Bob continued to help on the farm. My mother, who was an excellent seamstress, was able to make the four bridesmaids dresses. Roxy and I decided to attempt making her wedding dress. This required a lot of shopping on Roxy's and my part, but it was a whole lot of fun to work with my daughter on wedding plans and wedding apparel. I'm so thankful that I had one daughter to experience all these exciting things with.

Allen, Roxy and Vivian's Weddings

Toward the end of April I decided to quit my job at the nursing home. With several big events happening through the summer and, also, getting ready to go back overseas we needed more time.

Our first big event was Allen and Kim's wedding. Many of the relatives attended their wedding at the Wesleyan Church in Atkinson Nebraska on June 12th. This was also Ron's birthday. I remember so well, the kindness of Marilyn Hendricks and her husband Bob who allowed us to have the rehearsal supper at their home outside Atkinson on a farm. Bob and I were very pleased with the girl our son chose to be his wife. She is the fourth daughter in a family of five girls and one boy. We praise God for Kim and her Christian family.

Ronald was in his senior year of high school and was hoping to go to college and then med school to become a doctor. I remember one day as we were riding to school with my sister-in-law and, I believe, my mother-in-law, Ron and I were talking about what he would like to study. He said to me, "I would really like to become a doctor, but there is no money for all the schooling I need." I looked at him and said, "Ron, if God wants you to become a doctor, you will find the money to do it."

When Ron graduated in May, he received some scholarship money. One scholarship was fairly sizable and would help a lot if you went to school within the state. He made the decision to go to the University of Nebraska at Lincoln, Nebraska. Some of his classmates were going to be there, too, and after Ron and Roxy were married they planned to be pastors of our Omaha Wesleyan Church. This would make his sister close enough to visit sometimes.

So now with one wedding over we looked forward to two more. The next one would be our daughter's. What a busy time getting everything ready for this wedding. Roxy chose rainbow colors for her bridesmaids, yellow, pink, lavender and green. Sheryl Karnes came to be Roxy's maid of honor, then Ron's sister Shelley, her close friend, Francis and cousin Julie Cheney. My sister came and although Joyce French baked their wedding cake, Esther decorated it in the same rainbow colors, a beautiful triple tiered cake. The kids were married in the Lutheran Church at Oshkosh and the reception was held at the city auditorium. Bob walked Roxy down the aisle and also did the wedding vows for them to repeat. Rev. Lauber assisted and my other sister, Elaine, sang for the wedding. Truly it was a beautiful service that many will remember. The one family that attended as very special guests was the Israel Langa family. They were still attending Bartlesville Wesleyan College. Israel had only finished his second year of college. So now we have Ron and Roxanne Lauber married on July 24, 1982.

But this wasn't the end of the weddings. Bob's sister, Vivian, had met the man of her life and so now we prepared for her wedding on the 21st of August. Of course, we didn't have quite so much responsibility this time. It was held at the Methodist Church in Lewellen. Bob did perform the ceremony and our cute little nieces, Tara and Kristin, where the sweetest little flower girls. So now all of Bob's sisters were married but Wilma. Don Lark, now married to Vivian, became our newest brother-in-law.

Now we were on the countdown to August 31st, the day Bob and I would leave with our two youngest boys. But first, we had to take Ron to Lincoln for college and say goodbye to him. This was one of the hardest things I've ever done, leaving my son at a state university. He stayed in Farmhouse Fraternity house with several boys from the Oshkosh area so it wasn't that he didn't know anyone. It was hard because we knew we would be clear across the ocean from him. We could only pray God would keep him safe and help him in his lonely hours.

Suitcases were packed and drums sent on their way to Zimbabwe. We learned that Jim and Roxy Lo and their twin boys would be joining us in our third term in the country of Zimbabwe. So on August 31st, 1982, we flew out from Denver to New York where we met the Lo's before we caught our flights to Amsterdam in Holland. God was leading us into our third term of missionary work in Africa.

Chapter Five
Returning to Africa (1982-1987) - Our 3rd Term

As I mentioned, we did meet the Lo's in New York but did not get on the same flight to Holland. Rev. Lo's brother came to visit them so they got on a later flight. Our plane landed in Amsterdam, Holland about 8:00 AM, September 1st. We were pretty tired so we got to our hotel and went to bed for a while. Later we took a canal boat tour that was quite interesting. The next day we decided to go to Floriade – a large show of acres and acres of many different flowers. It seems that this show of flowers is only put on every 10 years. We came on the year the show took place and what a beautiful place it was! It was such fun to have our two younger boys with us – Rylan, age 13 and Randal, age 10. The Lo's were staying at a different hotel, but we did have the same flight to travel on to South Africa. We landed in Kenya at Nairobi for the first time, so we now have a new country to add to our list.

We stayed with Orai and Linda in Boksburg and got invited out quite a bit for meals. Jim and Carol Ramsey invited us for supper one evening. It was nice to visit with many that we knew in the Johannesburg area.

From my letter of September 13, 1982, I wrote: "We are so happy and pleased that the South African field has provided two very nice "Passat" Volkswagens which are diesel. We get the white one and the Lo's have the yellow one. We have quite a bit of business to see about here before going on to Zimbabwe. The Lo's have to get furniture for their house. The South African field is providing the money for this. Then we got both our boys bicycles, as well as groceries that will be harder and more expensive to get in Zimbabwe. We went to Swaziland for the past weekend and stayed at the Keels' in Mbabane. They have moved there from their farm near Ebenezer Mission near Siteki. On Saturday we had lunch with Dr. Paul and Martha Riley and then on out to Joy Mission to visit the Langa's and Bob and Brenda Bagley. On Sunday we attended the new Metro Move Church pastored by Rev. Samson Ndabandaba. It was nice to meet so many of the people we knew in Swaziland."

The Los and our family headed for Zimbabwe about September 18th. When we got to the Zimbabwe border we were told we needed residence permits to enter. It was a really big issue with the border people and so we had to make a call to Rev. Charles Sanders. We had to wait the whole long, hot day while Rev. Sanders worked on getting us into the country from the Bulawayo end. Rev. Sanders did work out about our permits enough for us to be allowed into the country. It seems there was a mix-up between what Rev. Sanders asked headquarters and what actually happened. I said in my September 26th letter, "We can't go back and change things; we just have to trust the Lord to help us. As far as safety is concerned, we are probably as safe here as in the States despite, what you may hear."

When we arrived, the Sanders took our family in and arranged for the Lo's to stay at the Brethren in Christ guesthouse while we looked for houses. We decided that since the place where the Sanders' lived was quite far out from the schools, we needed to locate a house closer into the city. Many houses were for sale because a lot of the European people were moving out of the country.

On September 26th, in the afternoon, we held a farewell tea for the Sanders' as they plan to return to Canada. Bill Morgan, our Mission Director, and his wife made plans to come up to see the Sanders' off. They were leaving Friday morning October 1st from the Bulawayo airport. Before they left the Sanders' tried to show us the ropes of what needed to be done. We found that there is a church that needs to be built and many other things to see about. Before we can do all of this we have to have work permits.

Rev. Inyoni (translated Rev. Bird) came down from Victoria Falls for the farewell tea for the Sanders'. He is the district superintendent over Zimbabwe. It was nice to meet him and get acquainted. The farewell tea was held at the Nazarene Fellowship Hall and a number of Nazarene friends attended. Rev. and Mrs. Jim Sage are missionaries from the States and pastor the Nazarene church in Bulawayo. We will probably attend this church on Sunday evenings. The Sage's are very lovely people and have two girls, ages nine and eleven.

After the Sanders left, the Lo's moved in with us until we could find a house for them. Roxane and I shared cooking the meals. I found you couldn't buy tuna or canned mushrooms. Also, oatmeal was very expensive, but most things you could buy. Rev. Sanders had some garden in for us and that really helped. Fruit was very expensive and scarce. The oranges and bananas were the most plentiful and cheapest. I paid $.65 for one apple in U.S. money. Gas also was very expensive at about $4.00 a gallon, diesel about half as much as gas.

In my September 26th letter I write: "Randal says to tell you it's boring here." In other words, I think he means he doesn't have enough to do. They miss school I think, although they wouldn't admit that.

October 6th letter: "We got the boys in school finally. They thought it was really bad yesterday, but today they sounded as though they were adjusting a bit better and were a little happier. Their school clothes were outrageous for price. In fact, it took nearly $145.00 American money to buy hats, clothes, socks and shoes. That was only one safari outfit for Randal and shorts and shirt for Rylan. Rylan has to wear a tie also. We get up about 6:00 a.m. and leave for school about 7:00 a.m. because we are so far out. They get to bed between 8:30 and 9:00 p.m.

Bob and I studied Ndebele language every morning. It is a little like Zulu so this helped us a lot.

The city of Bulawayo is all ablaze with color now (I wrote in October 6 letter). The Jacaranda trees are just a lavender hue amongst the yellow–gold blossoms of the Silver Leaf Oak, and all the different colors of Bougainvillea. It is just gorgeous!

Missionaries always long for news from home. It seemed like weeks went by before we got any letters from home. However, one of the October letters from my mother told about the wonderful revival they had at Lewellen. She told about Ron Howard and Jim Berglund getting saved, as well as Trudy French and John French. We loved to hear this kind of news.

In my October 22nd letter of 1982 it sounded like we were a little depressed about our search for a house. The Building Society told us we could not buy a house until we became residents. We didn't want to buy a house in our name, but just wanted it to be in the name of the Zimbabwe Wesleyan Church. There would be just so much more we could do if we were settled and had our permits. The man at the estate agency said he would look further into the matter of the church buying houses for us.

The boys like school much better at the end of October. In fact, at Randal's school I'm having a Scripture class for the children. To me it is so different that in a socialist country you can have Bible scripture classes when they wouldn't think of such a thing in our country. I also help with their snack shop at the school. Randal has taken up swimming and is starting to swim in the Gala competitions in which a number of schools participate. I think he is quite excited about swimming.

Finally Roxy and Jim Lo have rented a house in the Kumalo area of Bulawayo. They were supposed to buy a house and even had one picked out, but they could not get a loan without having a residence permit. However, we praised the Lord because we received a letter from the Chief Immigration officer in Harare that we would be allowed to stay in Zimbabwe while we waited for our permits. At least it gave us hope of getting the permits.

November 5th I write: "It seems like things are falling into place. We found someone to take over our rent at Richmond and were able to find a bigger house to rent about 2 km from Randal's school and about that far for Rylan's. That is one and a half miles, which is certainly better than 60 km every day. Now the boys can ride their bikes to school very easily. We won't be able to move in until the 1st of December. Our new home will be located at 95 Cecil Ave., Hillside Bulawayo.

We were very excited to learn that Orai and Linda Lehman and family would be coming to spend Christmas with us in December. Orai had to come for the Zimbabwe Conference anyway, so it would be a great opportunity for the whole family to come.

It is always a nice helpful deed to missionaries when a church decides to print off and mail out a form letter for a missionary family. Unfortunately, as of November 13th, we had no church offer to do this for us. So Bob printed up about 150 letters for us to send out to churches that pray for and support us. We always like to keep the home churches informed about our work and our prayer needs. Now my job is to address all these letters and get them mailed out. My hope was that eventually some church in the States would take up this project for us.

When Bob and Jim made a trip to Victoria Falls, Bob called back (it is about 400 km to the falls) he said they had looked at the church site there. The people want to have a church built for the Victoria Falls area. This meant we would be having two church buildings to build.

While Bob and Jim were gone, Roxy and their twin boys, Andre and Matthew, were staying with the boys and me. In my November 19th letter I wrote that the Lo's had moved into the house they are renting and that in ten more days we would be moving. The Lo's furniture came through and the barrels they packed should be arriving soon.

I go on to say, "We are having a moving company come in to take our things to the house on Cecil Avenue that we will be moving into. It costs $14 an hour. I hope they don't take too long doing the job." In the same letter I write: "We got our cars and pickup cleared at customs today so evidently they must be pretty certain of our getting residence permits. We got the licenses for the cars and pickup. We have a shortage of diesel now. I'm not sure how long this will last."

Continuing from the same letter: "Bob and Jim are going to hold Bible study at a new convert's house. We are just thrilled about him and his witness. He took the Bible we had given him and gave it to his family about 60 km from here. These people are really hungry for God and want us to come and start a church there. Truly God is working and the doors are wide open. Just keep praying."

It was in November that we met a couple, both teachers, who live in Bulawayo. She was American from Iowa and he was from the African Ndebele tribe. They met each other in the states through her brother while they were in college. They eventually married and taught a while in Zambia where Wilma Cheney met them. When they moved back to Zimbabwe Wilma told us about them. They had two little boys about Matt and Andre's age. A very nice family I must say.

How do American missionaries celebrate the holiday Thanksgiving in a foreign country? While in Zimbabwe this is how we celebrated. With about 50 to 60 other American missionaries here in the Bulawayo area so we made plans to all join together and eat Thanksgiving dinner. They asked me to fix one of the turkeys. It was hard for me to believe how much I had to pay for a turkey that was 12 ½ pounds. It was about $24 but everyone chipped in and helped pay. It was a big meal with pumpkin pie and even cranberry sauce. We really enjoyed it!

December 6th- We are moved and pretty well settled into our new home. What a nice house to live in with rent costing $160 a month! As I said before, a lot of European people built very nice homes in Bulawayo. Then when Zimbabwe got their independence in 1980 quite a number of these people decided to move to South Africa, Australia or other places. From my December 6th letter I describe the house: "There is a big front veranda with a red cement polished floor. There is one door into a large dining room/sitting room and the other front door goes into a long hallway. This passageway is really big. When you walk into the hall from the front door it leads to the left, then on into a large kitchen. If you go right it leads to Randal's bedroom, around a corner into our bedroom with full bathroom, and Rylan's bedroom. About middle way in this hallway is a door that leads into a study.

The kitchen is just fantastic! I'll probably never have another like it and have never had one before. It has lots of dark wood cupboards with a center island that contains an electric stove as well as a breakfast bar and working cabinet area. At the side it has an eye level oven and by the window a double sink and broom closet, also a place for potatoes and other fresh vegetables in a closed bin. I feel like I'm living like a queen!

Orai and Linda Lehman and their three children arrived on December 10. During this week up to the 17th we were busy in our Church Conference. It was a great conference and in my letter of December 17th I state: "We feel like things are starting to fall into place and we have a great work to do here in Zimbabwe." Still we have not received our permits but the Lo's did get their permits. We really aren't sure why we have not gotten ours or received any word about them.

I need to mention that on December 22, 1982 Bob and I celebrated our 25th wedding anniversary. Linda took care of our boys and got the evening meal for their family and our boys. Bob and I celebrated by going to the New Orleans restaurant in Bulawayo. We thanked God that we have celebrated 25 wonderful years together. God is so good! Bob gave me five silver Zimbabwe dollars and a silver spoon.

The Lehmans are having Christmas with us. On Christmas Day we had the Lo family over as well as Pastor Mhlala Phansi, his wife and daughter and another girl who was with them. Altogether there were 17 of us, but with a big house it all went fine and everyone seemed to have a good time. We did have roast turkey with dressing and several Jell-O salads. I baked a fresh peach pie and Linda made the traditional plum pudding. So everyone got to see how the Cheney family celebrates Christmas. We even found lemon flavoring to pour on the sugar cubes so that they would light up on the cake.

It rained on Christmas and we were very grateful because it had been pretty dry. Jim Lo was really wishing for some snow. But as you know, it is summertime in the southern hemisphere in December. Since Jim was wishing for snow the night before Christmas he sat down and drew us a snow scene picture as a gift. He is a very good artist so we were very happy to receive his picture.

Linda and Orai and family left the day after Christmas and were going as far as Mike and Carolyn Rumble's, our missionaries in Pietersburg, South Africa. They had been with us over two weeks so the kids had a wonderful time. They went swimming a lot and we went to a nice museum in Bulawayo, as well as visiting an animal park and Matopa Hills. So with our company gone things quieted down and we begin preparing for the new year of 1983.

1983 – A Fruitful Year in Zimbabwe

Our first event of the year was our Missionary Retreat and Council meeting the beginning of January. It was excellent this year, held in the Johannesburg area. We were really sad that the Lo's were unable to come because they didn't receive their South African Visa's in time. We had Rev. C. B. Colaw and his wife, and Rev. Cox, a Nazarene, as our guest speakers.

I know the Lo's were very disappointed, but I felt the Lord was in this situation. The man at our church out at the mines, whom we had been really praying for fell sick and was taken to the hospital. Jim went to visit him at the hospital and was able to lead him to the Lord. I stated in my letter: "We are so excited and happy about this. God is really working in Zimbabwe." In the same letter I said, "Jim called and said our residence permits had come through. Praise the Lord!"

One of the problems with receiving parcels in the mail is that the person sending it must list the value. This presents a real problem because so many list the value too high. If a package is valued at $50 or more then they want you to have an import license. Apparently the postal department thinks it might be items that the person receiving it is going to sell. This really made a problem for us when they sent Ron and Roxie's wedding pictures. They valued the pictures at $300. Of course, to us they were priceless but to others they definitely would not be of much value at all. We were going to have to pay over $100 in duty and get an import license. Later I wrote: "Finally we had them open it, then they sent us to original customs which cleared our stuff duty free since we were coming in as residents. This was a real problem to us and other missionaries when people sent parcels to us. So we tried to emphasize that people keep the value really low.

Our barrels came through and that means it's almost like Christmas when we take out our things. I had my sewing machine and ice cream freezer in the drums. It sounded like our crate would also soon be arriving.

Diesel and petrol (gas) have been very short here in Zimbabwe so we tried to cut travel as much as possible. Roxie and Jim did go to Victoria Falls for the Women's Meeting. Roxie Lo is the district leader for the Women's work and she felt she should go. It was nice for them to get away since they could not come to South Africa for our missionary retreat. I do state in this January 14th letter that the terrorist activity has picked up so we need to use precautions in traveling outside the city.

Bob began TEE classes (Theological Education by Extension) this month. I began to teach a Scripture class at Moray school where Randal attends school. I felt this was a real outlet to teach the gospel.

The boys began school January 18th. Rylan had started at Hamilton High School but at the end of the year we decided to try out the Catholic boys school called Christian Brothers College, as it seemed a better standard of education. When we went to check them out they didn't have a place for him in Form II, so we let him drop back into Form I. This probably was a good thing for Rylan to be a little older. Randal continued at Moray school where he started in October. He seemed to be doing fine at the school and got involved with swimming. Rylan also got involved with swimming and both boys really enjoyed the sports their schools provided.

In my January 21st letter I wrote: "We are having a baptismal service this Sunday. About eight new people are going to be baptized. This may sound rather strange but we are having it at a young Nazarene couple's yard, in a swimming pool, near where we go each Sunday." We had nearly 80 people present. Bob and Jim did the baptizing, all new Christians since we've come to Zimbabwe. It was really exciting and what was so wonderful is that six of these were men who are following the Lord."

Having left three of our children in the States when we came for our third missionary term was not at all easy. My mother was so faithful in writing almost every week, but I can't say this about our kids. So when we got word it was really special and uplifting. One of the events that I really hated to miss was our oldest son Allen's graduation from Marymount College in Salina, Kansas in May 1983. Allen did not have a high school graduation because he got his high school diploma through the University of Nebraska high school department. So I always felt really bad that he never experienced the marching with his class and receiving his diploma. Now that he was graduating with his class we couldn't be there. However Grandma and Grandpa Thornton filled that place for us, along with sister, Roxy and brother, Ron. Kim's parents, Don and Naomi Cavaness, and Kim's younger brother and sister, Bart and Amy, were also present.

I think our oldest son does get quite homesick at times. In a tape cassette we received from them recently they said they did have a nice Christmas with Kim's folks. Also their car's fuel pump gave out on them and they hit very icy roads and slid into a ditch some 70 miles from Atkinson where Kim's parents lived. Some of the Hendricks came along and helped them out by towing them to Kim's parents. I know the Lord had his hand on our kids.

Allen is applying to hospitals to finish his clinical training and is waiting to see which one accepts him.

While we were out in the northern suburb of Bulawayo called Alexander, the place where Charles Sanders lived when we came, the boys wanted to have a dog each so we went to the SPCA where they keep animals for adoption, to see what they had. Rylan got a Springer Spaniel which turned into a very good watchdog. It seems if you have dogs people aren't quite so apt to enter your place and steal. Randal got a puppy. Well, in the first few weeks each dog became sick. Randal's puppy died, but Rylan's dog lived.

When we moved, some people wanted to give us a Golden Lab named Lady. So now both boys have their dogs, "General Lee" and "Lady". Of course we figured Lady would present us with puppies and this is exactly what happened. One day Rylan was riding his bike in the neighborhood and this lab dog started following him and wouldn't go back to his house. Well, when he found we had a lady dog he decided for sure he wasn't going home. We couldn't make him either. So you can guess the rest of the story!

In my April 11th letter I write: "Guess what? Lady had her puppies; seven beautiful Golden Labradors, so they are a purebred bunch. Shane, who is the father, is a Golden Lab and the man who owns him has papers on him so we should get $20-$25 from each puppy. They were born last Friday. They are just going to be darling when they start walking around. Already several people have contacted us for one.

February 17, 1983, the Lo's and Bob and I left for the Pastors Retreat at Victoria Falls. The Lo's boys are staying with their house girl, Anna, and our boys are with the Nazarene couple where we baptized new Christians. This way they will not have to miss school. We are praying that this meeting will draw us all closer to the Lord. There are so many great needs here. "This week," I wrote, "we should be finding out what can be done about building the church. Bob and Jim are going to visit a builder on Thursday. We would like to have this building up by next November, so pray that we can accomplish this."

So many great spiritual things were happening in Zimbabwe that I want to share from my February 25th letter: "We got home safely from Victoria Falls on Sunday evening about 5:15 PM. We were very low on diesel too, but thank the Lord that He helped us to get home all in one piece. We had an outstanding meeting and the Lord really met with us. Roxy Lo and I didn't have interpreters but we had our lessons written out in Sindeble so we could read the lessons to the women. One lady did try to help us some, but her knowledge of English was very limited.

On Sunday we all got up very early, took down our tents and loaded our things. You see we were staying right in Victoria Falls the town, in a rest camp. After we got loaded up we drove out to Bethesda Mission, where we had the main service and then there was the baptismal service after that." I need to insert here that Bethesda Mission is an older mission begun by the reformed Baptists who joined the Wesleyans. They used to have missionaries there and a hospital and school, as well as the church.

The services were so good! Jim Lo preached and the church was really full. There were about a dozen that were baptized. The amazing thing is that most of them were under 25 years of age. The people in this country are very hungry to know God and are very receptive to the Gospel. Please pray for this country as it is very troubled.

Jim is going to get the English speaking church started very soon. He is having Bible studies right now and told us that six more people gave their hearts to the Lord. Today the children at school where I teach Scripture were so attentive as I told about Jesus raising from the dead, about how we need to invite him into our hearts. The children love to sing so I think I will take my accordion next week. We are planning for a VBS during the school holidays and so we do need prayer for this.

Now I go on to the March 4th letter and write: "I had such a wonderful class with the school children for my Scripture class. I have about 50 children to teach and it is so exciting. They are the ones I have been teaching the wordless book to. Today I did take my accordion and we sang with it. They really love this. I told Bob I really feel that I can serve God in this area. I love children and doing Child Evangelism. One never knows how much these children are influenced. I'm just really thankful for this opportunity.

I guess one never knows what they will be doing even on the mission field! In my March 4th letter I tell about playing for a wedding at the Nazarene church in Bulawayo. Since their missionary family left they have no one to play the organ, so I've been playing for them. I never dreamed I'd be playing music for weddings or I would have brought some of my music along. Anyway the folks are supposed to find music for me.

Here in my book I want to express a big thank you to Jim Lo. So many don't have a plan in mind when it comes to sharing about Christ and what he has done for us. So Jim had lessons for Bob and me to go through on Evangelism Explosion. It was a series of lessons, along with practical experience. Although Bob and I had led people to the Lord this gave us a simpler plan that was easy to explain to people what it means to receive Jesus as Savior and Lord. Jim took us with him in some of the visitation he was doing and after experiencing how he did the presentation he then allowed us to do the presentation to one who wanted to accept Christ. Knowledge is good but what I liked in his teaching was doing the actual presentation to people. After this training I felt very comfortable in talking to people about the Lord. Thank you again, Jim.

From my March 10th letter I write: "Jim and Bob are going to do visitation in the Kumalo area where Jim and Roxy live. There is no evangelical church in the area and it seems the doors are wide open. They will find those who want Bible studies, then have these studies for about three weeks. They will have the first service at a school in the area. Please pray for this endeavor. Our plans are to have the first service on Easter Sunday. We are really excited about the number of new Christians that have come to the Lord since our coming. Please pray for them as we try to disciple them. The other night Jim and Bob were so thrilled to have 22 people in Bob's TEE class. Not all of them are taking the class, but they seem so interested in the lessons and crave the spiritual truths they are taught."

March 15th letter: "This week eight more people have accepted the Lord. It is simply thrilling to see what God is doing. We are so excited to have our first English-speaking service on Easter Sunday. This week the boys are passing out flyers to announce this service in the community. Jim was able to get the school hall for our service. Jim has asked me to head up CYC for the English speaking church. So I've consented to do this. I told him I had never headed one up, but had taught a CYC class. So I will need to get some materials from headquarters. First term of school ends April 15 and will begin May 16th. Lots to do in the month of holiday!

From my April 11th letter. "What a wonderful weekend we have had! Bill and Elsie Morgan, Karl Gorman and his daughter Cora came up from South Africa. Bill has been our mission director but now they are returning to Canada and Karl Gorman will be taking his place. They came on Thursday arriving about 6:00 PM. Karl and Cora stayed with us and Bill and Elsie with the Lo's. Friday evening we had a special dinner in honor of the Morgan's. I got some bouquets of flowers downtown and fixed a most beautiful aster arrangement of pink and lavender shades for the table. We had turkey and dressing and I made apple and youngberry pies, with all the special things to go with it. We ate by candlelight. Bob had said I could get a copper candle holder that held three candles. I decorated the candles with blue bows and set it in the middle of the table with the bouquet. I set the table fancy and served in courses. Everyone seemed to enjoy the meal. At the end we presented Bill and Elsie a silver bell engraved with their names from the Los and us. They were quite surprised and pleased.

We had a nice Easter Sunday although it was quite a busy day with services. We started our services at the Mines Church at 7:00 a.m. and then at 10:00 we went into Bulawayo for our first English-speaking service. We had 31 people at the English-speaking church. Several new ones came in and another white couple came forward to be saved. We have mostly Blacks who attend the church. One of the men told me he really liked our church and was going to come all the time he could. By the end of this year we hope our church will be having 100 or more attending. I believe even before December we may reach our goal.

As missionaries there are three churches we are working with to develop. At the Farm and Mines churches we combined the services for the dedication. Bill Morgan preached the message for the dedication. About 80 people packed in the new building. The people had only a tree to worship under before the building went up. Rev. Inyoni and his wife came on the train from Victoria Falls for the dedication. He is the district superintendent for the Zimbabwe district. I need to add in here that the dedication and company came after Easter. For Easter dinner I invited the Lo family. I put in the oven a roast and cooked it very slow while we had church services. Our Roxane had sent some Easter egg dye for Randal and Rylan and so they and the Lo boys enjoyed dying Easter eggs.

First School Term Holiday

The school first term holiday was April 15th to May 17th. The Los went to South Africa to visit another young missionary couple who planned to furlough soon. Since they hadn't gone for a missionary retreat in January, it was good for them to get some time away from Bulawayo. We decided to stick around close to home, but take the boys to interesting places around the city. Although they haven't been to Victoria Falls yet, but I thought we would wait and take them when Orai and Linda come through in August on their way back to the states for furlough. We had a wonderful VBS in April with an average of 86 in attendance. Thirty 30 children opened their hearts to God.

For my birthday, May 12th, Jim and Roxy Lo invited us to come and have supper with them. In my May 12th letter I wrote: "I had breakfast in bed. Bob brought it to me this morning and now everyone is gone. Bob went with Jim to an evangelism seminar so today I decided I'd do just what I wanted to do, so I've read several pieces from the Reader's Digest and later I want to do some Tri- Chem painting and crocheting. It's quite cold today and rather misty outside, at least this is what Rylan said. They put the puppies inside their house and they are very unhappy. They are so cute now. Randy says they are little toddler puppies. We should be getting rid of them in about two weeks."

"The phone service in this country is terrible. In fact, they don't have direct dialing. You have to go through a telephone operator. In the morning's paper they say we should have better phone service by the end of the year.

From my letter May 19th, 1983: "Can you guess what we got today? The Lord really answered a want for us, for I don't really believe it was a need. That is just how God works for His children, though, and sometimes He just gives us something extra special. We now have a lovely piano in our house and Randal and I are both thrilled to death! In fact, right now he is playing some of the music from his music books and I really spent quite a bit of time playing tonight. I enjoyed it so much. We had been watching for a piano that was selling and had looked at about three different ones that were really rubbish heaps and the people were asking for each from $350 on up to $600. I decided if we couldn't find something better than those I just didn't want one.

Anyway, a lady who plays for the Nazarene church on Sunday mornings had heard that I was looking for one and she called me. I was quite sure that hers would be quite a good piano and I was right. It is an old piano but has had very good care and it is not an upright, so it doesn't look ancient. In fact, when she said she wanted $300 I could hardly believe my ears. I told her right off that we would take it. I just felt like it was an answer to prayer for us. Randal is going to start lessons probably next week with a lady here in Bulawayo. You see, here in Zimbabwe you can't buy a new piano that I know of so you have to take from someone who is leaving the country or pay a fantastic price to have one shipped in from South Africa."

From the same letter was this paragraph: "I got such a nice box from the Methodist youth which actually was instigated by Barb Glissman. She sent a box of craft material for all our holiday bible schools. It was so thoughtful of her to do something like this. It also included some candy for the boys and shirts and cake mixes. I really did appreciate it."

"Finally the puppies are going to new homes," I wrote in my May 26th letter, "We have sold three of our puppies and they are gone. We need to get rid of three more. The boys are keeping one of them and have named him Charlemagne."

In this same letter: "Jim Lo was here this afternoon and said that someone had written them that on one week of 'Wesleyana Phone' it was all about Zimbabwe. Please pray for us. We desperately need African pastors and leaders in this district. Even if we start churches we have no pastors to place in these churches. We just aren't sure where to go from here because we need good trained Zimbabwean pastors. We wonder if we should start a Bible School here to train them."

Back to the subject of the puppies from June 3rd letter: "We only have one little puppy left and he will probably go on Monday. We had an ad in the paper last weekend and I've never seen anything go so fast! I believe we could have sold two dozen of them if we had them. The people whose male dog was the father of the puppies didn't come to choose their little puppy and we thought that they didn't want one. After we had the others sold we found that they really did want one. So now the boys have to give the one they were going to keep to these people. Actually the man was really nice about it. We decided we would let Lady have another bunch of puppies by his dog; then the boys would keep one from the next batch. His dog has quite a pedigree, even some ancestors from England. We also thought if we waited then Ron could enjoy the puppy with us when he comes to visit next year."

"Tonight Rylan is at Nazarene youth service so Randal decided to bake some Cowboy cookies. He did most of it himself, even the baking. It is really nice when they can do this. Randal says to tell you they play their first soccer game at school on Tuesday. He is quite excited about soccer. Rylan doesn't play anything because of his knees. He has an appointment to see the bone specialist. "

June letters: "Another preaching point was opened on Sunday. Two lay leaders doing it were so thrilled. They had 12 in a house service. Please pray for these men and for another man who has been holding services at a place 60 kilometers from here. Bob and Jim went there on Saturday and had about 30 people."

"You will never believe what happened yesterday! We went to a funeral for the father of one of our pastors. We waited and waited for them to bring the body so we could have the service and finally someone arrived and announced they could not find the body of the man at the mortuary. Did you ever hear of the like? I really felt sorry for the family. I'm not sure what they will do. Someone said they thought the body had already been buried."

After Allen and Kim moved to Kansas City to finish his training, in a June 30th letter, he wrote: "The Lord has really been taking care of us." At this time Kim worked as an assistant manager at an athletic shoe store and Allen worked as a janitor cleaning an office building. Allen wasn't too thrilled living in the city and said he would be glad when his training ended."

It was last of May or first part in June that Ron and Roxane decided to make a trip to Canada with Grandpa and Grandma Thornton to see Aunt Elaine, Uncle Steve and April. At this time Roxy and Ron were trying to make a decision about Ron going to Seminary. They did finally make the decision to stay in Omaha to pastor in the Wesleyan church there. They had a two year recall.

Miss Esther Phillippe visited us in Bulawayo in July and spent about five days. She was having services at the different churches and conducting church education seminars. She was really good. After staying with us she went to stay at the Lo's.

Patti Bramsby wrote a very nice letter to us. She was in the States as an exchange student. She told about her plans to get together with our three older children Roxy, Allen and Ron. She was planning to spend a week in Omaha with Roxy and Ron.

Randal celebrated his 11th birthday on the 12th of July. Since he had soccer that day we celebrated his birthday on Thursday. He had four little boys from his class over and we invited the Lo's and Esther Phillippe to have pizza with us. I made him a football cake as well as a baseball mitt and baseball cake. Then we had homemade chocolate ice cream. For Rylan's 14th birthday on the 19th, I made pizza again at his request. (It had to be made from scratch.)

Esther had to leave on Sunday so Bob and I did the evening services so the Los could take her to the airport. That day we learned that next year we would have a tour group come through to visit our work, very welcome because we had so little company.

"This past Sunday we had 71 at the English speaking service. Pray that somehow we can get a church built for this work. We desperately need it. Dr. Lytle says there are no finances for building more churches, so maybe we will start our own building fund and God will somehow help it to grow. We do know we are in God's will here."

During August we had a great Scripture Union Camp. I wrote to our son, Ron: "I believe it is the best kid's camp I've ever been in. However, it wasn't really a rest because Bob usually got up about 5:30 AM to take two groups of kids game viewing, then they would have their devotions on a little kopie (hill). Stuart and DeAnn are really good leaders with kids. Stuart told the 'Adventures of Hiawatha' and worked them into a real spiritual application. It was really fantastic!"

"I should tell you about the bus hijacking that the leaders did. They all wore Indian headdresses and made tomahawks and took them to a certain place where they were to stop the bus. Then they got their kids into their special groups and had a walk back to the camp where we stayed."

"The camp was at a school about 20 km from Bulawayo. It's quite well protected with security. They even had police keeping watch for several days. It even had a security fence around it which was locked every night. We praised the Lord for protection. I had a Bible study every evening before supper and the children's message on Sunday. At this camp we had 72 kids and about 90 total with leaders and workers. I prayed with about five or six children."

Orai and Linda Lehman came after our camp finished. We then had our District conference Thursday through Sunday morning. At our English speaking service we had about 140 present. It was thrilling to hear some of the testimonies of our new Christians.

August 29th letter: "We plan to go to Harare to visit Jim and Barbara Sage and their two girls. While we are up there the boys have an appointment with an orthodontist and we have to try getting our South African visas." Later:"I must tell you about our trip to Harare. We had some restful days and it was really good to get away from home for a while. We stayed with some Nazarene missionaries, Jim and Barbara Sage and their girls." I told earlier about the Sage's living in Bulawayo. This is where we got acquainted. They invited us to stay with them in Harare. While we were there, they took us to a lion park and a small game park and went to an agricultural show. We heard and saw President Banana and his wife at the show. Then we returned to Bulawayo on Sunday afternoon."

"We had Hudson and Diana Mazwi and their boys over for supper on Tuesday evening before Wilma left for Zambia. In honor of Wilma's birthday, which is September 1st, I baked a cake and made homemade ice cream. That cake turned out a real flop. It was a Dixieland box mix that someone had sent in a parcel and I'm sure it was really old.

News from Nebraska: Rev. Duane Lauber was voted Nebraska District Superintendent. We wondered who would put out our missionary form letters now. The people renting us our 95 Cecil Avenue house want to sell it and we had to be out by October 31st, and if possible, even by September 30th. I dreaded moving again and had such high hopes that this term we could live in one house for the whole term.

We found a house not far from the one we were living in. The address is 9 Ulswater Drive and it is still in the suburb of Morningside and about the same distance to schools for the boys. It is a much smaller house but does have a lovely yard. Now I have quite a job ahead of me getting everything packed up again and ready to move before the end of September.

However, before we made this move we had visitors again. The Ramsay's came with their daughter Shari and their friends from Indiana. Roxy said she didn't know how to cook food for diabetics so they kept Ramsay's and we kept their friends. These people were so nice to us; they gave us $7000 for the building fund and also took us to the Holiday Inn for lunch. We also had the Ramsay's come for a meal and then on Saturday we all had a braai (cookout) at the Hillside Park. They left after lunch on Sunday.

According to my September 26th letter we learned that Ron and another boy were mugged in Omaha as they were on their way home from work. I'm so glad they weren't hurt badly.

October 4th, "We are pretty well settled into our new house, all except the kitchen. I have so much stuff that I just don't have any more room. The kitchen is much smaller than the other house." In fact, we did not even have enough room for the refrigerator so it had to go into the dining room. I wrote, "I think even though this house is smaller we will like it better. It also has a fireplace in the living room and all wood floors except the kitchen and bathroom. They look nice and shine beautiful." I don't know if I should say that we have a swimming pool now, but in this city probably three-fourths of the houses where European people lived have pools. So in trying to find a house without a pool to rent in the location we needed would have been rather difficult. Rylan and Randal put the pool to use. We really enjoyed our big yard and the privacy we had in it. On the 16th of October we used the pool for a baptismal service and 15 or 16 people were baptized. About 50 people came and afterwards we had a fellowship time. The ladies cooked hard porridge with "Umshibo" (gravy meat and vegetables) on the outside fireplace. I had fixed a cake and oatmeal bars and had tea. Everyone seemed so happy and blessed. At our morning service on the 16th we had over 130 people. We are growing by leaps and bounds and just thank the Lord. We hope to start building in about two or three months.

"Another thing which we are praising the Lord for is the lovely rains he gave us on Friday and Saturday. Now everything is going to green up so fast. All the Jacaranda trees are in full bloom so the city is a lavender hue with all the varied colors of bougainvillea scattered throughout. It is really just gorgeous when spring comes"

October 5th letter stated: "Last Friday I asked if there were any children who wanted to pray and ask Jesus into their hearts to just stay after the class finished. I was so amazed that 27 children stayed to pray. Then in my Sunday school class on Sunday I asked during class if there were any children who wanted to pray to receive Jesus and two little girls stayed behind and asked if I could pray with them. It seems to me that here the children are so receptive to the Gospel. Tomorrow I began a class for Scripture Union at the Kumalo school.

During October we conducted a Sunday School Convention asking all the teachers and workers to attend. On Tuesday evening we had a banquet and Wednesday and Thursday evenings we held classes. Bob spoke on "Are your students doers of the Word?" I stressed the point of memory work and different ways of doing it. Everyone seemed to get a lot of good. In fact, I could really tell our adult teachers had taken many things to heart and were putting them into practice.

"On Monday we had a braai here in our yard. Los, the Evans (Assembly of God couple), the Cornets and Mazwis all came over. They brought their own meat and carried in salads and desserts so it wasn't hard work for me. The children enjoyed the swimming pool.

"Last night I went to Rylan's parent-teacher conference at Christian Brother's College. He is doing very well and teachers commented on how mature he acts. He is one of the top in his class except math. He is about 14 down from the top of about 35 or 40 students so the teacher seemed pleased with his progress. His high classes are History, English, Geography and Science. His language classes are quite good.

This Saturday Randal had a swimming gala at Morray School and Bob was to be a timekeeper for it. We were so proud of him for winning the trophy."

November 3rd: "This is a terribly busy day. It is Roxy Lo's birthday. I'm fixing her a cake and birthday supper. I plan to make a cake in the shape of an umbrella if I can find all the stuff for decorating. Then I have a chiropractor treatment and will get my hair cut, besides getting groceries. Anyway, I'll manage, but sometimes I wonder why everything falls on the same day. (It still does sometimes.)"

November 9th: "Today was women's meeting at Roxy's house. We are sewing on quilts. We have two completed. I'm really proud of how they are turning out. Some missionary society sent us five quilt kits. Each kit contained all the blocks for the quilt, two spools of thread, yarn for tying them and the backing. I really have enjoyed working with this group. We have had as many as six machines going. The African ladies have hand turned machines, but it certainly is quicker than trying to do it all by hand. Out at the mines I plan to start a women's meeting and do sewing. There we definitely will do sewing by hand.

Israel and Victoria Langa and three children have been in the States about four years, so in November I wrote: "Israel gave their car to Allen and Kim. I thought that was really nice of them. They are getting ready to come back to Africa. They leave from Bartlesville and have Christmas with Bertie Lemley in West Virginia, then fly out and will be in Swaziland by New Years. Israel wrote a letter telling us that Victoria had some kind of sickness, but not related to her operation. He said they would have to wait seven months to see what it is. I thought this was a cute way of putting that a baby was on the way."

It is quite amazing to me as I'm writing this book that way back on December 1, 1983, I wrote to my mother, "I want to thank you for your encouraging words about my writing a book. I have always had this desire to write a book. That is one of the reasons I've been asking you to save my letters. I think it will be a book about our family, so it will be more for just our children and grandchildren to read. Your encouragement has inspired me."

On December 1st: "You'll never guess what happened to us two missionary families now!!! First the pickup broke a belt that runs the alternator or something like that, so we can't run it because we cannot find any belts here. Jim is supposed to bring one from South Africa. He flew down for a meeting on Monday and is coming back today. Second thing that happened, our car went on the blink. We had been out calling in the Kumalo area and then on the way home Bob put the car into reverse and couldn't get it out, so had to call the garage to come and tow us in. Third thing that happened; this morning Roxy called me and said, "You won't believe this, but I can't get my car started! When it rains it pours! Anyway, we hope that their car only needed the lines bled. Ours is probably going to really cost a fortune because the trouble was with the gearbox. Anyway, the Lord knows about these problems.

Fortunately, we have some good Nazarene friends who helped us out. I'm just glad that our boys have bikes to ride to school."

I'll be really proud and happy when December 22nd gets here. We will have been married 25 years on that day. Can you believe it? Hardly seems only yesterday I was preparing for our wedding. Anyway, they have been such wonderful years and I expect to reach 50 and maybe even 60 years, the Lord willing and he doesn't come back first.

Tonight the boys got the Christmas tree up. You'll never guess how we decorated it this year. I got red ribbon and had saved the cotton out of the vitamin bottles. The tree has on it red ribbons and cotton balls, a bit of tinsel and pinecones we gathered along the road. Really it looks nice and quite different.

Our Kumalo church made nearly $650 for their building fund. We sold the quilts that our women's group made at a yard sale. We have such wonderful people in the Kumalo church. We praise the Lord how we see they are growing spiritually. Two more new Christians who recently gave their hearts to the Lord got up and gave their testimony before the church. One was a man, the other a woman.

On Saturday I fixed a big dinner for the families of the women who helped me clean my house on Cecil Avenue after we moved. We had a braai, but it rained so I fixed five chickens in my oven. I had jello salad, potato salad and lettuce salad and baked rolls. About 26 people were present and everyone seemed to enjoy it and we had a great time of fellowship."

December 21st letter: "We have company! Jenny Madden and her son, Jonathan, are going to spend Christmas with us. We are really grateful for this because I always like to have someone special to spend Christmas with. She was planning to visit missionaries in Zambia, but she couldn't get a visa. So they came back to us intending to go on to Johannesburg. We convinced them to spend Christmas with us and the Los. Her son, Jonathan, is between our boys in age so it has worked out quite nicely. The boys have been camping in our front yard and sleeping out all night."

So now we closed out the year 1983. "We had a lovely Christmas Day at the Lo's. We had a lovely Christmas church service at Kumalo with all the Bulawayo churches participating. There were about 120 present, quite a good number considering so many go to their communal homes at Christmas.

It was so good to have Jenny Madden and her son with us. Yesterday, December 27th, we took them to the train station and they headed back to Johannesburg."

One last note for the year is that Lady had her second batch of puppies, mostly black ones because they weren't thoroughbreds. We sold most of them, but the Nazarene Pastor lost their other one, so we gave them one of these. The boys are keeping one of these puppies, too. So the year 1983 ends with our preparation to go to South Africa for the Missionary Council and Retreat in January.

1984

The year 1984 began with a trip to South Africa. Our Missionary Council meeting was January 3 - 6 in Brakpan. Brother O. I. Lehman invited us to stay at Boksburg where Orai and Linda lived before they went on furlough. We always enjoyed staying there except this time Orai, Linda and family were gone. Orai's dad was holding the fort for them.

We had a great time in South Africa. We did a lot of shopping for things we couldn't get in Zimbabwe and, of course, everything was much cheaper. The boys got things with the Christmas money they received, like watches, soccer ball, and things for their bikes, as well as clothes. In one of my first letters of the year I stated, "They had a happy time shopping."

Of course we had many friends in the Johannesburg area and so it was so nice to visit again. The Ramsay's were pastoring the Boksburg church so we had lunch one day with them. Then another night the Shackels, friends of Orai and Linda, invited us to have supper with them. Remember the lady and her son, Jenny Madden and her son Johnathan, who had Christmas with us when they couldn't get into Zambia because of no visas? She invited our family to come and eat with them. Then she took us to the Musical Fountains afterwards. It was so pretty. They play music while different kinds of colored lights shine on the water spraying up in many designs. It was beautiful and they played Christmas music.

January 11th we headed back to Zimbabwe. The boys then began school January 17th Randal is in the 6th grade at Morray School and Rylan enters Form II at CBC.

Zimbabwe is really suffering from lack of rain. In fact, the day we came back from South Africa the temperature was 40° centigrade, which is 104° Fahrenheit. It felt like we were in an oven as our car doesn't have air conditioning. In Bulawayo we are having water restrictions and one can only water with a bucket – no hoses allowed. People will suffer because there will be no food because of the lack of rain.

Alfred Cheney, Bob's Dad, Comes to Visit

We are very much looking forward to the visit of Bob's dad. He is bringing a suitcase of presents from the family. Of course, our boys are excited about this.

We had been thinking Grandpa could go to Zambia for Naomi Swan's and Eugene Vanhaus' wedding. They changed the date from the 14th to the 18th, so it wouldn't work. However, we do plan to take him to Victoria Falls February 3rd, 4th or 5th. We are hoping Wilma Cheney can get to Victoria Falls so that her dad can see her, too.

The folks from Zambia arrived about 5:30 Friday afternoon. We all stayed at a camp called Zambezi Camp, about five or six kilometers out of Victoria Falls. Wilma came with the Thompson's, Naomi and Eugene, and Leland Swan who had come for Naomi's wedding to 'give her away'. We all had a grand time together. This is the first time our boys have seen the falls, so they really enjoyed walking around. It is so beautifully green at the falls because they have had more rain. In Bulawayo strict water restrictions start tomorrow – only 800 liters a day allowed.

We showed Dad Cheney around the city of Bulawayo, taking him to a train museum and showing him where the new Kumalo Church would be built. He also enjoyed visiting with our neighbors, the Goodes. In fact the Goodes took him around some, too.

Naomi Swan's Wedding

Naomi is my mother's first cousin, although she and I were very near in age .She went to Zambia as a missionary teacher. During her missionary career she met a very fine single missionary by the name of Eugene Vanhaus. A relationship began between these two that eventually ended in marriage. These two decided to have their wedding day February 18, 1984, at Jembo Mission in Zambia, Africa. Naomi asked Bob and me to sing the song "Each for the Other" at their wedding. They did not have a piano there in Jembo, so I prepared a cassette tape on which I played the music. Then Bob and I were able to sing along with it. We stayed only one night at Jembo Mission. Then we went back to Choma to spend the weekend with Wilma, Bob's sister. We got back to Bulawayo on Monday.

Leland Swan was even able to visit us in Zimbabwe, too, after the wedding. It was so neat to be able to show him the mission work that was being done in Zimbabwe. He then took the train to Johannesburg to fly back to the States.

Building a New Church, 1984

From my letter of January 17, 1984 I wrote: "Very soon we are planning the groundbreaking service for our new Wesleyan Church in the Kumalo suburb of Bulawayo .Jim asked the mayor to be present for this service too, so we are just waiting to see which date he chooses that fits his schedule. Either it will be the 5th or 12th of February. Today Jim and Bob were out checking the prices of bricks and building materials. We are getting very excited about building. Praise the Lord we are finally seeing a dream fulfilled! We took pictures of the groundbreaking service and one was of me lifting a shovelful of dirt. The building as of February 24th had not actually been started yet, but we were expecting it to start soon.

Bob and I enrolled in an Evangelism Explosion III International class with Jim Lo, our other missionary here. I can honestly say that I have never, in all my life, been so excited and thrilled with evangelism. It is a class that takes about 17 weeks for full training. It is sharpening our evangelism tools and the Lord is directing our lives toward greater emphasis in personal evangelism. What is most thrilling is going out to witness with one who has been through the lessons. You learn the practical along with the book.

After our training we take a test and if we pass we then can take others to teach in this program. Really, I don't think Bob and I have ever been so excited, nor felt the urgency of getting God's message to people who really aren't sure they will go to heaven when they die. Our hearts cry out "Lord, help us to witness to everyone who isn't sure." Our goal has been, and still is, to touch at least 100 families per year."

It isn't that Bob and I have not been witnessing and winning people to the Lord. It is that this program has helped us so much in the presenting of

Christ to the lost. Bob and I have been so grateful to Jim Lo for his training in a very workable presentation for people who aren't sure of their readiness for Heaven. Still, to this day, I share with people with this method of explaining the plan of Salvation.

"As Bob and I shared with one family last Saturday, three accepted the free gift of eternal life. We had invited Bob's prayer partner, Isaiah, to go along with us. He was so delighted with the message and our method of witness that he acknowledged he could hardly wait to enroll in a class with us. He is very anxious to be able to witness to his handicapped friends because he says they feel God has no use for them."

Isaiah was born a cripple from birth and has had a lot to overcome. However, he is a very smart young man. We feel the Lord is going to use him in a mighty way. We are working really hard on the follow-up of new Christians. It is fine to win them to the Lord, but we must help them to grown in the Lord and become established. So in my March 2nd letter I write: "Please pray with us and for the many new Christians we are seeing won to the Lord each week. We know that without prayer we just as well give up for it is not in our power that we are doing this. It is in God's power and we must give Him the glory and honor."

Conrad and Susan Braun came here from Edmonton, Canada. He is here on a teaching assignment. I told her about my young sister and husband being at Lac la Biche, Alberta. I've talked to her about the Lord and she seems to really want to serve God. I'm hoping when they go back to Canada she will be able to look up my sister, Elaine.

The boys had their sports days on the same day. It was hard for us to attend both because Bob was helping out at Randal's school. Bob already volunteered for this before we knew about Rylan's. Anyway, Rylan did first in long jump, first in the 100-meter run and first in hurdles. He broke the record at CBC for hurdles. Randal got second in high jump at Morray School.

On April 8th I wrote: "We are really looking forward to our "Easter in Africa" tour group visit. We are having a baptismal service while they are here. Both our boys, Rylan and Randal, want to be baptized at this time. We are keeping one couple from Ohio – the Wards. Paul Swauger brought this group and Cliff and Naomi Ward are the couple we kept from Ohio. They are the aunt and uncle of my friend, Joanne Goodman, from college. Our visitors did come April 24th, 25th and 26th, and were able to attend the special combined service and the baptismal at the farm church. We had hoped to have our Kumalo Church building, but this hasn't started yet. We only had the ground-breaking service on February 12th with 160 people attending; hoping to start this building soon.

Letter to My Mother

P.O. Box 9058
Hillside, Bulawayo
Zimbabwe, Africa
May 13, 1984
Mother's Day

Dearest Mother,

You will be very surprised to get this special letter from me, I know. However, I have felt for some time how I'd like to express to you in words how I really thank God for such a wonderful Mother, as you are to me. As time moves on, I have become even more aware of just really how much you mean to me.

The other day as I was washing clothes, my thoughts went back to quite a few years ago when I was a girl. Remember how you taught us about cleaning the washer and leaving it shining, looking like a new one again? I'm so glad that in the little things you taught us the value and care of material things. I know you never had a lot of things, but what you had you took good care of. This, too, has reminded me to teach values to my own children, and appreciation.

Then do you remember what we girls used to do when it came time for doing dishes? I'm sure you do. How could you forget? It isn't an easy task to train three girls. When you called and said we were to do the dishes many times we would slip away to play. Just hoping, perhaps, mother would do the dishes. But always, when we came back later, the dishes were still on the table waiting. I'm sure many times you may have felt it would be easier to do the task yourself, and get the job over. But you didn't and that was good. Because you see Mother, dear, you were teaching us responsibility.

There are memories of our church. Thank you Mother, and Daddy too, for taking us to Sunday school and church and for teaching us about family devotions. I know Mother that you have spent many hours in prayer for me. Thank you for those prayers. Even now I know you and Daddy are holding us up to God in prayer.

As I grow older I realize more and more how much you have really done for me, Mother. Having children of my own has brought into sharper focus the things that one's own mother has faced and gone through. Thank you, Mother, for your patience with me. I know now that it really does take a lot of patience and perseverance. Thank you for not giving up, even though you felt like it.

Remember the time when as a young teenage girl I realized a certain boy wanted to date me? Thanks for taking time to talk with me and to listen. I feel certain if more mothers would take time to listen to their teenagers instead of telling them in short words, then many young people would not have the problems so many do. I'm sure your prayers entered in here at this stage of my life. You wanted God's best for my life and though I didn't actually understand it all at the time, deep in my heart I too wanted God's best. When I prayed that prayer one afternoon by my bedside, after coming from the high school, I really meant it. I prayed, "Lord if I can't have a Christian home then I would rather not be married." I praise God because I feel he honored that prayer. It is wonderful being married to Bob. I can never thank God enough. We have such a wonderful Christian home and five children who live and serve the Lord plus to more wonderful children, a son-in-law and a daughter-in-law.

And now Mother, more than ever, I appreciate the time you take in writing letters every week. You can never know how much it means to know that usually every week I find a letter in our post box from you and Daddy. Sometimes I wish we didn't have to be halfway round the world from you, but I also know God can watch over you and Daddy as well as our family here in Zimbabwe. Best of all is the fact that I know you want us in the center of God's will and that this is where we feel God has put us for now. But I must add, I'm really looking forward to August 1986 if Jesus tarries and hasn't come to take us all to heaven.

Mother you may feel you've done so very little for God, but really you have done one of the greatest jobs for God on earth. You have been a wonderful, praying mother of three girls. I really love you and thank you so much, though I cannot find enough words to express my true feeling of gratefulness and thankfulness and love. There are many more things I could say, but I think I'll close with this little poem I found in the Ideal's Mother's Day book.

For You, Mother

Pink roses for you, Mother
On this your special day.
I've wrapped them up with love, dear,
To greet you in this way.

You deserve the loveliest flowers,
The best that life can hold,
The best my heart can offer,
The best when all is told.

You mean so much dear Mother,
How can I ever say
The many, many thank yous
That are in my heart today?
Georgia B. Adams

(I wish I really could wrap some of my roses to give you. This time we will just have to pretend and then one day I hope I can.)
With All My Love and Prayers
Your Loving Daughter,
Eva

Ron Comes to Visit

We were all so glad when Ron arrived at the Bulawayo airport on June 3rd. Before he came, I searched and inquired around about him being able to visit some of the hospitals for some practical experience. The ambulance service already told me that he should contact them when he gets in and maybe he can do some volunteer work or at least observe.

Letter to My Father

Father's Day
17 June 1984

Dear Daddy,

Today is Father's Day! I hope it was a really good day for you As I sit here by the fireplace warming my feet I have lots of memories of home, the home you and mother made for we three girls This letter is just a special way of saying thank you for all you did for us

Speaking of memories – well, the fireplace reminds me of gathering wood, cow chips and bringing in the coal! Believe it or not, I even remember going to get those big loads of cow chips and making big piles at the house so we could keep warm during winter. I consider this an excellent experience – maybe not at the time – but now. We did it as a family – gathering up provisions for keeping us warm those long cold winter days and nights
Then I appreciate how you taught us girls about money. You were wise in giving us special things to do to earn money Like all those horrible Mexican sandburs which we pulled – for each pile of ten we got one cent and for each cow we milked five cents. I know you and mother didn't have the training along some lines of child rearing, but you seemed to know how it should be done in many areas I'm sure God helped you I also appreciated so much the facts you taught and showed by your example of tithing I shall always be grateful to you for this I know you and mother never had a lot of money, but you were faithful in your giving to the church and still are.

You, Daddy, were the spiritual head of our home. Every morning we had family devotions for as long as I can remember. This has greatly influenced my life and even Bob's. So many Christians today forget family devotions or say they can't find time.
With All My Love and Prayers,
Your Loving Daughter,
Eva

The Good News, 1984

In October I wrote to my parents and said, "I'm sure you may not know what the good news is, so I better tell you. About next June you should be great-Grandpa and Grandma again – Roxy had a lab test which showed she is pregnant, but she hasn't been to the doctor yet. I'm so excited! When she called us, I guess I made such a commotion of excitement that even our next door neighbors heard. I felt a little embarrassed when she asked me about it. But she told her husband it could only be one thing and that was a new grandchild on the way! Anyway, I've got lots of ideas in mind and wishes, too. If the Lord is willing and we can save up enough money, maybe I can come for your 50th wedding anniversary and a new grandchild too! Please pray about this with me."

Then on November 18th, we had another surprise call from Allen and Kim at 2:00 am. It was such exciting news, but this time I tried not to be too noisy as everyone else was asleep. However, Bob said in his sermon yesterday morning that he was sleeping with one ear and listening with the other ear. So now we are expecting to have two grandchildren, one due June 17th and the other on June 29th. I wrote: "How's that for timing!"

In Bob's sermon, the first one to preach in our new church, he told about the phone call. But he said he would tell about the bad news first. The bad news was that Nebraska lost their football game to Oklahoma and as soon as he said it, Dennis Engle yelled out "yippee!" Everyone laughed and then he told our good news

Now I had several reasons for hoping the Lord would allow me to take a trip back to the US. Our first two grandchildren, my parents 50th wedding anniversary and then, as time went on, we learned that Julie and Cliff would be married and I had my 30th anniversary for high school reunion. So we prayed a lot, hoping God would open the doors if it was His will.

When I asked our 12 year old son, Randal, how it seemed to know he is going to be an uncle he said, "It's better than being a grandma!" Well, I guess it is a matter of opinion!"

The New Church Dedicated

From my letter written November 12: "Our District Conference starts Friday morning, November 16th .Our guests will be arriving on November 14th and 15th. Orai Lehman, Dennis Engle, Karl Gorman and Rev. S. Sigwane, our Regional Superintendent, are coming. Women's Conference will be on Friday and on Saturday our District Church Conference meets. Then, On Sunday we will have our first service in the First Wesleyan Church of Bulawayo. In the afternoon will be our dedication service. We are expecting a church filled to overflowing. Tomorrow the youth are circulating flyers about the program.

There were quite a few last minute things that need to be done. The women and I were out today looking for flower planters to place in the front of the church. Bob and Jim were over doing touch ups and last minute painting and Jim fixed a church sign. The women were planning to wax the floors today. Then sometime we have to put all the chairs in the church, move a piano in and it's hard to tell what else. We are so happy that finally it is a dream fulfilled and not just something we are talking about.

The dedication day arrived. It all went great and we just praise the Lord. I feel the most exciting thing was that the Lord spoke to a woman's husband that we had been praying for, for a long time. He came forward and prayed to receive Christ. Also, another young man came forward. For the first service in the Church, this was so exciting. We had over 200 in the morning service and also around 200 for the dedication service. We had a special surprise about visitors. On Wednesday before, Linda Lehman called me from Boksburg in South Africa. She said they had visitors and wondered if we would like them to come to Bulawayo. The visitors were Bertie Lemley and Delbert and John and Carol Chisler and their son, Van. When she said who the visitors were I got so excited. She said Bertie and Delbert came out with the Chisler family mainly to visit in Swaziland where Bertie had served as a missionary nurse during our first term. Delbert is about Randal's age except a bit heavier. He and Randal got along fine and really enjoyed each other's company. The other boy, Van Chisler, was Rylan's age; in fact they are only a week apart in age. It was nice for our boys to have visitors their age.

The boys are getting closer to the end of their school year. Randal had his swimming Gala. He won the trophy for the Senior Boys Champion so we are really proud of him. Now he is practicing every day for the Interschool Gala at CBC on November 24th. This is when other schools participate. He is still on the cricket team and should be finding out soon if he gets to go to Harare to play. Rylan will be writing exams again this week. He didn't have school last week because he has been writing what they call his JC exams.

From November 26th letter: "I was hoping it wouldn't be such a busy week but Roxy Lo called and said the youth are planning a weekend retreat this weekend, so it sounds like we will be busy anyway. I don't think any of us have really gotten rested up from the conference and dedication. Last weekend I helped a couple days preparing for our Thanksgiving Banquet. We had a missionary couple stay with us on Thanksgiving night, on their way to South Africa. They are missionaries from Zambia, Alan and Myrna Houston. We were so pleased to have them. The Peeds were also with the Houston's, a young missionary couple from Zambia and their two young children. They stayed with the Lo's. We had our Thanksgiving Banquet at the Seventh Day Adventist Hall and about 64 people attended. It is really nice to have quite a number of missionaries serving in Zimbabwe who have come from the US. Mainly they are Nazarenes, Seventh Day Adventists, Assembly of God, Brethren in Christ and Wesleyans.

I mentioned earlier how it was terribly dry. Well, in this November 26th letter, I write: "Thank the Lord for rain. We got another lovely rain last night and everything is looking gorgeous." I told Mother I wished I could give her a bouquet of my beautiful roses from our garden. They are so pretty and just loaded with blooms and buds. I have dark red, pink, yellow, peach and yellow-gold roses. Our yards are beginning to look so much better now. I think it is more beautiful here now than I've ever seen it in Bulawayo.

The Month of December, 1984

Christmas was always such a special time, even here in Zimbabwe where we have hot Christmases. Rylan and Randal were growing up fast and doing well. They enjoyed the long school holiday, which seemed to go all too quickly. We were so thrilled to hear that our son, Ron, at school in the University of Nebraska, was able to spend Christmas with the Ramsay family and several other missionary kids in South Carolina. Some wonderful people sent him a plane ticket so he could do this. When he called us Christmas morning, he was just bubbling over with joy. God is so good!

Grandpa Alfred Cheney had arrived the 6th of December, bringing all kinds of gifts and goodies from family and folks in America. We had a lovely Christmas. Wilma Cheney, Naomi and Eugene Vanhaus and the Lo family all had Christmas dinner with us on the 21st of December. While we are in South Africa the Vanhaus' will stay in our house. We made plans to leave December 22nd for Boksburg, South Africa, to celebrate Christmas Day with the O.D. Lehman family, Wilma Cheney and Grandfather Cheney.

In my December 31st letter I gave a prayer request: "Pray for our outreach program in the western suburb of Emtumbane. We really do need a church in this area. Our building fund is growing slowly, but it needs to grow faster if a new church goes up in 1986. On December 16th, when we had our Christmas service under the tree on our church site, three women came forward to pray and give their hearts to Christ. Not only do we want to win new souls to Christ, we must help them grow and mature in the Lord.

We headed for South Africa for our Mission Council. December 22nd through January 4th. We received our two-year work permits and so this would not trouble us at the border like it did when we first arrived in Zimbabwe. The Los were hoping to get their permits very soon so they could also attend Mission Council. After our Missionary Council and getting our mission vehicles repaired in Brakpan, we returned to Zimbabwe. And so ends the year 1984.

The Exciting Year of 1985

We began the new year in Boksburg attending our missionary council meeting and the European camp. At our missionary council, Jim Ramsey was elected as mission director since the Gorman's will be leaving in May. Also at this missionary counsel, it was decided our family should furlough in May, 1986, and the Lo's in November so that we didn't leave the church body all on its own. This would give the church in Zimbabwe more time to adapt. At the European camp, Rev Farlow from the US and another man from the Johannesburg area gave us some wonderful preaching. It is always so refreshing to us as missionaries to get in on services like these.

The first thing on our list was to take our pickup and car into the garage to see what they needed to have done. It is better to get an overhaul of a motor here because Zimbabwe doesn't have that much know- how to do a good job.

We arrived back in Zimbabwe January 11th. I drove the car and Bob drove the pickup, all in one day, over 900 kilometers or about 500 miles. I felt quite exhausted from the trip. In fact, it was boiling hot down at Biet Bridge where we cross the border. We had to spend a little extra time at the border because Bob had forgotten to have our residence permits stamped in into our passports. Thankfully, we did have the permits. Wilma Cheney and Grandpa Cheney came back to Zimbabwe with us and then Wilma, Naomi and Eugene VanHaus traveled back to Zambia.

After hearing the wonderful news of two grandchildren coming – our first two, I started praying and making plans to fly back to the US for an extended visit. My parent's 50th wedding anniversary would be May 19th 1985. It would be so nice to make this a great celebration for them. Of course, I would need to coordinate this with my sisters, Esther in Oregon and my youngest sister, Elaine, in Canada. I would also need to find the money for a ticket. I found that if I got my ticket in January it would cost a little over $1,000. Bob found that on an Apex ticket you would not have the cost of the ticket changed after you paid for it. So Bob had our Mission Director buy the ticket before it changed. I had about $600 toward the ticket at that time and trusted the Lord to help me get the rest.

Besides my working with the Scripture Union classes at the school and the work of our churches, I did a lot of sewing, crocheting and Tri-Chem painting. I made a maternity dress to send to Roxy for her birthday and also during this time was crocheting two baby blankets for our two expected grandchildren.

In my January 12th letter I wrote of my concern for our parents. My sisters and I had heard that during a bad winter storm their car broke down and they had to walk home in the snow and cold. It was probably at least two or three miles that they had to walk in this bad snow storm. Daddy was having a lot of heart trouble, but Mother was able to keep him going until they reached the house. I'm so glad they didn't freeze to death out on the prairie. My cousin, James French, came to help get their car home, which was so nice of him. I urged my parents to always call when they got home or have some-one call to see that they did get home. Then I put in a suggestion that maybe they should come and live in Africa for the winter months. I said they could come as Gospel Core workers for the Wesleyan Church. Dad could help us with building churches and Mom could teach the women about sewing. My mother was an expert seamstress and quilt maker. I guess this was all just wishful thinking on my part.

Also in this January 12th, 1985, letter I wrote about our historical Re-gional Conference: "We had such a good conference. For the first time in South African history the Wesleyan Church has elected a national regional su-perintendent. The conference was held in Swaziland and about 200 people at-tended. It was held at a new teacher training college in Nhlangano. Our na-tional regional superintendent is now Rev. S. Sigwane.

By January 17th our boys were back in school starting a new year. We were back in language study again. (I think I failed to write about Jake and Nancy Shenk who are missionaries with the Brethren in Christ. They have been missionaries for years and Jake can speak like a national. He is teaching us the Ndebele language.) Bob is back on the school council at Randal's school. So as the term proceeds we seem to get busier by the day. I now have two scripture classes to attend and choir on Friday's. Bob is teaching two days a week some of our nationals and also doing visitation besides doing our regu-lar services. Last Sunday Bob and Jim had to drive to Gweru, about 160 kilo-meters from here, to visit one of our men who had been in a serious car acci-dent. So always there seems plenty to do. Yesterday Bob went out in the West-ern suburbs to a new school which is across from our church lot. We are trying to get a classroom to hold our services in until we are able to get our church built. So pray hard that we will be able to rent one of these classrooms. It's so hard meeting under a tree, especially at this time of year when we have lots of rain. Praise the Lord, though, for the rain! The dams are filling up quite quickly. Our garden is doing quite nicely. Yesterday Grandpa Cheney picked roasting ears for me. We had roasting ears, spinach and cucumbers all from our garden. We should have tomatoes soon. The Los have beautiful mango trees at the mission house where they live and we have been enjoying those too.

I often have back problems and so in my February 4th letter I write that I was able to find an osteopathic doctor and am hoping to get some relief, as I had to go to bed it was so bad. That very Saturday Bob had the District Board meeting at our house. Of all the times for my back to give out, it certainly wasn't an ideal time. But thanks to our wonderful, helpful, young son Randal, I was able to cope. He made tea and helped make the dinner. Bless his heart, he worked like a trooper. Rylan had gone to a friend's house before I knew my back was bad. By the February 13th letter my back was much better. We also learned we had a new nephew born February 5th to Don and Vivian Lark. So now Grandpa Cheney has 17 grandchildren and five great-grandchildren. Grandpa is planning to go up to see Wilma at Victoria Falls March 8th – 10th. He will fly up from here and then they will pick him up at the Victoria Falls airport. They will spend the weekend together before he leaves for the US on March 14th.

We have great news about Randal. He is becoming so grown up and responsible. The school chose him as a prefect, which means he wears a badge and helps the teachers with their classroom, keeping other children in line. They also (the student body) elected him as their house captain. They have four different houses at Moray School and every child in the school belongs to one of those four houses. The children try to earn points for their house by doing well in school or doing well in sports. They only choose children in their last year of primary school. Randal is in 7th grade this year and next year we hope he will get to go to CBC where Rylan attends.

The February 18th letter contained plans for my trip to the U.S. It seems we must have had to borrow about $400 to pay for the plane ticket. I state that I'm arriving June 6th in Houston, Texas then will fly from Houston to Kansas City. Also, plans for the anniversary celebration seem to be worrying my mother, but I assured her that my sisters and I would take care of everything. She only needs to make a list of the guests she wanted to invite.

February 24th Bob and his dad left for Swaziland to attend a minister's seminar. Bob is riding with missionaries from Pietersburg and leaving our pickup there to be worked on. They are planning to be gone a week.

"The Lord has been so good to us. We got an extra Christmas check from some people in Michigan which will almost take care of my plane ticket. Isn't it wonderful? The Lord does give us the desires of our heart sometimes."

From the March 6th letter I wrote: "I almost called Roxy and Ron, or my parents, but decided against it, knowing that you probably would worry too much about us. Actually, I felt a little insecure without Bob here last week, but we managed through the week (This happened while Bob and Grandpa were at the minister's seminar in Swaziland). I think what shook me most was a big army convoy that went by on our street in the middle of the night. There was a plane with a loud speaker telling everyone to stay inside for the weekend. This made me a bit edgy. They had a blitz in the western suburbs for the weekend so everything came to pretty much of a standstill and there were road blocks everywhere around the city. Fortunately, Bob and Grandpa were coming on Monday instead of the weekend. They got back safely. Please continue to pray for our safety because we can't get to the western suburbs to work with our church there. It makes things quite frustrating to say the least. I'm just glad we have our new church in the eastern suburbs because at least we can get to church there.

Randal went to the Scripture Union Camp last weekend that Roxy and Jim Lo led. This weekend some missionaries are coming from Zambia to visit, but they will probably be staying with Roxy and Jim Lo. We are to have a carry-in supper on Friday night at the Lo's. The other thing that will occupy quite a lot of my time is preparing lessons for the Scripture Union camp that takes place March 29th – 31st. Our theme is 'Treasure Island' and I found a neat story to tell the kids and it brings in a lot about the Bible and should be a real help to Christian kids. I'll have to fix my flannel board and pocket board, the prizes and a number of other things. Bob and I were leaders for the Scripture Union camp in the Matopas from Friday afternoon until Sunday afternoon. The cook didn't show up so I was left with the responsibility of cooking for 58 some people. This cooking had to be done over an open fire outside! Can you imagine?! Anyway, they did get a young girl as a helper and the caretaker out at the camp site helped a lot. It was a good experience and evidently the kids liked the camp because as they waited for the bus they were asking, "When will the next camp be? We want to come on the next camp!'" So Bob and I felt it was a very good camp. Sometimes I think I'd like to run children's camps. I love kids so much! Our theme was "Treasure Island" and the kids loved it. I told the story "Mystery of the Golden Key." We had treasure hunts and treasure hot seats and treasure Bible verses, which they could all learn to get points. We had four teams: The Black Beards, the Golden Girls, the Rumbas and the Cannibals, very exciting!? The kids all sleep in big tents and we will probably sleep in a dormitory nearby. Altogether, there were about 60 of us, counting leaders and helpers.

I've been spending some time at the hospital with Elaine Cornett. She was operated on over a week ago, but thinks she may get to go home tomorrow. I had her husband and two kids over for supper. I feel sorry when the father has to cook and do everything for the kids, especially when one is a little girl. I think Sheryl is missing her mother. I really wonder how Bob and the boys will do with me gone so much, but I'm sure they will cope. I know several will be inviting them over for meals.

This weekend Rylan and Randal both have their sports day. I don't know why every time they both have sports day scheduled on the same day. I guess I will try to go to Rylan's in the morning and to Randal's in the afternoon. Bob is to be a field judge at Randal's school so he has to be there. As it turned out, Rylan won the trophy for 'best sportsman under 16' at his school. He got first in 100-meter run, 200-meter run, the long jump, the hurdles and first in their relay. He got second in javelin and triple jump. Randal also did quite well, but because of his feet condition he didn't do as well as he'd like. He and his relay team did get first. Randal is House Captain and his House won the trophy so Randal got to receive the trophy for his House. Randal was chosen for his interschool competition just before the first term ended and Rylan was chosen for Rugby team to Harare where he stayed with the Nazarene Pastor's brother and family. The boys were back in school by May 7th for their second term of school.

Regularly, I wrote a form letter to the Mission Department of the Wesleyan Church and supporting churches and in April I made a special prayer request for our son-in-law and daughter, Ron and Roxane Lauber, who are pastoring the Omaha Wesleyan Church. They had been contacted about going as missionaries to Suriname in South America.

In my April 12th 1985 letter I wrote: "About two weeks ago Roxy called us to help them pray about what they should do. Suriname is where the kids feel God is calling them. It sort of hit me like a rock at first because, do you realize, this would mean they won't even be in the States when we come on furlough? So one wonders, I thought, when will we ever get to see our kids and have the whole family together. But of course we want God's will for them and know that somehow God will help us.

As Bob says: 'Our time on earth is very short and eternity is long.' So we want our kids in the plan of God. I think now I see why God is making it possible for me to come back to the States, but I feel so sorry for Bob and the boys because we don't know when they will see them. Anyway, we just must leave it in God's hands. As for Ronald, I really think it is necessary for us to see him get into a Christian school. He is really down."

"We are trying a new venture for this year. Jim Lo and Bob have felt the need for theological training among our African men who feel God is calling them. Since it is very difficult to get students to our Bible College in Swaziland, over 1,000 kilometers away, they decided to try a mini Bible College extension and train with TEE books. The end of January Jim and Bob began training two young men for Christian service. They not only do the book work, but are involved in the practical such as making calls, teaching Sunday school classes, preaching, etc. Cosmos and Jethro are two of the young men in this training. Some classes are held in and around the Bulawayo area for others too."

I continued teaching scripture in two government schools in Bulawayo. I truly thank God for this opportunity. The last term I taught about the Bible, as a wonderful library of 66 books. It was thrilling to hear them sing the songs about the books of the Old Testament. Do you know what the prizes were? They were THE LITTLE BIBLES, which were sent to us by a WMS group in the States. Thanks, so much, WMS Societies for all you do!

During this time, the national elections were to take place in Zimbabwe. They were cancelled for March and set for June. Now the paper is talking about another postponement. Much prayer is needed for the continued unrest in Zimbabwe."

The Month of May

With just a month before I leave, I'm getting so excited! There are so many things to do. I made myself three new dresses and I did some meal plans for Bob and the boys and made up some food dishes for the deep freeze, as well. It's my mom's birthday this month, on the 17th, so we both celebrate our birthdays and Mother's Day the same month. I told my parents in my May 12th letter that I had a really nice Mother's Day-Birthday. The Kumalo Wesleyan Church surprised me with a tea. I thought it was so nice of them. Roxy and Ron called me to wish me a Happy Birthday. Roxy also said they had sent a card, but I hadn't received it yet. Also, in this letter, I wrote that Roxy and Ron were appointed to Suriname in South America. Headquarters wants them in Suriname by September of October. Roxy seems to be getting concerned about packing. I write: "Maybe I can help her while I'm there with them."

In Matthew 7:11 it says, "How much more will your Father in Heaven give good gifts to those who ask Him." As I thought of this verse I asked the Lord for a special gift, a trip to the States. Of course, I prayed knowing that it would be according the His will. Ordinarily we missed many special occasions. But this time, I really wanted to be there for the birth of our first two grandchildren in June and my parents 'golden wedding anniversary in July.

The Lord is so good! He provided money for my ticket, leaving Bulawayo on June 2nd and returning July 26th, the Lord willing. There will be a big family reunion with my parents and the opportunity to see many relatives and friends whom we've not seen for years. Bob and the boys will remain in Zimbabwe to carry on, missed, but definitely prayed for.

My Visit in the U. S.

I found that South African Airlines does fly into Houston, Texas and so this is the one I'm flying direct on to the States. From Houston I fly to Kansas City where Allen and Kim will meet me, along with Ron, on June 6th. After spending a couple days at Allen and Kim's, Ron took me on to Omaha.

It was really neat that on my travels from South Africa I had the privilege of traveling with Sister Ruth Mehlomakhulu from Johannesburg to Houston. She is our Regional Women's Director for the Southern Africa field. She was coming to the States for the General WMS Convention in Marion, Indiana. It was her first time to travel by plane, but we had a very enjoyable trip together. In Houston I took her to the terminal where she could get a plane to Tulsa before I got on my plane to Kansas City.

In June 7th letter I tell how Allen, Kim and Ronnie met me in Kansas City and then after staying a couple days Ron took me on to Omaha. He had to head for Lincoln soon after we got to Omaha. He works nights at Gramercy Hill Retirement Home in Lincoln. He gets $3.50 an hour at this elite place. He doesn't have much to do since it is at night, so he studies. He's taking an English course, which he needs to complete his credits for college graduation. Ronnie helped me get my ticket changed so that I could fly out of New York instead of Houston.

I think this is rather funny the way I started out my June 11th letter. "I'm in the land of late nights, big cars and fat people! Sometimes I wonder how these people ever survive." I think I must have been having a bit of culture shock. Since June 12th is our Ronnie's birthday, he came up to Omaha from Lincoln on the 11th and we celebrated his birthday with a braai. We had steaks, baked potatoes, salad and corn on the cob. I made a German Chocolate cake and we got chocolate marshmallow ice cream. Ronnie then had to leave shortly after 10:00 p.m. to be able to get to work by midnight.

It is youth camp time so Ron, my son-in-law, has been going up to Atkinson. He said they had 62 campers, really more than they expected. He planned to go back to the camp if Roxy doesn't go to the hospital. I guess he will call back each day to see how Roxy is doing and if Roxy goes into labor he will drive back to Omaha.

So the exciting news for June – Our first two grandchildren arrived. Roxy and Ron's little one, Alicia Rochelle was born June 14th, weighing 7 lbs. 9 oz. and was 21 inches long. Our son Allen and wife Kim had their little baby girl born June 27th. Her name is Kassandra Nicole and she weighed in at 8 lbs. ½ oz. and was 18 inches long. Since I was staying with Ron and Roxane in Omaha I got to hold Alicia right soon after her birth. Little Kassandra I never got to see until she was about two weeks old. Allen had gotten the weekend off and since Kim had gone to her sister Rhonda's in Iowa to get back on her feet, he came to take Ron and me to Iowa to see her and baby Kassandra. What a joy to be able to hold each of our first two granddaughters. Little Kassie was so cute with her little button nose. She really looks like a Cheney. I'm so glad I got to see her.

In my July 2, 1985 letter to Bob I wrote about some of the concerns I had for our son, Ron. I wrote about spending time with Ron saying: "We have had some really good talks but I'm so worried about him being so busy and not getting to church. Please pray for me that God will help me say the right things. I think he has done quite well up until the 1st of June. When they were here on Saturday Ronnie was so tired because he works all night and if he doesn't sleep it really gets him down. Of course I remember how it is, so what happens is that he feels tired and doesn't get to church on Sunday mornings. I said something about going to church with him and he said something like, "Well, I never go to church anymore." When I thought on that statement I started feeling worse and worse. I even cried hard Sunday morning and told Roxy. I miss family prayer time so much. The one time we have been in prayer as a family was at my parent's on Saturday. I still feel family praying together is so important. Ronnie isn't trying to go back on the Lord, I'm sure, because I've been so amazed at some of his spiritual concepts, but I feel he desperately needs some Christian fellowship. So please join me in this prayer request for our son.

I need to explain what I understand Ronnie's feelings are. He seems to really want to finish here in Lincoln at UNL. I understand that this doctor he works with on a research project and Ronnie both wrote on this research paper. The doctor is called first writer and Ronnie is called the second writer. It is some research they have been doing in breast cancer. So they hope to get this printed and Ronnie says when this printing goes out it will make him look good and he hopes by working with another doctor in training that he has a good chance at being accepted in P.A. school. He told me that he got an A+ in his physiology and he was going through his book and explaining things to me. I can tell he just loves it! Ronnie's problem is writing essays and language, otherwise he does fine. But we just must pray for him. We may look into some student loans he can get while in Lincoln. He's hoping to save up some for his next year's House bill and I hope maybe he will get more help from headquarters." (Ron lived in Farm House Fraternity at UNL.)

During some of my time with Ron I had mentioned that maybe he should pray about going to Central Wesleyan College to finish his studies. Central Wesleyan College was the only one of our Wesleyan colleges giving free tuition to missionary kids. I felt this was a real blessing and so commendable of this Wesleyan college.

After Allen, Ronnie and I returned to Omaha from our trip to Iowa, our three older kids got into what I consider one of the most important conversations, encouraging Ronnie to transfer to Central Weslyan in South Carolina. I know Roxy and I had prayed a lot, and others were praying too. I know God was leading in this conversation. I was so proud of our oldest son, Allen. Usually he is quiet and doesn't say a lot, but this night God helped him in encouraging his brother to transfer to Central Wesleyan. Also Roxy, his older sister, gave Ronnie encouraging words. We all promised to pray for Ronnie to know what God wanted him to do. I know Ronnie listened very carefully and that his brother and sister's words were impressed upon him to seek God's plan. On Sunday, July 14th, we all went to church in Lincoln. It was such a good service. Ron went forward to pray. I know God is helping Him. I'm so happy to write that in the end Ronnie did decide to transfer to Central Wesleyan College. Since he already knew a number of missionary kids attending college here, it made it much easier for him. In fact, two of those MK's were Susan and Shari Ramsay, MK's he grew up with in Swaziland, Africa. It was a real answer to prayer!

Back to June 21st – Ronnie and I drove Roxy's little Honda Civic out to western Nebraska to attend Julie and Cliff Transmeier wedding. It was held at the Lutheran Church in Oshkosh June 22nd. First let me tell about seeing our two cute little nieces', Tara and Kristin Cheney. When Ronnie and I walked in the house Tara started screaming "Aunty Eva" and just laughing and crying all at once. It was so neat to see how happy she was to see me. Kristin was happy too, but I don't think she really remembered us. But it didn't take her long to warm up to me. Sue also was in tears. It just was so neat to see them all again.

At the wedding we saw so many people that we knew. Rev. Dunwoody was the minister at the wedding. We saw Uncle Jim and Aunt Kathy, but not Doug, as he was at a soccer clinic. Aunt Vivian and Uncle Don were there with their cute little Jimmy Don. Aunt Elaine Harvey and all her girls were present with their families. Aunt Charlotte and Uncle Frank were also present. This is Grandma Cheney's sister.

As we came back from the wedding I dropped Ron off at the University. Then I continued on to Omaha. When Ron got out of the car he said to me, "Now Mom, be sure you drive on the right side of the road!" I said, "Oh yes, I will." You see in Africa you drive on the left side. Sometimes, I should say, often, if one is not concentrating you automatically go to the side you are used to. Well, my intentions were good, but as I was looking for a street I would travel on to reach the interstate I did turn too soon and realized I would need to turn around. I saw a motel and decided it was a good place to turn around and get on the right street. As I came out from the motel I turned into the left lane then looking up I saw cars coming right straight at me. It suddenly dawned on me, "Oh, you are driving on the wrong side of the street." I quickly backed into the motel driveway and waited for all the cars to pass then pulled over onto the right side of the street. No wonder Ron warned me!!! It didn't happen again!

In my July 2, 1985 letter: "I had a chance to ride to Oshkosh with Wayne and Rebecca Osborne. They were coming through Omaha on July 4th, a Thursday, staying overnight then leaving for Oshkosh on July 5th. I was able to go to the Alumni Banquet in Oshkosh and also to my class of 1955 reunion out at Buffalo Canyon. It was our 30-year reunion. My mom's cousin, Aunt Rebecca, also graduated from Garden County High School. I caught a ride back to Lincoln with DeAntha Ashby and then Ron and Roxy picked me up to go back to Omaha.

The last and big event that took place in my seven-week visit here in the States was the 50th wedding anniversary celebration for my parents, Earl and Beulah Thornton. I had corresponded regularly with my two sisters, Esther and Elaine, probably six months or more to coordinate the timing for our parent's anniversary celebration. Although their anniversary was actually May 19th, we celebrated July 21st. All my parents' living brothers and sisters, and some of the cousins were present for this occasion. Isn't the Lord's timing wonderful? All these special occasions happening while I'm here has been beyond my wildest dreams!

I want to add a little about how we celebrated Mom and Dad's anniversary. I had contacted the pastor, Rev. Clayton Severn, who performed their marriage to see if he and his wife could come and do a reenactment of their actual wedding. So the wedding attendants, my dad's sister, Grace Sherwood and mom's brother, Jewell French, who stood up with them were here. My Aunt Chrystal, who sang, was able to sing with Orpha Severn, like was planned for their wedding. However, I understand Orpha was not able to be at the real wedding and so my Grandma Devasher sang with Aunt Chrystal. Our daughter and son-in-law also sang. It was so neat to have our three older children present and my parent's two newborn great-granddaughters, Alicia Lauber and Kassandra Cheney. What a wonderful celebration.

Time to Go Home to Zimbabwe

In Omaha, at the Sonlight Wesleyan Church, I spoke in the morning service on June 30th. Then in the afternoon I showed my picture. Also, I spoke at Allen and Kim's church on the 24th of July. My plane leaves Kansas City at 12:35 pm on the 25th. I fly Pan Am to New York and in about two hours depart on my SAA flight. This put me into Johannesburg on July 26th at 5:30 pm. Linda and Orai Lehman as well as Shari and Carol Ramsay were there to meet me. Then, my plane left for Bulawayo, Zimbabwe at 10:30 pm. I transferred a number of things to a smaller case to take on the plane. Linda will bring the rest of my luggage when they come for Conference in September. Bob and the boys were at the Bulawayo airport to meet me.

This is what I saw when I walked in the front door. A beautiful gorgeous bouquet of roses was in the middle of the dining room table. The house was spic and span and there was a sign on the wall above the sideboard that said: "WELCOME HOME MOM". Sitting on the sideboard was a most beautiful tea set that Bob had gotten for me. I truly felt appreciation from my family, especially later when they told me how good the meals were! Really, I don't think I cooked any different than I ever did! Anyway, it was good to be home

It took about a week for the jet lag to wear off. When I was feeling more normal I started back into exercise with my Nazarene friend, Elaine, even though I still had a few stiff muscles

The boys were coming close to the end of their second school term. In my August 5th letter I wrote: "Bob and I watched Rylan play his last Rugby game on Saturday. Christian Brothers College (Rylan's school) won against Hamilton 26 – 0. I have been so thankful Rylan has not been injured this term. Oh, he has had a few bruises and knocks, but nothing serious."

The Los are leaving on Friday for a month of holiday in South Africa so we need to stick around and care for things here Matt and Andre have been sick, as well as Roxy In fact, a lot of people have flu and colds.

My next August 21st letter says: "I've been without transport for over a week as Bob went to South Africa to have our car worked on. During this time I got really ill. It seems some kind of a virus is going around that affects the chest. I felt like I could almost cough out my lungs. But fortunately I believe the Lord touched me. I'm pretty much back to normal. I didn't have to go to the doctor, thank the Lord. Anyway, I'm sure my good neighbor, Mrs. Goodes, would have taken me if necessary. I was really happy to see Bob drive in from South Africa after being gone nine days. I was beginning to feel a bit like a widow. It took longer to get the car fixed because the parts didn't get in very quickly. Our pickup was at the mechanic here in Bulawayo but soon, the mechanic said, "We should be able to get to it."

During the second term holiday Rylan and Randal went to Scripture Union Camp out in the Matopas for about a week and won't be back until August 27th. Bob and I have the house to ourselves. It's a little quiet around here, I must say!"

It seems like we really keep busy, especially since the Los are gone They will return in about a week I plan to have the evening meal ready for them In fact, Roxy Lo called this evening from Joburg to say they were having a really nice holiday. During this time I attended three ladies meetings.

The Month of September, 1985

What a busy month this was. The boys start back to school for their third term and last of the year. Bob had to take our car back to South Africa because they never got it fixed. We need it to go to our conference at Victoria Falls. I hope it gets fixed properly this time. Wilma will be coming down to Victoria Falls for the conference with some Zambian Missionaries.

I need to add here that Dr. and Mrs. McCullum were with us Monday evening until Wednesday morning. They were on their way back to Brakpan from the Zambian Missionary Retreat. I was really nice to have them. We had something in common. They had five children like we do. Dr. McCullum let me take a psychology course by correspondence which I found very interesting. It allowed me to pick up three hours of college credit.

About this same time Rylan got his learner's permit so he was starting to drive. With a learner's permit he could drive as long as a licensed driver was riding with him in the front seat.

In September Jim and Roxy took over our church at Emtumbane where we had worked for about two years. Jim and Roxy will be starting a new work at Sigola where one of our national preachers had already laid the groundwork. Jim was going to help develop the church. As always, prayers were needed for new church development.

We took over the development of the Kumalo Church where Jim and Roxy had been serving. That involved taking on the responsibility of the Farm Church and working with Pastor Sonny Makusha in church development. We hoped the Kumalo Trinity Church would be strong enough to stand on their own without a full time missionary. This is a big job and we needed a lot of wisdom from the Lord as we worked through an interpreter. Our goal was to give leadership and training in these churches so they would eventually be able to function with national pastors.

The Wesleyan Women's Conference convened at Bethesda Mission on September 20th. We had a real treat because our regional director, Mrs. Ruth Mehlomakhulu, was able to be with us. Our district conference was held on September 21st. We were privileged to have our regional secretary, Rev. Robert Hlengethwa, as well as regional superintendent, Orai Lehman and his wife, our mission coordinator, Rev. Jim Ramsey and his wife. God gave us real help in our conference. Several of our newer members were able to attend and beginning to take a real active part in church planting in Zimbabwe. There were about fourteen people attending from Bulawayo besides missionaries. We had somewhat of a turnabout in administration on the district. Members of the regional board appointed our district board since we were small in membership. A new church in Victoria Falls was soon to begin under the leadership of Rev. Ben Mayo. We had had a church site in Victoria Falls for several years but at this time there was a vision to really build a congregation as well as a building.

Several times we asked the folks in Nebraska to pray for finances to build a church at Emtumbane in the western suburbs. Our God was not poor, is not poor and never will be poor! And, it is good when people are anxious to have their own church. They worshiped in a classroom at Emtumbane Secondary School and were about to burst out of the walls with 116 present for the service including many young people as well as adults. At that time Ramah and Belinda Ncube were pastors in training for Emtumbane. The Khumalo Trinity Wesleyan Church was still growing, with an average attendance of 100 and often as many as 130 present. Through the month of November we had special emphasis Sundays: Friend's Sunday, Neighbor Sunday, Children's Sunday and Parent's Sunday. During November we had membership classes and teaching about baptism. With a combined baptismal service for all the Bulawayo churches we really prayed that those joining in membership and baptism would really be committed to serving the Lord.

Also, in this time period evangelistic meetings were held with Lowell Sheppard and two young men. He spoke at the Khumalo Trinity Church and then at a big rally in the Bulawayo Park. It sort of made one feel like you were in a Billy Graham meeting. Someone said they figured there were about 2,000 present.

As new developments came up, Jim Ramsey, our Mission Coordinator, called our family and the Lo's together to talk over the plans for our work in Zimbabwe. He talked about a plan that was not set in stone but that seemed very logical. There was hope that soon there would be a new missionary couple and the idea was that they not be left by themselves any longer than necessary. So, if the Cheney family could furlough in May of 1986, the Lo's would stay until the end of November and the new couple would not be on their own no longer than six months. With that arrangement, our family would get home in time for Ron's graduation.

October 6: Yesterday we had a big wedding for Isaiah and Velisiwe. It was the first wedding to be held in the Khumalo Church. We decorated with bougainvillea and other flowers that I found in my garden. After the ceremony we had a reception at Makushas's home. Believe it or not, I baked another wedding cake which I never wanted to do again. It was only a small cake but with the big sheet cake I made, everyone had plenty to eat along with Kool-Aid. We were hoping that this would be an influence for our young people to have church weddings and not just live together without properly being married. It seemed rather terrible to us to see that the girl was already pregnant. This happens so much, but at least Isaiah wanted to have a proper church wedding. They did have a civil wedding about a month before. Often the parents don't agree on the bride price and things drag on and on until finally the boy gets the girl pregnant.

Maybe here I need to explain what lobola is. It is the bride price that the boy must pay to the girl's parents before they can marry. Most of the time the lobola was paid with cows .Since a cow was worth $100 or maybe $120, sometimes the parents would accept money rather than cows. The amount of lobola depended on how well the girl was educated. For instance, if she was a trained teacher or nurse, she would be worth 20 to 30 cows. If she only worked at home and had not had many years of school, she would probably be worth five or six cows. Now many young men are paying money for their brides because they have jobs in the cities and it is easier just to pay the price agreed upon by the girl's parents.

One of my responsibilities was training ladies in evangelism visitation. Another responsibility and privilege was to provide for visitors. Allen and Myrna Houston, Rev. Ed Wissbroeker (Ed later became our brother-in-law.), his daughter, Karen Wirth, and her child. I fixed breakfast for them and then took them back to the train station.

There were also times of fun! I baked a birthday cake for Larry Cornett, the Nazarene missionary. Their church had a progressive supper and invited our family to come. I made a cake in my big cookie sheet. It was a chocolate cake mix from the States. Then I decorated it by putting an outline of the state of Texas with a lone star and wrote 'Happy Birthday, Larry!" He really liked it. A few days later I made a birthday supper for Roxy Lo. I made pizza and a big birthday cake from scratch. We had homemade ice cream. It was really good, I must say. I bought Roxy a pretty light green dress from the shop. I felt I should do more because she had been so good to invite Bob and the boys for meals while I was in the States and I just wanted this to be extra special.

My Scare

From my November 20th letter: "I need to tell you about myself. I suddenly discovered a lump in my right breast and became quite frightened. So first thing Monday morning I tried to contact the doctor. I had thought that Dr. McCauly, the doctor whom we've been with, had gone back to Harare, but found he is still here. So I went to him this morning. He says he thinks there's not too much to worry about, as it is not attached or sore, so this is good. However, he says it must come out. I'm having surgery after I see the specialist that he sent me to. It's quite a minor surgery because I come home after surgery. I find out tomorrow when the surgery will be.

Bob is out on visitation tonight. Last night it was very exciting when we had our language study. This man who helps us study language had a couple friends come over, so Bob was able to witness to them and both received Christ. People are really so open to the Gospel, so we praise the Lord for this

Back to my minor surgery and the results: I went to the specialist who gave me the results of my biopsy on Thanksgiving Day. I truly thanked the Lord when the doctor told me the lump was benign and the area seems to be returning to normal. This is one Thanksgiving Day I'll never forget. How I do praise and thank my Lord!"

In our December form letter I wrote: "The Cheney household has had a bit of frustration recently, but we praise God that 'He works all things together for good'. In October we received a warning that the owners of the house we rent might be selling. Of course, we wondered what to do. Decent houses are now very scarce to buy and it's almost impossible to find a good place to rent. So many people are looking for homes now. We talked with our mission coordinator and he advised us to buy another house if possible. The mission does own one house now, where the Jim Lo family lives; however, the matter of finding a house to buy now is about like looking for a needle in a haystack. After much looking and a visit from our Mission Director, Jim Ramsay, we prevailed on the owner of the house to allow us to rent for four or five more months, which would put us up to the furlough time we had decided on. Praise the Lord, He does work things out. She has agreed to set up a contract with us. The Lord never leaves us stranded!

Beginning of December the boys, Rylan and Randal, are on their summer holiday from school. They will return to school January 14th. In the coming year they will be attending the same school since Randal has now completed Primary School. We have to pay $200 for Randal to keep a place for him at the school where Rylan goes, called Christian Brothers College. Each term we will need to pay $300 for Randal, which means $900 a year. We have to pay $200 out of our own pockets, but I'm very thankful that our mission headquarters will help pay the rest. School is expensive here I must say, when you go to a private school. But we feel they are taught so much better at this private school.

With Christmas coming there was a program to organize as well as church work and women's meetings. I really got the jitters about the Christmas program, fearful that the children would not do their performance well, but hopeful that with several more practices it would take shape and really be meaningful.

Then, we had a baptismal service at the Hope Valley Church with seven people from Khumalo to be baptized, two from Hope Valley and quite a few from Emtumbane. There were probably some from Sigola, too.

With never a dull moment, we had two English girls come to visit for a few days, girls we didn't know, but they were friends of our friend's, Bob and Sheila Smith. Sheila called me and asked about them coming and, of course, I said we'd be delighted. They had come on the train from South

Africa and gone to Victoria Falls. Now they were coming back on the train. We met at the train station and it proved to be quite interesting!

Bob's Dad Comes to Visit Again

Back in August Bob's dad started talking about coming to visit his kids and grandkids in Southern Africa. I really think he thought it was a good way to escape the cold Nebraska winters. My neighbor lady, Mrs. Val Goodes, is letting me borrow her twin beds and she is using our double bed while Grandpa Cheney is with us. What I plan to do is let Rylan and Randal take our big room with the twin beds and then they can each have a closet and bed. It should be easier for them to be peaceful with each other I figure. Grandpa will feel more at home if he keeps the same room he had last year. We then will take Rylan's room

Going back to my June form letter, I wrote: 'We are happy and pleased that God is leading our children in some big decisions that they are making. In May, Ron and Roxy were approved by our missions department of the Wesleyan Church to go as missionaries to Suriname in South America. Ron is going in September, the Lord willing. He will work with Metro-Move and find a house for them to live in. After returning to the States they will have some time to visit relatives and say goodbyes. Then about four or five weeks will be spent at the Missionary Institute in Michigan. On November 15th Ron, Roxy and baby Alicia fly to Suriname. The preparation becomes a bit overwhelming at times, but we know God can give special strength and that visa permits, etc., will be granted in time. I then ask people who receive our form letter to also pray for our children preparing to go to Suriname. Often I would say: "We would like to say how much we appreciate our prayer partners and those who support us. You are a very vital part of Wesleyan World Missions. Without you there we could not be here."

Christmas Time, 1985

We had a very nice Christmas Day with the Los. Several of the missionaries from Zambia came to celebrate with us. The Thompson family, and Wilma, Bob's sister, and her friend Rosemary came. With the Lo's family and our family, along with Grandpa Cheney there were 16 of us. Roxy asked me to cook the turkey. Rosemary and Wilma did a lot of baking and made salad. We even had sliced cucumbers from my garden.

We got a call from our son, Allen, and were hoping to hear soon from Roxy and Ron in Suriname. In my letter of December 27th I wrote: "We won't be in Boksburg today as we had planned. Our South African visas didn't come through, so we are sitting here at the airport with Grandpa Cheney." He was flying to Johannesburg to be with Orai and Linda Lehman. This same afternoon I wrote: "Karen and Mark Wirth are coming with their two kids. They live next to Wilma and Rosemary at Choma Secondary School. They will be staying in our house while we are away. We aren't sure when we will get away, but we hope maybe Monday.

On Christmas Day we had two services on Christmas morning; one at Kumalo and one at Hope Valley Farm. We ate Christmas dinner at the Lo's about 1:30 or 2:00 pm then we opened our gifts. We had really nice Christmas boxes from a church in Virginia who took us as their Christmas missionary family. Also a lovely pastor's wife in Canada sent a lovely box of used clothing – all dresses – that fit me quite nicely. So I have some quite nice clothing now.

Come Monday morning Bob and I were still in Zimbabwe. Rylan and Randal were on their way to South Africa with the Zambian missionaries and their two pastors going to Swaziland for the conference. We did get our visas but our delegate, Ramah, didn't get his. Before the day was over he also had his visas. Our boys wanted to go on to the South African camp and youth camp with Aunt Wilma and Rosemary. Bob and I, along with our delegate, headed straight for Swaziland for our Regional Conference. And so ends the year 1985.

Four Busy Months in 1986
January, February, March and April

After arriving back in Zimbabwe from being in South Africa our days began to fill up with a lot of activities. The boys began a new school year, both attending Christian Brothers College. This year I'm not teaching the Scripture Union classes at the two different schools which I did last year, but I have added a bible study and choir practice and will be going with some of our ladies doing visitation. I also am teaching a class course entitled "Ministries to Youth and Children" to our bible school students. There are some Sunday school seminars I want to do, besides get ready for a Wesleyan Women's Conference that takes place in April. In my January 21st letter I say: "We just must live one day at a time and try to do our best. I think the longer one is on the field and get closer to your furlough date, the more there seems to be to get done before you have to leave.

One of our goals is to help the Khumalo Church to be able to go on its own without a missionary having to be present all the time. More and more we are feeling that our purpose for being here is not to do the work, but to train nationals for leadership positions. We are working with the Lo's as quickly as we can to get a really good Bible school training set up for those who feel the need for Christian training. We and the Lo's are looking forward to a new missionary couple coming to serve in Zimbabwe, David and Donna Tolan. Bob and I are looking forward to meeting them at Missionary Retreat in August before they come to Zimbabwe.

In the book of James it tells us we should say we will do this or that and go to a certain place. Then it goes on to say we should say if the Lord wills we will do such and such. We had plans that on our way home for furlough we would go via Suriname so we could see Ron, Roxy and Alicia.

So, according to my January 21st letter, "We are planning to leave here by train May 6th going to Johannesburg. This is what the route will be we think, but of course there could be a change. We would fly KLM from Johannesburg to Amsterdam May 9th and catch a flight from Amsterdam to Paramaribo on May 12th, arriving in the evening. We may need to stay nearly two weeks in Suriname to make the right connection to Miami. We asked about stopping to see Jim and Kathy, but aren't sure that will work out It would only be a day or two, then on to Kansas City to be with Allen and Kim for at least a week. We would go on to Omaha to pick up a car to drive on to western Nebraska, getting there near the end of May. Well, so much for plans, for they did change on us, much to our disappointment.

My next paragraph said: "I have two women's meetings tomorrow besides having a Swedish missionary whom we became acquainted with in Swaziland coming for lunch." I continued telling about Grandpa Cheney. "He has now set his date for going back to the States as March 10th, unless he decides to change. It seems that each time Grandpa comes I can tell he is failing in health and mind. It seems hard for him to remember things. He is talking of going into the rest home when he goes back. We dare not say too much for we want it to be his decision and not ours. However, we do feel that he is getting to the place he needs extra care. Grandpa finally decided he is leaving on February 25th, going to Orai and Linda's for a couple days, flying out for London and on to Denver arriving March 1st."

We made a plan to go visit in Zambia before Grandpa Cheney left. We left on February 4th and came back February 9th. The boys missed three days of school but we figured since they don't remember being in Zambia (Rylan was only 17 months when we were there in November 1970), and Randal has never been there. It will be educational for them. We saw Wilma and Rosemary Maddox and Eugene and Naomi VanHaus and had the evening meal with them.

Randal's Accident

Randal had an accident riding a horse. We drove out to this ranch near Choma to have tea with a European rancher. He let the boys ride his horse. Randal was riding slowly across the field when the horse stumbled, causing Randal to come off. Then the horse actually rolled over Randal, or at least on part of him. Randal's left side was quite badly grazed. We were very concerned about this knee because it was so swollen so we took him back to Choma and one of the missionary nurses looked him over. She felt we should take Randal to the hospital for x-rays the next morning. We did this and fortunately the x-ray machine was working. We found he had a cracked ring finger at the last joint but his knee x-ray didn't look too bad, at least it didn't show any breaks. So they bandaged him up, gave us some pain tablets and antibiotics and I started giving him lots of Vitamin C. We started back to Zimbabwe in the afternoon.

It was an enjoyable stay outside of the fact Randal got injured. On our way back we held a service for our new church in Victoria Falls. We had 60 present in this service. They meet in a primary school but we are hoping we can soon build a Wesleyan Church in Victoria Falls. We arrived back in Bulawayo about 5:00 p.m. Thank the Lord for safety on the road.

After getting back to Bulawayo we made an appointment for Randal to see the doctor who put his leg in a cast. It seemed to be healing okay. However, about a week later he came home from school violently ill. He had a temperature of nearly 104 degrees, so I tried to get it down with double strength Tylenol hardly fazed it, so I gave him another double strength Tylenol. His fever went down just a bit, but I decided I had better call the doctor. He said to bring him right down to his office. Bob took him to see the doctor and when they didn't return very soon I called the office. The nurse said, "I think the doctor has put him in the hospital." Sure enough, the doctor did put him in the hospital. The symptoms seemed much like malaria, or maybe typhoid, so they got him in and started IV's and taking blood samples. It was several days before we found he had neither malaria, nor typhoid. Praise the Lord! It seems there is quite a bad flu going around, so evidently this is what Randal had gotten. Soon he was much better and chomping at the bit to get back home. My summary of the whole situation is that Randal had such a traumatic experience with falling off the horse and horse rolling over him, that he was in a weakened condition and run down. On the phone his Uncle Orai said to tell Randal that he just got "run down by that horse." He did have to take physical therapy treatments on his knee and soon he was able to ride a bike. He had to see his doctor two weeks later.

Bob and I had the privilege of attending a weekend marriage seminar with Pastor Sonny and Annie Makusha, our pastors at the Khumalo Wesleyan church. A couple from the Nazarene Church conducted this seminar. There were about five couples who attended this seminar. It was really good for all the married couples who attended. I'm so glad Bob and I got to go. I'm hoping it will benefit us in counseling others in marriage problems. It was mainly one evening and through the day on Saturday.

From February 19th letter I wrote: "This last Sunday the Los and Bob and I exchanged churches. We attended services at Emtumbane and Sigola and Los went to Kumalo and Hope Valley Farm. At Emtumbane we had 174 people for church service at Emtumbane and at Sigola there were 88. At Emtumbane there were a number who came forward to pray. We still do not have a church building at this place but desperately need it. The classroom was wall to wall people. At Sigola, Jim has started building the church. Truly there is so much to do that one wonders how it will ever get done.

Notes from Home

My parents, now in their 70s, had lived for over 50 years on our ranch. In my March 11th letter I wrote, "I <u>hate</u> it when you get snowed in! It was good to hear from Esther and she tried to assure me you were okay."

One time my parents were snowed in for about seven weeks. Grace and Clint Reeves really looked after my parents and I appreciated this so much. It was such a relief for me when my parents had a phone and could call out if they needed help.

My mother expressed her concern to me one time. She said, "Eva, I don't know what I should do if something happens to your dad? What can I do to get help?" Later, when we were on furlough I took a walk with my dad and said, "Daddy, Mother is really worried. She told me she didn't know what she could do if you got really sick or had a heart attack. She is really worried about you, Daddy. You should talk to her about this to let her know what you want her to do in an emergency.

The next Sunday Mother shared with me that Daddy had talked to her and she was greatly relieved. You see, to get an emergency vehicle into the ranch would have taken at least an hour. The roads were only trail, two track roads for seven miles off the main road. Our ranch was certainly in an out-of-the-way place in the sand hills of Garden County.

Continued Preparations for Furlough

Again, in my March 11th letter: "I've been trying to hold extra Bible studies. I want to train another woman in our church to lead so we will have more than just Mrs. Makusha, the pastor's wife, leading. Anyway, today it was so exciting because a Zambian lady was at the house where we held the Bible study. We were able to witness to her and she prayed to receive Christ. She has promised to come to church on Sunday with her children. Tomorrow is the ladies meeting and we are going to be sewing quilts for a while.

I have two Sunday school training seminars to prepare for, one March 14th and one March 22nd. Our farewell will be at Bethesda Mission on March 23rd. Then the following week the Lehman's will be coming up to spend Easter with us. April 14th – 18th is a VBS and I'm planning it as a project in which the Bible School students can participate. Then, we must prepare for the Wesleyan Women's Conference.

Well, we had a very happy Easter with Orai, Linda and the children. They came on March 27th and left on April 3rd. They spent some time with the Los. Paul went along but Mike and Valarie stayed here with the boys. We have all had a great time together and basically have taken it easy. Yesterday all the older kids went to the Matopos early. Then we went out about 11:00. I just fixed sandwiches and carrot sticks because Roxy planned to fix the main meal. We had the Los eat with us on Friday and Saturday evenings and so

Roxy said she would fix our main meal for Monday night. This gave us time to really enjoy the Matopos. They had a craft market out there and we traded used clothes for grass woven things and wood carvings. It was really nice seeing all the crafts that the people there in Zimbabwe make from grass and wood. The next day Orai and Bob took the kids back out to the Matopos to crawl in a cave. Later we went back to this same market in the Matopos and purchased some grass woven clothes baskets. All this was written in my April 1st letter.

In this same letter I gave our flight schedule which actually in the end didn't turn out the way we had hoped. We planned to ride the train from Bulawayo to Johannesburg May 6th and then leave May 9th from Johannesburg for Amsterdam. We planned to have two nights in Amsterdam then fly to Paramaribo to be with Ron, Roxane and baby Alicia for about two weeks. From Paramaribo we would fly into Miami, then to Kansas City to meet up with Allen and Kim. Sad to say this schedule did not materialize!

I continue in this letter saying: "Time is running out so fast and this house doesn't even look like we are leaving yet! This coming weekend we go to Victoria Falls for a Sunday school teacher training meeting and our farewell. Then we have VBS coming up and a Wesleyan Women International Conference. When do you think we will ever get packed up? I wonder myself! The closer it gets the more I dread it. I've learned to love these people so much I hate to leave them. But then I want to see our family too, so here we are being pulled in two directions. Tonight we were out with one of the members of the church, witnessing to some of his relatives and both the husband and wife prayed to receive Christ in their hearts. They were so receptive to the Gospel. We hope Liberman can get a Bible study going for them to help them grow stronger in their walk with the Lord. Sometimes I think, Oh Lord, how can our time end so soon when we still have so many to witness to?"

There were farewells for us at a number of our churches in the Bulawayo area. Finally we arranged to leave Bulawayo on April 28th by plane, flying to Johannesburg. We would wait at the Lehman's in Boksburg while we tried to get visas to fly into Brazil, then flying from there to Paramaribo, Suriname.

A Great Disappointment

My letter written May 8th begins like this: "You won't believe this but we are still in Boksburg! Our Brazilian visas didn't come through so we delayed a full week keeping the same schedule, meaning that we should be in Suriname May 15th. Now if they won't let us have a visa in Rio for Suriname, we may only be able to stay at the airport and catch the next flight into Miami. So we still aren't really sure of seeing Roxy, Ron and Alicia. Sometimes we have to face great disappointment in this life, which is hard to understand.

Really, we are having a good rest here at Boksburg. We both were so exhausted when we got on the plane in Bulawayo I don't think I could have taken one more week like that last week. It's so hard to say goodbye to people and having farewells. We got so many lovely gifts from people

The Lehman's went down to Swaziland to take a deep freeze for the Bible College and also Linda needed to help Israel Langa with the Southern Africa field books. Bob, the boys and I stayed with Valarie and Mike who are in school. If we weren't waiting for visas, perhaps we would have gone down with them. I was afraid Roxy and Ron would call from Suriname and wanted to make sure I was able to take the call. I declare, I never saw such a ridiculous country that didn't have international phone service for private people. They have to use public phones.

We learned that a young girl, Sheila Edmondstone, is planning to visit us, arriving June 6th in the States. She is a Zimbabwean. We met her at the Nazarene Church in Bulawayo. She got to know the boys because she was the Nazarene Youth Leader at the Nazarene Church where we attended Sunday evening and the boys were involved with their youth group.

Again from my letter of May 19, 1986 I write: "Well, we are still sitting here in Boksburg waiting! Today Bob called and learned the visas didn't come, so we asked the travel agent to see if she can get us on a direct flight tomorrow evening for New York. I'm looking forward to staying with Allen, Kim and Kassandra. I think we will probably stay about a week with them."

So our plans to visit Ron, Roxy and Alicia in Suriname never worked out. It was a great disappointment to our family and to them. Sometimes in this life we face great disappointments and we wonder why God doesn't work out plans for us. In James 4:13-15 the Bible says, "Come now you who say, "today or tomorrow we will go to such and such a city...v14 whereas you do not know what will happen tomorrow. For what is your life? It is even as a vapor that appears for a little time and then vanishes away. Instead you ought to say, 'If the Lord wills we shall live and do this or that.'" I really had to battle with a bad attitude for a while, but the Lord helped me to get over the hard feelings.

Our Third Furlough

After our great disappointment of not being able to fly via Suriname on our way back to the U.S., we flew straight from Johannesburg to New York; from there on into Kansas City where Allen and Ron met us. They then took us to Trenton, Missouri, where Allen and Kim lived. Allen worked in the hospital there. Since we did not get to Suriname to see Ron, Roxy and Alicia, we decided to do something special for our boys. We took a day to go to Worlds of Fun in Kansas City. It really was a fun day for everyone. My fun was being Grandma to Kassie. While the others did the rides I got to wheel Kassie around in her stroller just watching all the excitement. We stayed with Allen and Kim about a week then headed for Omaha. We decided that we should get a vehicle of our own and then we wouldn't drive the one from headquarters. We found a brown Chevrolet Cavalier in good condition and one which we felt our pocketbooks could handle.

Then we proceeded on to western Nebraska and the Cheney farm. Again, it was our choice to live in the old Cheney farmhouse. It has been fixed up some since our stay there in 1980-1982 for about 2½ years. I think my father-in-law would have liked us to stay with him in the pink house. However, Bob and I felt that with two young boys and their activities, it might be too stressful for him.

During the summer of 1986 Ron worked for Bud Swan in hayfields. Rylan and Randal helped Uncle Charles on the farm. It was nice being close to my parents and also having the three boys home for the summer. Bob and I attended some of the camps and conferences. I guess one of the things Ron did with his two younger brothers was to take a trip to the Rocky Mountains, where they camped out in a tent. They didn't realize how cold it gets in the higher elevations of the mountains and so they said they almost "froze to death"! So they didn't really stay that long, but it was an experience they won't forget.

Rylan decided he wanted to play football in his last year of high school. He had played rugby in Zimbabwe as well as doing track. So now he had to get used to American football. Randal entered 8th grade and got to be on the grade school football team. When I could, I went to their games to give them support. While Bob traveled to many churches around the country I stayed home to care for our boys. Linda and Charles were very supportive of the boys when they had football games. Bob and I really appreciated this since it was very seldom that Bob could be present for one of their games.

As Christmas drew closer Roxy and Ron decided to take a holiday and come home so we could see all of them – they wanted so much for Bob, Rylan and Randal to see little Alicia. We had Christmas with them from Christmas Eve to January 2nd. Then all our family went to Trenton to spend a little time with Allen and Kim and little Kassie. I had made two little dresses for Alicia and Kassandra. They looked so cute together in their little red Christmas dresses. It truly gladdened our hearts having them all around us, for it was rare that this happened these days.

Our three younger boys, Ron, Rylan and Randal attended PACE, a youth conference for the Wesleyan denomination. They had a great time there thanks to Aunt Wilma who helped them have the funds to attend. It was an experience that really helped them to grow spiritually. We are grateful to the Lord for this.

After our time together at Trenton with Allen and Kim, Bob headed for another mission tour in the Tri-State District. On January 12th he was in Scott City, Missouri, and then had a number of churches in Arkansas and Oklahoma. On the 12th of January he said St. Louis, Missouri had six inches of snow. Bob returned home on January 26th.

In a letter that I wrote for January 12, 1987: "We were refused a temporary residence permit to Zimbabwe, but they said we could apply for a temporary work permit." We are trying to get back into Zimbabwe to work with the Zimbabwe churches that we had gotten started before we left in May of 1986. It seems that the Tolans, other missionaries, weren't allowed into Zimbabwe either. Instead they were sent to Zambia, which I'm sure the people there really appreciated.

Ron, Roxy and Alicia went to Omaha to spend January 4th through January 15th with Ron's parents. From there they will leave for Suriname. Ron's sister, Shelley, was also home for Christmas and she left January 10th to go back to Puerto Rico.

Headquarters asked Bob and me to tour the Northwest District from February 1 – 15. I was really excited to think I'd get to be with Bob this tour. Since Linda and Charles agreed to look after Rylan and Randal we knew we would not need to be concerned for their well-being.

We went to the church in Hamilton, Montana, then on to Idaho and Post Falls. One of Bob's old college friends, Lester Boone, and his wife were pastoring the Coeur d'Alene church. From there we were scheduled for the church in Hermiston, Oregon, on a Sunday morning where James Rosentrator and wife pastored. That same day we were scheduled for one of our churches in Salem, Oregon and just barely made the evening service at Capitol Park Wesleyan. However, we did make it by the "skin of our teeth", as they say. Bob and I really enjoyed sharing about our work in Zimbabwe, how Zimbabwe was a whitened harvest field and many souls were saved during our time there.

Sometime after the beginning of the New Year we learned new babies were on the way and we would become grandparents. Julie's baby was expected around April 26th, Kim's baby was due May 11th and Roxy's baby, June 14th.

Wilma, who has been a missionary in Zambia since 1964, was expected home on furlough the spring of 1987. Dad Cheney is really looking forward to her coming. He seemed pretty lost without Grandma. He did go back to Florida with Kathy and Jim the day after Christmas, but didn't stay very long. He flew back to Denver January 17th and took the bus from the airport to Big Springs, where I met him.

During the month of March, Rylan, who loved track, got very involved. Randal, however, preferred wrestling, At a district track meet in Bayard, Nebraska, Rylan qualified to go to State. He participated in the 100-meter run. A number of relatives decided they should go to the Omaha state track meet to support Rylan and other Garden County High students. In May we found that babies don't always come on their due date. Allen and Kim's baby, due May 11th, decided to come May 1st. Our niece Julie was due on April 26th and her baby arrived May 4th. I guess these little baby boys wanted to go to the Nebraska state track meet! Even the two recent babies attended: Kyle Cheney from Missouri, our first grandson, and Evan Transmeier, our niece's new baby boy. Others who went included Uncle Charles and Aunt Linda, Ron,

Randal, Allen, with his wife, Kim. As you might know, Bob and I were also there to see Rylan get 6th place in the state for the 100-meter run.

After Kyle was born, about one week later, my sister-in-law, Wilma, and I decided to drive to Missouri to see him. I really enjoyed having Wilma join me for the drive to Missouri where Allen and Kim lived. It was nice for Allen to be able to see his aunt again, as well as for her being able to see baby Kyle and little Kassie, the big sister.

At this time, Ron was in Omaha doing his training to be a Physician's Assistant. He had gotten quite sick and was diagnosed as having mono. So on our way back to western Nebraska I decided we should check on Ron in Omaha. When we got to Omaha, I found my son to be very sick. I said, "Ron, I'm taking you home with me." I wanted to start giving him some good vitamins and food and make sure he was getting plenty of fluids to drink. Within a week of being home, he was well enough that he thought he could get back to school. He really liked training as a PA and didn't want to miss any more schooling than was necessary.

During the month of May we were also packing up to head back overseas. Wilma was such a help to us during this time. In one of my notes to her I said, "It was so pleasant to be with you those four or five weeks. Thanks for going with me to Allen's and for all the packing of boxes you did. I'd never have gotten it done I'm afraid, without you."

We said our goodbyes to family in the Lewellen area and headed for Missouri. It was a real privilege and delight to us to be present at Kyle's dedication in the Nazarene Church at Trenton, Missouri. We had planned for Randal, Bob and me to fly via Suriname on our way back to Africa. However, when we checked what was required for us to get into Suriname we found that each one of us needed to bring $300 into Suriname to change into their currency, the gilder. This was absolutely out of the question for us. We didn't have that kind of money. So Bob said, "Why don't you go and spend two weeks with Roxy, Ron and Alicia, and be there when their baby comes?" He continued, "I'll spend the time here with our sons, then Randal and I will meet you in New York and we will fly together to Africa." So these plans were put in place. Kim took me to Kansas City to fly out to Miami and then on to Paramaribo, Suriname. I arrived there on June 6th, 1987.

My Suriname Visit

When I landed at the Paramaribo airport, Ron, Roxy and Alicia were there to meet me. It was so good to see them again. Alicia had grown so much since I had seen her at Christmastime. One of the first things I had to do was change my $300 U.S. dollars into guilders. The airport was about ten miles away from the city of Paramaribo, so it was interesting to see the terrain – very much tree covered, so not the wide open spaces like Nebraska. When I walked down the steps from the plane a puff of hot humid air just hit me head on. The airport was really old and dilapidated. In fact, the whole country looked quite a wreck and ruined mess. There were beautiful flowers and some beautiful homes, but not many.

The house my kids lived in was a double story. In fact, it sort of reminded me of a house on stilts. One reason houses are built up high was because the breeze could go through better. The main living quarters was up a long flight of stairs. Here was where the kitchen, living room and bedrooms, as well as bathroom, were located. Below the main living quarters was the garage. Besides parking for the car, it was a place for hanging clothes to dry. It also contained a guest room with a bathroom and this became my room for two weeks. I don't think they even had hot water in the guest bathroom, but that was fine with me because it really felt good to cool down. I don't usually perspire much, but seemed very hot and beads of sweat would run right down my face. The humidity was really high because this city is located right on the ocean front.

Paramaribo it's definitely cockroach country and I mean the roaches are huge. So yesterday it was the time for the "kill-it-man" to spray the house. Everything had to come out of the cupboards, especially food stuff and dishes in bottom cupboards. Needless to say, the next morning we found several large cockroaches lying on their backs. This was hard for Alicia, a little girl who was really afraid of frogs, bugs and anything that looks like a bug."

Here I would like to insert an incident that my daughter wrote to us about. It happened, I believe, after I had been there a while. When I was at home in Africa, I had made a nice big crocheted tablecloth to be a special gift for Roxanne. She had it in Suriname. Well, they had a young man working for them and one day he decided to sneak away with some of Roxy and Ron's things. Roxy said when she and her missionary friend returned to their house they saw this young man take off with one of their suitcases and so they proceeded to chase him down the road. When he went running into a nearby road, they just continued following in their car until finally the young man dropped the case and ran for his life. They picked up the case and halted their chase. And, yes, you guessed it – inside that bag was the crocheted tablecloth. Those two missionary ladies had done their own police work!!

I visited several of the churches in the Paramaribo area and also saw where they had the classes for Bible School. It was a privilege to meet some of their missionary friends of other denominations.

Roxy and I prayed that her baby would arrive before I had to fly back to the States. On the morning of the 10th of June they awoke me with the news that baby was on the way. Of course, Grandma was there to take care of big sister Alicia while mommy and daddy made their way to the hospital. I believe it was afternoon when Ron came back to the house and reported they had a baby sister for Alicia. Michelle Renee was born at 2:00 p.m., weighing 8 lbs. 8 oz. on June 10, 1987. We were so happy to hear that Roxy was able to deliver normally this time and did not have to have a C-section.

One of the occasions when we met together with some of the other missionaries was to celebrate Alicia's second birthday on the 14th of June. Grandma was delighted to make her a birthday cake for the celebration. I made a Care Bear cake which delighted her.

I described to the great-grandparents their little great-granddaughter. "She is such a cute little blond, curly haired, blue eyed child. I wish you could see her. You don't need to curl her hair on rags. It just hangs in ringlets down her back. She is absolutely beautiful. She is a very expressive child. The new baby is quite the opposite. Michelle, or as they plan to call her, Missy is so quiet and is such a good baby, doesn't cry much, and sleeps a lot, even through the night. Roxy keeps worrying that something is wrong with her since she isn't like Alicia, but I said to her, she should be very thankful for such a good baby."

I was told by headquarters that before I returned to Africa, I had to lose at least ten pounds. I had lost about six pounds before I arrived in Suriname. So with the heat, perspiration, and a flu that causes me not to eat, in the two weeks I was there, I lost five pounds and made the goal they had set.

On June 21st, Sunday afternoon I had my suitcases packed and was ready to go. Bob and Randal flew into New York on Monday evening, and I was to arrive Monday night so we could fly out together on British Airway to London. The last morning of my Suriname visit, I attended the big church in downtown Paramaribo. Most of the service was in Dutch and Creole, so I didn't understand too much. The church where Ron and Roxy worked was farther out of town, in a good area to start a church.

The next morning, Monday June 22nd, Ron and Roxy took me to the airport to catch my plane back to Miami, Florida. They left me there and went back home. My plane kept delaying. In fact, it got to be noon and still the plane had not left. They kept saying something about mechanical problems. Eventually, they announced that our plane would not leave until the next day. Was I ever in a predicament - I did not have a number to call Roxy and Ron and really wondered what I was going to do. There happened to be another mission couple there, taking the same flight, so I talked with them and told them my problem. They said I could ride the bus back into Paramaribo with them and the man offered to take me to Roxy and Ron's house. I was so thankful God had prepared a way for me.

Of course, the Lauber family was shocked to see me back but it was so cute what Alicia did. Roxy said she went out on their stairway and prayed that God would let Grandma come back. Well, God answered Alicia's prayer and Grandma was back for one more night. Next morning the kid's again took me to the airport and this time the plane took off with us to Miami. I must add, though, that Ron and Roxy didn't leave the airport until they saw the plane fly off.

I arrived in Miami and was to catch a Delta flight to New York so that I could meet up with Bob and Randal. So guess what? The Delta flight had several delays. I knew I would miss my flight with my husband and son, so called headquarters to see if they could change my flight to leave from Miami to London. Of course, they said, "No, I would have to fly to New York." I guess the reason was that my ticket would be waiting in New York for me. Finally we left Miami for New York and I was definitely on pins and needles, realizing I would be late. About 15 minutes before our plane was to land a voice came over the intercom, "Mrs. Robert Cheney, you are to check in at the British Airways desk as soon as you arrive." Oh dear, now what? As soon as I got my luggage, I checked in and was told my flight had left about 5 minutes ago. My husband and son had gone on ahead of me. I was so disappointed. It was the plan that all three of us would fly together and I was looking forward to catching up on family news. They would be telling me about our sweet dear granddaughter, Kassandra, Allen and Kim's daughter, and baby Kyle. I would be telling them about Alicia, Ron and Roxy's daughter, and baby Missy. But it didn't happen this way.

The British Airways clerk told me I would have to catch the next evening's British Airways flight and he gave me my plane ticket. He said I would need to get a hotel so I took a bus to Kennedy Hotel and got a room for the night. I truly was glad that Ron had exchanged the guilders I had left back into two hundred U.S. dollars; otherwise I would have had a problem. It took $100 for my hotel room.

So I flew out the next evening for London all on my own. Good thing I had traveled quite a lot so it didn't scare me at all. In fact, while at the London airport I called our friends, Bob and Sheila Smith, and I visited with Sheila to pass some time away. That night I again boarded the plane for Johannesburg, South Africa. It wouldn't be long now until I'd be meeting my dear husband and son, Randal. It was exciting just thinking about seeing them. The flight went smoothly and soon we were landing at Jan Smuts airport in Johannesburg. I was able to get through customs quickly and head to where I would meet my family. But, guess what? Not one soul was there to meet me. What a letdown!

Well, it wasn't really a problem because I just went to a telephone and called the mission house where the Lehman's lived. Linda Lehman answered and with a rather shocked voice said, "We were told that you were coming in tomorrow morning!" I said, "Well, I arrived this morning!" Rev. Karns, Bob and Randal came as soon as they could to pick me up. Finally, we had our happy reunion. Thank God we did all arrive safely – though not at the same time.

I was really tired after two nights of travel. Several of the missionaries planned to go to Petersburg where they were having a new church dedication. Bob, Randal and I were allowed to stay at Brakpan with the Karns'. He was our Mission Director at the time. This gave me time to rest up. We attended the Boksburg Church on Sunday. Jim and Carol Ramsay pastored the church there and invited us to have Sunday dinner with them. The Lehman children had stayed at home in Boksburg and didn't attend the church dedication so Randal enjoyed being with his cousins for the weekend. On Monday I was able to pick up the two lost cases at the airport and then did some grocery shopping before heading to Swaziland.

Here I need to tell why we wouldn't return to Zimbabwe. We were refused temporary residence permits and told we should apply for temporary work permits. Of course, this process can take a long time and even then you are never sure of getting these permits. So the council decided we should go to Swaziland and teach at our Bible College. This is not at all what we had hoped for. Randal really had his heart set on going back to Zimbabwe and attending Christian Brother's College where he was familiar with the school and knew some of the boys going there. But the decision was made that he would go with us to Swaziland and then in August he would come back to Boksburg and stay with the Lehman's so he could attend school in South Africa.

Daphne Niemack and Esther Phillippe were two single lady missionaries at Emmanuel Wesleyan Bible College. We would be working with them at the college. So Daphne took our suitcases and other things for us to Swaziland on Monday and on Tuesday Bob, Randal and I rode to Swaziland with Esther Phillippe. The region did not have a car for us yet. One of Orai Lehman's cars had been stolen and they had not yet gotten the insurance settlement. So we would just have to wait for a while. Daphne and Esther were good about letting us borrow one of their cars, but it meant we had to pay mileage.

Chapter Six
Our Fourth Missionary Term Begins
July 1, 1987- May of 1991

Again there were changes we had not anticipated. Our fourth term had brought changes to the family. We came back to Africa with only our youngest child, Randal. In fact, we celebrated his 15th birthday on the 12th of July. It didn't seem possible that 15 years ago he was born in Swaziland at the Raleigh Fitkins Memorial Nazarene Hospital in Manzini. Randal was feeling very lonely and dreading entering into a new school again. Our plan was to let him board with Bob's sister and husband, the O. D. Lehmans in Boksburg, South Africa. School would begin for him on August 4th.

God knew we were needed as teachers here at Emmanuel Wesleyan Bible College. In fact we were thrilled to find that three of the men students were from Zimbabwe. Because of the training the Lo's and we gave them in our last term in Zimbabwe, they would be able to graduate from the college here in Swaziland in November. The second semester of the Bible College here started on July 8th. There were 20 students enrolled and another one would be coming soon.

Just a bit more information on our son, Rylan, whom we left in the States: He worked for his Uncle Charles Cheney the rest of the summer and saved his money for college. His cousin, Valarie Lehman, had gone to South Africa to spend time with her parents. On August 12th she flew back to the U.S. and Rylan met her at the Denver airport. After spending a few days in western Nebraska with Grandpa Cheney and Aunt Wilma, Uncle Charles and Aunt Linda, the two of them headed for college in Bartlesville, Oklahoma.

Now back to the Bible College in Swaziland and the students who began their second semester on July 8th. Bob taught about the book of Romans, the Pauline Epistles and church history. I was teaching music and typing. On the weekend there was a Wesleyan Men's District meeting. The speakers were Rev. S. Sigwane and Rev. Hleta, head of the Swaziland Council of Churches. We felt it was a real honor to keep Rev. Hleta in our home.

There had been a real change in our campus since we lived there in 1978 and 1979. You would hardly believe it was the same place! The trees, of course, really grew so the place didn't look barren as before. Buildings had been painted and, soon, a lovely guest cottage would be finished with a small bathroom, two small bedrooms and a kitchen-living room area. It was made from a water tank that Daphne Niemack had built when she first came. One great thing was that now there was electricity all the time and the water system worked great. There was a pump on the windmill so that you could just plug in when the wind didn't blow or the tanks got low. Another wonderful thing was that there was hot water in the taps, much better for washing dishes, making it much more enjoyable to live there.

During July it was really lonely for Randal. He missed Rylan so much. Randal did have his keyboard so I let him show his keyboard to my music class. He even played at church. We let him call Rylan for his birthday on the 19th of July but it made Randal more homesick than ever just hearing Rylan's voice. They talked for four minutes and it cost us E15! We didn't make many calls back to the U.S. in those days!

One other project we took on was pastoring the church in Manzini. That was rather hard to do for two reasons: number one, we didn't have a vehicle and number two, there was no church building. Bob and Israel Langa were looking for a site, just the right place where the potential of 400 persons could meet.

Carol and Jim Ramsey conducted a Metro-Move at the college and then the students helped do the practical in Manzini as part of Evangelism Week. At that time we had twenty Bible Study groups going in Manzini. We met at one of the high schools as they waited for space at the fairgrounds to open up.

Getting Randal into School

Now I want to add what I wrote about getting Randal into school in South Africa. "Daphne Niemack took Randal and me to Boksburg in her car because as yet we had no car. When I went through the border I only put two days for my stay and tried to explain we were getting a student permit for Randal, but that didn't work. So Randal, too, had only two days for his stay. I thought to myself, I won't trouble these border people too much and just get this fixed in Germiston where Orai Lehman always goes to see about permits, visas, etc. We arrived in Boksburg around 12:00 noon and had tea and a sandwich with Linda, then rushed over to Germiston.

There we came upon another obstacle! They told us that Randal could not get a student permit for at least six to eight weeks – so now what do we do??? We all went back to Linda's rather heartsick and wondered how we could solve this problem. Daphne, bless her dear heart, began praying. Finally she called up an office in Pretoria that takes care of these kinds of things. The people were really nice and the man even said if we could come by 7:15 a.m. he would help us get the permit that day. We stayed at Karns' that night and got up very early the next morning and headed for Pretoria. Believe it or not we had the permit by 8:20 a.m. and headed back to Boksburg. I say here, "Bless Daphne's heart for all her efforts and thank the Lord for answering prayer." It was terrible to think of leaving Randal! Both of us were in tears. I wrote, "It just tears my heart out to leave my children." He did call on Saturday and was doing quite well and getting adjusted.

Our Visit to Zimbabwe

God answered our prayers for a car. We were able to get a 1986 Toyota Corolla station wagon to drive to Zimbabwe. While on furlough we had raised money for a car for Zimbabwe. Somehow this car ended up in Swaziland, but we thanked God that now we had the privilege of driving it to Zimbabwe. We were always so thankful for the people who gave to the projects that missionaries presented. We assured the people of our home churches that without their help and prayers we could not serve as missionaries.

So in our (new to us) vehicle we took off for Zimbabwe. It was Bob's, Randal's, and my first time to go back to Zimbabwe since we had been back on the field. The people gave us such a welcome at our return. Our hearts cried out because we couldn't understand why the Lord had not allowed us to go back. Just before we left for this visit our Mission Director gave us the sad news that our work permits were refused again. We were very thankful, though, that our churches were still holding their own.

We arrived in Bulawayo Saturday night about 6:30. On Sunday we attended the services at Trinity Wesleyan and then drove to Emtumbane for another service in the Western suburbs. We were there until about 3:00 p.m. and Bob preached for both services. That evening Liberman and Thandiwe Ndlovu invited us for the evening meal. She did a candlelight dinner and also invited Pastor Sonny and Annie Makusha. We had missed all these dear friends so much. We still had the mission house in Hillside so I had Belinda, who had worked for me while we were living here, to come and clean the house. Then I invited her and her husband, Ramah, to have supper with us.

Stewart and DeAnn invited us to their farm on Tuesday night for dinner. The last night the Goodes, who lived next door to us our last term, invited us for dinner. I state in my October 9th letter: "It has simply been marvelous to be here." I also say: "Our permits were rejected a second time so we don't know what God's plan is. Pray that Jim and Roxene Lo will be able to get back into Zimbabwe with work permits." I need to add about one more friend. We were able to see Sheila while in Bulawayo. She also introduced us to her special friend Kevin Thompson. He is an assistant pastor of the Presbyterian Church in Bulawayo. Sheila is the young gal who visited us in the States while we were on furlough. We enjoyed so very much being with all these dear friends in Zimbabwe!

End of the School Year

The first few days of November exams took place. I gave my finals in typing class and had to check them and turn in the final grades. I gave a final in Music, but really it wasn't much of a final because students only had to take it for credit. However, I did give ten questions just to see how much music theory they picked up from the class. In one of my letters I wrote: "I was quite proud of how the choir sang for the graduation. I think it was almost the best choir there.

Graduation and a wedding took place the same weekend, November 7th and 8th. On Saturday the 7th Helena, one of the students got married. Of course, the wedding cake is one important item for the wedding in African culture. Daphne Niemack helped me get the wedding cake made and it turned out quite beautiful. The cakes were round fruit cakes which Daphne had made. It was decorated in pink and white icing. Israel Langa said that he wished he could get married again because it was so beautiful! Then on Sunday we had the graduation. There were 11 students who graduated. We had 22 missionaries and some of their children here for the graduation. The Lo's came down from Zimbabwe, and the Dennis Engle family from Pietersburg were present. It was a beautiful day for this occasion with about 400 people attending, representing at least seven districts. The church was packed wall to wall and even down the aisle with children. In my letter of November 10th I write: "I tell you we need desperately to have a bigger place to conduct a graduation. Please pray about this in the coming year. We are also desperate for a new classroom block and a library and chapel. Pray that somehow money will come in for building."

Visitors

Now that school was out for this year at the Bible College, things were a bit more relaxed. We decided to go to Boksburg the 19ᵗʰ of November so we could have some time with Randal before Barbara Glissman arrived. Barb had become my very good friend in Oshkosh during the early 80's. She came with Sue Green, her son's girlfriend. Barb's son, Todd, was already in Africa where he had come to go on a Safari. Barb and Sue arrived on Sunday, but their luggage didn't come in until Monday. So we had to wait before going to our house at Joy Mission.

In keeping with our usual treat for guests, we took them to Kruger National Game Park. It is really interesting with many different kinds of animals. This time, we saw lots of African buffalo, also elephants and lions. The lions weren't very close to the road so we didn't see them very well. We saw two giraffes that were drinking water. That is quite a sight to behold! They spread their legs and bend their knees to get their heads down to water. It seems like even though I've gone through this park numbers of times there still are so many interesting things to see." After our excursion to the Game Park, we were delighted to have them celebrate the U.S. holiday of Thanksgiving with us.

Teaching at EWBC

As I mentioned before, typing was one of the classes I taught. At times it was quite frustrating because we had manual typewriters that didn't work well and we didn't have enough typing books alike. At one time I sort of made up my own booklet for the students to follow. During this time I also had the job of being secretary at the school office. Israel Langa was our principal at the school and would ask me sometimes to do typing for him. Then I did some typing for Bob's classes as well. So my hope and prayer request was maybe someone would send me at least some typing manuals that were the same. I wrote in one of my form letters; "Would it be possible that any of you high school teachers know of a school replacing their old typing books with new ones? Would it be possible to get these old books and maybe some Wesleyan Women's group take it upon themselves to help us get these books to our College?" This prayer was answered when we had visitors from the U.S. The high school in Bayard, Nebraska gave us typing books and our friend Barbara Glissman brought them to us. I was so grateful!

Early December, 1987

When we drove to Johannesburg to see Randal again, you'll never guess what we found!!! Our son had chicken pox! So this caused him to miss most of his final exams. It seems that what is done in a case like this is to just average his grades for the two terms and give him his final grades. He had a note from the doctor to stay out of school for ten days. So he only had three days of school left to attend. The school year in Southern Africa ends early December.

At this time we were at Mission Council. It was a real shock to get a call from Randal that my mother had been taken to the Scottsbluff Hospital for an emergency appendectomy. Her appendix ruptured and she was taken by ambulance to Regional West Hospital. In my letter of December 8th I wrote: "We are sitting here in Missionary Council meeting at Linga Langa in a business meeting. We were at Warm Baths, South Africa for this meeting December 5th - 14th. During the morning we do business and in the afternoon we have time for rest and recreation, then in the evening we have a service with Dave Tolen speaking."

I continue: "While we have been here, Mother, I don't think a day has gone by without mentioning you in one of our services. We want you to know that the whole missionary family here in Southern Africa has been praying for your quick recovery. It thrills my heart to know how close we become as a missionary family that when one of our loved ones at home needs prayer we all join in." It is times like this that are so hard when you would like to be near to help your older parents but you are halfway around the world, not able to be there. We have to just trust God and pray!

Christmas 1987

We spent a nice Christmas with Orai and Linda Lehman at their friend's place. Then Bob had to attend a mission executive council meeting. We decided to stay for a couple days of camp meeting before heading back to Swaziland. It had truly been an eventful year and turned out so much differently than we thought but praise God, He has been with us all the way!

Our Placement for the Coming Year

It seems that the council felt we should plan to stay on at EWBC for the coming year. The Bagley's were to be at the school, but because Tracy Bagley still didn't have the trach out of her throat they wouldn't be able to come for some time. This also made things uncertain for Randal's schooling.

We did check about getting him into school at Waterford in Mbabane. This would make it closer to home for him. In the end it seemed best to keep him in Boksburg High and staying in the Lehman home. The new school year will be starting on the 13th of January, 1988.

A New Year – 1988

As we move into the new year, there seems to be some uncertainty about our placement on the field. The fact that we did not get either a temporary residence permit or a work permit has led to the wondering of where to put us. This, too, causes some concern for our son's education. In one of my first letters of the year I expressed the plan for us to stay in Swaziland until June. One good thing is that Randal will be able to stay in Boksburg High because after Linda and Orai leave Jim and Carol Ramsay are willing to have him board with them. They will still be pastoring at the Boksburg Wesleyan Church. Randal did take the test to see if he could be in school at Waterford School in Mbabane Swaziland. However, though he passed the test, he was told they had no room for him for the new year. It probably was just as well because this is a boarding school and he would not be able to be at home anyway. Bob and I had determined before we ever came to the mission field that we would not put our children in a boarding school. The way things had turned out he could continue in the same school in Boksburg.

After New Year's and a couple days at the camp we headed back to Swaziland with Randal, as he still had some vacation time left. We decided to send Randal back by plane to Johannesburg and Lehman's would meet him at the airport. I tried to spend as much time with Randal as possible. One night we were up until midnight playing Scrabble. Can you believe it?

We began a very busy month. Miss Esther Elliot was at Joy helping us organize our school library. The Regional Board and a number of pastor's were also coming. I was assigned the cooking position; this meant not only the buying and preparing of food, but preparing and cleaning the school kitchen and dining room areas. Daphne was a big help to me in organizing this job.

It is hard not to have concerns and some worry about one's parents when they are in their 70's and living far from town and people. My mom seemed to have gotten over her ruptured appendix operation, but then I began hearing about all these terrible snowstorms taking place in the U.S. My parents lived 30 miles from town and at least nine miles from people around them. This gave me concern as to what would happen if they needed medical help. At one time I believe Mom and Dad were snowed in, unable to leave their place for around six weeks. Of course, I never worried about their food supply because Mom had a cellar filled with canned goods and she always kept a good supply of flour, etc. One thing I felt so thankful for was our good friends, Grace and Clinton Reeves. Since Clint and Grace were mail carriers for the route my folks were on it was a big relief to me. In fact, Grace wrote several letters to us during these bad weather times. She would call my mother and read my letters to my mom. I asked her to do this. Then, over the phone, my Mom would dictate to Grace what she wanted to tell me. In fact, one time Clint rode his snowmobile in the seven miles to my parent's home, bringing mail and supplies. Oh how we praised God for these wonderful friends helping out my parents!

Toward the end of January we had a work team coming from the Tri-State District and a lady who will take over the secretarial job and teach typing. The work team men were Jim Ridings and his son Joshua, and John Murray. The lady was Mrs. Moraga; however, she had to delay because her daughter was sick. She came about a month later and really lightened my load. The men were building tables and benches for classrooms and fixing electrical lines. Since they were building a house for the Regional Superintendent they were also building trusses for the roof of this house.

Now I want to give an incident I wrote about in my January 25th letter that really disturbed me. "Saturday we attended a funeral for Louis Nkambule. This man was only 39, but it seems he just drank himself to death. His family lives just outside the mission grounds. They are Catholic and so the priest did the service. It was the first funeral I have ever been to where I actually saw and heard a member of the family go through the village down to the grave calling out the praise names of their ancestors. It really was disturbing. And to think these people are right here on our doorstep."

Bible College began February 2nd. I was not teaching since I had been assigned to the school kitchen and doing the cooking. I learned how to buy for the school meals. I state in my February 3rd letter that I feel like we are in a rat race at times. It always settles down and things get into a more smooth routine after the students arrive and get registered. We learned in early February that our son Ron would be doing some rotations in medical experience here in Swaziland, at the Nazarene Mission Station hospital. His school in Omaha allowed him to do this for clinical training. We were excited to hear that Ron will be arriving March 2nd. It truly was a special blessing to Bob and me to have Ron come. He was able to stay with us except on the nights when he was on duty at the emergency room. He even recovered some of his lost SiSwati language. He loved the work even if it was long, hard hours.

Before coming, Ron broke the good news to us that he is engaged to Karla Langemeier. We were thrilled to know he would be marrying a Christian girl who also was preparing to be a doctor. Last year while we were on furlough, Ron brought Karla to our home several times. We hoped and prayed that we would be able to attend this wedding. "Ron and Karla have set their wedding date, December 17th.

Ron's News

God does work in different ways and the word does say he wants to also give us the desires of our hearts. Of course it depends on what those desires are. We had decided to look into a loan from our stateside bank so I wrote: "Daddy and mother could you find out if we could get a quick loan from our bank? What we are thinking is that now the exchange rate for the Rand is $2.27, more or less, for every dollar which means if we purchased our tickets here while the exchange rate on the Rand is this high we could borrow the U. S. money and pay it back in payments. Ron is going to take over payments on the car. We want to borrow money for our tickets to come home for the wedding. Of course if the exchange rates go up to $2.30 then our tickets would be even less. The travel agent here is to let us know in time so we can pay for the tickets before they go up. It sounds bad maybe to borrow money to go to our son's wedding but to Bob and me it's most important to be at their wedding and witness this once-in-a-lifetime event than almost anything else. So I hope people will understand!

Our kids are so wonderful. Rylan gave us $500 for our tickets and Roxy and Ron $300. It was in my November 3rd letter that I said: "Mother and Dad can you guess what? One of our good friends sent us $1000 for our tickets! It was so unexpected, but I felt the Lord would somehow help us get there. Tickets paid for! The Lord is so good."

The new school year seemed to be busier than ever with visitors pastoring the Manzini church and teaching at the college. February 27th I mentioned in my letter: "The youth have planned a youth camp out here at Joy

Mission on March 18th so we are hoping to have a good number out. We will just have them come for the day as we really don't have any place for them to stay at night while school is in session. We will have a big picnic for them. Bob went out to Maliduma to one of our house churches today. Someday we hope that we can see a church built there. I stayed here to help the cook and give her a break from being in the kitchen. This year we used one of our student wives to help in the kitchen, as well as each day of the week in the evening and at early morning before the cook comes. She really only has to cook on the weekends but she does clean up the kitchen and dining area every day. I thought that she really needed a rest but besides that, Langa asked me to help her out so she could accompany her husband and four daughters to one of the churches where the husband is going to be preaching for the school year.

February 28th Roxy and Ron called us. She said they were sick and that their car had broken down because the thermostat had quit working. So they were feeling quite down. At this time Ron was attending the Nazarene Seminary after returning from Suriname. They had the two little girls, Alicia and Missy, and were living in an apartment. They planned to all get together at Allen and Kim's in Trenton for Easter. Ron and Karla planned to go down from Omaha and they were hoping Rylan could come from Bartlesville. Easter is a wonderful time to be together with family!

So March finally arrived and we made a special trip to Johannesburg to pick up Ron from the airport. Of course, while we were there, there was shopping to do. Many times in Swaziland one could not find the things that are needed. It was always easier to find what we needed in a bigger city.

Then there was the issue of finding a place for Randal to stay. In May the Lehman's were to go on furlough. We approached the Ramsey's about this. When we went to see them we said, "We have a question to ask you." They said "yes" to our question before we even asked it. They also were keeping Paul Amos, another South African missionary's son. They readily agreed to keep Randal for the rest of the school year. He would begin his stay at the beginning of the second term which began April 19th. This wasn't really that big a change for Randal for he stayed in the same Boksburg high school. Randall had known Auntie Carol and Uncle Jim all his life, so they were no strangers to him. Jim and Carol were living at Ebenezer Mission when Randal was born in July 1972.

Ron arrived on a Thursday so we decided it would be best to wait until Saturday to go back to Swaziland. Then he could have a little more time with his brother, Randal. He was able to bring a new 7000 Minolta camera for us from the States. We truly were thankful to the Nebraska district for giving us $500 toward this camera. Ron said the total cost was $529. Here in South Africa it probably would have cost us R2000, which we could not have afforded. Ron took pictures of my pretty flowers to try the camera out. I said in my March 8th letter, "I wish you could see the flowers I have in my yard. The Jasmine is blooming as well as the Tiboshina. The Jasmine is a creamy white and has a sweet fragrance. The Tiboshina is a beautiful pink." The weather is not as hot now and we are having more comfortable days and have been getting some really nice rains. Remember March is fall for us and springtime for you!

This is what I wrote March 14th. "Ron had worked a 24 hour weekend shift at the Nazarene hospital and was too tired to go to church Sunday morning. The weekends are really wild for doctors on call. So many people drink, drive and fight. He had someone who was stabbed in the chest. They tried their best to save him, but couldn't. Ron's been doing things like lumbar punctures, suturing lacerations, and seeing all sorts of patients with malaria, leprosy, pneumonia, etc. He is getting a lot of good experience."

We had the Malihambe Conference toward the end of March. Daphne said she thought about 70 women would attend from across the district. According to my March 30th letter 200 people were present at the Sunday morning worship service.

Sometimes missionaries have the job of transporting not only the living, but also the dead. According to my April 7th letter I wrote: "Bob has to carry a body from the mortuary to the village had Thimbutini and then he and Fernando, one of our helpers, will have the funeral on Saturday morning."

From the April newsletter: Former missionaries to Zambia and South Africa, Rev. and Mrs. Paul Ragsdale, arrived the second week of March. Rev. Ragsdale helped us with many small jobs that needed to be done so badly. He made a large storage cupboard for the college kitchen, put in a hot water heater in our guesthouse, laid ground electrical wire for our water pump, and fixed many leaking pipes. Mrs. Ragsdale was a great help in the sewing line. She sewed around 22 or 23 pairs of curtains for the college classrooms, dining room, and office. We were so thankful to these Christian friends who came to help us.

Events in May, 1988

In my May 10th letter I wrote: "Today Ron called me and asked if he could bring out some medical students to have tacos with us. Three of the students were doctors and one of them had his wife along. They enjoyed the food very much."

Ron is scheduled to leave May 29th and the Lehman's flight leaves May 28th. Bob and I were so grateful that we got it worked out about our flight back to the United States for Ron and Karla's wedding. Ron said to me, "It's so amazing that you write to your mom and dad every week." Then I said to him: "You must really be in love because you write to Karla about every night, besides talking on a tape." Ron is so funny! I reported in this May 10th letter that our flight on Zambian Airways was confirmed. Praise the Lord!

For my birthday Bob cooked breakfast and then Bob and Ron took me out to eat. My mother was able to call me. At least on May 12th our phones were working! The rest of the day I did painting with my Tri-Chem paints. I told my mother I was trying to save money by making the gifts I wanted to give.

For Mother's Day the boys, Ron and Randal, were so nice to me. They got breakfast Sunday morning for all of us. We had scrambled eggs, Beor Vors (this is a farmer's sausage), juice and toast. It tasted so good (maybe because I didn't have to cook it). I enjoyed so much having two of my boys with me on Mother's Day.

I took Ron to Ebenezer Mission so he could see it again. This mission was where he lived from eight years old to 10 years old. He seemed rather in a daze looking at all the things where he used to live. He said, "It seems strange how much smaller the mission house has become, where we used it to live." Things do seem so much bigger when we are children. That's just the way it is! The Rev. Sigwane's were living in the house at this time. While Ron was there Chrystal and the nurse had him look at several of the patients they had at the clinic. Then Mrs. Sigwane's daughter fixed dinner for us. It was a delicious dinner of fried chicken, rice and pumpkin, with cake and tea as dessert. Mrs. Maphanzeni also was invited to eat with us.

Themba and his bride got married on May 20th. "The cake I made turned out beautifully even though I do say so myself I decorated the cake in white, lavender, and pink with light green leaves. They were really pleased with it. The cake had to travel many kilometers. In fact I prayed that I could get it safely to Swaziland and the Lord answered my prayer. Even the groom's mother was praying for me. You see the wedding cake is a very important part of an African wedding. They have it sitting right in front of the church where the couple and the wedding party are standing before the preacher. So if they did not have the wedding cake there it would be a great tragedy.

Toward the end of Ron's clinical training in Swaziland, Randal came back from Johannesburg with Uncle Orai Lehman. This made it possible for him to spend a bit more time with his brother. In one of my letters toward the end of April I wrote, "Ron is doing maternity ward so I expect he will report he has delivered a number of babies by the time he returns. It's so nice that, here, doctors don't need to worry about being sued. He surely is getting valuable experience."

Finally it was time for Ron to say his goodbyes to the Swazi people. We took him up a few days before his flight left. We got to help the Lehman's do their finishing touches to packing before their flight left on May 28th. Our things from Zimbabwe had been stored at the Boksburg mission house to. So we hoped to be able to fill our Kombi with the five drums and the piano, besides a number of boxes. We decided to stay on into the next week as Randal had Monday and Tuesday as holidays. Since Grandpa Lehman is married again, he and Orpha plan to live in the Boksburg mission house. So now we head back to Swaziland, our empty nest. But what a great privilege it was to have Ron almost 3 whole months!

The Busy Days of August through December, 1988

I'm looking over my letters for these months and wonder how I ever got everything done. I know in my own strength I could not have accomplished all there was to do. Philippians 4:13 has been such a wonderful promise from the Bible to me. It states "I can do all things through Christ who strengthens me." Many times the Psalmist David mentions the strength God gives. I can certainly say it is true in my life back then and even now. Psalm 27:14 says "Wait on the Lord, be of good courage, and He shall strengthen your heart, wait I say, on the Lord!" But I also stated in the August 7th letter the need for prayers. "This month I really need your prayers because it is probably the busiest we've had since coming. There is a Regional Board meeting, a District Board meeting, and the District Conference all here at Joy Mission-EWBC. I have the responsibility to oversee the kitchen and feed all the people who come. Of course, I have people doing the work. The District

Conference will be the hardest to do as there will probably be up to 200 people." Having a school garden definitely helped in feeding students and in providing food for special meetings. "My garden is looking so nice. The tomatoes are now ripening, but either the chickens or the birds are trying to eat them too. We had a small head of cauliflower. The old lettuce is finished but new is coming on. We are getting onions and spinach and should soon have green beans."

At the close of my August 14th letter I wrote: "We made a flying trip to Johannesburg Wednesday. Bob had his Council meeting on Thursday. Then we drove back to Swaziland on Friday. Randal was so happy to see us at Boksburg. We had supper with the Ramsay's, where Randal stays now. We were very late getting in because we started out with the Kombie and it stopped on us at Mbabane. After it finally started again we drove it back to Joy Mission and got our car. I much prefer riding in our car anyway, but it doesn't carry as much. I did a lot of shopping for the school for Daphne and for the Region and I had to speak for a Malihambe service at Daphne's church. One of the ladies from Manzini was to speak, but she didn't show up."

The Regional Board met at EWBC August 15-19th. We had about 45 people to cook for. Bob and I had the joy of having Jim and Roxy Lo and their two boys come a few days early so we could visit with them before the board meeting sessions. I need to mention here that Roxy and Jim did get their permits to go back into Zimbabwe. We truly praised the Lord for this answer to prayer.

"I got through Regional Board meeting. Cooking for that was quite a job, but I made it." Saturday was rather an anti-climax because I had to cook for the District Board Meeting. Then the District Conference began on Wednesday. "I wish so much we had someone to do the maintenance work because Bob has to spend time working on fixing things. Many times he doesn't have time to spend on his lesson preparation. Anyway, as I said, the Lord is helping us through. Yesterday they butchered the cow for conference so today Daphne is cutting it up. What she can't cut we will take into the butchery and have them cut it up. Then I asked for prayer for Israel Langa as the RBA appointed him as principal of EWBC and he is also District Superintendent of the Swaziland District. We, the staff, were really happy that Israel was appointed because we felt if an African was not appointed to this position it would be a downward step. What we as missionaries are trying to do is work ourselves out of a job."

August 30th we were on our way to Zimbabwe for their District Conference. We planned to stay with Dan and Patty Connor on the way. We had not met them before so we looked forward to this introduction. The next day we traveled on to Bulawayo. Just Bob and I went because Rev. Segwane had to stay for a funeral in Swaziland. It was the funeral of Rev. Nhleko. We just praise God because he said he was ready to meet Jesus. Since Rev. Sigwane had to stay for the funeral, Bob and I needed to help Jim Lo with this Conference by having lessons, messages and Bible School services. It was so good to be with Roxy, Jim and the boys, and wonderful to see so many people and friends we knew from before. We had 160 – 200 people the last Sunday of Conference. There were 21 baptized and ten children and babies dedicated. The Lord really touched and melted hearts – a real sense of revival. We came back via Boksburg and stayed a couple nights, which allowed us to see Randal. Ramsay's were gone a couple days, so one night I fixed supper so we could eat with Randal and Paul.

A nice surprise that I mentioned in my September 17th letter, I stated that "Wilma Cheney is getting married to Ed Wissbroeker, another missionary in Zambia who lost his first wife to cancer." Also in that letter, I mentioned the cost of air tickets, round trip from New York to Omaha and back. Ron found them for $208 each and the cheapest I ever had was $329, a big difference and a real help for us. So Ron got tickets for us, flying Zambia Airways.

September 16th Pope John Paul II came to visit Swaziland so Israel Langa let the students out of school and took them to the stadium in Ezelwini Valley to see the Pope. I didn't want to go because there would be abantu baningi (many people). Then it turned out that the school cook, who was Catholic, wanted to go, so I needed to do the cooking anyway.

My mother and daddy were so faithful in giving to the Church and to missions. I wrote to them in my 27th of September letter, "Do you know how much you gave to missions in South African Rands? Bob figured it would have been about R1700 – that's really good! We appreciated how you support missions. If every church member gave like you do, we wouldn't have to worry about missionaries being told they could not go back to their field because of lack of funds." We learned that Roxy and Ron would not be going back to Suriname because they said the Mission Department is in a bad way financially. Several other missionaries had been terminated besides Roxy and Ron.

Roxy, Ron and the girls were booked to fly out of Suriname October 3rd. In Suriname missionaries have only a three year term so they could be home for Ron and Karla's wedding.

The October 3rd letter gave details about Wilma and Ed's wedding. "They decided that their wedding date should be December 24th. Wilma asked me to be her matron of honor. I do feel so honored to get this position. She wants me to wear a medium blue velvet dress. She has asked Alicia to be her flower girl, and Jimmy Don the ring bearer. Tara and Kristen will light the candles. Wilma says she wants the ceremony at the church to be mostly for relatives and the church people; then she will send out announcements afterwards. "

Randal got home for his ten day school break. He came back with Esther Phillippe October 1st. The secretary who came to help at the school, Helen Moraga, had never seen our mission at Ebenezer. Since Bob had to deliver a message to Sigwane about an emergency meeting, we took Helen and Randal to Ebenezer with us. Ten days of vacation from school went all too quickly. He left by plane October 10th at 12:30 p.m. He would be in school from the 12th until December 7th.

October 18th – "Well, today is a 'walking in the rain', day. Praise the Lord for all the good rains. My garden should really do well now. I pulled some small little carrots yesterday and we had beets for supper, besides the head lettuce and onions. I have an older man student now helping me for a while in the garden, so it's beginning to look much better. If the old bull who chewed off my green beans would have stayed out of the garden we could have lots of nice green beans now. "

This month Miss Phillippe, Bob and I went to Johannesburg with five students to represent the school at the Reef District Conference. As it turned out Regional Superintendent, Rev. Sigwane, was unable to make it. He lived at Ebenezer and we had had so much rain that when he tried to leave Friday he got stuck. Then the tractor which tried to pull him out got stuck and he couldn't do anything about the problem. Saturday evening he was able to get a message through to Brother Lehman, Sr., and to Rev. Karns. They conducted the conference until midnight Saturday. We had our part in the service for the Bible College on Sunday morning. The presence of the Lord was very close. I believe eventually we are going to have many students whom God is working on to train for the work of the Lord.

We had a praise this month because Bob talked to the headmaster of Central School in Manzini and he was willing to allow us to meet at the school for Church services until the end of December. In the meantime, we continued to look for and hoped to get a church site, or at least a more permanent meeting place. At this time I asked for prayer for one of the mothers in the Manzini church. We thought that maybe her daughter was demon possessed. Her mother was a wonderful Christian, but this girl caused her mother so much heartache. She was only about 15 and had a baby. She was a beautiful singer and if only God could control her life she would be such a blessing.

November arrived beginning with lots of activity. But first I want to add here a paragraph from my daughter's November 1st letter: "Two weeks before we left Suriname we received news that the Department of World Missions was experiencing severe financial difficulties and therefore we were asked to terminate our contract. This meant a total change of plans for us since we were packing with plans to return to Suriname after a year's furlough. In the two weeks that remained, we sold all our personal belongings and tried to tie up loose ends as best we could. Through this we sensed that God was in control and trusted that He would guide our future. He has not disappointed us as the Downey's (missionaries in Guyana) are now planning to move to Suriname, perhaps as soon as March. We see this as God's leading, for Brother Downey will be able to fill a desperately needed role at a critical time in the life of the Suriname District."

In one of my form letters written in November, I made this statement: "We know many hands have worked hard and sacrificed by giving during Mission Emphasis and Self-Denial, and even given of themselves to come and work here." Some of those coming to work here were the Tri-State work team, Rev. and Mrs. Paul Ragsdale, and Mrs. Helen Moraga. In my November 3rd letter I say: "Helen and her daughter are going back to Johannesburg on Sunday and then they will leave Tuesday or Wednesday. We will miss her so much, especially since she has been doing so much typing for us. She is a dear person. I took her and her daughter out to the Game Park yesterday. It was a perfect day to go. We left early in the morning and saw lots of animals."

November 5th and 6th was a big weekend. Graduation took place on the 5th and seven students graduated from EWBC.

I had mentioned earlier about a house being built for the Regional Superintendent. Our first National Regional Superintendent was Rev. Samson Sigwane who originally comes from the Ebenezer area. On November 6th, the day after graduation, we had the dedication of this house. Of course at a big celebration, the dedication of this Regional House and Headquarters, a big feast is held. My November 3rd letter states: "I've baked hundreds of cakes from scratch, actually 500 cupcakes and nearly 40 double size cakes. Now I must frost all of them. I really don't care to bake another cake or cupcake for a long time! The men killed a cow and there were stacks of meat, rice, salads, and cakes to fill everyone to the brim. There were approximately 450 people attending. Seven districts of the Southern Africa region were represented. Praise God for those helping hands, both from America and on this field who made this dream a reality. Our dear Rev. Samson Sigwane, Regional Superintendent of the Southern Africa Region, now lives near the Joy Mission and Emmanuel Wesleyan Bible College in a large beautiful home, well able to accommodate many visitors and meetings."

After the big events earlier in November there were things to do to finish up our year before leaving on vacation to the United States. I had correspondence to take care of and had to do the inventory for the school kitchen. Then one weekend we had a pastor's meeting for the district which meant I had to help some in the kitchen. But it isn't so bad when you have only 15 to 30 people to cook for. The school cook came to help me. She always is such a blessing because she does an excellent job. I was also trying to do some sewing for myself.

It was middle of November that we heard about my brother-in-law Steve, my youngest sister Elaine's husband. He was in a serious hunting accident and nearly lost his life. Of course this was of great concern to us. A lot of praying was going on and we asked many in our missionary family to pray as well. He and his friend were out hunting for moose. They separated in different directions. Not wearing bright colored jackets made them easy to mistake for a moose. This is what happened. So being shot by a rifle doesn't give one much chance. But praise God he allowed our dear brother to live!

One of the teachers we hired to teach at EWBC was Caroline Kongwa from Zambia. She went with me to the capital of Swaziland, Mbabane. I wanted to get some Christmas gifts for family to take with me to the U. S. So we visited the market and the Swazi Flame. I gave quite a number of African craft gifts this Christmas. Then we planned for our Christmas program at the Manzini church on December 4th. After this we prepared to go to our Missionary Counsel at Linga Langa near Warm Baths in Transvaal. It was held December 7th through the 11th. We will meet Randal after we make our flying trip back to Swaziland to pick up our luggage on December 11th. Then we will make our way to Boksburg via Swazi Air December 12th. At the Jan Smuts airport in Johannesburg we transferred to Zambian Airways and headed to Lusaka and from Lusaka to New York. We arrived in New York at 7:30 AM December 13th; we changed airports and flew into Kansas City and by evening of the 13th we were meeting our family at the Omaha airport. What a happy reunion!

Our dear friend Barb Glissman gave us her house to stay in while we were in Omaha. During our stay there we did some shopping. We took Wilma to some bridal stores so she could find a wedding dress. She found a beautiful dress. Only four days was a pretty short time to get everything done. Since I wasn't writing letters during this time I'm not remembering how long we stayed at Barb's house. I do know Ron and Karla's wedding was December 17th so we had to be at O'Neill, Nebraska by December 16th. I was to have the rehearsal supper. I fixed ham, scalloped potatoes, peas and salad. Roxy and Kim helped me. Kim's parents, Don and Naomi Cavaness, let us stay with them. We served the rehearsal dinner at the Fellowship Hall of the Methodist Church where Karla's folks go. This is the church that Ron and Karla were married in the next day, Saturday, December 17th, 1988.

The week before Christmas was a busy one, visiting many loved ones and preparing for Ed and Wilma's wedding. It was delightful to be with our four lovely grandchildren, Alicia and Missy Lauber and Kassandra and Kyle Cheney. We were able to be with our children, my parents, and Bob's dad as well. In fact Bob's family had not been all together since the early 1960's. This was a real treat! So the 24th of December 1988 arrived, the wedding day of Ed Wissbroeker and Wilma Cheney. Bob performed the ceremony for them at the Wesleyan Church in Lewellen, Nebraska. The reception was held at the fire hall in Lewellen. It truly was a happy Christmas for all of us. We felt so blessed by the Lord in the fact that we were able to attend both of these weddings and visit with family. Truly the Lord gave us a happy ending to the year 1988!

Beginning a New Year – 1989

We said our goodbyes to our families in western Nebraska around January 7th and headed for Omaha. Then we went on to Allen and Kim's in Trenton, Missouri to say our goodbyes. We got to their house at about 7:30 in the evening because we had terribly slick roads and thick fog. It was fun being with Allen and Kim, Kassie and Kyle. We played with our grandchildren and even had a tea party with them. From there we drove back into Omaha. Again we had bad roads, but made it back into Omaha. We were so grateful and thankful to be back safe spending our last few hours with Ron and Karla.

Here I would like to say a few words about my friend Paula Boquist. She lived in Omaha with her husband. I had first met her when I came for the birth of our first granddaughter in 1985. She got us the most wonderful useful gift that was so helpful and time-saving. She purchased a new Smith Corona DeVille 750 typewriter and gave it to us. As I have stated before I had lots of typing to do for the Bible School, as well as our own correspondence. On this typewriter you could type up a letter and store it in memory to type later or you could use it to answer a number of letters. I stated in one of my letters: "I think that this is going to be a great addition to the Joy Mission house and should really save me some time." This typewriter did use fuses and if they burned out it was hard to find this item unless you traveled to bigger places. I guess this was the start of computers! Anyway, I really enjoyed the gift my friend Paula gave us.

Ron took us to the Omaha airport and we flew out to New York on January 9th. I wrote to my parents that we mostly sat in the JFK airport in New York for the rest of the night and waited for the Zambian flight to leave at 11 a.m. on January 10th. When we flew into Lusaka we had to claim our luggage and get on another Zambian plane that would fly us into Matsapa airport in Swaziland. At the airport there in Lusaka they evidently opened into Randal's suitcase and stole his little alarm clock which he had gotten for Christmas. That was very disappointing to him. I have to tell about the plane we rode in to Swaziland from Lusaka. Of course it was a much smaller plane. When it came time for us to load the rain was really coming down so we tried to hurry to our plane. As we climbed the steps and headed in the door of the plane I will never forget the sight that met us! I wasn't sure we should even be getting on this plane. Up above the seats there was water streaming down onto the seats. A pretty scary thing to face when you expect the plane to protect you from the rain! Anyway, whatever was the cause of this water pouring onto the seats, they got it stopped. But you better believe we were praying this plane would get us safely to Swaziland! What a sigh of relief when we arrived safely at the Matsapa airport!

January 17th I wrote: "It's been almost a week now since we arrived in Swaziland. We have been so tired since getting back and waking up at

queer hours and feeling sleepy at odd hours, so I guess we're in the recipro-
cating stages of "jet lag".

On the 13th we took Randal to Boksburg, South Africa so he could
enroll for Standard nine which is junior year of high school. Then on Jan 31-
Feb- 4 we had our retreat with Mr. Mike Metz of Trans World Radio as our
guest speaker. As the school year at the Bible College got underway at Joy
Mission, I was appointed to serve as school secretary.

First of all, there was a staff retreat to attend mornings and evenings.
It didn't leave much time for doing other things. We were expecting about ten
new students. Also, one of our young missionary couples, Mark and Diana
LaPointe, planned to come and spend a few days with us. They were from
Canada and they were expecting their first baby about August or maybe July.
They brought a young man from Venda as a student for the Bible College. We
also had visitors from the Free Methodist missions, Rev. and Mrs. Henry
Church, and Rev. and Mrs. Phil Kapp. They were meeting with us to discuss
about accepting some of their students from Zimbabwe and Mozambique. At
that time I thought they probably couldn't get in until second term or maybe
the next year. For the first term in 1988 we had 18 students.

Bob and I had to work on the course called "Personal Devotional
Life" that we would team teach and I had to type up the course syllabi among
other things.

Carolyn Kongwe and I started a Kid's Bible Club at one of the neighborhood homes of one of our church members. As often in my letters I include
a prayer request. "Please pray that somehow we can reach out to some of
these really needy children in Manzini. They so desperately need to know that
Jesus loves them. "

I went with Esther Phillippe to get a copy machine for the school. I
mainly wanted to accompany her because I wanted to see Randal. He misses
us and we miss him terribly. We went up on Monday and returned on Wednesday." It poured rain most of the day. I'm really glad that we got home from Johannesburg yesterday before all the rains came. We may be drowned before
long if it keeps up this rain!

I'll have to tell you about our flat tire on this trip. Miss Phillippe
didn't have very good tires on her truck and so on the way out we had a flat
tire. We had this flat tire after we had gone about 50 kilometers past the bor-

der. So we got out and found the tire really ruined. I was going to go ahead and try to change it myself thinking that probably someone would come along and help us. Esther said she had never changed a tire but I said I had and could probably do this one. Anyway as I was putting up the jack a man stopped to help. A few seconds later two more men stopped. It happened by a sawmill and the one guy must have been the foreman or some head man. Anyway he told us that we really needed another spare tire because the other one was too ruined. So we asked him if there was a station around to get it fixed. He said, "No." but then offered to take us to their workshop and he had another man fix it for us. They even put in a different tube for us as the other one was shot. I told him it just showed how God took care of His children and he agreed. I was really thankful that the flat tire happened there rather than further down the road where we couldn't have found help. The Lord even knows where to let us have flat tires!

In February we got heaps of rain. The countryside turned gorgeous and my garden did well. From the trees we got guavas, mangoes and even oranges, grapefruit and lemons.

Last night, March 6th, Bob and I had the Tom Riley's out for supper and they brought their small TV so that we could see the video that John Karns brought of Bob and Brenda Bagley and their family. The staff came at 7:00 p.m. to view it. We kept the TV and video so that students could view it if they wanted to. In the same March 7th letter I mention about the blizzards and snow Western Nebraska was getting. It concerns me that my folks live so far from anyone in the Sandhills. My mom was about 72 years old and my dad close to 77 years old. Having cattle to feed and care for in blizzards is not really something people their age should be doing. In looking back to that time I know we prayed and God took care of them!

On March 7th I wrote: "I taught the class for Bob today so he could work on some other things for classes. Next week I'm not sure if I will go with him to Johannesburg or just stay here and get things ready for Randal's return for the school holiday. He gets out of school March 17. Bob has a meeting with the Missionary Executive Council at Karns'. I'd like to go but I probably need to stay here to do classes and Bible studies."

Bob went to Brakpan to attend the Missionary Executive meeting on March 14th. Early the morning of March 15th they were to travel up to Venda to look at a place for the LaPointes to build a house. Earlier I mentioned the LaPointes, a young couple who had recently come to help us here in the

Southern Africa region. They really needed to have a better house than what they had been living in. It was very hard to find good houses in Venda. A work team came from Kansas to help with this project.

Bob brought Randal back to Swaziland as it is time for school holidays. He just waited an extra few days so as not to make another trip. Randal then wouldn't have to go back to school until April 12th. There was a bit of news about Randal in my March 15th letter: "He is doing okay in school but is getting rather tired and ready for a holiday. He told us that he had gotten a small trophy for getting third place in the shot put out of eight different schools. We felt that was very good because he was in the above 17 age group and he is still 16. He has ordered spaghetti for supper Friday night when they get home. He says he likes my spaghetti best of all! This has been my son's favorite meal for a long time!"

Is there such a thing as getting too busy? Well I guess there is because I wrote in one of my letter: "Yesterday I forgot to go to class! Can you believe it? I was seeing Bob off to Johannesburg and then we had two phone calls booked; one to Zambia and one to Zimbabwe, so someone needed to be at the house. (You see in those days, you couldn't dial direct. You had to go through a telephone operator). Rev. Sigwane was also waiting for a call and talking, so I guess with so many things on my mind I just forgot about the class. Anyway, I apologized and we had class in the evening in place of Bob's English class.

March 28thwas a good afternoon on a very hot day in Swaziland! I really did not feel much like writing letters. We are all doing well, just very busy. Last week was Easter holiday time so the post didn't go out for four or five days. On Thursday I invited a Nazarene missionary family to have supper with us. Then that evening we also had the Naudes come in from Brakpan to be here for two or more weeks. Roxy and Allen would remember Lynn. She was Lynn Hurley. She went to WES and was on a YES tour in the States in '74 or '75. She is now Mrs. Naudes and they have three children and another one on the way. She has come down to teach our ladies sewing for two weeks. They are planning on making a skirt and blouse, each of the ladies. It will be a part of their school uniform which is a gray skirt and white blouse. Lynn really sews well and does so many things. I think I could really learn from the class too, but I need to babysit her little 14-month-old baby girl. One little boy is seven years old and the other is five years old. The sewing class starts at

2:00 p.m. and ends at 5:00. I'm cooking the main noon meal for them and Esther Phillippe is fixing the evening meal."

We had a nice Easter dinner, but I must say I really did miss an Easter service. The King had called people to the Stadium for a big Easter service. I felt with Lynn and the three children being here, it was best to stay home. Randal wasn't keen on going either. So I fixed roast chicken, dressing, apple pie, and several other things.

Randal seemed to be enjoying his time with us. He found that he was the hero of two little Afrikaan speaking Naudes boys. This definitely improved his Afrikaans. He went back a little early with the Naudes, so then I didn't need to go up to Boksburg until about the 17th of April. Paul Amos was also staying with the Ramsey's, but this time they each have separate bedrooms."

This week I needed to get many other things done before going up to Joburg on the next Monday. I'll be staying with Randal and Paul there on the reef for the month while Ramsays are gone. Randal is really looking forward to it, as well as me. I hate being away from Bob so long. Knowing how he cooks for himself or rather doesn't cook, helps me to know that it isn't good to leave him alone too much. I'm trying to fix up some things to help him have something to eat."

My April 4th letter begins, "I'm about ready to fall asleep. Last night I stayed up with Randal and we talked and talked until after midnight. Then this morning I had to get up shortly after six to take a girl into the hospital to have her stitches out." I think I need to explain that we had the responsibility of caring for our student's health. This girl, Maggie, had gotten sick right at the beginning of the school year. "Maggie is the one who had an appendix operation last month. She seems to be doing all right but is healing just a bit slow. I really don't know how she is going to get everything made up from missing so much school. But she is determined she is coming to Bible college and definitely doesn't want to be taken home."

The young couple who couldn't come back to school because of sexual misconduct have really repented. They have written letters and met with the staff to tell how sorry they have been for such a thing to happen. They are planning to get married very soon, as quickly as the damage has been paid by a cow from the boy's side. If a boy gets a girl pregnant he has to pay the girl's parents one cow for the damages before he can even think of paying lobola for the girl. Lobola now is anywhere from 15 to 20 cows, depending on the education of the girl and where she comes in line. If the boy doesn't want to marry the girl after getting her pregnant then he is required to pay five cows to the girl's parents. One good thing about this couple is that they say they know God has forgiven them and they still feel God is calling them into his ministry. They will not be unequally yoked together and we felt good about their marriage. If this couple gets married soon then the college plans to let them re-enter the school and continue with their education."

The group of eight people came from Pretoria on Friday evening and I had supper for them. Daphne helped me a lot by making the curry.

"We had a very nice weekend with the people from Pretoria. One of them was Stanley Benjamin formally from the Johannesburg area. They now live in Pretoria. Wayne Smith and his wife were with the group. We took all of them to see the church that was recently dedicated at Mkhweli and they went to a revival there in the evening. Then on Sunday six of them went with us to Manzini for our services. The other couple went with Daphne to her church. We had a wonderful service in Manzini. The Lord is working, I believe, and people are beginning to respond. Tonight we began a new Bible study in the Mamba home. This will make three Bible studies we have going in Manzini. Last Saturday I was talking to one of the Post Office workers and I think that we may have an opening for another Bible study in his home."

After I arrived in the Johannesburg area coming from Swaziland, at about 2:00 PM, I decided to do grocery shopping at the Pick & Pay Hyper Market. The boys, Randal and Paul Amos, had soccer games so I knew they wouldn't be home until after 4:30 p.m. Actually they didn't get back until 6:00 and I had supper ready. Carol had left spaghetti prepared so it wasn't difficult to get. The next night I made pizza for the boys, and after that, tacos.

While in Boksburg with the boys I did two wedding cakes. I found a shop in Edenvale that rented cake pans for baking all kinds and shapes of cakes. It cost R2.00 a day to rent the pans and for this I was really happy. I won't ice the cake for the Sigwane's daughter until I get back to Swaziland. But for the Nhleko's son I must have the cake ready in two days. I made Themba Nhleko's cake in three round tiers with four heart-shaped cakes at the side. The one for Sigwane's daughter was heart-shaped. I hate baking fruitcakes for a wedding, but this is always what they expect in Southern Africa. I guess they do keep better in the warmer weather.

241

Another small paragraph of this letter states: "I'm making Themba
Nhleko's wedding cake, so please pray I can do a nice job. He is really depending on me. I plan to do it while I'm in Boksburg with Randal and Paul. I
should not have quite so many interruptions I hope!"

We had a work team coming from the Kansas district. There were 13
members on this team. I was able to go over to our Mission Director's, the
Karns', and meet them. I entitled my letter of April 19th, 1989 "The King's
Birthday in Swaziland". Although I'm not in Swaziland at this date because I
drove up to Johannesburg by myself on April 17th, I wrote about King
Mswati's III. He turned 21 years old today, the 19th. They are having a big
grand celebration in Swaziland for him today. Even the Bible College is not
having classes and even Bob should be able to get caught up on some of his
bookwork. He had to get the Regional treasurer's book caught up to date for
there will be a Regional Board meeting in May. While I'm gone Daphne is
looking after the school kitchen. It's really wonderful to be free from that for a
month. This morning I've been sitting here in the sun trying to get my blood
to run more freely! It's been quite cool up here on the reef. One of these days
we are going to wake up and see frost."

Rylan's Visit, May of 1989

Rylan, our fourth child, who was attending Oklahoma Wesleyan University, came to visit us for his summer vacation. He landed in Johannesburg
on May 14th. It really was a nice Mother's Day gift! He also came with me
back to Swaziland on May 19th. I had to get the wedding cake back by May
20th for Themba Nhleko's wedding.

While I was in Boksburg with Randal and Paul Amos, the Ramsey's
had flown back to the States for their daughter Sheri's graduation from college. They were flying back into Swaziland on the 23rd of May. We were to
pick them up at Matsapa airport. They had left their car with us at Joy Mission
and after picking up their vehicle would travel back to Boksburg. They had a
wonderful time and were so happy to see their daughter graduate. I also had a
happy time with my son and Paul. I enjoyed staying with the boys. It was
good to be a part of getting them to school, fixing lunches, watching them
play soccer, and helping them study for exams. I was even able to attend a
parent-teacher conference for Randal and meet some of his teachers. Randal
and I came back for a long weekend May 3rd through the 7th. It was a nice
break in my stay. This way Bob and I weren't separated so long. Then to end

my Boksburg stay I arrived back shortly before the Ramsey's, around May 21st.

Now at school we are in the week of final exams for this term. The coming week the students will be going on the Evangelism and Work week for the students. This year the Qhubekani district invited the students for this project. Each district is invited to apply to the school for this team of students.

Then we entered June. I was so preoccupied with preparing lessons for the Wesleyan Women's Convention held at Ebenezer Mission that the first week of June didn't see any writing. I spoke on relationships. The first relationship is with our Lord Jesus Christ. This of course is the relationship that affects all other relationships. The next lesson was on our relationship with mother- in-laws and daughter-in-law. I was happy to report to the ladies about the two wonderful daughters-in-law that I have. Here in this country this is the one relationship that needs a lot of help. Many women like to use their son's wife as servants in their homes. Also another thing that takes place is the son gives his money to his mother and if his wife gets any money she must go to her mother-in-law and ask for it. But many of the Christians do try to be kind to their in-laws. One of the ladies I talked to is Mrs. Rosalina Thwala, a pastor's wife who is such a radiant Christian. I said to her, "I know that you are a wonderful mother-in-law." and she said, "Oh, yes, I have a wonderful daughter-in-law." They are more like friends and they love each other.

While I was away at the Women's Convention Bob and Rylan had no vehicle for transport. So on Sunday morning they decided to ride the bus into Manzini so they could be at church. Fortunately Rev. Sigwane came along and didn't let them sit by the roadside waiting for a bus. He took them clear into Manzini. But they had to find a bus coming home. I guess that was quite an experience. If you ride a Swazi bus you always expect it to be very crowded, not only with just people but often chickens or even a goat or two. Of course, you will never forget the smells! But the important thing was they made it home to the mission.

It would be so nice if Randal could be home more while Rylan is with us. He gets out of school for a holiday on June 29th. We are talking of taking the boys down to the Port Shepstone area on the South Coast. It has been years since they have seen the place. Rose and Chris Motley told us to just let them know and they would have a place for us to stay.

From my June 27th letter: "We finally made it up here to the Johannesburg area. We didn't get our visas until Wednesday afternoon about 3:30 so this was why we got such a late start. Jim and Carol told us we could stay at the Bible College in Brakpan. We have two bedrooms and can use all the other facilities. Randal is staying with us. It's so nice to have the boys together. We aren't able to do much shopping, but we are enjoying one another. Rylan even wants to put us on a prison diet, so we can save even more!" "I'm not sure what special thing we will do for Bob's birthday June 29th, but I think Bob and the boys will go down to the Indian market, downtown Johannesburg," I wrote.

We moved Randal's things over to the Cinderella Mission, Boksburg, where Grandpa and Grandma Lehman are now. Randal is going back over to Orai and Linda's where Orai's folks are right now. Orai and Linda will be back about August 2nd. When Randal goes back to school the Lehman grandparents are willing to keep him the few days before Linda and Orai arrive.

We went to Port Shepstone on June 30th. Leaving very early that day, we got ahead of the big line of traffic that usually goes to the South Coast for July holidays. We arrived around 1:30 PM and drove to Eden Park where we lived in 1976. It still looked about the same. Then we drove into Port Shepstone, on 221 Alamain Drive, where we lived in Don Miller's house. We drove by the lower primary school where Rylan started to school. When Rylan saw the playing field it was so funny. He said something like: "Man, oh man, is that ever small!" We just laughed and laughed. It is rather funny how things look so big to you as a child and when you see them again as an adult they aren't very big at all. We drove them to Manaba Beach where the Motley's live. They were so nice to put us up and we did enjoy our stay there so much. We had a chance to go down on the beach. To me it seems the Indian Ocean is one of the most beautiful oceans of the world. Although it rained all day on Saturday we had a chance to go down to the beach and picked up pretty shells washed up by the waves. Sunday turned out to be a beautiful day with hardly a cloud in the sky. That deep, deep, blue sea against a blue sky is almost beyond description.

After getting back to Swaziland we made plans to help Rylan and Randal get to Zimbabwe, where we spent our third term. The bus was too costly so it was decided I would drive up to meet Jim Lo in Venda. All three of us then will ride with Jim Lo to Bulawayo, leaving our car in Venda. Then Jim plans to come back in a week's time so we will ride back to Venda with him. Jim is doing some Theological Education by Extension lessons in the Eastern Transvaal, Venda and Casteel districts. This has made our visit so much easier in Zimbabwe. We truly appreciated Jim helping us in this travel.

The second term of school began July 4th at EWBC. We enrolled 18 students, two more than last term. Bob, Langa, and Esther have somewhat of a heavier load as we are freeing Daphne Niemack to go to Fuller School of Missions in Pasadena, California. However, Robert Bagley's will take these extra classes when they arrive. Their arrival date is September 10th.

We celebrated Randal's 17th birthday in Zimbabwe. It's July 12th and I asked Randal after he woke up if he would like to go with Rylan and me to a tea room downtown and celebrate his birthday. He said he would like that so Rylan, Randal, and I went downtown Bulawayo. Randal ordered a great big chocolate milk and sausage roll since it was his breakfast. Rylan had a berry shake and I had two cups of very nice hot tea. It was so nice to get away with the boys and do something different for his birthday. At noon Roxy Lo fixed a scrumptious dinner of pizza, then apple cake with ice cream. Even Randal's friend John, who used to visit us a lot while we lived in Zimbabwe, came for lunch.

Yesterday, the 16th, I went to Sigola with Jim Lo and got to visit quite a number of the church people whom we knew from the Farm Church and Sigola area. Then today Roxy asked me to speak at the WWI meeting in the Kumalo Church. I had not really planned to come with the boys but in the end it seemed better for me to go, especially since Bob made the suggestion. This coming week Jim is returning to South Africa to conduct more seminars. So this way it hasn't cost us so much and we really do appreciate what Jim and Roxy have done.

We came back to Venda July 17th with Jim Lo and picked up our car at the LaPointes. Then we drove to Palaborwa to see the Amos's. Since Paul was there with his folks, the boys wanted to see him. They convinced us to stay the night before driving on to Swaziland. I'm glad that we did stay for I think the Amos's needed some encouragement. The next morning we drove to Badplas where Rylan and Randal enjoyed swimming at the hot mineral springs. I stayed in our car and painted some quilt blocks. Then we drove on to Swaziland and arrived at 5:00 PM that evening.

When we arrived we had missionary guests, Don and Patty Connor, and their children staying at our house. They were missionary speakers for our

College Missionary Convention. They brought one of their men, William and his wife and little girl, who had graduated in 1987 from EWBC. The students were pleased to see this family who are doing missionary work in Lebowa. Lebowa is a new area in which the Connor's are working. It was nice having the Connor's, but we had a terrible water shortage because the pump on the windmill wasn't working. In fact when Bob and Dan took it back to the people who were supposed to have fixed it, they found they had left some part out of it. No wonder it didn't work! It really makes one thankful for water after having gone without for two or three days. So now we praise the Lord the windmill is fixed and we have water!

Friday the Connors left and then we had to get ready for our annual Malihambe meeting. It started Friday evening and went through Sunday. This is where the churches collect money for the yearly conference. The money goes to help in different projects across our district. Mrs. Sigwane, our Regional Superintendent's wife, was our speaker.

In my July 25th letter I mentioned that early the morning of July 26th Roxy, our daughter, called us. She reported the news that they were taking the Wesleyan Church in North Platte, Nebraska to pastor. The other news was that we would again be grandparents because they were now expecting their third child. We as missionaries, far from home, always enjoy getting news like this!

On Monday morning Daphne Niemack took Randal with her to Boksburg. Randal then started school. He moved in with Grandpa and Grandma Lehman until Orai and Linda arrived the 4th of August. I wish we could be there to meet them, but at this point it looks like we will be unable to. Bob has an Executive Meeting on the 8th and 9th, so perhaps I'll go along and get to visit.

August 7th letter: "Seems like I'm always hurrying here, doing this, doing that, called here, asked to do that, and also trying to prepare for my teaching. I teach a typing class and another class called, "Ministry to Children", so I'm quite busy this term. I do have my typing syllabus done but I need to make one for my class, "Ministry to Children". "Anyway, I have our suitcase packed so Bob and I will head for Boksburg. Rylan went up to Johannesburg earlier with some TransWorld Radio missionaries, Linda said it helped her so much to have Rylan there since she didn't have either Val or Mike to help. Last week we took Rylan to Milwane Game Park and also over to Ebenezer Mission. We hope to spend time with him this week while we are on the reef in the Johannesburg area.

We are so grateful to our Mission Department in the States for making it possible for our children to visit us at least one time while they are in college. Rylan flies out of Johannesburg August 14th, arriving back in the United States at Kansas City, August 15th. We will not be able to see him again until his graduation from Oklahoma Wesleyan University in May 1991.

In my letter of August 11th to my parents I write: "I decided to send a letter with Rylan and have him mail it in the States. Randal was able to be at the airport to see Rylan off as well as the Lo's, Mrs. Karns, Linda and Paul, and Grandpa Lehman. I always hate so much to say goodbye to our kids, seems like it gets harder each time.

From my August form letter: "Today has been one of those days! A day when it seems everything goes wrong. Our Toyota car could have burned up, but praise the Lord it didn't! Miss Phillippe and I were planning to drive into Manzini to choose a farewell gift for Daphne Niemack. Before we left the school campus the car refused to start. It always started very well before. I sent someone to call Bob but before he arrived I decided to investigate for myself. I lifted the hood, the bonnet as they call it here, and right away I saw the problem. The battery brace had broken, allowing the battery to slide off into the radiator and belt. As Esther and I watched we could see a slight smoldering of the wires and I knew I'd better do something and do it quickly. I grabbed the battery and pulled it up on the shelf where it belonged. The wires had already burned some, but soon the smoldering stopped. By this time Bob and Israel Langa arrived and they were able to repair the damage and wire the battery back in place. We went on our way, praising the Lord for his protection once again.

The students and staff planned a farewell for Daphne. She will be greatly missed around the school. She first came to EWBC in 1980. This past Wednesday I took Daphne to the US Embassy to get her US study Visa. She was so amazed that she could get this all in one short morning. She will be leaving here from Joy on the 3rd of September and going to visit her people in Natal. Then on September 15th she will fly out for Pasadena, California.

September 5th - the college students have gone to Zimbabwe with Israel Langa, the principal, for the conference. Then they will travel to Lebowa, where they plan to help build a church. So there will be no school for the next two weeks. Bob and I however are going to Zimbabwe with Rev. Sigwane, the National Regional Superintendent. We just don't plan to be gone as long as the students. Taking our students out to different districts across the region gives them practice experience in ministry as well as expose the different districts to what students are learning at the college.

Ten days later I write in my letter: "We had a safe trip to Zimbabwe but it was terribly tiring. We traveled all the way from Joy Mission to Bulawayo, 15 hours of constant travel, only stopping for border gates, changing drivers, and getting petrol (gas). So it was good to climb into bed at Roxy and Jim's. Praise the Lord for his wonderful help in our conference at Victoria Falls. We spent three nights at the Falls. We slept in a school and believe it or not we slept in sleeping bags on a hard cement floor. I didn't rest well at all, but it was nice to be with the women and girls. The men and boys were in a separate classroom. I think this is why Bob and I have been so tired since we got back. Anyway, the Lord gave a real revival Spirit and people were making things right and asking forgiveness. I really believe Zimbabwe is on its way up again even though we aren't planning to have a missionary present for a while. Jim and Roxy are moving to the Republic of South Africa to work with the TEE program in December. They will be renting the mission house in Bulawayo rather than selling it. So if we want to put another missionary in Bulawayo we will have a house available. On our way back to Swaziland we stopped in Petersburg and stayed overnight with Mark and Di LaPointe and their new baby girl. She was born September 6th - such a little doll. They call her Kristy Nichole.

September 15th - the Bagley's arrive. I fixed supper for them. They will be staying in a house at the Nazarene Mission in Manzini. When we get the house enlarged we will move them out to Joy Mission.

From my September 21st letter – "This week we had the Karns come to visit us. Yesterday we met for breakfast with the Bagleys, Karns and Miss Phillippe. After the meal we had a meeting to discuss about our housing situation. Although the Bagleys are staying at the Nazarene Mission station in Manzini we would like to see them come here to Joy EWBC as soon as something can be arranged about their housing. It now looks like we will be living in Daphne's house because they feel like it is going to be easiest to build on to. Orai and Linda, Paul and Randal will be coming from Boksburg next weekend since it is the shorter holiday time for Randal. Orai is going to draw up some plans for adding on to Daphne's house. I thought maybe this term we wouldn't have to move but it looks like we are going to move anyway. But it is just down the hill, not far, so that is one consolation!"

It is nice to have the Bagleys here with us. Little Tracy Hope is such a sweetie. It just seems a miracle that she is so normal and full of life. Bob B. has taken over the classes that other teachers were holding for him, so now my Bob doesn't have quite so heavy a load.

The first part of October I have another wedding cake to bake. This time it is for Victoria Langa's sister. The Lehman's and Randal are here at Joy Mission for the whole school holiday. Randal and Paul have to be back for school in Boksburg on October 4th. It is a joy to have them here with us. This whole week is going to be very full.

The wedding cake got made and decorated and I even got my talk prepared and given to the Christian Women's Club. We enjoyed having the Lehman's with us for the ten days of school holiday. I forgot to mention another thing I had to do was type a 20-page term paper for one of the students.

I want to tell about a Bible study I'm doing in Manzini with some of the students helping. We were doing one of Jim Lo's TEE books called "Bible Studies for New Christians". We were so happy because the husband gave his heart to the Lord. Then we asked for prayer in my letter as we were planning to visit a lady that doesn't go to church. We hope and pray she too will come to know Christ.

In one of my October letters I write: "I think I may have broken the toe next to my big toe on my right foot. I was running along down by the kitchen dining room area when I kicked a big rock. It really hurt at first, but I didn't think much about it. However, as the day progressed and by the time I had finished Kid's Bible Club, it was really hurting. We stopped in at the Bagley's and at Dr. Page's where Randal was visiting, and Dr. Page happened to be home. He looked at my foot and said that it looked like I might have broken the toe. Today it is all black and blue and is quite swollen and painful. Anyway, I'm hobbling around but I'm sure it will mend!

October 18th - we heard on the news about the terrible earthquake in San Francisco. It must have been awful. So many terrible things are happening in the world. Just last Friday our neighbor lady had her car taken during the night. This family only lived about a mile from us and so we are filling a bit edgy these days. The Bagleys almost had their car stolen in Manzini on Sunday evening. Their alarm went off and scared the thieves away. They called Tom Riley and he shot his gun a little later so as to scare the thieves. It really doesn't seem to matter if it is in the town or the country. But thank the

Lord we have the promise from his word: "What time I am afraid, I will trust in Him."

We had a call from Ron in Omaha. He and Karla will be arriving about January 28, 1990, in South Africa. This is so exciting to us! Then there came a letter Allen telling of their new venture, moving to Guthrie Center, Iowa to take up a new job as head of the lab at Guthrie County Hospital. We also heard from Bob Sweet that Sue and Keith have gone into the ostrich business. Some great news from home! It helps us to keep informed about our family. Wilma told us some rather sad news. She said her and Bob's dad just isn't well at all. She says his mind is really gone. We are so sorry to hear this about Dad Cheney. Bob and I have been writing to my mother and dad about renting the little house they have close to their home on the ranch. This is the house where I grew up. It was used as a storage area for furniture and things they had gotten at sales. Anyway, in November they decided to load up their pickup with much of this stuff and drive out to Oregon to my sister Esther's. Quite a bit of this belonged to Esther and Nathan, so making the trip with this load left the little house available for restoring and making livable. Since we would have no young children in school, I felt it was a wonderful opportunity to live close to my parents for our year of furlough. Of course we would be traveling in Home Ministries quite a lot, but there would be times we could spend with Mom and Dad. They were very thrilled to hear we wanted to do this and worked hard to make the little house very comfortable for us.

Now back to my November letters and all that was happening toward the end of 1989. In my November 8th letter I write: "Well, all my exams are given and so are all the other teacher's, but Bob has to grade his papers yet. EWBC closed November 10th this year. We had one girl graduate, but because she chose to go through graduation exercises with next year's graduates we did not have a regular graduation event. Not having a graduation service this year saved a lot of work for us. I did make cakes for our school party. We had ice cream and Jell-O in addition to lots of fried chicken, rice, and salads. I think everyone was quite happy.

I want to explain what is happening with the housing at Joy Mission and Bible College. Since the Bagleys returned in September they needed housing. We had been living in the Joy Mission house, but this was to be for the principal of the Bible College. Israel Langa, who was principal, resigned and Bob Bagley took his place. Since Israel had his own home near the college, Bob and I were allowed to live in this house. Since Daphne Niemack had gone overseas to the US to further her studies, her house was available. The only problem was it needed to be bigger for a missionary family to live in. So my December 1st letter reads: "Do you want to hear about our new house? Actually it is Daphne Niemack's made-over house, but when we get finished, it is going to be the newest house and nicest, probably, that I have ever lived in, except some rented houses in Bulawayo, Zimbabwe. They are starting to paint the rooms. A cabinetmaker is making the kitchen cupboards and closets. Then we will be laying carpet. There will be tile in the kitchen. When these things get completed, I will feel very good because we can start moving in. The problem is that we want this to be all completed so we can leave for Johannesburg by December 20th. Right now it looks impossible, but "nothing is impossible with God!" Israel Langa is the one who is responsible for the building. He has some young man working for him as well."

"You will never guess what I am doing for our new bedroom! I have decided that since I have not ever had a nice bedspread, I'm going to make one. Our room I'm doing in lavender, so I am doing a candle wicking bedspread in lavender and cream colors. The drapes will have lavender and pink floral designs. It will look quite pretty but what a big job I am undertaking! (I still have this lavender and cream bedspread and it's on my bed today)

Bob has been busy, too, going with Israel to buy materials and trying to find good buys. Since we must also furnish this house, Bob and I have been looking for furniture. You see they did not move the furniture down from Bulawayo and so we have been using the Bagley's furniture. Now we need our own. We found some bookcases and a filing drawer and the Mission Director is collecting some things for us from the Republic. Daphne did not have that much stuff to use as furniture, so that is why we can't use hers. It will be nice to have our own things.

From my form letter of December 1989: "Concerning the Bagleys and Cheneys: It will be moving time in December for both families. The Bagleys will be moving from Manzini into the Joy Mission house and the Cheneys from Joy Mission house into the enlarged house of Daphne Niemack. Miss Niemack's house was first built with one person in mind and so needed some extra room for the Cheneys. Hopefully the moving can all be completed before Christmas."

In my December 17th letter: "On Tuesday the DeBeer's from Brakpan, South Africa came to help us. They are taking their holiday here. He is helping on some of the cupboards in our house and she has been making curtains. I really appreciate what Mrs. DeBeer has done. She has my bathroom, bedroom, and kitchen curtains all made. Tomorrow she wants to work on curtains for the lounge. I made dinner for them today. It was an easy dinner of pot roast, potatoes, and carrots which cooked while we were in church. They went to the Nazarene church so that the kids could understand better. They actually speak Afrikaans, so the children don't know English that well. One of the little girls was so surprised when the Sunday school teachers spoke Afrikaans to her. This evening we took them to the Living Waters Nazarene Church for the service. Now tomorrow I want to do some more packing of all our things into boxes and put them into one of the bedrooms here in the mission house, hoping to move in when we come back from Mission Council."

We spent Christmas in Boksburg with the Lehmans and LaPointes. All the missionary family will be in the Johannesburg area for Missionary Council meeting, which starts December 26th to finish the year 1989. We will be back in Swaziland for the Regional Conference December 30th through January 4th. We were privileged to have our General Superintendent from the States, Rev. Harry Wilson. So with this we end our year 1989 on a positive note, looking forward to a new decade!

The Beginning of a New Decade, 1990

Over the Christmas holidays I had a lot of back trouble. There was a lady who did massages that went to the Boksburg Wesleyan Church, so I went to her for a massage. It seemed to help me a lot. However, I learned that there was a chiropractor in Benoni, which isn't too far from Boksburg. He took x-rays of my back and gave me a treatment or two. It has really helped my back and I feel so much better and think I'm ready to go back to Swaziland.

While we were in Boksburg we had news that our home church in Lewellen, Nebraska burned down on January 4th. I asked where they were having church now. They were able to save the annex to the west of the church and are using it for services at this time. I wrote: "It must be a terrible shock for the whole community."

In my letter dated January 9th it reads: "The boys, Randal and Paul, began school today. Randal is a prefect this year. He looks quite neat in his new blazer and basher (that is a special hat that separates him from looking like the regular students). Being a prefect is a real honor because the teachers place their trust in these helpers to keep order and report anything that should not be happening. So we are very pleased about our son having this honor. Bob and I headed back for Swaziland soon after Randal started his new school year. We not only had our own car, but were driving a car back for Israel Langa. This meant we both would be driving a vehicle. Sure glad my back got better."

At this time an older couple, Bob and Betty Rosas, from Minnesota are in Swaziland as WGC workers. They are working on our house, trying to get it finished enough for us to live in.

When we arrived Friday evening we found our bedroom almost complete. The bed was made and the carpet on the floor. Only the curtains were not up! So Bob's and my first project was to put up curtains in our bedroom and the bathroom. We still need a table and chairs and my piano needs moved down from the mission house. The carpenter put Formica on my countertops and breakfast bar. It really looks nice.

I stated in my letter: "I've been really frustrated trying to live in this mess while we get the house fixed, but when it's finished it will really be a nice house. Today I painted pink primer paint on some of the cupboards. The carpenter said it was really important so that the wood would be waterproof. The cupboardswill be white with what is called a biscuit color for trim. The floor tile is beige."

"The Rosas are really a blessing to us" I write in my January 25th letter. "In fact, I don't know what we would have done without them. Right now Mr. Rosas is laying the carpet in Randal's room. Bob (my Bob), (you see during this time we had three Bobs on the campus) is building cupboards in the bathroom and Randal's closet because the carpenter is just too slow. Our closet needs to have the shelves painted and some carpet put on the floor. When everything is finished it will be nice."

"We are hoping that our furniture will come tomorrow. Orai and Linda are planning to bring it for us. I still have quite a pile of stuff here in the corner of our bedroom, but I think that when our furniture comes I will be able to put more of it away. I'll be glad to have a stove to cook on".

"We are getting Roxy and Jim's stove because they are renting a house in Springs which already had a stove. Also, I think there will be some of their bedroom furniture coming to us as well. You see the Lo's have moved to Springs near Johannesburg. Jim is doing TEE for the whole region. Pray for them, as well as us, for they are having some adjustments to make too. Jim Lo and Esther Elliott were here for our staff retreat. I kept Esther and the Bagleys had Jim stay with them. We had 20 students enrolled this year."

While the Rosas were with us they stayed in our guest house. They were away for a while and she told me during this time I could use the stove in the guest house. That was really helpful! Brenda had been fixing the main meal for us and this really helped her out. The Bagley had just gotten their shipment and Brenda has been working on putting her things away. Little Tracy hurt her hand and finger quite badly a week ago and they had to rush her to the emergency room and get it stitched. Thank the Lord it is coming along and looking better. She is three and really quite the girl. She looks so much like her mother, even the color of her hair. Their son, Joshua, goes to school in Manzini. He is eight years old." This was all from my February 5th letter.

Then in the same letter I wrote about Rhoda. She was a dear lady who worked for me at Ebenezer Mission during our first term. She died from a ruptured appendix. It was such a shock. The Good Shepherd Hospital never tried to do anything for her. Maybe it was too late to do anything, but I do feel terrible about it.

Ron and Karla Cheney's Visit, 1990

"Thank God," I write in my February 5th letter, "Ron and Karla arrive safely on January 31st, here in South Africa." The Lord protected them from a bad accident while in flight when a crane hit the window of the pilot and cracked it. This made it necessary for them to turn around and go back to Amsterdam." They plan to arrive in Swaziland about February 10th.

Since Ron and Karla had not taken much of a honeymoon they decided to use this first part of their African visit as something special for just them. They flew to Cape Town then went to the Motley's in Port Shepstone. Rose and Chris Motley then drove them up to Swaziland and spent the weekend with us.

Karla, I think, has had a bit of culture shock, but she is doing fine. She has even learned a number of words already. Ron is so proud to show off his makhoti (Swazi word for new bride) and today when he introduced her at Joy Mission Church everyone just clapped. The people seem so proud to see a missionary's son's wife. We are really enjoying having Ron and Karla stay with us. February 18th letter says: "Yesterday they had the day off so I took them and the Rosas to the Swazi candle factory. Then we visited another small craft shop on the way to the Mahlanya market. There we found lot s of nice fresh pineapples. We bought several to bring home with us to let the kids enjoy it. Just wish we could share some with all of you. This is the time of year when pineapple gets so good and sweet that it just melts in your mouth!"

We had Randal fly into Matsapa on Thursday so he could go with us to the Kruger National Game Park in Transvaal, South Africa. Ron and Karla got off for the weekend so we all went to the game park. We saw about 20 different animals. We saw a lion trying to catch a warthog. It was very exciting for Karla. Actually we prayed about it because I so badly wanted Karla to see some lions. We also saw close ups of elephants and the usual giraffe, zebra, and impala. One unusual thing we saw was the sable antelope. Another thing was the mother hyena and her pups right along the road.

I want to explain why Ron and Karla came out to Africa. Karla is doing her practical clinic work for her MD. Omaha medical school was willing for her to come to Swaziland to do these rotations. I think the medical school in Omaha was impressed with what Ron learned when he came before he and Karla were married. So they were quite willing for Karla to do some of her training here in Swaziland. She will be graduating from medical school on May 12th in Omaha, Nebraska.

Randal came home to Swaziland for his short school holiday. It was so nice to have Ron, Karla, and Randal here with us. From my April 1st letter: "One Thursday night we were privileged to go with Ron and Karla to Dr. Merke's home for supper. It was a great time. We relaxed and played games after supper. I played Pictionary for the first time. It really is quite fun!"

From my April 23rd letter I apologized to my mother for not writing: "I'm sorry, mother, I've been so bad about writing. I've had so much going on. I guess it does make extra with three kids at home. I'm afraid we are going to feel a bit lonely with them all gone. This evening we all went to Pizza Hut at Eastgate shopping mall. It really was a nice sendoff for Ron and Karla. They do have nice pizza here, just like in the States. So with this their visit ended and they headed back for the States.

Backing up a bit, I want to tell about our new grandson, Andrew Laverne Lauber. He arrived March 13, 1990. Now Roxie and Ron are the parents of two little girls and a little boy - our second grandson! This makes five grandchildren for us.

So continuing about babies, I want to tell you about Albert and Gladys. They had their baby on March 11th. It was a tiny baby boy. Albert was so happy you could hear him all over the campus this morning telling everyone. Bob and I took baby clothes down to them. Albert works here at the college and I know they don't get a lot of money. So I got down my box of baby clothes that I try to save up to give to students and workers. By the way, these come to us as used clothing from the States. We sure do thank you! I chose several things from this collection and Bob and I went down to visit them for a few minutes. Gladys said to her baby, "You are a rich little boy with all these clothes!" They were so grateful. Now we have two other student couples who will be having babies this year. I told the nurse at the hospital that Swaziland is going to be full one of these days. She told me yesterday they had dismissed 16 babies and today 12 babies. They keep busy in the maternity ward with so many babies coming. Gladys had her baby last night and came home today.

It is morning now and what a night it was! Actually the couple, Albert and Gladys, who had their baby and brought it back from the hospital, had a hard night. Bob and I had gone to bed early, fortunately, but we got woke up about midnight by the husband coming to our door and saying, "The baby is hungry and the mother isn't having any milk." I tried to reassure him that the mother wouldn't have milk for about two or three days, but of course anxious parents with a firstborn child kind of go to pieces. I told them to boil some water and give it to him. In about a half hour the father came back. So I told him to go get the baby and bring him to me and I would keep him the rest of the night; they should go back to bed and get some sleep. Fortunately someone had sent a Playtex bottle with three plastics so I had saved them thinking I just might need it sometime. It really did the trick. I gave the little one boiled water and he went right to sleep and slept the rest of the night.

1990 - June Arrives, Then July

Thief problems-June 6th I write: "We have been having some real problems with thieves around here. School finished for first semester on June 3rd and most of the students have gone home, so it's easy for thieves to break in. They broke into Esther Phillippe's house last night. Before this they broke into the kitchen at school twice and into Bob's office, the school office, and Daphne Niemack's house. The people across the road were also broken into. Please pray that we will catch him or something will make him stop stealing.

Maybe praying for old-fashioned conviction is the best way to pray. As of tonight at 10 PM we have hired a night watchman to come on duty. I hope this helps. I hope the watchman has a good knobkerrie. You don't want to be hit on the head with one of these! Israel wired the kitchen and Esther's house. If he tries to get in again hopefully a real good shot of electricity will cause him to do some serious thinking. Also we are trying to get some big dogs."

Randal came home for his mid-term holiday from school July 11th. He had gotten pretty sick. The winter months of June and July seem to be a time when sickness, colds, etc. hit a person. His birthday was on the 12th so I made him a chocolate fudge cake with blue decorations and various colored candles. There were about 15 of us present to celebrate. We served vanilla ice cream with the cake. I painted a big beautiful Eagle that I had gotten from Tri-Chem for Randal's gift. It was for hanging up in his room. He got several more cards and some gifts, so he felt pretty happy. I played a game of scrabble with him and we were up pretty late, but it was fun. Also, that is when we got a new dog from some missionaries going on furlough. She will make a nice watch dog. We called her Millie.

After school began at the college for second semester we had Missionary Emphasis week. Rev. and Mrs. Don Karns, our Mission Director, came for this special time with our students. The Karns' told about their experiences in South Africa and about serving as missionaries in Liberia, West Africa. It was good for our students to hear and hopefully they will catch the missionary vision. The end of July the Bible College students were away for Work and Evangelism week. They chose to go help at Mpholenjani, where the Nhleko's use to pastor. Now they have a young man named Sam, a former student of EWBC who pastors the church now..

Our Cape Town Trip

We returned to the Lehman's in Boksburg on December 19th and got ready to travel on a trip to Cape Town, South Africa with Orai, Linda and Paul, Ed and Wilma Wissbroeker, Bob, Randal and me. There were eight of us traveling in Orai's Hi Ace. By doing this we could share the cost of our vacation. (It has occurred to me as I'm writing our story, that these are the three missionary children of Alfred and Ella Cheney, serving with their families as missionaries in Southern Africa. God called them to the countries of Zambia, Zimbabwe, South Africa, Swaziland and Mozambique).

I wrote a letter of greetings from the Cape Province. It reads: "We seem to have problems with vehicles when traveling long distances. In fact, we just barely crippled into Cape Town. The next morning Orai worked on the van, helping it to run much better. We drove all over Cape Town. We rode up beautiful Table Mountain in a cable car. Going up the side of the mountain was quite a thriller and made me think of Manitou Incline in Colorado Springs that Bob and I went up before we were married. Just looking out over Cape Town from the top of Table Mountain is amazing. We were also able to drive down to Cape Point. This is where the Atlantic Ocean meets the Indian Ocean, the farthest point one can go south in Africa. From Cape Town we traveled along the southern tip of South Africa, going toward Knysna. This is where we stayed the night. While in Cape Town we stayed at City Lodge, the same place Ron and Karla stayed when they visited Cape Town. It was a lovely hotel. From then on we stayed with different people. In East London we stayed with Orai's cousin, Gladys. Her father lives there too and we were able to see him. However, Faith Sorensen had passed away November 8th. Rev. Thomas Sorenson and his wife, Faith, were my mom and dad's pastor and family when Earl and Beulah were young people. Faith Sorensen was a sister to Orai Lehman's dad. It was so neat to see these folks who had connections with my folks years before. We then drove through the Transkie and on into Pietermaritzburg. There we stayed with Rob and Patti Church (the former Patti Bransby) for the night. The next day, December 22nd, we drove on to Swaziland. This was Bob's and my 33rd wedding anniversary.

Christmas in Swaziland, 1990

Here at our home in Swaziland we had such a nice Christmas with the Lehman's, the Wissbroekers, the Bagleys, and Bob and Betty Rosas, who were back. We had an outdoor dinner on our veranda. In my letter to mother and daddy I said: "It was a delightful Christmas because we never worried about buying gifts for anyone, or wrapping them. Our Christmas was our trip to Cape Town, hearing Christmas music, and attending Christmas programs and services. It was a wonderful Christmas to remember!

On December 26th we all went up to Boksburg; the Lehmans, Wissbroeckers, and us, so we could see Randal off on December 28th. Randal had shopping to do and friends to see before leaving. It was a busy time before he left. At 7:10 p.m. my lastborn son flew out on UTA Airlines. I'm sure there were tears, but we committed him to the Lord and knew God would take care of him. In my December 31st letter I say: "We are happy to report that Randal arrived safely – missing no planes, no lost luggage and arrived only one hour late at the Omaha airport, December 29th, in 10-degree below zero weather. Thankfully, Ron loaned him a coat and gloves because from here he left in warm, rainy summer weather."

So I end the year 1990 with an excerpt from my Christmas letter which I think is quite appropriate: "In the New Testament Survey class which I taught this last term, we had an overhead diagram of the Book of Revelation. At the bottom I had in big bold print, 'WE WIN' and then I added, 'WITH CHRIST'. Bob and I were glad we were on the winning side with Jesus.

1991

1990 has become history and we are now well on our way into 1991. January 9th we had a terrible electric storm with rain and so our electricity was out for about 24 hours. This often happened in Swaziland during a storm so of course my typing came to a standstill. We also had concern for our refrigerators and freezer, but to keep things cold we only opened the doors and lids as little as possible. While the rain poured down outside we were inside our warm house writing letters by candle light. Thank the Lord for candles!

Tuesday night while the electricity was out and rain was pouring down the Israel Langas had thieves come and steal their car battery and tire. We were so thankful they didn't harm someone or take any more than they did. I was afraid that the next night they might come to the mission but they didn't. It makes a difference I believe when electricity is on and of course we have dogs.

At this time I had in mind that during January I should start sorting our things for packing away and getting rid of. Plans were official that now we would be furloughing May 1st.

I wrote earlier about being able to see the lights of Maputo, Capitol of Mozambique when we lived at Ebenezer Mission during our first term. Now we were actually planning a visit to Mozambique with Israel and the Rosas. The Rosas had come back a second time to help with building the Bible College buildings. So we were planning this trip for Jan. 18-20th. Israel Langa went to Mbabane to pick up our visas for this trip.

Another exciting happening is that we were getting a fine Christian national couple, the Ron iNkosis, coming to teach here at the college. The Rosas have been preparing their apartment so that they can move in. It was all freshly painted and cleaned and now the couple and their two little girls have moved in. We had them come to our house for their first three meals so that they could get moved in. Then we are having the David Depews from California coming to teach.

Our Mozambique Trip, 1991

We left Joy Mission January 18ᵗʰ at about 10:20 AM and arrived at Mafalala Church in Maputo about 5:00 PM. Those of us traveling to Maputo were Israel Langa (our driver), the Regional Youth Director, Bob and Betty Rosas, and Bob and me. We were so excited to be doing this trip to a new country we had never been to before. As we neared the border of Swaziland and Mozambique there were two borders to go through. First we filled out papers on the Swaziland side; then drove a short ways over to the Mozambique side. Here we had to fill out more papers and let the border guards check our van and what we were taking into the country of Mozambique.

After all this was done we began our journey toward Maputo. As we were leaving the Mozambique border our driver, Israel Langa, spoke up and said: "Alright, I want to tell you that if perhaps there is shooting, you are all to get down!" Oh my, what are we getting into? Everyone became very quiet. All along the way we saw soldiers guarding the road. It was a little scary. From the Swaziland border, after you pass the town of Namahasha, the country is very deserted and you see very few people. People don't live in an area of about 25 kilometers because of Renamo attacks. These are men fighting the present government of the country. We saw many cars, buses and other vehicles that had been attacked and left to rust away by the roadside.

The safest time to travel on this road seemed to be between 10:00 AM and 2:00 PM, the very hottest time of the day. Oh, was it ever hot there in Maputo. Being on the ocean front made the place have a high humidity. We were so happy to make our way to a better highway into the city. The roads after crossing the border were in terrible condition. You could imagine what a tarred road would be like after 20 to 25 years of no maintenance. Pot holes, grassed over parts, and a surface you would not want to even travel over going 50 miles an hour. It was bad!

On Sunday morning, in the church service, we felt like we were in a sauna. The men's shirts were actually dripping wet and the ladies' dresses were wet and clinging. Despite all of this we had such a wonderful meeting with the young people. This weekend was their youth camp. The regional youth leader, Rev. S. Ntshangaze preached Friday evening and Sunday morning. Bob Cheney preached at the Saturday evening service. The people gave us such a royal welcome. The WGC couple – Bob and Betty Rosas also participated in this gathering. On Sunday morning the ladies surprised Betty and me with some material that we could wear to look like Mozambican women. It was so neat! Then the youth presented us with some gifts. My gift was a Mozambican musical instrument which I had wanted for so long. The Lord really blessed in our services and many people came forward to pray. You could tell there was a real hunger for spiritual things in that country.

Now for a little bit about the living conditions. You can hardly imagine how people live there in Maputo. Many people have fled from the rural areas because of the war and have built temporary living quarters from reeds, old iron roofing, and whatever they can find. So flies and rubbish are terrible in many places. Even in the city the big rubbish bins are full, running over, and smelling dreadful. The place where we stayed called Mafalala was an area of corrugated iron building pretty much temporary. Even the church and the pastor's house where we stayed were made of this material. The mosquitoes were awful in this area because of the rains. It's swampy and we were hoping we wouldn't get malaria from this trip. We did take tablets to help prevent it. We didn't rest very well because of the heat. Our windows couldn't be opened because of the mosquitoes. We did, however, have a good bed to sleep on. The people fed us well. We had plenty to eat but the food was different from what we were used to. About every meal they fixed French fries for us. One morning our breakfast consisted of French fries and lettuce salad. Actually, it was quite good! Their main staple food is rice, mealie meal (corn meal) and fish.

They have an outdoor hole for a toilet and a place next to it where they bring you warm water so you can wash. We asked if we could have the water brought into our rooms since the bath house was open and airy. We knew a lady who lives in Maputo in a very nice apartment who let us use her shower on Sunday so I was able to wash my hair. This part reminded me of Suriname. They only had cold water in the taps, but you didn't mind because it is so hot and humid. This same lady fixed breakfast for us on Sunday morning. I've failed to mention that Israel Langa is a Mozambican. This is his home area. His cousin fixed another meal for us of national food. We saw the home of Israel's parents in Maputo as well.

I just want to add this part about the lady who lived in an apartment and our experience when we left. In a way it was rather funny, but also quite scary. We bid farewell to the dear lady and left her apartment which was probably two or three stories above ground floor. There were quite a number of us who decided to ride the elevator to the ground floor. I don't know if the elevator told its capacity or number of people who could ride or not, but we kept crowding into that little boxed area and finally got the door shut. We pushed the button for ground floor. Then guess what? The elevator kept going half way past the ground floor. So now we were packed in like sardines and wondering what we were going to do. Betty said to her husband Bob, "Can't you do something to get us out?" Finally someone did hit a hook on the door and it came open. So people started stepping up around 18 inches and crawling out of that elevator. After this I was always quite aware of how many people got on an elevator with me. I certainly don't want to be in an elevator packed like sardines that stops halfway between floors!

The most exciting thing of this trip was to see the couples that the District of Mozambique are sending to our Bible College in Swaziland. Two new couples were coming for our new school year and one couple was returning for their third year. Then in July another couple was planning to come for school. We praise God for calling out these couples as workers in God's great Harvest Field.

Mary Elizabeth Bagley

A new, tiny baby girl was born to Bob and Brenda Bagley, January 22, 1991. They call her Mary Elizabeth Bagley. She weighed 4 pounds, 15.5 ounces and was 19 inches long. Brenda had her at the Nazarene Hospital in Manzini, and then came home to Joy Mission about four hours later. Brenda's mother, Elizabeth Karns, came from Brakpan to help Brenda and the family. So now the Bagleys are parents to a son, Joshua, and daughters, Tracy and Mary Beth. Thank the Lord for this baby's safe arrival.

School Begins for 1991

Beginning of February the Bible College got off to a good start. We have 16 students enrolled at the present time. We feel so blessed this new year because we have the Ron Nkosi family as well as David and Pat Depew. It is great having new teachers here to take a number of the classes. David and Pat have made a number of trips to the Holy Land. It was refreshing to have new insight given to us on a number of Bible subjects. I even audited one of the Bible classes that Pat taught and learned so much. The class I took was called "Bible Customs".

I've been trying to teach Beginning English. What a challenge! The students (five of them) can hardly speak a word of English, and some of them can barely speak Zulu. So I felt like I was teaching both Zulu and English in the same class. Sometimes I think that we need to teach three different languages here at E.W.B.C. because we have so many students coming from Mozambique. I did rather enjoy it and I think I learned even more Zulu for myself so that is beneficial.

At the beginning of each new school year we schedule a school Revival. This year our Regional Supt. Rev. S. Sigwane is preaching for these meetings. He preached at the chapel services and then each evening.

The latter part of February I began going through things deciding what to take and what to sell. I sorted through all my old letters making a decision of what ones to take and the ones to leave. I stated to my mother and Dad in my letter: "Of course you know what I'm planning to do. I want to save these letters so that in a few years I'll be able to write a family history for our children and grandchildren. The family letters will help me recall many things as I'm writing. Sometimes I think I have too many things I want to do so let's hope I get some of them accomplished."

In March I made another comment in my folks letter: "two months from today we should be leaving Swaziland for Joburg. Our itinerary calls for us to fly from Joburg May 3rd at 7:30 p.m. And arrive in Indianapolis May 4th at 7:22 p.m. We are scheduled to fly Air Portugal so will be landing in Lisbon this time. That will be different."

Bob and Betty Rosas, who have been with us did some traveling to Capetown and Zimbabwe. They got back March 1st and did the college kitchen shopping for me. What a relief!!!Buying for the school is such a job. But all the students must be fed. Bob Rosas has been working on the school library building. It is going up quickly. You would never recognize the place any more. The building for the library goes up two stories high. The chapel is on ground level and then there is the basement for classrooms.

In another one of my letters home I stated: "I still want to write a letter to Grace Reeves and send her a card. Please tell her that I am praying for her." "We were so happy to read in the Pioneer (News from the Nebr. Dist.) that Ron and Roxy's church is doing so well. It is always so good to hear that souls are being saved, baptized and taken in as members. I wish that all churches would be saying this. Ron was pastoring the North Platte Wesleyan Church at the time."

It was at this time that the war had ended and we heard several times on BBC London, President Busch talk. It was good to hear him mention praying and saying, "God bless each one who helped."

March 10th I wrote: "Praise the Lord for one answer to prayer! Bob came back from services today and said that we are to go to the chief of the area next Sunday with Israel Langa or Rev. Mohale and they will see about giving us land for the daughter church of our Manzini Church. We are planning to take a gift, a quilt that Betty Rosas will sew together this week. What would we ever do without Betty and Bob Rosas!!! They are staying longer because Zambian Airways canceled all their flights to the U.S. Now they are booked to leave March 25th. I think the Lord knew we needed them to help us some more. They will fly this time Zambian Airways to Frankfurt Germany and then fly Pam AM to New York. Bob is working on the new library and chapel complex. They want to get the roof on as soon as possible. I hope it is all done before we go home so we can see what it's going to look like.

March 13th is our grandson Andrew's first birthday. He is walking now. This is our youngest grandchild at this time and the one we have not seen yet.

Today March 17th, it has been a very rainy day—in fact so much rain that we didn't get to our church Mphembakati. We were to see the chief about a piece of ground for this church but with so much rain the roads would have been impassable. We hope that we will have another chance. So we decided to visit the Manzini church and were blessed and thrilled at how the Lord is working in the church. Pastor Mohale and his wife are doing such a good job. Although the attendance was down, still the service was excellent. It was great to meet a young man who attends there regularly. He was recently saved under Henry Mohale's ministry. Then another young man was present who had been recently saved. It's good to see how God is building His Church!!!

We had a delightful surprise this month. Roxane Lauber and Ron Cheney called us on the phone. They actually got through to Joy Mission – surprise of all surprises!! It was wonderful to talk with two of our children. It is a good thing they didn't call on Mar. 17th because I doubt that they could have gotten through to Joy Mission. It seems that day there was too much rain and the phone drowned!!!

We truly appreciated Dr. Pat and Chris Page who allowed us to receive calls on the phone in Manzini. We thank our Nazarene missionary friends so much. May God give them great blessings! It seemed like the letters that were sent to us were coming very spasmodically during this time. One letter that Karla wrote to us took about a year to get to us. We weren't sure why this was happening but wondered if the Iraqi War might have had some influence. Anyway we truly enjoyed getting letters from home! We did learn that Rylan, Randal and Mike Lehman spent some of their spring break with Ron and Karla in Omaha. Here I might add that whenever anyone visiting our mission work was returning to the States we often would write a bunch of letters and send them back to the States with our visitors. Then they would put on U.S. postage and mail the letters for us. Another couple we would like to thank is Rev. and Mrs. Duane Lauber for putting out our form letters. There were a number of people who did this for us. It was such a blessing and help to us. Another dear friend was Colleen Mullanix from the Imperial Nebraska area and another church in the state of New York. These were all dear people who helped inform others across the U.S. about the need for prayer support as well as financial support and gave the news of our work in Southern Africa.

One of the last letters I wrote before our 4th term finished told about our Mission Council that went so well. It was written April 16th and told about Dr. and Mrs. Wayne Wright being with us for this meeting. I stated: "We were able to talk about some of the issues that were troubling us as missionaries. I think that Dr. Wright now has a better understanding of where we are coming from and we understand our leaders better." We went up to

Brakpan on April 8th and came back early Saturday morning April 13th. Our hope was to attend Lena Manana's wedding at Joy. I had made their cake the week before we left. Veronica, who use to work for me, also had a Christian Wedding the 6th of April. I tell you we seem to be so busy around here I don't know how the packing is going to get done. Now I have started on the last wedding cake that has to be done before I leave. It is for a couple in Mozambique who are planning to marry in May and come to school this coming July for second term. Well, if I live just one day at a time I'll be fine!!! Just want to add here that many couples go to the D.C. and get married but then they want their marriage to be done in the Christian way and blessed by God. Many are not Christian at first and they truly want to do it the right way after they become Christians.

There is one more thing I want to add to this ending of our 4th missionary term. Early in January I began encouraging my Dad's side of the family to have a reunion May 24-31st of 1991. In one of my letters I said: "I must add that we are planning for everyone to come the last week of May for the THORNTON FAMILY REUNION. So May 24th-31st is to be marked in red on your calendar!
We are excited about getting to see the family and many relatives. I hear the fatted calf has been killed so it sounds like things are getting in order. Those who have tents and campers or motor homes we will be happy to see but don't stay away if you don't have a house to bring with you! We will find a place for you. The Thornton ranch is big enough to have everyone come!"

And so we brought our 4th missionary term to a close and made our way to Johannesburg. We flew out of Jaun Smutts Airport on May 3rd on Air Portugal flying to Lisbon. From there our flight took us to Indianapolis where we landed May 4th at 7:22 p.m. Our 4th missionary term had ended!

4th Term Furlough Begins May, 1991

Now, as I'm writing my story, I do not have written documentation from letters or diary as I had while we were in Africa. I'm writing from memory and also questioning my children for the record from May through December of 1991.

We landed in Indianapolis Airport on the evening of May 4th and were met by one of the people working at our mission department. The next morning we met with the department heads of our Mission. They arranged for us to take one of the mission vehicles to drive during our home ministries.

Our plans this term was to rent a small house that my parents had in the same yard as their house. They had fixed the little house quite comfortably and it was nice to be near Mom and Dad.

At this time all our children were married or in college. So their schooling was not an issue. Although this small ranch where my parents lived and owned was about thirty miles north of Lewellen, it was a nice quiet place for us to be while we were not on the road. Of course during the winter the roads sometimes were impassible because of snow. The last seven miles into my folk's ranch was just trail roads. When you traveled them you really needed to know where you were going and how to get there. But during the spring and summer and fall months we were able to get in and out of this place. It was just so neat to be at my childhood home. I know my mother and daddy enjoyed having us nearby.

There is one thing I want to mention. In these hills one could see some of the most beautiful sunrises and sunsets. The cloud formations were outstanding at times. During one summer evening Bob took a most gorgeous picture of cumulus clouds with beautiful pink golden linings. We used one of these pictures for the title page of our missions presentation and entitled it "A Living Hope" using the scripture from I Peter 1:3-5 "Blessed be the God and Father of our Lord Jesus Christ, who according to His abundant mercy has begotten us again to a living hope through the resurrection of our Lord Jesus Christ from the dead, to an inheritance incorruptible and undefiled and that does not fade away, reserved in heaven for you who are kept by the power of God through faith for salvation ready to be revealed in the last time." Bob gave a most beautiful message over this passage of scripture. We felt God directed us to these verses for our theme on missions as we traveled from church to church across the U. S. telling of our work in Southern Africa.

As we traveled across I-80 interstate it was quite easy to visit our three older children who lived very close to this road. Allen and family lived west and a bit north of DesMoines, Iowa and so we visited them first. How fun it was to be with 6 year old Kassie and 4 year old Kyle. They had grown so much since we'd last seen them. From Guthrie Center we went on to Omaha where Ron and Karla Cheney lived. Again we had a great visit. Rylan and Randal were in school at Oklahoma Wesleyan University. Since Rylan was graduating May 11th, we planned to ride with Ron and Karla to the graduation in Bartlesville, leaving our mission car at Ron's place. Our other children would be coming for this occasion and so it was quite a family reunion. This was the first time we were introduced to Amy Garritson, a girl from Idaho, who was Rylan's girlfriend. I remember so well her generosity. She worked at a nice restaurant in Bartlesville and invited all our family to come and have lunch there and she paid for it all. We were quite impressed, I must say! I believe we did leave a good sized tip for her.

The next day was my birthday. We stayed with Grandpa and Orpha Lehman. She so kindly surprised me with a lovely birthday cake. From there Ron, Karla, Bob and I went back to Omaha where we picked up our car and headed for western Nebraska. Randal, also, came with us. Rylan stayed in

Bartlesville where he had a job with roofing. In August he got a job with ARC group homes working with mentally and physically handicapped individuals.

By late December of 1990, I had contacted many of the Thornton relatives, planning for a family reunion Memorial weekend. To get ready for this we headed for the Earl Thornton Ranch. On the way we stopped at the Cheney farm and to say hello to Charles, Linda, Grandpa Alfie and others. My sister Esther and some of her family had come earlier to help put a face lift on the old ranch house.

One of the great memories about this reunion was seeing my dad's living siblings and their spouses. Aunt Grace and Uncle Homer came from Delaware in a motor home, along with their son Neal and his wife, Joyce. Uncle Bill (Dad's youngest brother) and Aunt Virginia came from Indiana. I believe this was the last time Dad's siblings and spouses were together at the ranch, the place where all three of them were born. (Uncle Loyal, Dad's brother next to him, had passed away in the later 70's.) The neat thing I remember happening was my Uncle Bill's birthday was May 27th. My sister, Esther, our expert cake baker, made his birthday cake and we all celebrated with him.

The children at this reunion enjoyed playing in the sandhill blowouts. These were places in the grassy hills where the wind took control and blew out all the grass. This left big wide holes, sometimes as big as fifty or a hundred feet wide, where there was nothing but pure soft clean sand to dig in. This was great fun for all the children. They could make sand castles; dig holes and even cover each other with sand—total body cover accept the head. Of course we won't say how much sand appeared in the bath tubs when it was time for clean-up. In all, it was a wonderful reunion time.

When June arrived so did our summer schedule for home ministries. One of the places we visited was the yearly camp at Clarkston, Washington. Randal was able to travel with us on this tour and it was such a blessing. We traveled from Clarkston, sightseeing on our way, to meetings in the Southern part of Oregon. One place we wanted to show Randal was Crater Lake. This was close to Medford where we were scheduled for a Sunday evening meeting. It was so encouraging to meet many new people who showed a great interest in our mission work.

Since Medford was not far from where Esther and Nathan lived at Kerby, Oregon, we decided to pay them a visit for a couple or three days before returning to Nebraska. They lived close to the northern border of California and we went to the area where the giant Redwoods grow. If you ever want to see one of these majestic trees you, visit "Trees of Mystery" in California. They reminded me how great our God is! While we were there, Randal went to the beach on the Ocean Front with some of the youth. It was a great three days of rest and relaxation.

The rest of the summer was filled with camps, conferences and another visit to our headquarters in Indianapolis. We attended our missionary retreat at Wesleyan headquarters. Several of us missionaries had to give presentations. Bob and I gave our home ministry presentation with slides and movies that we had taken as well as our written story to go with it. As I mentioned earlier, we entitled it "A Living Hope". Bob and I felt God led us to this title in order as a way to portray our work at the Bible College and churches in Swaziland.

September rolled around and there were a number of churches to visit. Of course Randal was back at college. He and Rylan saw each other quite often. It was during September that Randal started going with a girl named Candice Clark. She was the youngest daughter of Wilbur and Sandy Clark who pastored the North Gate Wesleyan Church in Salem, Oregon.

Part of September we were at home and I was able to help Mother in harvesting her garden. My mother always canned green beans, corn, and tomatoes and fruit that they bought by the bushel, coming from Colorado. By the end of September the cellar was filled with canned vegetables and fruits. The potatoes were dug and sacked, cabbages wrapped and carrots put into sand piles all down in the nice cool cellar. I believe we could have survived the whole winter without even leaving the ranch. Mother also canned a lot of meat. There was nothing better than my mom's beef and noodles or chicken and noodles! Just ask her grandchildren and they will tell you!!!

During October we were on the road again, visiting many churches. We went to Rochester, Minnesota for a week-end missions conference. This is where Rev. and Mrs. Doll pastored. Mrs. Doll showed me how to make little gift boxes from old used greetings cards. It was the neatest thing and so simple to make. You only needed a pair of scissors, a straight edge, and a pencil. All you had to do was cut the cards in two pieces making squares— one a bit smaller than the other. Then you began folding them to make boxes for small gifts. In fact, as Bob did the driving, I made many little gift boxes.

Since Grace Reeves was not doing well with her cancer, I decided to do something special for her Christmas. I bought an inexpensive imitation Christmas tree, then took 25 of the little boxes and put either Bible verses, a quarter or some small little thing inside the box; then tied them to the tree. On the bottom of the each box I put a number, 1-25 so she could look for a box with each day's date and open it. Every day before Christmas she had a box to open. She told me she liked it so much that she did this for another lady of the church who had cancer.

While we were traveling, I also made a large crocheted afghan for

Roxane. It had around300 squares, like granny squares only each square was crocheted in a different crochet stitch. That truly kept me from becoming bored as we traveled from church to church across the U.S.

While we were visiting the churches in Minnesota, we were fairly close to where the Rosas lived, across the river in Wisconsin. We contacted them and made arrangements to stay with them a couple of days before going on to a church in St Paul. (Bob and Betty Rosas had helped build our Bible College in Swaziland.)They took us up the river in their boat and to the other side where another little town was located. Here they tied up the boat and took us into a special restaurant along the water front. That was a fun ride on the river in their big boat. You never know what you might be doing even in Home Ministries!!!

We visited the capitol building in St. Paul, Minnesota. That was quite a neat building. Then in the evening we shared with one of the Wesleyan Churches located there in St. Paul.

There was a feel of fall in the air by then and time for us to head for a tour in South Carolina. We drove through Illinois and made our way into Kentucky and Tennessee. It was late October and flaming colors of red, yellow, orange, browns and greens nearly took our breath away. The mountains and hills were covered with beautiful trees. We had to stop and take pictures of this most beautiful scene before we reached our destination in South Carolina and began our tour of churches, meeting new people and sharing our story about the work God was doing in our beloved Africa.

Then it was Thanksgiving time. In our communication with family it was decided the Allen Cheney family in Guthrie Center, Iowa would host this special Thanksgiving Day. I was so delighted even my parents were able to drive to Iowa and our boys from Bartlesville came. Our daughter and son-in-law, the Laubers, came from North Platte as did Ron and Karla from Omaha. It was very neat to have our two youngest sons bring their girlfriends, Amy and Candice, from Bartlesville. What a fun filled week-end with family. Bob and I were pleased to be able to spend time with our five little grandchildren Alicia, Kassie, Kyle, Missy and Andrew.

We learned later that Rylan had proposed to Amy right after the Thanksgiving holidays. We, as parents, were very pleased with his choice just as we were with our other children's spouses.

Bob's dad, Alfie Cheney, now in the Lewellen Nursing Home, was beginning to fail quite quickly. This was the beginning of December and our schedule was not filled with meetings or at least had very few. It was nice to be getting ready for Christmas holidays. Randal came home to spend his vacation with us in the sandhills and with family and friends around the

Lewellen area. After Christmas we knew Grandpa Alfie was nearing the end. In a way Bob and I were glad it was happening while we were close and not out in Home Ministries half way across the U.S. On Dec. 30th, 1991 Dad Cheney passed into the next life, joining others who had gone on before.

The Year 1992

Many of the relatives in western Nebraska started the New Year by joining together at Charles and Linda Cheney's home: Linda's folks, Evan and Georgia Rittenhouse, her Aunt Sarah Mae and husband Pete and Julie and her boys, Also, my parents, Earl and Beulah, our daughter Roxane and husband Ron and children; Sue and the girls also joined us as did Jim and Kathy Oakes and son Doug and even neighbors. Everyone brought in food so we had turkey and dressing and all kinds of good stuff! In the afternoon we watched Nebraska Huskers play Miami but it was very disappointing. Nebraska lost 22-0 so it wasn't much fun to watch. We went back to the hills with Mom and Dad and Randal. I stayed up pretty late talking to our son.

On January 2nd and 3rd, many of the Cheney children started arriving for Grandpa Cheney's funeral. Ed and Wilma came from Florida and Don and Vivian from New Mexico. Bob and I decided to stay with Eldon and Genilia Drown so we could be with family for planning Grandpa's service.
Some of the grandchildren arrived: Valarie, Mike and Janelle and our children, Rylan, Ron and Karla, and Allen. On January 3rd we met at the lawyer's office in Oshkosh to discuss the future of the Cheney Corporation and for the reading of the will. After we were finished with this business everyone went to the funeral home to see Grandpa. The funeral home had done a really nice job.

January 4th 1992—William Alfred Cheney's funeral was at 11:00 a.m. Elaine (Cheney) and Earl Johnson, their daughter Carol Jean and her husband Alan along with their children, Scarlett and Anthony arrived from Denver early that morning. There were many people who attended the funeral. I counted 140 people and perhaps there were a few more. The service was held at the new Wesleyan Church in Lewellen. Grandpa was buried in their plot at Ash Hollow Cemetery.

In the next few days many of the family departed for their homes. We went back to the hills and had some good quality time with my parents. Bob and I caught up on our rest and I took down our Christmas decorations. I fixed dinner and ask my parents to come and eat with us and then mother fixed a meal and ask us to come eat with them. I had a lot of mail that needed attention and it was quite a challenge keeping addresses up dated. Bob also helped my dad with feeding so Mom didn't need to. I think my Mom was feeling, "How can this get any better?" She was loving it!!

Of course it was January and the snow did come. It also got much colder. I really wanted to take the toboggan out on the hills and ride it down the hill but I didn't get to.

On The Road Again

On Wednesday the 8th, Mom asked us to come and have a prayer meeting with them. We had a great Bible Study and time of prayer. Then, on January 9th we loaded up our things in the Subaru and Daddy and Mother started out with us to get out of the hills. We got stuck in a big snow drift in the road only once. It was kind of fun trying to get out. I'm glad I convinced my Dad that we needed to take two shovels. They took us to Linda and Charles' place where I did my washing. We said our goodbyes and headed for Ron and Roxane's at North Platte.

Our first assignment was the Wesleyan churches in Phillipsburg and Englewood Kansas with their pastors Patrick Skinners and Kent and Carol Longnecker and children. I would so much like to name all the wonderful people we met in our travels but it is impossible. Anyway, like I mentioned before it was great to be able to visit our children along the way.

There was a missions convention to be held at Harrison, Arkansas for Jan.19, 1992. On the way down to Arkansas we were able to visit our boys, Rylan and Randal. Both of them were in Bartlesville, Oklahoma at the time. Mike Lehman and Rylan had a house in Bartlesville and they arranged for us to stay with them. Randal was in school there also and he and Candy came several times to eat and just be with us. We were able to see Phil and Lucille Nettleton and Grandpa and Grandma Lehman too. From there we traveled to Harrison, Arkansas. There we had Sunday morning and evening services then the next day early we headed back to Nebraska. On our way we visited Myrna and Alan Houston, former missionaries, at Holdrege, Nebraska. January 21st we drove on to North Platte to our daughter's home and we got to see our grandchildren again—Alicia, Missy, and Andrew! We stayed all night. We suggested Ron and Roxy go out for a date and we would stay with the grandchildren. Roxy informed me that she had Egyptian Flu (she was with child again). She did look a little peeked but is doing ok!

Next day we drove to Linda and Charles', doing a little shopping on the way. Mother and Daddy came down for their prayer meeting and we then went back with them to our "Little House in the Hills". The little house needed a good cleaning, so next day I began a thorough attack of the place. Besides this we also had lots of mail to look over. I baked a cake for Roxy's birthday and on Jan.24th we took the cake to North Platte where I fixed her birthday dinner. Paula Boquist, our friend, was also there to help her celebrate.

Sunday, January 26th, we held a missions service at Oshkosh. Mother and Daddy came up for the preaching service. It was a nice surprise that our friend Doris Rickstein also came to our meeting. Afterwards we were invited to the Eldon Drowns for dinner, Mom and Dad as well as my cousin, Ardis and her son Jeff and wife Dee with their tiny baby girl Sara Ann. The baby is such a darling child. In the afternoon we visited my mother's cousin, Audrey Briscoe, who had cancer. This was our last time to see her alive.

Our next meeting was at Atkinson Nebraska. Bob and I seemed to suffer with colds a lot. We stayed with Don and Naomi Caveness this time, our daughter-in-law's parents. We got in on Wednesday evening about 9:00 p.m. I didn't feel well and neither did Bob. Thursday morning I prayed God would heal us. I read from Nahum 1:3 "That God is great in power" so I asked God to touch us with His healing power. I spoke at LIFT for the women in the afternoon. The Lord really helped me. We had 50 to 60 women. On Friday evening for the church service we told about our family, Faith Promises, our work at our Bible College in Swaziland and we thanked the church for their involvement. Again on Saturday night we told about the language we learned called Zulu, sang songs and taught them Bible verses in the Zulu language. Our big service was Feb.2 Sunday morning. We both had a Sunday school class we talked to. Then Bob showed our slide presentation of "A Living Hope". Feb. 3rd we left Atkinson making our way back to Lewellen. We arrived there on the day of Audrey Briscoe's funeral. Bob was still not feeling well so Linda made an appointment with the doctor. February 5th we had doctor and dental appointments. This was the first time our family made connections with Carol Packard, a P.A. who worked at the Family Medical Clinic. She knew Ron and Karla as they did some training together in Omaha. Bob got some help with his sinus infections.

One of the things we did before we ever left for the mission field was store a lot of our things in an old house on Grandpa Cheney's farm. Grandpa was gone now so they decided the old house needed to be destroyed. During some of our free days in February we started going through things, sorting out what needed to be burned and what we wanted to keep.

We enjoyed seeing Ted and Sue's girls, Tara and Kristin. They grew up so fast. On Feb. 6th Oshkosh grade school played Potter-Dix and Oshkosh won 36-22. It was good to see Tara in action. She was a good little player!

Our next meeting took us to Sabetha, Kansas for a week-end missions convention. Pastor Andy Smith is the minister but we stayed with an older lady they called Pansy, a lovely lady, so hospitable. At the first event we attended I spoke for their Valentine Banquet at the Hiawatha Inn. Then on Sunday we spoke to a congregation of about 60 people. In the evening we showed again our video presentation. Their faith promise offering was $3728.00. Pansy fixed breakfast for us the next morning and we headed again for western Nebraska. I seemed to have a really hard time trying to get rid of a cough. We tried to rest and relax more after we got back to Charles and Linda's. Then there was a Valentine Banquet to attend at Lewellen on Feb. 11th. It was quite cold that evening so my parents did not attend.

Bob and I headed for the hills on Wednesday, Feb. 12th. Bob worked on reports and I took care of correspondence. I called Ron and Karla in Omaha because I knew that Rylan was there. He had an interview at Omaha Medical School. That night I hardly slept because of the terrible cough I had. Bob finally called the doctor in Ogallala and got an appointment for me the next day. After Bob helped my dad feed cattle, we all left in Mom and Dad's car for Ogallala. The Sandhills Holiness Convention was on this day in Ogallala. Bro. Dunwoody preached in the morning service and Ron Lauber in the afternoon. I went to the doctor and she thought I might have something like walking pneumonia. She put me on antibiotics and cough syrup.

Then it was Valentine's Day! Bob gave me a gift certificate for Walmart, a beautiful card and a nice chocolate heart. I saved the chocolate heart because I wanted to lose 10 lbs. At this time I was heavier than I had ever been. Then we packed our things again and headed for Johnson, Kansas for a week-end missions convention. First we stopped in Lewellen and I got a pot of tulips and heart shaped balloons for Grace Reeves and we dropped them by their house.

We arrived in Johnson City about 9:15. Pastor Dave and Jan Kaufman gave us a nice room with half bath. The next morning Bob was involved with the men's breakfast and I spoke at the Women's brunch. On Sunday I spoke a little and then Bob gave the sermon. It was neat to meet some friends we had known before we married, Roger and Doris Slaven, and to catch them up on our family news.

From Johnson City we drove to Raton, New Mexico so that we could pay a short visit to Don and Vivian, and their son, Jimmy Don. Since we were only 178 miles from them it was a good chance to pay them a visit. We arrived at their place around 10:00a.m. After lunch they took us up to the lakes and on to the mesa where Don grew up. It was really snowy up there. The fences were nearly covered up with snow. We then went back to Raton and Don and Viv took us to Domingo's for enchiladas. We showed videos in the evening and had a good visit. Vivian fixed a turkey dinner for us the next day then we left for Grand Island, Nebraska where the Ministerial Convention was being held. We stayed with Duane and Lita Lauber who lived in Grand Island. In fact, Ron and Roxane Lauber and the kids were also staying with them. Rev. Mull is the guest speaker for the convention. It was so nice for us to attend the ministerial. Rev. Lauber spoke on the Colorado and Nebraska districts merging as one district. They gave Bob and me a few minutes to speak and emphasize the Heart of Missions, Self-denial, and Faith promises.

After lunch we left from the Ministerial Convention and drove to Omaha. However, Ron and Karla weren't home so we drove on to Allen and Kim's in Guthrie Center, Iowa. Kassie, our little granddaughter, had a "Welcome Grandpa and Grandma" sign up on the wall of her room. She always gave us her room to stay in. We got to see their dog, Guess's cute little puppy, Daisy May. Next morning we left for Covington, Indiana where my Uncle Bill and Aunt Virginia live. Aunt Virginia had a big meal waiting for us at 7:30 when we arrived. We watched old movies and didn't go to bed until after midnight. Next morning Aunt Virginia had a great breakfast for us before we left.

There were some people by the name of Fred and Louise Jones who wrote faithfully to us while we were on the mission field. We wanted to meet them because Tipton, the place they lived, was not far from where we were headed for another missions' service. She was bedfast but it was good to see them after all these years. From Tipton we traveled over to Colfax, Indiana. We found the place of Marjorie Wolfe and her son Dave where we were to stay. That night they had a pot-luck meal at the church. The service that night was the first service to be held in their new church. Rev. and Mrs. Howard Barefoot were the pastors. We showed our video slide show and both of us spoke some. Here I would like to make a comment about Marjorie and her son Dave. Bob and I felt these dear folks were making big sacrifices just so they could give to missions. We truly were grateful for people that gave so generously. They were laying up treasures in Heaven!

Monday Feb. 24th we got up at 6:30 packed for the road again that led to Guthrie Center Iowa. This time Kassie was sick. How we enjoyed these grandchildren watching them grow and develop. The little puppy Daisy Mae had found a new home though. We tried to do some work on Allen's computer getting all the addresses for our March tour down on paper. After supper we headed for Ron and Karla's home in Omaha. The next day we had letters to get out. Then we called on my friend, Paula who took us out to lunch. We drove to Target to pick up the new radio, cassette, CD player she was buying for us. She really spoiled us! About 4:30 p.m. We took off for North Platte, getting in around 9:30 p.m. Some more time with grandchildren and then the next day back to Lewellen.

The first thing we did in Lewellen was to go to Clint and Grace's home. They were so happy to see us. Grace was failing but we continued to believe God would work a miracle. She needed scriptures to give her assurance so we helped her find some and we all prayed and cried together. After doing a few errands we took off for the hills where we ate supper with Mom and Dad.

Sale Day for Grandpa Cheney's Stuff

Feb. 28Th was a very lovely warm day. We had breakfast with Mother and Daddy then loaded up to come to the sale being held at Billy Gordon's place. Grandpa's things were sold along with Paul Forney's farm things. The Wesleyan ladies served lunches. I helped some in serving coffee. Many people came from far and wide. After things quieted down, Cynthia, Mom and I drove to her place and she fixed us a meat loaf sandwich. It was really good. We then went back to Grace and Clinton's to see how Grace was doing. After this we went back to the sale and it had finished. Many people were loading up. It was kind of hard for Bob. I really hadn't realized how it would be to see the things you had been around most of your life, now disappearing from your life forever. We then said goodbye to Mom and Dad, Charles and Linda and went back to the Reeves again to visit and pray. From there we went on to North Platte to stay overnight with the Laubers.

This was leap year so Feb. had 29 days. Since we were at the Lauber's I helped Alicia and Missy with their work charts. We got to listen to Alicia play the piano before heading for Ottawa, Kansas. We got into Ottawa about 10:00 p.m. where the Paul Turner pastors.

The Turners had been missionaries in the Philippines. They put us up for the night. Sunday morning, March 1st, Bob gave the sermon at the Ottawa Wesleyan church. I worked with the children, telling them about missions at their level of understanding. Then in the evenings we presented our slide show telling about our work. This is pretty much the pattern we would follow at all the churches where we visited. I have to say that we appreciated all the people we met and really thanked them for their part in missions. I wish I could mention every church on every district and name every person we met. My son suggested that we do it like the Bible does in telling the genealogies— name every church and all the people. I'm not sure how many would read it if I did that! Anyway we truly loved meeting the pastors and the people in each church.

It was especially interesting to meet the Kansas Church Builders and to hear about the work they did. This group had a big part in rebuilding our home church that had burned down in Lewellen. One of the services of this missions convention in Ottawa was conducted by Marvin Bissel. At this week of Missions the people met in different homes for coffee hour. Bob and I would give a little talk on something about Africa—here at Ottawa one of the subjects we spoke on was African weddings. Then we always took time to pray for different African leaders. We prayed for Israel Langa, principal of our Emmanuel Wesleyan Bible College, for Robert Hlengethwa, one of our church leaders in South Africa and Nesta his wife who had cancer. Then there were evening services. Wednesday evening service ended this missions convention at Ottawa.

From this place we took off for Eldorado and Wichita Kansas to see some of our longtime friends, Claude and Twila Livingston and Dr. Pat and Chris Page. One thing we did with Claude was watch a TV program about democratic candidates for president. The candidates were Gov. Clinton of Arkansas and Senator Harken Brown from California and another man from Mass. It was rather interesting! Twila let me catch up my washing and then gave us lunch before we left for Salina, Kansas. It was also very nice to visit with their daughter Chrystal and family.

The services at Salina were Friday night through Sunday. At these services we shared our speaking time with missionaries to Native Americans, Wayne and Darlene Brown. After the evening service we drove back to Wichita to stay with our friends, the Pages. We got to their home around 10:00 p.m. There was a tornado warning and all of us went to a neighbor's basement. You never know what's going to take place next in missionary life!

Next day we were on our way to Bartlesville to see Rylan and Randal. We had breakfast with them and then started making our way to South Carolina. After an over-night in West Memphis to sleep early the next morning, March 10th, we made our way to Nashville. The couple who were Nazarene friends in Zimbabwe, Larry and Elaine Cornett, lived in Nashville so Bob called Larry. He came to have breakfast with us; then we drove to the school where Elaine teaches. It was so good to see them. It's neat to have friends all over the U.S.!

We were on our way for a District tour of South Carolina again. This tour was from Mar. 10th through March 30th. We held services in 18 different churches. The Edwards, Hal and Lillian and the Grigsbys were some who gave us places to stay and took us sightseeing. I especially want to mention how Bear and Cathy Grigsby took us around the Charleston area. From my diary on March 23, "They took us in their car into Charleston and drove to the old part of town, the market, and Battery where you could see Fort Sumter. A lot of history has taken place in that city We had a delicious fish dinner with them at a nice restaurant. It was all quite impressive!!

I want to mention that it was great to see Dr. George Failing and to have breakfast with him at Shoney's Restaurant in Easley, South Carolina. Dr. Failing had spent some time with us in Swaziland teaching at the Bible College. While in this state we were able to meet with Susan and Shari Ramsay, the missionary kids that our kids grew up with in Swaziland Africa. They were married and we had the privilege of meeting the couples, Chris and Susan Potter and Kerry and Shari Lammi. Chris and Susan had a baby girl named Rachel at this time. What fun we had recalling old times in Swaziland.

March 30 we left South Carolina and headed for Pensacola Florida where Bob's sister Kathy and husband Jim and son Doug lived. Jim had just gotten back from a mission trip to Costa Rica. The next day I wrote in my diary: "Kathy decided to take us to the Navel Museum to see all the planes, space capsule and air craft carriers. We saw so many interesting things. She took us over to the Light House Restaurant to have lunch. Then we walked out on the beach where the sand is so white and beautiful. Bob and I stuck our hands in the Gulf of Mexico water." That night we celebrated Kathy's birthday since we were leaving on her birthday April 1st. I fixed a cheese cake and we had a wonderful meal. It was so nice to be in Jim and Kathy's home!

Next morning we made our way west and north driving through Mobile Alabama, New Orleans Louisiana, Baton Rouge, Shreveport and on into Texas. One of the things we noticed was the Interstate highways were often built out over the swamps and marshy areas. As we came into Long View, Texas we decided to get a motel for the night. This is where the Letourneau College is located. The next day it was on to Bartlesville, Oklahoma where we wanted to meet Rylan and Randal for lunch at 1:00. It didn't work out because Rylan was working and Randal had class. However, after waiting a bit Rylan was able to eat with us and when Randal came back we had a hot cup of African tea with him. It was so good! Bob gave Randal his papers to turn in for a Pell Grant. Even if we only saw our boys briefly it was good! We drove on the Salina, Kansas before stopping for the night. From there we went to North Platte, getting there about 12:30 p.m. When we arrived we learned that Roxy's stove was not working so we all drove to Amigos. This really pleased Missy and Andrew. Their favorite was Amigos' tacos!

We hurried on to Gordon, Nebraska where we were to have a week-end convention. Our arrival time was 5:00 p.m. We set up our display and then they invited us to share with the church in an international supper. Bob showed our slide presentation. We were really tired from traveling on April 1st and now for this service April 3rd. That night we were the guests of Judy and Leo Zuver.

Next morning Bob attended a men's breakfast with Leo and I went with Judy to a Ladies Luncheon where I was the speaker. There was a Saturday evening service and then a Sunday a.m. Service with a carry-in meal at noon. We visited with a number of people and then left for our 'Little House in the Hills'. This time we drove down the narrow tar strip from Ashby. It was so nice to be in our little home again and to see Mom and Dad. We had put on a lot of miles since March 1st.

On April 5th we received a call from Ron. Praise the Lord, he had been accepted at two medical schools. Ron decided that God wanted him to be a surgeon. He was already a PA but now that Karla had graduated he felt he wanted to train in surgery.

During the month of April my mom helped me with the dresses that Alicia and Missy would wear for Rylan and Amy's wedding. Often I would fix the noon meal and Mom and Dad would eat at our little house or we would eat at their house.

On April 8th I wrote in my diary: "This afternoon we stopped a few minutes to see Grace Reeves. She is a real miracle. Hard to believe that she is up and around with no tubes or oxygen attached. God has performed a wonderful miracle in Grace's life. Doctors say her lungs are better than they have been for a year."

On April 14th the Lewellen Wesleyan Ladies put on a Mother-Daughter Banquet with the theme "April Showers". This was a fun banquet because not only was my mother with me but so were my daughter and granddaughters, Alicia and Missy. This doesn't often happen so it was a very special occasion with four generations. I mentioned in my diary that Grace Reeves even felt well enough to come.

Even though Bob and I lived in the sandhills we had quite a number of visitors who came to eat with us. Leland and Joeretta Swan came April 17th and I fixed sweet and sour pork with rice. Then on the 18th I invited Sue, Keith, Tara and Kristin to come for a birthday dinner in honor of Kristin's 12th birthday. Her birthday is actually on April 20th but I wanted them to come so they could see our 'Little House in the Hills'. 'Of course Aunt Eva had to make the birthday cake for Kristin and we all had the birthday dinner by candle light.

Easter Sunday was April 19th. After Bob helped my dad feed cattle, we had a wonderful breakfast of eggs and ham. Then we drove to the Lewellen Wesleyan Church for Easter morning worship. There were about 60 people present for this service. After the service we drove to Oshkosh Wesleyan for their Easter morning worship because this was the Sunday of Baby Sarah Ann Wilhelm's dedication. Mom and Dad were to stand up with Jeff and Dee. At the end of this service we drove back to Lewellen to my Aunt Nellie and Uncle Howard's for Easter dinner. The community choir sang their Easter Cantata at the Oshkosh Lutheran Church so we drove back to Oshkosh to hear them. In my diary it stated: "by now I have a headache—then back to Lewellen Wesleyan for the evening service. We drove home after service and got back before dark. Dad rubbed my feet after we ate some sandwiches and this seemed to help my headache."

The next morning we got ready bright and early to take off on another tour. We headed for Omaha after a brief stop in North Platte. I had finished crocheting Roxane's afghan and wanted to give it to her. Weather was good until we passed York. Then we hit a real blizzard. I prayed hard that we would arrive in Omaha safely. There were cars, trucks, and vans off the road.

It was a mess and we just crept along. We did make it to Ron and Karla's around 7:30, thanking the Lord for a safe arrival. There were between 9 and 12 inches of snow in the Omaha area.

That evening we drove over to the hospital where Ron worked. He was working that night so we took pizza and ate together and talked until about 10:30. Bob and I stayed with Karla for the night. Next morning we prepared to go to Spencer, Nebraska for a missions night. The Byron Summers and their two little girls pastored at this church. They took us out to supper at a restaurant and then we conducted the service. That night we stayed with Roger and Edith Loocks who have two girls and one boy. We enjoyed their beautiful home. They took us around to see their farm.

The next morning we left for LaPorte, Iowa where a missions week-end was planned. Pastor Randal Peterson opened the church for us but we stayed with Jim and Susie Hanna near the church. This is where I really learned a lot about the Pro-life movement. Mrs. Hanna was very involved with this organization. In fact, I talked with a lady at the church who told me it was Mrs. Hanna who led her to Christ. This lady's little boy was so sweet. He brought a ball to me and ask if I would give it to an African boy who didn't have any toys. I was so touched by this! Sunday evening April 26th was our final service there. It was a great Missions conference.

The next day we left for Rockford, Illinois where our friends, Oscar and Mary Lou Scamihorns lived. It was good to see them again. Mary Lou showed great interest in cake decorating so we looked at many cake decorating books. The next day they wanted to take us to the "Sweet-Pan". This shop had cake decorating equipment galore. Oscar paid for me to get some things I needed to help me with decorating cakes. These people were truly a great blessing!

On Wednesday, April 29th, we took leave of our friends and drove to Milwaukee, Wisconsin where we stayed with Peter and Peggy Stanes and their two children and visited several churches in the area, the West Brook Church, Hale Park Wesleyan, and West Allis Wesleyan Church. The Lietzels, and Leslies worked with us during this missions conference. The missions offering on Sunday morning, May 3rd, came to $21,000.00. We did enjoy working with these other missionary couples.

Going Back West Again

From there we headed back west again to be with Allen and Kim, and our grandchildren, Kassie and Kyle on May 4th. Kyle had his 5th birthday on the 1st of May but since we weren't here then I decided to bake a birthday cake and fix supper for him anyway. In my diary I said: "I got a chocolate cake mix and some round cake pans to bake in. I then iced the cake and decorated it with clowns and cowboys and a big number 5 candle. Kyle seemed so proud of his cake. For the birthday supper we had chicken breasts filled with cheese and bacon and all the trimmings. It was all so good.

It was so lovely spending time with our kids again. We stayed with Allen's family until May 9th. During this week we had some health procedures done by Guthrie Center Hospital. Of course Allen did my blood work up and my cholesterol was 303—very high. My blood pressure was 108 over 72 and the hospital did an EKG which turned out good. I have been doing a lot of walking which is helping but eating out and having church dinners are hard on one's health.

We drove on to Omaha where we stopped to visit my friend Paula then on to North Platte to Ron and Roxane's. May 10th we celebrated Mother's Day with my mother and Roxane. We all got orchids to wear. Bob and I went to church in North Platte and then Mother and Daddy drove down for dinner. I wrote in my diary: "Ron preached such a wonderful message today about Hannah, entitled 'From Brokeness to Blessing'. Bob and I attended the Sunday school taught by Bro. Hunn. Then I went to the house and fixed Mother's Day dinner." Mom and Dad went on home in the afternoon but Bob and I stayed so I could get my Driver's license at Oshkosh on Monday the 11th. After this it was on the hills to our "Little House". I felt so bad for my mother as she explained Daddy didn't feel well enough to get the cows and calves in for branding the next day. But on my birthday, Tuesday morning, Brian Cheney came to help us get the cattle in the correl. In fact Grace and Clinton came, Ron and Roxane, Missy and Andrew and Chris Daily so there were enough men to get the calves branded. Mom made a wonderful dinner with roast beef and then an angel food cake with strawberries for my birthday. She also made a cherry pie especially for Ron Lauber. They finished branding around 1:30 p.m. Then we ate dinner. After dinner I showed our house to Grace and Clint. That evening Mom, Dad, Bob and I went to vote in the primary election.

Then we were back on the road again, May 13th, first to Red Cloud, Nebraska, then back north to Carthage, South Dakota where Julie and Cliff Transmeier lived. The following day we even got to watch their son Evan run in the races at the school grounds.

"Rylan's and Amy's wedding was coming up and so we stopped in Huron, South Dakota to shop for some gifts for them. We bought a knife set, an angel food cake pan, a guest book and a motto for their home. While we were in Huron we decided to visit the Sherman Mills. We had not seen them for a long time. Sherman was the minister who performed our wedding back in December of 1957.

Our next missions convention took place at Redfield, South Dakota, where Rod and Judy Griffin and their boys pastor. There was a banquet on Friday night, a men's breakfast on Saturday morning and a brunch for the ladies. On Saturday evening we showed our video "A Living Hope". Bob gave the message on Sunday morning. Monday morning we were on our way back to Nebraska.

Going to Rylan's and Amy's Wedding

Our journey to the Northwest started May 19th. Roxy and Ron had recently gotten a new van so we met at Charles' and Linda's leaving around 10:00 p.m. It was late but the kids wanted to spend the night at Ron's sisters in Scottsbluff. The next morning we started about 7:00 a.m. and drove as far as Bozeman, Montana staying the night at the Lewis and Clark Motel. The grandchildren had felt really cooped up; so they had a ball at the swimming pool in the motel. Before leaving we ate breakfast and also called Lela DeCock. I told her we would pay them a visit on our way back from the wedding. Our destination was Weippe, Idaho where Rylan and Amy would be married. We ate our lunch in Missoula and arrived in Weippe about 5:00p.m. Since Allen and Kim were not there yet Bob and I stayed in a Caravan and Roxy, Ron and children stayed at Pastor Don and Patti Blains. Rylan and Amy came in late. I got their gifts wrapped and let Amy open the one of the gifts, an angel food cake pan.

On May 22nd we had to fix the rehearsal dinner. I made four pineapple upside-down cakes. This is one of Rylan's favorite cakes. The kids were getting married in a hall there in Weippe so a number of people helped clean and set up for the wedding. I made salads and then we felt it would be easiest to serve pizza. We ordered fifteen large pizzas costing $175.00. It was definitely plenty for the rehearsal dinner. Then other relatives from the east began arriving, Mom and Dad, Allen, Kim and children, Linda and Charles and Julie and Cliff and boys, Aunt Chrystal and Uncle Ken from Whitefish, Montana, Elaine, Steve and April from Canada. Bob and I stayed at Headquarters with Nel and Rick, Amy's parents. Some boys took Rylan out on a bachelor camp that night.

May 23rd 1992 - The Wedding Day

We were up early preparing for the 10:00 a.m. wedding. The bachelor party had gotten in around 7:00. and Esther, Nathan and their family, Neal and Craig, Sharon and Celia arrived about 7:30. Grandpa and Grandma Thornton went ahead of us and, unfortunately, got on the wrong road. They were late so the ceremony was a few minutes late getting started. When they were ushered in the ceremony started.

The wedding was conducted primarily by Don Blain; however, Bob did the communion service and prayer for Rylan and Amy. They each had two attendants: Randal was his best man and Chris England was his groomsman. Amy had Shandra Daily and Andrea Lejameier. The reception went pretty well. After cutting the cake and reception, Rylan and Amy opened their gifts and then invited everyone for a cookout at Headquarters. The newlyweds had help loading some furniture and then we sent them off on their honeymoon.

The next day, Sunday, early in the morning Esther helped me clean the stove parts that we had used for the cookout. We then packed and headed for Weippe. Our family went to Timberlake Café for breakfast. This included Esther and her family; Elaine, Steve, and April; Ron and Karla; Roxy and Andrew; Grandma and Grandpa Thornton. We then said our goodbyes to everyone and went to the the Weippe Wesleyan church. Rev. Blain had asked Bob to do a missionary service that morning. Mom and Dad drove on to Whitefish to spend some time with Aunt Chrystal and Uncle Ken. The Laubers and Bob and I had lunch with Don and Patti Blain. I was not feeling very well by afternoon, so I stayed with grandson Andrew Lauber and Andrew Blain while the others went to church Sunday evening.

Heading Back to Nebraska

On Monday, about 4:30 a.m., we started back to Nebraska. Our first stop was in Belgrade, Montana to see Lela and Gary DeCock and their two girls. They prepared lunch of grilled hamburgers and hotdogs for us. It was so nice to see them again. The weather was nice for traveling and we arrived in Sheridan, Wyoming around 8:00 p.m. where we ate at McDonalds. Then we drove over to our friends, the Rex Weltys. They let us stay in Laura's parents' house for the night and invited us for breakfast. Paul and Arlis Slaughter were also there. They talked with Ron and Roxy about Surinam since they planned on going there as missionaries. We left Sheridan about 9:00 a.m., traveling to our homes in Nebraska, thanking God for a wonderful, safe trip with our kids, for Rylan's beautiful wedding and for a lovely daughter-in-law named Amy.

Trip to Indiana

Often we stayed with Charles and Linda after returning from a trip. Bless my dear sister-in-law, Linda, who let me do my washing very often. This was such a blessing because my mom didn't have an automatic washer. Then, it was to the hills again to our "Little House in the Hills". This didn't last for long because our next plan was to take Mother and Daddy with us to Indiana so Daddy could see his brother Bill and wife, Virginia. They planned to be with them while Bob and I did a missionary meeting at Mitchell, Indiana. Following these services we made our way to headquarters in Indianapolis. We learned that John Connors and Dan Connors were there. It was now 1st of June and a great time to visit with other missionaries. Phil and Elsie Myers are near Marion and so we stopped in to see them.

Elsie(Kilmore)Myers is the missionary who taught in Zambia with Wilma Cheney. On Wednesday evening we had a missionary meeting scheduled with Chapel Pike Wesleyan Church. Since we were in this area Bob and I had a chance to visit World Gospel Mission headquarters. It was our privilege to meet Fred and Rosetta Rietz and Roman Miller. These were folks we became acquainted with in Wilmore, Kentucky while Bob was attending Asbury Seminary.

After this service at Chapel Pike Wesleyan, we were introduced to Dave Lietzel and part of the team he was planning to take to Zimbabwe to build the new church building at Victoria Falls. That night we stayed with Suzanne and Bob Vardeman in Marion. The next morning we were on our way back to Covington, Indiana to pick up my parents and head back west. On our way we stayed at Allen and Kim's. We really saved the mission department by staying with relatives along the way as we traveled for home ministries! All the way along Interstate 80 we had children, and grandchildren —Guthrie Center, Omaha, and North Platte. We arrived back home on June 5th.

It's hard to name all the churches and the people that we held services in and saw the people, but churches where we had more connections I have to write about. Our next meeting took place in the Imperial Wesleyan Church. Our dear friends Verlon and Lucille Dinnel had us come for the Saturday evening meal. We had a lot of catching up to do on family news. Remember the Imperial church was the last church we pastored before going to the mission field. Colleen Mullanix, the Dinnels oldest daughter had taken on the project of sending out our missionary letters to all the churches on our mailing list. This was such a blessing for us. In fact, all the churches that took on this project for us we can never say enough thanks to them. From my diary on June 7th I wrote: "The Pastor Larry Shaw and family were away and so Bob preached in the morning service and we showed pictures in the evening service. At noon they had a church pot luck dinner. We saw Miss Fanning— Allen's and Ron's kindergarten teacher. Verlon and Lucille wanted us to stay until Monday and so we did. We drove to Wauneta with Dinnels and visited the rest home to see Mrs. Ina Martin, her sister Ruby and Mrs. Scriven." Bob had taught in the Wauneta school system and had known Mrs. Scriven who also taught in the school. Ruby and Ina were in our church when we pastored at Imperial in the late 60's.

From Imperial we traveled to Atkinson for the youth camp. Here we spoke to the youth on Tuesday, June 9th. Bob visited about the missions day for camp meeting with Rev. Dale Drown. Bob and I traveled from the youth camp to our home. I must add that Mom and Dad had been improving on the Little House and now had another room for us—a bedroom with a large closet. They even put carpet on the bedroom floor. It was so nice we hardly knew how to act with the additional space!!! We had some extra days to do some sorting and looked through boxes and boxes of stuff that Bob and I had stored in the old house at the Cheney farm. I must say it was a mess to go through. At the pink house, the place where Grandpa and Grandma Cheney had lived, we had to do more sorting. Others helped with that since Dad Cheney had been gone since January, Vivian, Kathy and Linda Cheney. Among the things we found was Bob's high school diploma.

On June 14th some of the Cheney cousins and the Vick cousins decided to have a mini-reunion. After church we went with Charles and Linda to Roy and Jane Vicks house. The Rekers were there, as well as the Andreas and Vivian and Jimmy Don. We had a delicious dinner and a wonderful visit. We looked at the books that Vera McDonald had made up for the Vick family. What an interesting book of the family genealogies. We got back to Lewellen quite late that night and Randal still had to drive back to Maranatha Bible Camp where he worked for the summer.

I want to tell something that happened to Randal so as to help others not to have this experience. About midnight we were at our house in the hills. We were pretty late getting in so I don't remember if we were in bed yet or not. We got a call from the police saying our car(I guess they looked up license number and found it belonged to us)the person driving it had gotten gas at the Hitching Post in Ogallala and had not paid for the gas. I was shocked! The man on the other end of the phone said they planned to put out a call to stop this car and pull him over. I said, "Oh, please don't do this. We will come to Ogallala early in the morning and pay for this gas." The policeman said, "We will then erase the call we have made to have this car pulled over." I thanked him and was very relieved when I finally went to bed. What was this call all about anyway? Randal would never do anything like this.

Early the next morning I called Randal and told him about the phone call. He was shocked and upset. Randal said to me, "Thanks, Mom for letting me have a good night's sleep." He also told me he did pay for the gas with a $50.00 bill but he failed to get a receipt. I then called the hitching Post and talked with the manager and he didn't know anything about the situation. He said he would look into the matter and call me back. When he called back, he said the guy working couldn't count the right amount of money and thought Randal hadn't paid. I called the Ogallala and Oshkosh police to let them know we had taken care of the matter. What we learned from this incident is, if you pay cash or even use a credit card or check, always get a receipt!!!

The next big event for us was the Festival of Missions and the General Conference for the Wesleyan Church in DesMoines, Iowa. The Mission Department had a hotel room reserved for us during the Missions Festival. The rest of the time we stayed with Allen and Kim in Guthrie Center and drove back and forth. Some of our speakers were: Tim Elmore, Dr. Earle Wilson, Dr. H.C.Wilson, and Rev. Paul Hontz from Holland, Michigan. Ken

Osborne, my cousin, was the special song evangelist for the conference. On one of the days we met our son Ron Cheney for lunch. He was in DesMoines looking for an apartment for himself and Karla. Ron was going to enroll in the surgery program there in DesMoines, learning to be a surgeon.

On the 24th of June I decided to stay with the grandchildren in Guthrie Center. Kassie would soon have a birthday on the 27th and so Grandma decided she needed a birthday cake, too, since I had done one for Kyle in May. She was very pleased with her Dog cake. In the evening we had taco salad and celebrated Kassie's 7th birthday. Now I had made cakes for Alicia, Missy, Kassie and Kyle. Grandma uGogo's goal was to make at least one birthday cake for each of her grandchildren. I didn't know then how many that was going to be!!! But I loved doing it.

Back to the conference—I want to tell about the new officers for the church that were voted in.
At this conference there were three General Superintendents elected: Dr. Earle Wilson, Dr. H. C. Wilson and Dr. Haines. Dr. Wayne Wright retired and Don Bray was elected as General Director of World Missions.

On our way back to Western Nebraska, we stopped long enough to have lunch with Ron in Omaha and then drove on the North Platte. We got in around 8:00 p.m. and I was able to do my washing at Roxy's. The next day, Saturday, we traveled on to Lewellen. Charles and Linda were in North Dakota attending their son-in-law's ordination service but they were having company from Denver coming in before they could get back. There company was our niece, Susan and husband, Jim Chidley and their three children. I wrote in my diary: "We had a cook-out although it was not real warm. Little Phoebe is so cute. She is 5 months old now. Matt and Connor have really grown too."
On Sunday morning we attended church then the family had a picnic in the park. Sue, Keith, Kristin and Tara joined us. Even Ron and Roxy drove up from North Platte and were able to visit with Chidleys. After this Bob and I visited with Aunt Nellie and Uncle Howard and Grace and Clint Reeves. Then we took off for "the Little House in the Hills".

Bob celebrated his 58th birthday with my mom's special meal. He received a number of cards and I gave my husband his special card. We ended June trying to get our house in order. There were lots of papers to go through, some of them back before we married, checking accts., bank statements etc. What a Job!!!

Our Next Meetings

On July 3rd Bob and I drove from North Platte to the Sandhills Holiness Camp, a short distance from Tryon, Nebraska. In the afternoon Bob spoke and after the service the ladies had an afternoon tea where they ask me to speak. The regular speakers for the camp were Rev. and Mrs. Duane Smith. They were also the singers and I must say very good too! Bob and I stayed in Tryon with Susie Bond, the sister of Olive Neal. She treated us royally. The next day we attended the morning and afternoon services. In the evening Randal invited us to the Maranatha Camp where he worked. It was a very nice celebration for the 4th of July. Bob and I enjoyed the fireworks. The North Platte Wesleyan Band played music for this event. Roxy and Ron and children also enjoyed this event. They called it a "pig feed, fireworks and singing" service.

On Sunday morning, July 5th, Bob, Randal and I traveled back to the Sandhills camp. Bob drove our car and I rode with Randal. It was so nice to have Randal along with us. He spoke in the afternoon service and gave his testimony. It was the first time I remember that he publicly confessed his call to missionary work. He gave such a good testimony and the people enjoyed it. The next day we drove back to North Platte before returning to the hills.

The sorting continued. On July 9th I packed our first drum to ship overseas. We were going to have three grandchildren visiting soon and were trying to get as much done as possible. That day Bob drove to the mail box seven miles from our house. When he returned he had three grandchildren and their bicycles. We had lots planned to keep them entertained. They liked riding with Grandpa on his three-wheeler, especially Andrew. Alicia and Missy liked running through the sprinklers. The next day we had a picnic and fixed hot dogs and roasted marshmallows. Yumm! When Roxy called in the evening, Andrew heard her voice and began crying until Great Grandma Thornton rocked him to sleep.

On Saturday morning Andrew woke up about 5:30 a.m. so we got an early start to the day. At lunchtime, I fixed spaghetti and Missy said: "It tastes better than mommies." Tomorrow is going to be Randal's birthday so while I baked his cake, Bob took all the kids to the big blow out where there is lots of nice soft sand to play in. After supper we took them all up to Great Grandma Thorntons to have baths in her special folding tub. The grandchildren were easy to get to sleep that night!

We got word from Randal that he had rolled the brown Cavalier car on the gravel road going to Maranatha Camp. Thank the Lord he wasn't hurt.

Next morning Sunday July 12th we all got up early to make sure we got to Lewellen church service by 9:00a.m. We got all the kids and our stuff in the car. Bob also took our audio visual equipment so he could post it UPS from North Platte. The kids were anxious to get home to see their mom and dad so we left right after morning worship service in Lewellen and drove to North Platte. We had planned to celebrate Randal's birthday but he had to work at Maranatha camp. Bob and I went out after dinner to visit him. He felt so bad about the car. Kind of a difficult 20th birthday for him! We stayed all night at the Laubers.

Monday morning Bob and I drove out to the camp to access the damage to the Cavalier and get it in for estimates of how much it would take to repair the car. Ron and Roxy left for CYC Camp. While Bob was taking care of the car issues, I decided to do our washing and clean Roxy's house. Bob found that it would cost us about $2000 to fix the car, more than it was worth. He decided to check on other used cars and found a 1983 Buick Century Ltd. for $4350 plus our wrecked car. We decided to take this offer. That Monday evening we drove on back to Linda and Charles and stayed overnight. The next morning Bob did the banking business in arranging the payment for the Buick. We drove up to the hills arriving about noon. Since Mother was helping Dad with haying, I told her I'd fix lunch for them. In the afternoon Bob went out to help stack the hay. Daddy did the sweeping. Mom raked and Bob stacked. It worked out quite well!!! By Thursday they had four stacks of hay for winter feeding.

Now back to the brown car—Bob and I left our home early July 17th going to North Platte. We planned to get the 1983 Buick Century Ltd and turn in the brown car to the Bob Spady Car dealers. We took the new car out to Randal. I wrote in my diary, "his eyes were shining with approval." Randal's last day of work at Maranatha Bible Camp would be July 18th. Then he would go to Ron and Roxane's.

We drove back to the hills after running a few errands in Ogallala. The next day Pastor and Mrs. Bennedict came to the ranch for the first time. We had dinner at mother and daddy's house. Then Daddy and Bob decided to attend the funeral of Lois Dunwoody's mother Lenore Crouse. Mom and I stayed to show the Bennedicts around the place and the little house Bob and I lived in.

Sunday, July 19th, Bob and I drove to Sidney, Nebraska to hold services, morning and evening. The Browns were trying to keep the Sidney Wesleyan Church open but had very few members. Bob's cousin, Victor Reker and his wife, Polly, and Vera McDonald were all in the morning service.

Bob's 3rd and 4th grade school teacher, Miss Masters, stopped to say hello. I wrote, "It must be rewarding to know that one of your former students has turned out to be a missionary." We returned to Charles and Linda's to stay the night. Randal also came from North Platte. Since July 19th is Rylan's 23rd birthday we all sang over the phone the Happy Birthday song. Monday morning Bob and Randal went to the Lewellen Bank for business and to get traveler's checks for Randal's trip to South Africa.
Then back to the little Thornton Ranch in the hills. Randal came along and sorted through a lot of his things.

On Tuesday the 21st we learned that Aunt Grace and Uncle Homer were at Ash Hollow but had some trouble with their motor home. When they got to Jeff and Dees in Oshkosh we drove down to see them. We had decided we should all eat at the S and S cafe but there was a storm brewing and tornado warnings were out. We even saw a funnel cloud and decided to take cover. We went to the Hendersons, Pastors of the Church of Christ, as they had a basement we could all get into. We learned that the tornado had touched the Snows, the Johnsons, and some other farm. After all this passed we went back to the S and S cafe to eat. We enjoyed being with my aunt, uncle and family.

On July 22nd I arose about 5:00 a.m. to fix lunches and we began our trip to Bartlesville, OK for Valarie and Wayne Callaghan's wedding. On the way we stopped briefly at Ash Hollow cemetery to see Uncle Homer again. They were in the process of getting the motor home fixed. Then we drove on to North Platte. Randal was with us. We had just a few minutes to say hello and goodbye to Roxy and family and then journeyed on to Wichita, Kansas.

We arrived just about 8:00 p.m. at Dr. Pat and Chris Page's home just in time for supper and a good visit until about 11:30 p.m. It was nice to be in their home at Willow Bend Circle in Wichita. From my diary I wrote July 23rd: "Dr. Page signed some of Randal's health papers and we left for Bartlesville about noon."

We got to Rylan and Amy's about 3:30. How nice it was to be in their home at 517 ½ Quapaw in Bartlesville. During that evening a reception was being held for them at the Pat and Debbie Livingston's home; Rylan and Amy got some really nice gifts!. A number of people came, including Orai, Linda and Paul. It was our first time to see them since they had arrived in the states on July 1st. Even Annette Callaghan was there.

Valarie Lehman's marriage to Wayne Callaghan, July 25th

The following morning after having breakfast, I went to the college to help Linda make filling for 100 milk tarts. They already had sausage rolls made. Bob helped Orai set up chairs for the rehearsal supper. Ed and Wilma got in so we were able to visit with them. There were about 40 present for the rehearsal. They grilled hamburgers and hot dogs and had salads. It was nice that Rylan didn't have to work that night. Saturday, the day of Wayne and Val's wedding, Rylan and Amy took us out to breakfast at the Holiday Inn. Randal was also with us. Afterwards Amy and I went shopping. Amy, who was in charge of reception, got a bow for her hair. Rylan, Bob and Randal took off for the driving range at the golf course.

The wedding took place in the Bartlesville Wesleyan Church at 4:00

p.m. It was a very nice wedding. The reception was held at the college cafeteria. After everything ended for us, I helped Randal finish all the letters he was sending out and we got his packing done. Actually, Randal and I got very little sleep that night. Sunday morning we were up at 5:30 and left for Tulsa where Randal caught his plane to Indianapolis. His plane from Indianapolis would be leaving at 8:30 p.m. He was going with a YES Corp team to Africa. We had prayer with him and told him goodbye.

We were able to get back in time for the Sunday school and worship at the Bartlesville Wesleyan church. In the afternoon Rylan and Bob went boating with Mike Roost. Amy and I visited Mike's sister, Kim. She does color make up to see what colors go with your type of skin. Funny enough we found that a good color for me to wear is purple; actually any of the darker colors like blacks, whites, navy, maroon or plum and forest green suit me well. She told me I'm in the winter category.

The next day, Monday, we visited with Rylan after he came from work. Then we visited the McCullums, the Nettletons, and went to the Albertsons store where Amy worked to tell her goodbye. We were off for North Platte late that morning and arrived about 11:00p.m., staying the night with the Ron Laubers. Roxy talked to us about the merging conference of the Nebraska-Colorado Districts and that Rev. Phil Harris was elected as the new District Superintendent.

On our way back to Lewellen we stopped in Ogallala to get our x-rays and medical forms filled out. Once that was done, we went to Lewellen for lunch. Then it was on to Oshkosh where we got police forms filled out and licensed our 1983 Buick. We took it to the hills but it didn't go quite as well as our Cavalier had done. Once home, we had supper, looked at our mail and visited with Mom and Dad until about 11:30 p.m.

July 29th we got forms from Sonny Makusha so we could apply for work permits, trying again to see if we could get back into Zimbabwe. We attended the Wednesday prayer meeting and afterwards drove up to Clint's and Grace's to see how she was dong.

Seems like so much happened in the month of July. The camp at Weeping Water, Nebraska for the Missionary Church is going on and Mom and Dad took off on the 30th to attend it. We couldn't go because we still had many things to do. For one thing, we wanted to talk with Ed and Wilma about buying the Pink House where Grandpa and Grandma Cheney had lived. Grandpa had given the house to Wilma and since they wanted to sell, Bob and I hoped we could make arrangements to buy it.

Weeping Water Camp was the camp I always loved going to as a child and in my youth. I was glad when Bob and I got there on Friday, July

31st.The speaker for the camp was Frank Krispen. It was such a pleasure to meet once again, Brother Gray who was District Superintendent when I was a girl. He would come to visit our church north of Lewellen. He was 92 years old and his mind very clear. I got to meet his daughter, Mary, and her husband, Larry Secor. They were in college with me at Bethel.

The next day we met other people I had known as a girl: Goldie (Severn)Boese, Orpha Severn, Ethel and Roy Starkey. Ethel and Orpha pastored the Lewellen Missionary Church when I was born. They presented a special program called "Vote for Sunday School". Their candidates to vote for were 'Mr. Hookey' and 'Mr. Fill-a-pew.' Mr. Fill-a-pew was the winner by far when votes were counted. At the Sunday morning worship service we were privileged to listen to the Benally Family, an Indian family from Wyoming. They were very good singers. We also met a man who knew Debbie Miller, the daughter of Norma and Hilbert Miller, Nazarene missionary couple who became good friends with us in Swaziland. She played for his church for two and a half years — what a small world!

On Monday morning, August 3, Bob and I left for our camp at Atkinson, Nebraska and Mother and Daddy went home to western Nebraska. Later, on Thursday my parents came to the Atkinson camp and we all stayed in Hubby Hall on the camp grounds. On Tuesday they focused on Missions. Other missionaries besides us were Paul and Janet Turner, missionaries to the Philippines, and Rev. Gale was representing the Native American work in South Dakota. Bob and I had the evening service and we told about Randal being with a YES Corp group in South Africa doing a revival in the Alexandra area and a youth camp at Casteel Mission. I thought Bob had a great message using an acrostic with the word world. W-Worship, O-Organization, R-Resources, L-Laborers, and D-Defining Event. We also showed our slide show, "A Living Hope". Rev. Joe Seaborn and his family were present as he was the main speaker. Bob and I met with our new District Superintendent, Rev. Phil Harris and his wife BettyLou. They are so nice!

Allen, Kim and the children Kassie and Kyle came from Guthrie Center, Iowa. They stayed at Kim's folks, Don and Naomi Caveness. We had to go into Atkinson so on way back to camp we picked up Kassie and Kyle to let them play with their Lauber cousins. Then while Roxy took the four older kids to swim I watched Andrew while he took a nap. After Sunday morning service we packed up to go to our home.

Through the month of August I did quite a lot of studying on a course I took in "Day Care Management". One of their requirements was to visit and observe in three different day care facilities in my area. At the time Karen Wall had a day care in Oshkosh and Barbara Webster had one at Lewellen. I made arrangements to visit both of these. The other one I visited was in North Platte close to where Ron and Roxane lived.

We were still doing some Home Ministries. The Wesleyan Camp at Rapid City, South Dakota asked us to come for their missions day. The Paul Turners, Dudas, George Nallys and the Yellowhawks, as well as Kate Kindle, were present for this meeting. It was a great Missions Day!

Earlier I mentioned about Ed and Wilma wanting to sell the pink house. Bob and I felt it would make a nice retirement home for us. On August 16th Ed and Wilma came up with a contract for us to sign. Linda and Charles would take the land south of the highway.

I did a lot of walking during this furlough, especially since we lived in the sandhills. I loved walking those hills that I had roamed over as a child. It was especially nice when Bob and I took walks together. One day we took off in a westerly direction and came to the site where I first started to school. Of course the buildings are no longer there but it wasn't hard for me to remember how I walked that one mile and a quarter to school and then back home again. When I was out walking by myself one time I saw two adult deer and a baby deer. Another time I had the privilege of seeing two turtle dove nests. One had two little eggs and the other nest two baby birds. There is just something about God's creation and nature in these hills that captures your heart!!!

My dad had six stacks of hay by August 18th. On the 20th Allen and Kim and their children came for a visit. Also Ron Cheney came. It was quite an arrangement for sleeping. Bob and I let Allen's family take over our house. Ron slept in Grandma Thornton's guest room and Bob and I slept on the sofa in Mom and Dad's living room. The next day Ron and Roxy came with their three so now we had all five of our grandchildren together. That evening Ron left with Bob for DesMoines. Bob was scheduled to speak at Hamilton, Indiana so he flew out of DesMoines. I didn't go this time.

While Allen and Kim were visiting, Allen helped my dad in the hay field. We got pictures of the kids, the haying, and Kassie and Kyle playing in the sandy blow outs. Saturday night everyone had to get a bath in Grandma Thornton's folding plastic bath tub, quite an experience for Kassie and Kyle.

On Sunday morning I rode down to church with Allen and Kim and the grandchildren but they didn't stay for church because they had to get back to Iowa. Now it is just Mom and Dad and me, a little lonely after everyone left, I must say!!! On Monday I took Mom and Dad's car to Charles and Linda's. I planned to take our car that had been left there and go to North Platte. For some reason the car would not start, not even with a new battery. Later we learned the battery was faulty and they had to exchange it for another new one. In the meantime, I drove Mom and Dad's car to North Platte. About 9:30 p.m. Bob was to fly into North Platte airport but the plane was 45 minutes late so we decided to just stay in North Platte for the night at Ron and Roxy's.

On Sunday August 30th we did a Missions service in the North Platte Wesleyan Church. We had a group of 149 out for the service. Before we left on Monday morning I helped Roxy fix breakfast for Alicia, Missy and Andrew. Alicia and Missy were to start school that day. Missy was so excited about school she could hardly contain herself. Alicia went to school all day Monday through Friday but Missy only on Mondays and Wednesdays.

September of 1992

On September 1 we drove back to Lewellen to find that my Aunt Chrystal and Uncle Ken had come for a visit. They came to the hills to visit a few days. While they were here we decided it would be nice to see the old French place where Mom and Aunt Chrystal grew up. It was beyond Racket a few miles. The place was well kept and I'm sure it brought back many memories, even to me the oldest grandchild. Then we drove some four or five miles to the old Jeff Devasher place where my Grandma Thornton lived after she married my step-grandpa. It was in very sad shape for no one had lived there for some time.

It was nice to have Uncle Ken and Aunt Chrystal visit in our "Little House". They had breakfast with us one morning. Uncle Ken helped Dad with his haying. When we took them to the mail box next day (remember the mail box is seven miles from Mom and Dad's house) and who should we meet but Claude and Twila Livingston! It was quite amazing that our paths crossed right, same time, same place!

A lot of Bob's spare time this month was packing our steel drums to take our stuff back overseas. He continued to help my dad stack hay some days. I tried to spend quite a lot of time on the Day Care Management course I was taking.

It was getting closer for Roxy to have her baby. Labor Day week-end so all of our children accept Kim met at North Platte to be together again. Randal had gotten home from his YES Corp work team. He and Rylan and Amy came up from Bartlesville to be with us. Ron and Karla slept in a tent in the back yard. Allen, Kassie and Kyle came in around 1:00p.m. on Sunday. We were all together for Sunday evening church. The kids had a great time together. One thing our boys did along with their dad was sing Zulu songs. That was really neat and I got some pictures of them doing it. Next morning Rylan, Amy and Randal left early because Randal had to be back for soccer practice. Bob and I and the other kids left on Monday afternoon.

I decided it would be nice for me to have a surprise 80th birthday party for my dad. I fixed the announcements and stuck them in people's mail boxes at church so Daddy wouldn't see them. I planned the surprise on prayer meeting night Sept. 23rd which was the actual date of Dad's birthday. After the prayer meeting people began coming at 8:00 p.m. When we sang Happy Birthday to Daddy, he was so surprised and pleased. People brought in birthday cards and I served the cake I had baked and decorated with ice cream. There were about 25 people present.

Bob had to send in our applications for Zimbabwe work permits again. We've also called headquarters to see if any word had come on our South African visas. Although we hadn't heard anything, we just kept on packing the drums to send. Bob also helped Charles by hauling ensilage. Since we were renting our pink house, Bob had to go over the rules and regulations that we required of our renters. Our renter didn't want to paint for part of his rent so Bob and I did it. Then we had to pass medical exams before we could be accepted to go back overseas. One of my problems was I needed to lose weight and get my cholesterol down. I tried to do a lot of walking to help this.

A New Baby, Micah

Along with our preparation for going back overseas this month we were waiting for Roxy to have her baby. It was Sept 18th and we were going back to North Platte after our medical exams. We planned to stay the night but Bob decided to go back and paint on our house. I felt I should stay with Roxy and help her with house cleaning and preparing for a new baby.

On Sunday Sept 20th I wrote in my diary: "This a.m. Roxy woke up with contractions so I timed her. They were quite sporadic and not hard enough. She stayed home from church but the contractions sort of stopped. I really think she had in mind it was Ron's busiest day and too many people kept coming around to check on her. She couldn't relax.

About 1:45 a.m. Monday morning early, Ron and Roxy left for Gothenburg hospital. Bob was back with us and so we stayed with Alicia, Missy and Andrew. We just prayed for a safe delivery and a healthy baby. Micah James Lauber arrived at 6:50 a.m. September 21st weighing9 pounds and 14 ounces. Ron brought Roxy and the baby home that evening. The children were so excited to see their new baby brother. Shelly and Butch came around to have a look that night as well. We took a video of the occasion, too. In fact, the next day a lot of people stopped by to see how Roxy and baby were doing. The church organized for meals to be brought in. This truly was a blessing.

I stayed on to help Roxy get on her feet again but Bob went back to

Lewellen to finish painting our house. Another excerpt from my diary, which I thought rather amusing, stated: "Alicia had to come back from school because she coughed so much but I'm kind of wondering if she had more than that reason. She just wants to hold her new baby brother all the time. She asked a friend to come in and play so I really don't think she is as sick as she's letting on." By Saturday the 26th I tried to get everything organized so Roxy could manage. Then Bob and I drove back to Lewellen and on to the hills.

On Sunday Sept 27th Bob gave his farewell message at the Lewellen Wesleyan Church. There was a picnic at the James and Joyce French's for the whole church. In the evening we attended the New Comer's supper at the Methodist Church since it was a community event and a chance for us to see quite a number of people in the area.

I'm glad we got to be with my parents so much through the warmer months of the year. I hated leaving them to go back overseas but I knew God would take care of them. I'm sure Dad especially appreciated a strong man's help in some of the things that needed done, not that Mother didn't help, but of course, a man is stronger. One of the last days in September Bob helped my dad pull out an old pump that had given out. Dad was going to see about putting down a new pump.

On the 29th of Sept. there was a baby shower in North Platte for our newest grandson, Micah. On our way we stopped in Oshkosh at the court house to get absentee ballots for voting in the election. It was a joy to have Mom and Dad riding with us. Before the shower we took them out to eat at Bonanza. This was the first time for Great Grandma and Grandpa to see their new great grandson. Needless to say we were really late getting back to our home in the hills. We ended September with getting more packing done and putting addresses on the drums for shipping.

Two Grandchildren Come to Visit

October was really a busy month for us. But then what month isn't busy? We met Roxy in Ogallala for lunch at Wendy's. Then we took Missy and Andrew with us as we planned to keep them while Roxy and Ron attended a special meeting. Since Alicia was in school she stayed with her Aunt Shelly. This same day we picked up a new keyboard at the Kraus Music store with speakers, microphones and all so that we could take it back overseas with us. Bob's sister was so kind to give us the money to get this key board.

Of course our packing was still going on. Headquarters would not allow us to send our drums until we had medical clearance. This meant we had to get appointments for EKGs and the doctor had to give us the report on them before we could be cleared to go overseas. We got this done in Ogallala on Oct 9th when we took Missy and Andrew back to North Platte. The kids were so glad to see their parents. It was cute what Andrew said, "My brother is growing."

We stayed only briefly as we wanted to be on our way to Bartlesville to say goodbye to our two younger sons and daughter-in-law. We arrived at Rylan and Amy's about 11:00 p.m. Rylan was working and Amy was staying with another lady, but Randal and Candy were there. Seemed like Rylan was working so much we hardly got to see him. We did get to spend time with Randal and got to see him play soccer. BWC played against North Eastern State but BWC lost 3-1. After the game, Bob, Amy and I went to the place where Rylan worked and had supper with him. It was so nice to be together, another moment to savor in preparation for the coming years of separation. We went back to Rylan and Amy's and Randal and Candy came to visit with us.

On Sunday October 11th we went to early church with Rylan and Amy, Randal and Candy. Rev. Joe Colaw preached the sermon on Persecution. We also saw Val and Wayne, Mike and Janelle and then attended the Sunday school class. All of us ate at the school cafeteria and then rested in the afternoon. It was a great privilege to hear Rev. Wumbrandt in the evening service.

Next morning I wrote in my diary: "We had breakfast with Randal and Candy. Rylan and Amy had to meet their K-Life group, and then they came back to their house and visited awhile. We said our goodbyes to Rylan and Amy and Randal and Candy. We wouldn't be seeing them again for four years. It's so hard!" We left Bartlesville at about 10:00a.m. and drove as quickly as we could to North Platte. Here we decided to stay overnight as it was quite late when we got in. We let my parents know we would be coming the next day. In the morning we left at 7:00. Bob and I had told the children goodbye the night before. When we arrived at Charles and Linda's we found them just leaving. This would be our last time to see Linda before we left but didn't realize it at the time. We took Mom and Dad's car and headed for the hills, getting in about 10:00a.m. Bob got all eight of our drums loaded in Dad's pickup. We called the doctor for the results of our EKGs and the doctor informed us we were both fine. Bob then called headquarters and they gave permission for us to ship our things.

Mother had been doing a lot of sewing for me, making a suit and another dress. I had such a wonderful mom who would do anything to help me. It was Tuesday Oct. 13th and we were to be in Iowa the next day, but no way could we make it! On Tuesday evening I talked with Mother quite a long time. She asked me to write out a witnessing plan for her. It was just so good to spend some private time with my mother.

Wednesday, Oct. 14th, was a hard day. It seems like as one gets older the good-byes are harder. Our suit cases were packed and loaded. We had our noon meal with Mother and Daddy and left about 2:00p.m. The last place we stopped to say goodbye in Lewellen was at Grace and Clint Reeves. We realized that probably we would not see Grace again on this earth. Mom and Dad had come to their place too. Bob and I had special prayer with them and tried to give encouraging words. This picture is still in my mind. There on the steps of Grace and Clint's home stood my mom and dad, bravely waving their goodbyes as we drove out of the yard.

Bob and I made our way to North Platte to say our goodbyes to the Ron Lauber family. In my diary written Oct. 14th I wrote: "We told the children goodbye tonight because we must leave early tomorrow. Little Micah is developing so quickly. I hate missing his baby stage. Lord, you know how hard it is! Please help me". Oct. 15th: "One by one, family by family we are getting the goodbyes said. I kissed each of the children in their sleep and held little Micah. He'll be so big when we return."

In Omaha we stopped to see my friend Paula. She took us out for lunch at Bishops. We had a lovely visit and then we were on our way to Allen and Kim's. Arrival time in Guthrie Center was about 3:30. Kassie and Kyle were always so glad to see Grandpa and Grandma Cheney.

On the16th I went with Kassie to school and had lunch with her and met her teacher. Bob had lunch with Allen and Kyle. In the evening Ron and Karla came over for a spaghetti dinner. Ron and Allen played a computer game called 'Doctor'. On Saturday morning Wilma and Ed called to say goodbye, as did Kathy and Jim. In my diary I wrote: "This morning it was hard saying goodbye to Kassie and Kyle. Kassie looked so sad." We went up to the hospital where Allen works and took pictures and video. He did our blood work. My cholesterol is down nearly 100 points. In April or May it was 305 and now it is down to 214. I've lost 8 pounds. Then we drove on to DesMoines to spend time with Ron and Karla.

Fourth Term Furlough Ends Oct. 18, 1992

On Sunday morning I was not feeling very well. My throat was very sore. We were trying to get everything into our suit cases. Finally Ron let us borrow a couple of his cases. I called Mom and Dad and ask for prayer. Then I called Elaine asking for prayer and finally I called Colleen Mullanix and she requested prayer at the Imperial Wesleyan Church. I truly praised God for praying people! Ron fixed a lovely breakfast and Karla came back from doing hospital rounds. We were finally ready to leave at 11:50 a.m. for DesMoines airport. We took our cases and things to check and all was ok. I carried the key board and they didn't say much till we boarded our KLM flight. Since they allowed us to be in business section we were allowed to have the key board with us. Finally we were on our way to Amsterdam.

Chapter 7
Our Return to Africa

October 19th we arrived in Amsterdam Airport but had to spend the day in the airport waiting for our evening flight to Johannesburg. My diary stated: "We are spending the whole day in this smoky airport—shortening our lives because we have to breathe this second hand smoke." I walked about 20 minutes in the airport. We did get a sandwich and some mineral water, an apple and some oranges. I also had a cup of tea. Because of the rain our plane was a little late taking off. On Tuesday morning we woke early and prepared to land at Jan Smutts Airport. We landed about on time and had no trouble getting through customs. Those waiting to welcome us were Orai and Linda Lehman and Rev. and Mrs. Don Karns. We went to their place for breakfast. It felt good to be back in Southern Africa beginning with a wonderful prayer meeting that we attended that morning and learning of so many answers to prayer. We had to catch up on sleep in the afternoon and then Linda fixed a lovely evening meal for us.

The next morning, Oct. 21st, I called my parents to let them know we had arrived in South Africa. That would have been the evening of October 20th for them. Bob and I went back to bed again for the jet lag had really gotten to us. About 5:00p.m. Rev. Karns came to pick us up in a 1990 Toyota Cressida, a very nice car with air conditioning. He took us to their home in Brakpan to visit and talk about what our assignment would be. We stayed in the granny flat where Orai and Linda live while trying to sort out what we would be doing this term. We did go with the Karns to Lebowa for their conference that week-end where we got to see the William Selamalelas, Sigwane and Ngobeni as well as missionaries Marc and Di LaPointe and their two girls. We were really impressed by the church at Leboahomo and the area. What great potential we saw in that place because there were no other churches around, a brand new area. Bob preached twice at his conference and then we returned to Brakpan with Rev. Karns.

One of the things I mentioned in my diary was that I had lost 9 pounds and weighed 176 now. It really was a process for me to lose weight but headquarters had required that I lose at least 10 pounds. Bob and I did a lot of walking so I know that was helpful. We walked every morning while we were in transition. I also read a lot. I read "The Prophet" by Frank Peretti and Ben Carson's book "Gifted Hands". Both were very interesting books.

For the next prayer meeting, Don and Elizabeth, the Lehmans and Bob and I all went to Alexandra (suburb of Joburg) to the Engles. At this prayer meeting we also met a young Zimbabwean hoping to go to EWBC. That evening Bob and I went to Kempton Park to have dinner with a couple by the name Lionel Goslings. These folks became friends with Carleta Anderson who lived in Western Nebraska. The Goslings came to pick us up and then brought us back after our meal. I gave Carolyn, the wife, a gift Carleta had asked me to take to her.

The week-end of Oct. 30-Nov 1, we had the privilege of again attending a conference that was held on the South Coast for the Nkosinathi District near Port Shepstone. We were invited to sleep at Bill NieMacks near Ramsgate. We got to meet Helen, the sister of Daphne and Bill NieMack. After breakfast we went back to the Immanuel Mission Church. It is quite amazing how many youth and children attended this conference. One of the things the youth liked these days was music on the key board—and was it ever loud! We left to go back to Joburg after the evening service.

On November the 2nd, Bob and I decided to attend the South African Pastor's fellowship in the evening. This was very nice as it was held at the Stanley Benjamin's in Pretoria. We got to see Chris and Rose Motley. In fact we got to see quite a few of the white South African pastors

The U. S. elections for president was being held November. We prayed for these elections. Next day I got up early to watch President Bush give his conceding speech to Clinton. Now Bill Clinton, democrat from Arkansas is President Elect. He won only because Perot got 16 electoral votes. The popular vote showed Bush getting about as many votes as Clinton.

Before we left for Swaziland to attend the graduation, Bob and I went shopping to get gifts for the graduates, Esther, Israel, and Fakazile. The gift for Esther was a candle, for Israel, a torch, and for Fakazile, an umbrella. About 3:00 p.m. we began our journey to Swaziland and arrived around 8:30. Orai and Linda and Bob and I stayed in the guest house and Paul Lehman slept in the van. November 7th we had breakfast with Esther Phillippe at her house(the house that we lived in last term). We got to see many people we knew. At noon we ate our lunch at the school dining hall, and then we made a tour of the new library and chapel. After this we went into Manzini to see the new shopping malls and to visit the Emmets and Shirley Mordant. We came back to Israel and Victoria Langas for tea and a nice visit. In the evening Brenda Bagley invited all of us for supper at their house to honor Esther Phillippe's birthday. There was an evening service at which my Bob (remember, there were two Bobs)preached for. That evening Jim Lo brought

Daphne's sister Betty and Ray and their family and their brother Bill. Daphne NieMack was so surprised!

Sunday, November 8th, was Graduation Day at Emmanuel Wesleyan Bible College. We visited the Sigwanes briefly that morning and had prayer with them. After this we all joined in the graduation. The two of the graduates were Fakazile Langa and Khanyisile Xaba. We saw so many people that we knew and so many were happy to see us. We left Swaziland about 4:00 p.m. on a five & ½ hour trip back to Joburg. A couple Zimbabwean boys, Dan Cossa and Honwana, rode with us.

The missionaries on the reef welcomed a wonderful dedicated couple from the North West and Indiana districts, Mike and Cindy Helvie and their children Eric and Melody, with a summer cook-out at the Karns on Nov. 9th.

Rev. Karns was able to purchase a very nice Toyota Hi Ace that might come to us if we get our work permits into Zimbabwe. Things moved so slowly when connected to the government there. Our hopes were still that we might be able to work in Zimbabwe with the new Christians and churches that were started.

Bob took our passports into Boksburg Home Affairs to straighten out the holiday sticker and they said we needed to apply for work permits and gave him papers. We hadn't realized we would need them but since we did, on November 11th Linda Lehman went with us to Home Affairs and they gave us the same forms. Then went back to Rev. Karns and he called Pretoria. We left our passports with the lady at the Home Affairs who was going to call back at 1:00 p.m. and went back to Boksburg. Karns called us after lunch and said we better come and get our passports so we did. When we got to Boksburg it was just barely in time before closing at 3:00 p.m. Finally they explained to us that what we had in our passports was a multiple visa that allowed us to apply for a either a work permit or temporary employment. They will try to have it for us soon after we fill out the papers. My Oh my, what a process!!! On November 12, Bob got all the papers filled out and took our passports into Home Affairs in Boksburg. In mid-November we packed our cases for a two week stay in Zimbabwe. On the way we stayed at the LaPointes in Petersburg. The Helvies were also there as they were taking over for the LaPointes who were going on furlough. We drove on to Zimbabwe on the 16th and had no problems at the border.

Finally the wonderful rains are coming. Zimbabwe had been desperate for good rains so it was a great blessing from the Lord. We stayed at Youngways the BIC guest house while we were there. While we were there, Bob tried to get our papers organized for work permits in Zimbabwe. We also visited many of our old friends and the churches. Again we worked on what was required for us to move to Zimbabwe. Chipo Makusha was a big help in this area. She went with us to immigration. The man was very nice and really gave us some helpful suggestions. I typed the letter for immigration and we took it the next day into them. When they called immigration at Harare they could not even find our file. The man at immigration said our letter was great. Now he just needed to find out why we had been refused.

During this visit we traveled to Victoria Falls. It was so dry in the area. In fact very little water was going over the Falls. While we were there Bob tried to see the architect about the design for the new church, but he wasn't in his office. On Saturday we met Mr. A. Ngwenya and spent the morning discussing the building plans. Bob went with Mrs. Semente to see the town council inspector to get an estimate of the cost of the church building. On Sunday we went to the morning service where I gave an object lesson about being lights for Jesus. Bob preached a wonderful sermon on Colossians 1:15-20 about the supremacy of Christ. Seven people came forward to pray, one man, three ladies and three children. After having Sunday dinner with the Sibandas there was a women's meeting at 2:00. Again, I was the speaker and my topic was "Having a Clear Conscience". Several of the women ask for advice on how to live with non-Christian husbands. That night I made a list of Bible verses for them to study.

Monday morning Bob went with Miss Sibanda and Mrs. Semente to see the architect for the church building plan. He had to redo the plans and bring it to Bulawayo where we would take it to the Mission Council. We left Victoria Falls for Bulawayo and arrived about 3:30 p.m. We were exhausted but it was nice that Sheila and Kevin Thomson invited us to supper. They had a sweet little eight months old boy, a very lively fellow.

On the morning of Nov. 24th Chipo Makusha went with us again to immigration and the man there had still not gotten information from our files. They still said they could not find them. Our next move was a letter from the National church asking for us to come to Zimbabwe. Then we could re-submit everything on Thursday. From there, we drove with Janet Kalenge and Elmon Dlodlo to Mvuma where Isaiah Kalenge and his wife live. It was so good to see Isaiah and his lovely family again. Velesiwe, his wife, cooked a delicious meal for us and sent us on our way, back to Bulawayo.

It was a wonderful two weeks spent in Zimbabwe. How our hearts ached to be there with our dear Christians to help them grow spiritually and to be able to do outreach to win more Zimbabweans to Christ. Nevertheless, back in South Africa we kept busy. Two main things for me was putting time in on my course of "Day Care Management" and then Bob and I spent time in studying Shona, the other main language in Zimbabwe.

We had a very nice Christmas Day at the O. D. Lehman home. The temperature was just right to eat outside. A long Christmas table was set for about 30 people under a big red and white tent. What a Christmas dinner - even homemade ice cream! What we really liked in these Southern African countries is how they hold a beautiful morning Christmas service. It helps to think of the real meaning of Christmas, God's gift to the world, His Son Jesus'. So ends our year of 1992!

The Year 1993

    As 1993 started off, we found ourselves in a holding position. We were waiting for our work permits to come through from Zimbabwe. While waiting we stayed in South Africa at different places. Carol and Jim Ramsay were gone for awhile and during this time we were at their house. Then Orai and Linda also had a place for us at Cinderella Mission in Boksburg.

During this waiting period I worked a lot on the "Day Care Management" course. I felt that this time could be utilized by trying to get the course finished. I did find that the last three units I needed to finish up were missing. In trying to figure out what I had done with them, it came to me they were packed in our barrels that we had shipped. I hoped that soon our shipment would arrive. It should be here by the end of January.

There was an incident that happened in Swaziland with one of our young pastors that was quite frightening. Henry Mohale was kidnapped along with the pickup that belonged to our missionary, Esther Phillippe. Some men took him at gun point, demanding money. They blind-folded him and took him toward the Mozambique border. Fortunately for Henry, they saw a police car and abandoned the pick-up and Henry. They ran into the bush and even left one of their guns in the vehicle. Henry talked to the police but they told him they couldn't really do much about the case and advised him to report it to the Manzini police.

Do you know what I thought might really have happened? I wondered if God didn't make that police car appear and worked a real miracle to get Henry free. These men have threatened Henry and his family and they are full of fear. They beat Henry and said if he did not do as they ask they were going to kill his family! So I asked people in America to really pray for this couple, to pray for the Holy Spirit to get hold of these wicked men's hearts and make them so miserable that they would turn themselves over to God. Nothing is too hard for God. I ask people to pray for Henry and Bethel to have peace knowing God would protect them. Miss Phillippe also needed prayer as she was not feeling well and losing weight. I believe it was from having a lot of stress in her life. Having your pickup stolen by wicked men planning to kill a young pastor is very traumatic. In fact we all needed prayers for protection. The prayers of God's people releases God's power to do mighty things!

Toward the end of January we made another trip to Zimbabwe. On our way we stopped at Petersburg to stay overnight with Mike and Cindy Helvie. The Helvies are a new young couple from Oregon doing missionary work here in Northern Transval.We planned to stay about a week in Zimbabwe and hoped to bring students back from there to go to Bible College in Swaziland.

Another one of our projects while waiting for our work permits was to learn Shona which is spoken in Harare and the Eastern part of Zimbabwe. I was learning both Zulu and Shona. So here is a little example of Shona. "Masikati"! (Greetings.) "Maswera Seyi"?-(How are you?) "Taswera Maswerawo." (We are well.) Shona contains many rolling r's and zv, zw, sv and sw sounds but we found it very interesting. A young Zimbabwean couple lived very close to us while we were in South Africa and coached us in the language. We also continued to expand our Zulu and Ndebele—the two languages we worked with in past terms. I hoped we wouldn't confuse them one day. Studying the language kept us busy while we waited for our Zimbabwe work permits.

After returning from Zimbabwe to South Africa we prepared ourselves to go to Swaziland. We stayed in the little round guest house there in Swaziland. Orai Lehman was scheduled to be guest speaker for EWBC's Spiritual Emphasis Week. He also stayed with us in the rondovel (guest house). I told Brenda Bagley that I would cook for Orai as she had her hands full teaching Joshua and Tracy and little two year old Beth, besides all the other things she was doing. While we were there I did some teaching with two typing classes and some typing for another teacher.

We were always so glad for letters from home. On Feb. 18th I wrote, "What a wonderful day! Randal sent his school pictures and Kassie and Kyle sent school pictures and some of their special art work for Grandpa and Grandma. They made special valentines for us." This term Colleen Mullanix is putting out our form letters for us from the Imperial Wesleyan Church. We always appreciated every letter we received from home, especially family loved ones but also those from prayer partners and supporters.

We will leave Swaziland again on Feb. 27th driving to Joburg for one night and then head for Zimbabwe once again. We are to be in Zimbabwe Mar. 1-21. Bob has to teach on the night of the 26th of Feb. here at EWBC. During the day he had to be in an executive meeting. Bob was put on the Executive Board of the mission council.

One of the subjects brought up in the executive meeting was sending Bob and me to Beira, Mozambique, to help teach the new converts in the churches that are springing up. In our Home Ministries in the States, Bob and

I did ask people to pray for Northern Mozambique, a region that needed to be reached with the Gospel. Orai Lehman and his parents had just returned from that area with such a stirring report of the work in the Beira area. The council talked of us going as "College on Wheels". In my letter to my parents I said, "We are excited about it but we want to be where God wants us. Maybe God is opening the door we don't know. But whether it's Zimbabwe, Swaziland or Mozambique we are ready to follow where the Lord leads." This letter was written Feb. 27th and also contained this: "Guess what? You know the drums we sent October 13th last year? When they traced them, they were still sitting in Florida! Isn't this something??? So maybe because we are not settled about where we will be stationed perhaps this isn't a bad thing to happen!"

One unexpected thing that happened was my front tooth which had a cap on it started getting loose. I had eaten some corn on the cob that was quite hard and thought this may have been the cause. It was so loose I decided I better find a dentist. Here in Bulawayo the Seventh Day Adventists have an emergency clinic. They see patients on a first come first served basis. I had my front tooth fixed and then I ask the Dentist about one of my teeth at the back of my mouth that had become so sensitive. He suggested I get a new filling in it. The fillings in these teeth had been done in 1964 or '65.

Well, the very afternoon after I had my front tooth fixed, I was eating whole wheat bread and I crunched down on something which made my back tooth feel terrible. A few seconds later I commented to Bob, "My tooth has cracked in two pieces!" It didn't come out but I knew it meant another trip to the emergency clinic. The next morning, at 7:00 o'clock, I was waiting at the gate of the Dental Emergency Clinic. I was the first one so he took me right in and put a different kind of silver filling in it. It was quite sensitive at first but eventually felt much better. This dentist was from California and was very good. My total bill was just under $30.00 U. S. money equal to $170-00 Zimbabwe Dollars. I just could not get over how good God was to me. A lady whom we knew from the Nazarene Church in Bulawayo was in the clinic at the same time. When she heard about my problem she wanted to pay my bill for me. Now isn't God so Good! One cannot out-give God!

During our time in Zimbabwe, March of 1993, we noticed a lot of sickness which we were pretty sure was the result of AIDS. One young man with six children who used to attend our church said he had constant diarrhea and vomiting for three months. I visited many others in the western suburbs of Bulawayo who were sick, out of work and very poor. Many children were just running the streets. The Aids outbreak was truly serious. This disease was among the younger couples who had children at home. Often the parents would die and then the grandparents were left to raise the children. The young man I just mentioned did die and eventually his wife died.

During our March visit Bob was teaching a class on "Doctrine of

Holiness" at the Kumalo church in Bulawayo. There were about 14 students attending. At the end of this class ten students received credit. It was exciting to hear people saying, "This is just what we need. We wish we could go on." and "We want you to come again." were some of the positive remarks we heard about "College on Wheels"!

On April 12 Rev. Bob Bagley and Rev. Israel Langa took the class to the Victoria Falls area. We were praising the Lord for this outreach that Emmanuel Wesleyan Bible College had. There was a request for 50 students to be trained at EWBC in 1993. God didn't answer quite the way we expected. Since we had started this new program and the system of three week modules at the school the number of students had already passed the 50 mark. Right at this time, April, 1993, the number of part time and full time students had grown to about 70. Esther Phillippe informed us by July when our second semester started that we had already enrolled over 100 students for the year so far. Praise God, He was answering our prayers!

In April we were back in Swaziland. We were still waiting for our Zimbabwe permits. At times we almost felt God was closing the door, yet we knew "nothing is impossible with God". More and more we were getting involved on campus at EWBC. Bob was teaching a 3-week module April 12-30 on Bible prophecy –Daniel and Revelation. I was busy with typing classes and it sounded like Brenda Bagley was going to turn her music classes over to me. A class study for the women students called "A Woman's World" was held on Wednesdays which was also turned over to me. One of the Wednesdays I was asked to speak at a Mozambique Refugee Camp at Mpaka, Swaziland to some of the women on the subject, "How to be a Good Mother". This, of course, was right down my line. I loved talking about the home and children. God knew I loved children. I guess that is why He allowed Bob and me to have five of our own. They are all so special, as are our daughters-in-law and our son-in-law. At that time we had six wonderful grandchildren.

I had a new adventure during this time in Swaziland. I was trying to learn how to run the computer at the college office. Bob Bagley wanted me to learn it before he and Brenda went on furlough in May.

One of my frustrations in Swaziland was phone service. It seemed like the phone was always out of order especially at times when I wanted to contact my parents or one of our children. I stated in one of my letters to my parents: "I guess if I call I'll always have to remember 2:30 – 3:30 a.m. is a good time." Then I go on to tell Mom, "The phone service here is atrocious and makes me frustrated. In fact I've been so angry and upset about the phone that I'm grumpy as a snake and it's hard for me to be positive with my family. Anyway the Lord spoke to me about this when I read Job 40:11 "Disperse the rage of your wrath…" It hit me right between the eyes. So I've asked forgiveness from the Lord and am trying to be more positive now."

Randal's Visit, 1993

Our mission department made it possible for our children to visit us one time during our missionary term and we especially thank them for this blessing. During our five terms in Africa all of our children except Allen came for a visit. In 1993, Randal left the U.S. on May 6th. He flew via Holland so he could visit his friend Marc and then flew on to Southern Africa. Randal arrived May 19th and returned to the States on August 11th.

Bob and Brenda Bagley went on furlough in May. Before they left, however, Brenda organized a 40th Anniversary celebration for her parents, Don and Elizabeth Karns, who were living in Brakpan. I had the privilege of making the anniversary cake, a three tier cake iced in white icing, decorated with red roses. The reception was held at the Boksburg Wesleyan Church. Brenda did a great job of organizing the program.

Our drums and shipment finally arrived in South Africa about the middle of April. While Bob went to see about our shipment, I had to teach his class, Daniel-Revelation, and I enjoyed doing it. Bob got back to Joy Mission about 5:00 p.m. so he had made good time. He got the papers all signed for our barrels and now they will be delivered to Karns in Brakpan to wait until a decision is made about our placement. In the end it was quite clear that we should be in Swaziland. We received word again that for the second time our permits were not granted for Zimbabwe. It seemed the Lord wanted us to work at Emmanuel Wesleyan Bible College in training workers. We knew that "God's ways are higher than our ways and that He knows best." However, the folks in Zimbabwe were so disappointed! Later in May we were again in South Africa to pick up our drums and boxes to bring them back to Swaziland.

The mission vehicle we now had was a Toyota Hiace 10 seater. We had lots of room to haul people. At first I wasn't too keen about having this van but I got used to it. We got five of our barrels and a number of boxes loaded into this vehicle so we could take them to Swaziland. Since we knew that now we would be making our home at EWBC we wanted to prepare the Joy Mission house where we would be living. By the last day of May all the rooms had been painted except the kitchen and one bedroom. We had a carpet put down in the Living room, the dining room and hallway. We had new curtains made for the living room and dining room. I was truly looking forward to moving into our home. It is somewhat difficult to not be settled for six months.

It seemed like we did a lot of traveling during this term. By June 7th we were back at Boksburg in South Africa. Our purpose for going to Boksburg was to bring up some furniture to store for the Bagleys who had left on May 16th for furlough. We have now been appointed to fill their place at the Bible College in Swaziland. The few days we had in South Africa we helped the Lehmans pack to leave on furlough to the States. They were to leave June 20th.

A women's convention was held in Zimbabwe, June 16-20. When we arrived in Bulawayo we stayed with our friends Kevin and Sheila Tompson. This is the same Sheila who came to visit us in the States back in 1986. She and Kevin were now married and had a little boy. We did some sight-seeing in the Bulawayo area with Randal. We visited the Matopas and saw Cecil Rhodes' grave. Then we went to the natural History Museum which is very near to Sheila and Kevin's house. The next day we drove to Victoria Falls for the convention. Mrs. Shandu, our Director, couldn't arrive until Friday, so Annie Makusha and I had to be quite involved at the beginning.

We got to take Randal to the Victoria Falls before leaving. On Sunday evening we drove back to Bulawayo. Then on Monday we drove on to Phalaborwa, a town close to Kruger National Game Park. At Phalaborwa Randal got to visit with Paul Amos, his missionary friend who stayed with him at the Ramsay home in Boksburg while they were in school there. The month of June is always a holiday month between semesters at EWBC. This made it convenient to take Randal around to visit the different places.

We were assigned a neat place of ministry in Swaziland. Besides being involved with training at the Bible College there is a group of people living upon the Bulunga Mountains, about twenty kilometers from the college, who are excited about their church under the tree. The chief Induna introduce us as the missionaries who would help them build a church for their community. We along with some of our students from the college worked with these people of the area reaching out to many who did not darken a church door. Pray for these people on the mountain!

On Bob's birthday, June 29th, some Nazarene friends invited us to have a barbeque with them. John Sprunger is a pilot and flies for missions of the Nazarene Church. Randal wanted to talk with him and hear what he does. It was a real blessing and help to Randal as he had considered being a missionary pilot. Randal brought some box cake mixes so I made one for Bob's birthday cake. Guess who decorated it? Randal decorated his dad's birthday cake and did an excellent job!

A number of times in my letters to my parents I would inquire about Grace and Clint Reeves. Grace died on June 22 but when I wrote the June 29th letter, I had not heard about her death. Then on my July 21st letter I said, "I wrote a letter to Clinton and sent a card and check." So I knew by that date I had heard about Grace's death. Also during the month of June we learned that Evan Rittenhouse had passed away and that the Lewellen and Oshkosh churches were getting a new pastor and family, the Lynn Lutz family.

Randal was with us to celebrate his 21st birthday on July 12. I made him a cake shaped like a castle. We invited the staff and students to the college dining room to have cake with us.

After this Bob and Randal went to a youth camp at Altona Mission near the Southwest border of Swaziland. During their absence I was not alone. The LOVE Africa team was there for our Missions Emphasis week. There were nine members on the team and two of the girls stayed with me. They were there to do evangelism in the Phonjawane area. One of the purposes or perhaps I should say two purposes were to represent the school and the other was to have a class for the youth on "Spiritual Growth". At this camp they showed the "Jesus film" twice and many accepted the Lord.

Israel Langa is now our acting principal and he wants very much to see our Bible College represented throughout the Regional Conference. A youth camp is a good place to talk about further education in Christian training. As of July 8th we had 18 students at the school.

From one of my later July letters, I told how I'd been in the classroom most of the day. After I had my typing class, I taught for Esther Phillippe on Story Telling for Children's Ministry. There was chapel service this day, too. During the afternoon the ladies had their sewing class. I typed and printed a test paper for Bob to give in English class.

August arrived and again it was such a busy time. Randal returned to the States on Aug. 11th. What a wonderful time we had with him, almost three months. On August 19th Don and Elizabeth Karns brought Don and Joy Bray to be with us for the week-end. Then on Monday the men left for Altona Mission and Joy and Elizabeth stayed for the week. We had a great time together. On Monday we went into Manzini so I could get groceries and I took Joy to the market so she could see what they had to offer. On Tuesday Joy prepared for chapel service as she was the speaker. Also she shared with us at our Women's World. This all happened on Wednesday. During that time too, I was typing lessons for Bob, trying to write letters and up-date our address list. Our next issue of our prayer letter was to go to some new folks on our list.

The next day Joy, Elizabeth and I headed for Manzini. There the ladies went to the market and got the handcraft they wanted. After they finished we drove out to the Swazi Candle factory and then over to Tisheshi Craft place. We were invited to Sigwane's home for lunch—what a meal that was! From there I had to go to my typing class. At about 2:30 p.m. we took Mrs. Sigwane, Joy Bray, and Elizabeth Karns to Ebenezer Mission on past Siteki on the East side of Swaziland. It was interesting to see the mission again but it was sad to see how run down it had become. From the Mission we drove on out to Ndlelane and over to where Sigwanes are building their retirement home. We drove back to Joy Mission just in time to go to Israel Langa's home for supper. Now, have I made you tired for the day??? It was such fun having Joy and Elizabeth and doing things together. They were so helpful to me and I really appreciated these two special ladies.

My Father's By-Pass Surgery, 1993

It was during August that my father was having real heart problems. Actually it had been coming on for several months before. So My Uncle Homer and Aunt Grace came out to western Nebraska during this time to visit and to see if they could help my parents with some of the haying. My Uncle Bill Thornton also came to help them during hay time. One Sunday morning Mother and Daddy didn't arrive at church as usual and everyone was wondering what had happened to them. Someone called up to my parents and mother told them Dad was very sick and in bed.

Clint Reeves told me later that he felt he should go up and talk Dad into going to Denver for a heart operation. I'm so glad that Clint did this. Otherwise I might never have seen my daddy again. Aunt Grace and Uncle Homer were there and that very Sunday afternoon they loaded Dad and Mom into their car and headed for Denver. I believe they took Dad straight into the emergency and he was able to see his heart surgeon. Mom, Aunt Grace and Uncle Homer stayed with one of Mom's cousins in Denver.

On the 19th of August, 1993, Dad had a heart operation, a three way by-pass. Many people were praying. Even in South Africa and Swaziland many were praying for Dad's recovery. I'm not sure how long Dad had to stay in hospital but Uncle Homer and Aunt Grace brought them back. My Aunt Nellie offered for them to stay in Lewellen but my dad is a determined man and he insisted on going home to his ranch. I certainly do appreciate my Uncle Homer and Uncle Bill helping get the hay put up for Daddy. Soon after this they left to go back to Delaware and Indiana and my sister Esther was able to arrive in September to help our parents during Dad's recuperation. God is so good to His children!

Back to Swaziland

Back in Swaziland our visit with Joy and Elizabeth came to an end. Bob and I took the ladies via Pretoria to let Joy off at the Stanley's and then we drove on down to Brakpan with Elizabeth. We stayed with Grandpa and Grandma Lehman in Boksburg. They were staying in Orai and Linda's place while they were on furlough. We had such a wonderful visit with them. In fact we even played scrabble—and the winner, of course, was Grandma Orpha!

We had such a profitable meeting at Karns with Don and Joy Bray, our Wesleyan Missions Director. Don and Joy are so wonderful and right down to earth. We love them! They told us about the meeting with the regional Board and the decisions made there. One exciting decision the National Church made, maybe I should say overwhelming decision, was for us to be missionaries to Mozambique until Orai and Linda returned from furlough. Don asked us, "How does it feel to be wanted in all these places?" Swaziland wanted us to work in the Bible College, Zimbabwe wanted us there and now Mozambique also wanted us! The Regional Board made a plan for us. We would continue living at Joy Mission and teaching at the Bible College but making periodic visits to Maputo, Beira and other places as much as possible.

Beginning September found us in Zimbabwe again for their annual conference. Israel Langa chaired this conference because Rev S. Sigwane asked him to do it. He has done a wonderful job. This conference was held at Victoria Falls. At this conference the District Board approved five new students to come to EWBC in Swaziland.

On Sunday afternoon we drove back to Bulawayo and stayed overnight with the Goneras. The next morning we headed for Hararwe, planning to spend the night with some dear friends who are like a son and daughter to us. Liberman and Thandiwe live in Harare. We had not seen them since their wedding in December, 1990, so it was a great family reunion.

The next day we headed for Mozambique going out through the Mutare border. Unfortunately Israel Langa didn't have a Mozambique visa in his passport. He had never gone through this border before. We found out that they would not grant a visa at the border like they do at the Swazi border. They told us to go back to Harare(this is the capitol of Zimbabwe) and get the visa. So back to Harare we went only to find it would take five days. We did not have this kind of time. We drove back to Mutare hoping maybe someone could help us, but to no avail. We decided that since Bob and I had visas, we should go on to Beira in Mozambique because they were expecting us. Israel Langa would go back to Swaziland by bus.

The Bible says, "All things work together for good to them that love God, to them who are called according to His purpose". Romans 8:28 God had all things worked out for Bob and me. At the Mozambique boarder you don't find many people who speak English—most people speak Portuguese or Ndau. But the Lord had an English speaking man there who helped us. Just before we left immigration, a white man approached us saying he was a missionary from Beira and needed a ride. Right there, on the spot, the Lord provided a guide to Beira!

Our work in Beira was conducting "College on Wheels" for college credit. Also, I gave classes for the women. Since Langa was not along to interpret, we had difficulty in communicating. Our missionary couple, the Honwanas, knew the Zulu language and so we could connect in this way. Rev. Malate, one of the pastors ,and one married lady who originally came from Zimbabwe knew English. We could only leave the results with the Lord but we knew we encouraged the Honwanas, our missionary couple working in the Beira area. Because Langa was not along to guide us down to Maputo we came back through Zimbabwe and on to Swaziland on September 18th after traveling 5844 kilometers in four different countries—Swaziland, South Africa, Zimbabwe and Mozambique. We praised God for the safe trip and for connecting with many of our Christians in these countries!

At the end of September we had an exciting call from the States. Rylan called us on Saturday the 25th. He sounded so excited. The phone wasn't working very well and he had to really shout it out. He told us we were going to be Grandpa and Grandma about the 1st of May. I stated it would be wonderful to have another May birthday. Later we found out this grandchild was going to be an April baby. We prayed that Amy would have a healthy pregnancy. This would be our 7th Grandchild!

Finally in October, I was able to complete the course on Day Care Management. I wrote my final exam on Oct 7th and then had to wait for my diploma. I wrote the school asking if I could get a degree so I waited to see what they would say. Earlier in my story I wrote about wanting to be trained in Child Day Care so that I could teach a course here at the college. A number of churches across the Southern Africa field have day cares or would like to start one. This, however, did not work out in the end. However, I did receive my diploma in "Day Care Management" at the end of January, 1994.

Mike and Cindy Helvie and their two children were with us at the Bible College during October. Mike taught psychology here at the school. We had a marriage seminar on Friday evening and Saturday morning with Mike and Cindy as facilitators. It was really good. There were twelve couples counting all of us. It truly was very helpful to all the couples. The Helvies have been here for a year working in the Pietersburg Area as WGO (Wesleyan Gospel Corp) workers. They are such a lovely family. They plan to go home for a year to raise their support and then return as full time missionaries.

Our Canadian Cultural Exchange Teacher

Here I would like to write about a young lady from Canada who came to us as a cultural exchange teacher. She was sent here to teach in one of our mission outstation schools at Phonjawane. Michelle got lonely at times and spent weekends at the Bible College just to be among English speaking people. We prayed for her a lot. One day I had the opportunity to share with her about Jesus and the relationship He wants to have with each one of us. We prayed and it was a life changing moment for her. To this day we are friends.

She even came to Nebraska to visit us one Easter week.

The Paul Meeks also came to teach a module for the bible college on "Wesleyan Discipline". It really was interesting to us to have all these visitors helping to train our students.

EWBC Graduation

At the Bible College work was beginning to wind down. We had our last Women's World Class. Mrs Nkosi had asked me to speak to the ladies about menopause. You find here in Africa the women have some really weird ideas about such things. Afterwards we had a party and exchanged gifts with our secret sisters. I fixed cake and Mrs. Nkosi got drinks and ice cream and oranges.

Before school closed I began thinking about how near we were to Christmas. This year we would have none of our family close because Orai and Linda Lehman and family were on furlough. Miss Phillippe would probably be the only missionary at Joy Mission. So I began to feel sorry for myself. I wanted to celebrate but we wouldn't have more than one or two to celebrate with. Then an idea came to me. I began wondering how our cook at the college celebrated Christmas with her family. I decided to go to the college kitchen and question her.

So off to the kitchen I went. I said, "Mrs. Gwebu, what special way do you celebrate Christmas with your family"? Mrs. Gwebu had about 10 children and she pretty much was the bread winner. Her husband drank a lot and didn't have a job most of the time. So she said, "I usually try to save enough to buy a big package of rice so that all the children can have a plate of rice." I thought to myself, "Now is that really that special?" But of course if you always had only hard porridge (that's stiff corn meal with maybe a bit of soup over it) then maybe having rice was special. So a plan began to form in my mind. We were going to plan a special Christmas for this poor family!

Graduation Day for Emmanuel Wesleyan Bible College was November 7th. We had a wonderful graduation with ten graduates receiving their diplomas. Rev. F. Stanley was the guest speaker and he gave a powerful message. The chapel was packed out with many guests attending. Two of the graduates were Zimbabwean young men. We decided to take them back to Zimbabwe and make our last visit for the year. This would make five times we had visited this year. We left on the 10th of November and would be there till the 25th.

While we were in Bulawayo we were able to talk with all our children in the States accept Randal. It was very relaxing to be in Zimbabwe visiting many friends and people of the churches. We also were able to visit in

Victoria Falls. We met with the church people there—in fact for three nights we had services at one of the homes. The people are very excited about building their new church. Prayer was definitely needed to obtain the right builder who would be honest and do a good job. One of the young graduates, Sikhumbuzo Ndlovu, would be the new pastor for this Victoria Falls Wesleyan Church. The other graduate would be pastoring in the Bulawayo area. We also needed prayer for the District Superintendent Rev. Sonny Makusha and his wife Annie. They were carrying a heavy load since no missionary was there to help them.

Toward the end of November we learned that the Canadian cultural exchange teacher, Michelle would be celebrating Christmas with us. It was getting even more exciting as we made our Christmas plans. I planned to fix a special Christmas dinner with chicken and boreVors(a farmer's sausage) prepared on a grill and all kinds of salads and desserts. Probably counting up everyone including us there would be about 20. We were missing our own family but really excited about our Christmas project. In my form letter I said, "Some of you have also had a part in our project because you have sent used clothes, some have sent stuffed toys, pencils, notebooks, sewing kits and various other things to make lovely gifts for this family. We truly appreciated what people in the States were doing!

Our Annual Missionary Council, Dec. 7-12th

On Dec. 7th the missionaries met at "Come together Guest Farm" in the Transvaal for our annual missionary council Meeting. This year I guess you could describe it as a historic missionary council. We thought it would be our last since we were merging into the Regional Board of Administration. But now the Regional Supt. Rev. Sigwane, The regional treasurer Rev. Israel Langa, and our Assistant Regional Supt. Rev. Robert Hlengethwa attended our council. They told us, "No, we must not close our mission council for now because the regional board sees it as the Heart of the Region". So now they recommended that Robert Cheney act as Mission coordinator. What a great surprise to Bob and me! We were willing to do it if the Lord wanted us in this position. They even voted on this recommendation and it passed nearly unanimously.

What had to happen next was for the recommendation to go to our general headquarters at Indianapolis and they would either approve it or recommend someone else. Almost everyone is talking like they are sure it will be approved but we won't know for a while. If they do approve it then Bob and I would be moving to Brakpan, South Africa to live in the Mission coordinators house. Rev. and Mrs. Don Karns would be retiring in June if headquarters appointed us. I never dreamed this could happen but if it's the Lord's plan then we are willing.

We had such a good council meeting. It was so nice to have Rev. Sigwane and his wife, Israel Langa and Victoria and Rev. Hlengethwa and his wife with us. It was our first time to come together like this but it was great! The African pastors gave the devotions and messages and we truly appreciated their ministry.

After returning from the council meeting Dec.12th we got busy preparing for our Christmas with the Gwebu family. Every child (remember there were 10 of them) needed a Christmas gift to unwrap. Also the Mom (our college cook) must get a gift. It was such fun wrapping all these gifts of clothing, stuffed toys, notebooks, pens, pencils etc. Then there was the meal to plan. Mrs. Gwebu said she would cook the rice we bought in her big black pot over the open fire. Esther Phillippe, Michelle and I would fix a number of salads and desserts and then Bob and I would buy the chicken and BoreVors from the store in town. Bob would load up the ½ barrel that had a grate over it for cooking the meat. It was so exciting getting ready for this special Christmas!

Christmas Day, 1993

Finally the day arrived. Of course, always on Christmas morning you celebrate the birth of Jesus by attending one of the Christmas services held in each of the churches. Since Bob and I helped in the church up on the Belunga Mountain, Ethlane, we attended the service there. Many people came out to worship. Michelle also attended the service. It was such a nice service and then they had a gift exchange. The Christmas tree was a big tree-like bush brought into the church and decorated with wrapped candies and tied by string to the tree. You can imagine how the children eyed that tree. After the Christmas story was told Bob gave the message. The high light of the service was the presentation of a wheel chair to Thembasile Mamba, a crippled girl who comes to the church. How I wish you could have seen the joy and excitement in that girl's face when she saw the wheel chair, a gift from an organization who gave money to buy it for her. What a beautiful event it was to happen on the day we remember the greatest gift God gave to the world, His son Jesus! The girl's mother was so grateful that she brought a live chicken to the service to give to us as her thank-you gift!

After the service and driving back down the mountain we headed for the mission to pick up all the food stuff for our Christmas dinner and boxed up all the gifts. Michelle offered to tell the story of Christ's birth after our dinner. We drove into the plot where the Gwebu home was located. Joyful children came out to meet us. Down from the grass thatched mud hut they led us to a tree where a table was set up under the shade. The oldest boy helped Bob move the home-made grill a little distance from the table. They got the fire going in the grill and put many pieces of chicken and the farmer's sausage on the wire grating to cook. I wish you could have seen the children's faces as they viewed all this food being brought in. They very seldom got a piece of meat and to see all this on the grill being cooked caused them to gaze wide-eyed. All the children filled their plates and got a special drink of Kool Aid, something they didn't get very often.

Before we handed out the gifts, we gathered everyone around to hear the Christmas story. Michelle did a great job of telling about Jesus' birth. Then we had prayer, thanking God for His gift of love, for Jesus whom He sent into the world to die for all our sins. The children listened intently!

Then it was gift time. As the name of each child and adult was called they came forward to receive their gift. Some of them didn't want to open their gifts because they were wrapped in such pretty paper. It was such fun watching these children's eyes sparkle with excitement.

I can say from my heart that this Christmas was one of the most memorable in my life time. Just seeing the joy on these children's faces made it a most blessed Christmas for Bob and me as well as for Michelle and Miss Phillippe. It is clear to us why the Bible says: "It is more blessed to give than receive." It was a Christmas we shall never forget!

To end our year we prepared for the Regional Conference held in Natal, South Africa. The dates for this conference were Dec. 27-January 2nd. It was so good to have with us one of our generals Rev. Earle Wilson and his wife Sylvia. The conference went well and even finished early. Rev. Robert Hlengethwa was elected as Regional Superintendent since Rev. Samson Sigwane wanted to retire. And so our year 1993 ended with praise to the Lord!

Beginning a New Year, 1994

Early in January, we had the delight of having our General Superintendent Dr. Earle Wilson and his wife visiting our Regional Conference. He brought great messages of encouragement to our field. After the conference the Wilsons traveled with us to Swaziland. They wanted to see the Bible College. While they were with us we offered to take them to Kruger National Game Park in the Transvaal. We also took Prudence Langa and Michelle Miller with us. It was such fun! We saw a lion walking right alongside the road. Also we saw rhino, hippo, elephants, giraffe and many other animals. It was a great day for all of us!

Next on our calendar January 25-28th was our staff retreat and on Feb.1st school began at the Bible College. One thing I was trying to get done before school started was to write 33 or 34 letters to answer all the Christmas mail we had received. One of my problems was that our typewriter ribbon was bad and we needed to get some new ones. Visitors were coming from Pretoria so I ask them to bring some typewriter ribbons. In February, John and Marge

Connor flew into Swaziland on a Sunday evening and we picked them up at the Matsapa airport. We also had Jonathan Madden for about three weeks doing all kinds of maintenance work and the work of taking green mealies (sweet corn) to the market. They sold like hot cakes!

The Connors planned to help at the school and also worked on a church discipline for the Southern Africa Region. Then on Sunday Rev. George Failing arrived by plane with his pastor. Rev. Failing taught one of the classes at the Bible College. He didn't seem well when he arrived on crutches so we have been trying to help him a lot.

The first week of February was our Spiritual Life Emphasis week and orientation for the students. By the end of February we had enrolled 22 students. Dr. Failing taught Introduction to theology and I decided I wanted to take this class. This definitely didn't help me to have time for all the things I was involved in. I also wanted to take Theology I from Dr. John Connor but I realized I couldn't spare the time. I mentioned in one of my letters "Maybe one day I'll get a degree in Biblical Studies. I'm not sure that will ever happen but it was a thought! I'm teaching one English class twice a week and also help Miss Phillippe with her Children's Ministry Class. However Mrs. Madden is going to help her with this class so I won't have much to teach accept the lessons on 'Day Care Management', a class I am qualified to teach now that I've gotten my diploma."

After John Connor finished with the Theology Class we took him and his wife to Kruger National Game Park. Bob and I always enjoyed doing this for our guests. We saw quite a few different animals this time. There were six rhino, cape hunting dogs and a sable antelope which were unusual to see. But the lions, cheetah and leopards were hiding from us! We saw giraffe and elephants—one elephant was acting like a police on the road! He was really big!

When we arrived back at the college in Swaziland we had a Canadian Work Team arrive. There were thirteen members, five of them former missionaries that we had known from earlier times, Rev. and Mrs. Bill Morgan, Rev. and Mrs. Charles Sanders, and Rev. Eric Haywood. We were delighted to see all of them again. At this time we were in the process of building three new churches in the Swaziland District. One of those churches was the one we were overseeing on the Bulunga Mountains. Some of the men began digging out for the foundation the next week. The ladies all prepared food and we had a carry-in dinner—my, what a feast of mealies, mealie bread, samp, etc.!!!! I made cornbread, salad and the meat was boer vors. Seven of the team members went to Altona Mission in Transvaal and the other six stayed with us here at the college while they worked at building the churches. I felt sorry for these folks coming out of the snow in Canada and into an oven for March is late summer in Southern Africa. The Work team was able to get a church built along the road to Phonjawane called Msabane. This was one of the first places we worked with when we first arrived in Swaziland. We as missionaries were always so thankful for people who were willing to come and work!

Plans for a Wedding in April, 1994

Earlier in my writing I referred to our son Randal striking up a relationship with a young lady at Bartlesville Wesleyan College, Candice Clark. This relationship developed over a couple years and Randal and Candice wanted to get married April 30th. Bob and I had attended each of our other children's weddings and we certainly did not want to miss this one.

Not only was this wedding coming up, but the birth of our 7th grandchild was supposed to happen about this same time. We needed to find a flight that was within our means. A lot of prayer was going up. We found that Austrian Airlines was the cheapest way to fly home. How thankful we were that we had not taken any vacation time yet because now we could take a full month to be in the States.

Besides getting three church buildings up, Bob wanted to finish giving the rest of the membership classes to the ones at Ehlane before we left for the States. He also had to attend a meeting in Joburg on April 11th. I decided to not go with him because I wanted to sew the blocks for the quilt we were making for Bartlesville Wesleyan. The ladies at our Bible College were sewing the blocks by hand. Then I planned to put all the blocks together by machine. This quilt had a real African flavor. I called it the 'African Hut Quilt'.

. By April 6th we got confirmation for all our flights on Austrian Airways and TWA. We would be flying into St. Louis, Missouri on April 22 at 8:20 p.m. It was exciting thinking about seeing all our children and grandchildren again. We were especially looking forward to spending some time with Randal before the wedding. Having happy plans in place added joy for celebrating Easter.

Marge and John had known Candy since she was a baby. Candy's folks, Wilbur and Sandy Clark pastored the North Gate Wesleyan Church in Salem, Oregon. Orai and Linda had also gone to school with Sandy and Wilbur at BWC. Candy's sister Chrystal was graduating from college at this time and also our nephew Michael Lehman and his wife Janelle. So this seemed like a good time for Randal and Candy's wedding. Putting these relationships all together was a blessing for us and, also, looked forward to being in the States for the birth of Rylan and Amy's baby. "Amy, Rylan's wife is such a special girl. She has been writing to us and I love it!" (written in my letter of April 6th, 1994.)

Our visit in Bartlesville, Oklahoma

Our trip to the U. S. began April 21st boarding an Austrian Airways plane and heading for Vienna. It was an all-night flight and we arrived in Vienna airport early in the morning. We had several hours before our TWA flight would begin, taking us to St. Louis Missouri. That evening, on April 22, Randal met us at the St. Louis Airport. It was so good to see him and to ride all the way back to Bartlesville. We arrived at Rylan and Amy's where we were to stay until the wedding. How exciting to see our son and his wife. Of course Amy was very pregnant with their first child. It took a while for us to become adjusted to the eight hours differences in Africa time and the U.S. Central time zone.

On one of the days I was invited to a Bridal Shower for Candy. Quite a number of ladies attended and she received many lovely gifts. It was nice for Bob and me to see people we had known in former years.

Anlan Louise Cheney Arrives

On the morning of April 28th we were awakened early. It appeared that Amy was going into labor. Her midwife worked out of the hospital in Tulsa, Oklahoma so they felt they should probably head that direction. Tulsa was 40-50 miles south of Bartlesville and they certainly wanted to get there in time. They asked me to go along. I considered it a real privilege to be with my daughter-in-law. Some of Amy's girlfriends also came. When her midwife checked Amy she decided she wasn't very close to delivery yet. So Amy and I decided to do some walking in the mall. It seemed like that day she and I walked for miles! We wanted this baby to come before Randal and Candy's wedding on April 30th at 4:00p.m. Saturday afternoon. Amy was certainly not keen about returning to Bartlesville only to have to return to Tulsa. Finally, we decided to eat supper and wait. As the evening progressed the labor was getting more and more pronounced. About 7:00 p.m. they decided it was time to head for the hospital again. This time it was for real! Amy's midwife said, "Baby has decided to come this time." So Amy was taken to a special room at the hospital. I felt honored that she wanted me to be present when baby came. And so we waited. A couple of the girl friends were present as well as was Rylan. A few minutes passed midnight April 29th our little Anlan Louise Cheney made her appearance. What a joy we all felt! I was so privileged to be present at this sweet granddaughter's birth. Now Bob and I had seven grandchildren: four granddaughters and three grandsons. God was so good to all of us!

Randal and Candy's Wedding 1994

The day of our son's wedding arrived April 30th. The wedding took place in one of the smaller Wesleyan Churches in Bartlesville, Sooner Park. It was a beautiful ceremony. Rylan stood up as best man for his brother and Crystal, Candy's sister, stood up with her. Candy's father Wilbur and my Bob did the wedding program along with great music. Our daughter Roxane was able to come down with the children and bring Grandpa and Grandma Thornton. Our other sons Allen and Ron and their wives from Iowa came for this special occasion. Of course Rylan and Amy lived there and surprisingly enough Amy was able to attend the wedding with baby Anlan. Also a number of the Clark relatives attended.

One thing I promised Randal was to make a Southern Africa wedding fruit cake. I made it before we left Africa since it was solid enough to travel in my carry-on luggage. After arriving in Bartlesville I assembled the two tiered fruitcake with fondant icing. Of course they had the regular American wedding cake but it was nice to have a taste from Randal's cultural upbringing. After their wedding and reception, Randal and Candy left on their honeymoon.

Bob and I made our way to the Lewellen, Nebraska area so we could spend a little time with my folks. While we were at my parents, one of the events we were able to take part in was branding the baby calves. It was so nice to spend a bit of time with Mom and Dad, Charles and Linda Cheney and some of the church people. From here we made our way to North Platte where Ron, Roxy and Alicia, Missy, Andrew and Micah lived. They pastored the Harvest Christian Wesleyan Church there.

We wanted to visit each of our children's homes, so from North Platte it was on to Guthrie Center, Iowa where Allen, Kim, Kassie and Kyle lived. (I think I must insert here how thankful I was that we had visited in each of our children's homes, my parents and others in the Lewellen area. It would be their last time to see Bob, but, of course, at the time we didn't know that.) Ron and Karla lived in DesMoines at this time and so we made our way there. We were not able to spend a lot of time with each one but it was just a good to be in each home. Then it was time for us to head back to Bartlesville for a quick visit with Rylan and Amy and to be guests at Randal and Candy's new home, a very nice apartment in Bartlesville. It was great to have a meal at their house!

Then, it was time to pack our suitcases again and fly back to South Africa. It was a little hard on us being out of bed for three nights. We didn't go to bed because of packing and getting ready to fly out. Also, I rocked and prayed over baby Anlan. She is so sweet! Amy was quite tired that night. They are getting ready for a big move to Nebraska where Rylan is planning to work for his Uncle Charles.

Randal and Candy took us to the St. Louis airport. I will never forget the picture in my mind of Randal saying goodbye to his daddy. Our plane headed out for Vienna, Austria. This time when we arrived in the morning Mrs. Wright, one of the missionaries, met us at the airport and took us to their home. We were most grateful for their kindness in giving us a bed to sleep in for a few hours. It was a great privilege to get acquainted with the Wrights and to meet Brenda Babcock for the first time. That evening the Wrights took us back to the airport to get on our scheduled flight to Johannesburg. On Saturday, May 21st, we arrived in South Africa at about noon. Then we went to the Lehmans to freshen up and attend a farewell party for Don and Elizabeth Karns who were retiring.

On Monday May 24th I wrote: "Last night the area of Johannesburg has experienced its first frost of the season. Today is bright and sunny with a rising temperature and the feeling of fall in the air." I continue in the letter: "Recently we have received a report from the Dept. of World Missions that reflected our past support, our present support and what is projected in faith promises for the future. It would be great to be able to say that our situation is as bright as our southern African sunshine, but reality dictates that our present level of support needs attention." With the change of policy each missionary family is responsible to raise an assigned amount for their support. While we were on furlough in 1991-1992, we endeavored to raise support for the building project at Emmanuel Wesleyan Bible College and support for other missionaries. Now we were responsible for raising our own support. Bob and I never liked asking for money but we needed to find a way to do this. So we outlined a plan and sent out letters, praying that God would direct hearts to our present need. It was exciting to see how God brought in our support. During June headquarters listed the amount that had come in for us at $7,088.35. This probably was the highest that had ever come in for us in this short a time frame. It would cover for about two and one half months so we really praised the Lord. My job, of course, was to write thank you letters individually to each donor. This kept me really busy for a while.

Moving to Brakpan, South Africa

We had a new assignment beginning June, 1994. Bob had been appointed as the Mission Director for the Southern African Region. The Karns were retiring and returning to the States and we were to move into their house in Brakpan. This meant that within the next two weeks we would be packing up in Swaziland and arriving in our new home in Brakpan.

We left Swaziland with Karns helping us transport our earthly possessions. Everything went so smoothly and I commented to my husband, "I know that a lot of people must be praying for us. We praised God because He made an easy transition for us." One thing that was hard for us to get use to was the winter climate. I stated in one of my letters: "It is cold Cold COLD here!!!" Then I reminded people that Joburg is nearly 6000 feet above sea level so about every morning we see thick frost outside and even snow sometimes. Since the houses were not built with central heating it gets pretty chilly in our homes. You learn to wear layers and layers of clothing. Of course we do have little electric heaters that help some. Swaziland was much warmer because of being closer to the sea and at a lower altitude.

Don and Elizabeth Karns flew out June 21st for the U.S. Before they left Bob and I tried to learn everything we needed to know about our job. Although I had unpacked our barrels there was still organizing to do. The very day they left, a YES Corp, Vaughn and Cindy Telfer and five young folks, came in from Warrington, Missouri. They only stayed two nights and a day before heading for Venda and Lebowa where Marc and Di LaPointe worked.

For July we had a number of events to attend. First, from the 5th through the 8th Bob and I were speakers for the Missions Emphasis Week at EWBC in Swaziland. During that week we tried to clarify what was meant by Faith Promise Giving. At this meeting the offering amounted to R1322.00 for the coming year. We really praised the Lord that the students were beginning to catch the vision.

July 13-17, Mrs. Annie Makusha from Zimbabwe and I attended the Wesleyan Women's conference at Altona Mission. There were 244 ladies who registered for this meeting, coming from eight different districts of the Region.

Bob and I accompanied our Regional Superintendent, Rev. Robert Hlengethwa and his wife to Mozambique, July 20-24th for their conference. This meeting was held at Chokwe, about two hundred kilometers from Maputo the capitol. I want to share an incident that happened to us on our way back from this conference when we nearly had a serious accident. In our lane of traffic a car with a drunken driver had stopped and another car behind this one decided to pass just as we were passing. I could just see and feel us plowing into the back of the red car that was passing the stopped car. Rev. Langa. our driver, tried to avoid an accident and pulled onto the side of the road. When our vehicle hit the sand it pulled us down the embankment and we thought the car was going to roll. BUT IT DIDN'T! We sat there sort of suspended on the side of the bank and all we could do was PRAISE GOD we didn't go over! We carefully disembarked from the car so as not to let it tip over. The car didn't have a scratch and someone with a 4-wheel drive pulled us out of the ditch. All eleven of us realized that the angel of the Lord protected us from a terrible accident!

It was very interesting to be able to attend a John Maxwell Seminar in the Joburg area during August. Years before while we were at Ebenezer Mission in Swaziland I remember listening to tapes from Skyline Wesleyan Church and John Maxwell preaching the sermons on these tapes. I got so much good out of his sermons. So it was a pleasure now to finally be able to meet him and be in the seminar. It was especially for lay people as well as for pastors.

The Month of September

It was always a blessing to hear from my parents and about what was happening in Nebraska. From my mother's letter she kept us posted as to the news around Garden County. She informed us that Roxane and Ron and their four children planned a Labor Day visit with them. It is so nice for Rylan and Amy and their baby, Anlan, to also have time with them since they now live near Lewellen and go to the same church as Grandpa and Grandma Thornton. Mom told us how Aunt Grace and Uncle Homer Sherwood planned to come for a visit. I wrote back and said, "I wish we could be there, too!" Dad was celebrating the one year from his by-pass heart surgery. He turned 82 on Sept. 23rd and seems to be in better health than he had been for some time. For this I truly praised the Lord. It was hard for us to miss out on seeing our grandchildren growing up so fast while we were away on the mission field. Little Micah who arrived Sept 21, in 1992 was now turning two years old and the youngest grandbaby, Anlan, was already 4 months old. But thank the Lord for videos, letters and I must say much better phone service in South Africa!

There was a young man whom I will call Peter (not his real name) and whose story I would like to share. He actually is from Zimbabwe but came to South Africa to look for work. We knew this young man in Zimbabwe as he attended one of our churches there. He came to our home, not really having any place to stay. So we invited him to stay in our home and help with our yard work while he looked for a job. We started having Bible Studies with Peter. He came to know the Lord. One week our lesson was on baptism. After we had discussed the subject of baptism, Bob asked Peter if he would like to be baptized. He said, "Yes, I believe I am ready for baptism." We knew that the next Sunday at the Brakpan Wesleyan Church the pastor was planning to have a baptismal service. Bob called her and ask if she would mind if he baptized Peter after she had baptized two young ladies from her church. She readily agreed. It was very special to witness this important time in Peter's life. He seemed so happy and blessed to be taking this step in spiritual growth. We prayed for his continual growth in learning God's word and we praised God that this young man had decided to serve Jesus!

By the end of August and into September, a number of district conferences were held across the Southern Africa Region. It was our privilege to attend the Zimbabwe conference. We drove all the way from Brakpan to Bulawayo, Zimbabwe and took Marc LaPointe with us as well as the Regional Superintendent and his wife. Marc went with us because he now is the district missionary for Zimbabwe. It truly was an exciting conference at Victoria

Falls. What made it exciting to us was to see the progress that was being made in the district despite the fact we were unable to get into Zimbabwe as missionaries. Almost exactly twelve years had passed since the Lo's and our family went to Zimbabwe as church planters. At this conference thirteen new members were taken in. Nine people were baptized and nine young people gave their hearts to the Lord. The church is pastored by a young man who graduated from EWBC in Swaziland. Construction of the new church was in progress. The people were excited and the church was growing. This is what we as missionaries praise the Lord for!

At this conference the Regional Superintendent's wife and I worked together teaching the ladies, the youth and children. I gave out quite a number of award cards for the Sunday schools. Then it was a thrill to give out enough quilt blocks for each zone to be able to make a quilt which they could use to generate funds for their Wesleyan Women's groups. These awards and quilt blocks were sent by some of the North American Wesleyan Women's groups. I wished you could have seen the happy faces of the ladies and their excitement about making the quilts. You at home in the U.S. were definitely a partner in our mission work and we were so grateful!

The responsibilities were great in being Regional Mission Director of the Southern Africa Region. This included the countries of South Africa, Swaziland, Mozambique and Zimbabwe. There was the placement of missionary personnel that would be brought before the Regional Executive Board. Many of us were stunned to learn of the appointment of Jim and Roxane Lo to Cambodia but we praised God for the open door He had placed before the Los. The Los spoke at the Conference in Pretoria and told the people goodbye since they would not be seeing some of them again. They would be leaving after Mission Council, January 18-22, 1995.

Then at the end of September we learned of the death of Miss Esther Phillippe's father. Her furlough was due in mid-November so Bob had to see about getting her ticket as soon as possible. I guess one could say there were no dull moments in our household at Brakpan!

The end of October came almost before we knew it. There was a special Board Meeting with the Regional Superintendent and other members, making nine people staying in our house. I was really glad the Regional Superindent's wife came along for she helped me so much in preparing dinner for ten people. At this meeting a decision was made to have the Bob Bagleys go to EWBC. We were a little uncertain whether Mike and Cindy Helvie would be at WES (Wesleyan Evangelical Seminary) or be sent down on the South Coast near Port Shepstone. The Helvies were a wonderful young couple who had spent one year on our field at Petiersburg, Transvaal as "GO Net." workers.

Bob at this time was having trouble with a swollen ankle. I was afraid it might be a blood clot so I made a doctor's appointment for him. I mentioned in my mother's letter that the church had prayed for him on Sunday evening. We had gotten a call from our son Ron on Oct. 5th so I was able to ask him for some advice about his dad's swollen leg and ankle. During this time we had to get the Regional Statistical report done for the whole Region. I was able to help Bob some. What a job this was especially when so many districts didn't report in the right way. Finally it was finished and faxed to our Mission Headquarters in Indiana.

As the month continued Bob seemed to be doing much better but his ankle and foot still would swell some. We did try to take walks each day, Monday through Friday. We thought this might help the swelling. In one letter I stated: "His lower leg seemed better but the heel and ankle were purple and that I guessed he would have to go easy on them."

On October 15th we made a quick trip to Swaziland for the dedication service of the Msabane Wesleyan Church. It was a beautiful day. We had a near-tragedy happen but I believe the Angel of the Lord intervened. A small child, the son of the Mohales, got run over and nearly killed. In fact it seemed the Lord really performed a miracle before our eyes. This little one was pinned under the wheel of the pick-up and when the ladies picked him up, he began crying and vomiting. They prayed over him and rushed him off to the hospital in Manzini. When Pinto Langa came back he was asked how the child was and he said, "Oh, he is sitting up and playing." It reminded us of the incident Paul had in Acts 20:7-12. What we encountered at this church dedication was a modern day miracle! We all praised the Lord!

During October, the Bible College Work and Evangelism Team went to Zimbabwe. Principal Langa and the Student Dean and teacher, Daphne Niemack, reported a wonderful spirit of working together in building the new church at Victoria Falls. Twelve young men and women, students of EWBC, made the trip with their staff members. They gave their HELPING HANDS to this new church of the Zimbabwe district for two weeks. Revival services were held each night and the work was done during the day. The pastor was one of the students we had taught and had graduated in 1993, Pastor S. Ndlovu.

The graduation for 1994 was held Nov. 6th at the Bible College. Two young pastors who had graduated last year, one from Zimbabwe and the other one from Joburg area rode with us. What a happy reunion it was with the alumni and with the current students, seven of which graduated. When we arrived the students came to greet us with many hearty handshakes and great big bear hugs. It was like a real welcome home. Bob and I felt like the school was a part of us. The Nkosinathi district had not had a graduate from their District in years. It was a real celebration. There were students graduating from four districts of our Region. Rev. Jim Lo was the special speaker. What a powerful message he gave! The school chapel was packed out with probably 250-300 people. It was very thrilling for us to see former students coming back to the college graduation and to hear about their outreach for Christ in the areas where they worked.

Some six years before this we were pastoring the Manzini Wesleyan church in Swaziland. Then later, students Henry and Bethel Mohale, were voted in to take our place. At this time, November, 1994 the church was having 150 or more people attending each Sunday. They had 40 some full members and others studying to become members. Not only all that, but people were paying their tithes and offerings. They had a building fund established and already had a church site, (Remember, earlier I was asking people in America to pray about this church site.) Oh how exciting it was to listen to this Godly young couple tell what God was doing.

This month we had a very special message from Bartlesville Oklahoma. The message was that Baby Nathaniel Anthony Cheney arrived on November 11 to bless his missionary grandparents. Now we had eight grandchildren, four grandsons and four granddaughters. It was times like this when I got homesick and wished we could be home in the States for Thanksgiving and Christmas holidays. It was much better for calling overseas while we lived in Brakpan. The phones were always working but calling was costly!

I'm going to add a paragraph from one of my November letters: "It was nice to talk with Roxane about three minutes this morning. We were glad to hear the family is well and very busy. Roxy told us that they would probably spend Thanksgiving with the Laubers; Rylan, Amy and Anlan with Grandpa and Grandma Thornton; Allen and Kim with her Mom and Dad; and Ron and Karla sounded like Randal and Candy would have Thanksgiving with them. But plans changed for Ron and Karla. They came to western Nebraska to have Thanksgiving with Grandma and Grandpa Thornton along with Rylan, Amy and, Annie. Ron and Randal were able to fix the roof on Grandma and Grandpa Thornton's house.

Not only did our children's plan change but we had our own changes. Our plans were to be with Jim and Roxane Lo and their boys in Petermaritsburg. The Kitners, missionaries with TransWorld Radio were also to be there. We had a call from Zambia asking us to help with a medical emergency. One of our missionaries needed medical attention right away and they were flying down the next day. Bob had called for an appointment for him. I was disappointed about not getting to go to the Lo's, but sometimes plans get disrupted. We did have an early Thanksgiving with Miss Elliot and Grandpa and Grandma Lehman and the Dr. Emmetts. We made a plan to go to the Lo's and stay overnight. It was our hope to spend more time with them since they were leaving in January. Our plan also included looking for another house in Port Shepstone for the Helvies.

Another paragraph from the Nov. 16th letter: "I've baked the first layer of the wedding cake that goes to Zimbabwe for Gladys Makusha's wedding. Tomorrow I hope to do the other two tiers and finish getting my Thanksgiving dinner ready. Oh my, the aroma of baking pumpkin pie is getting to me. I hope it is as good as it smells. Today I was looking for stuffing mixes and didn't find any. I thought for sure I could get these in South Africa. Maybe I should have tried Pick and Pay. I wanted to go shopping with Bob today at East Rand Mall but we had the copy machine out being serviced and the men didn't bring it back until about 4:00p.m. so I didn't get to go where I wanted to. Oh well, I guess there will be another day."

One more thing to mention for November was the baptism of two young men who came from Northern Mozambique to work in the mines. Now they were going back to their homes and wanted to take the Gospel to their families and neighborhoods. I wish you could have seen their glowing faces as they gave their testimonies. Rev. O. I. Lehman gave a wonderful message for their farewell. I realized that some of the prayers we requested for Mozambique during our home ministries were being answered. These two young men have a deep burning desire to share God's Word with their people.

December of 1994

We mentioned earlier about finding a house for the missionary couple coming, Mike and Cindy Helvie and family. It did not work out about the one we had gotten. So, Bob called an emergency Executive Meeting to decide what should be done about a place for them to live. The Jim Los and Marc LaPointes came for this meeting making a house full for the evening. One couple stayed the night.

Then there was the wedding cake that I made in November that had to be decorated. It would be going with us to Zimbabwe when we visited the people there, the second week of December. I told about decorating our house for Christmas in one of my letters. I said, "It smelled very nice as I was burning a Christmas candle which was putting a perfume throughout the house. I told about our small bedraggled Christmas tree but that it would be good enough for Bob and me. Then I mentioned and quote from my letter: "Maybe next year if our children come we will have a bigger and maybe even a real tree. I hoped that if the Lord tarried I wouldn't be disappointed." (This of course did not happen because of Bob's death in September of 1995.)

For our Christmas of 1994 we invited Brother and Sister Lehman, parents of our brother-in-law Orai Lehman. It was a quiet day with a wonderful Christmas dinner. We were all looking forward to Orai and Linda Lehman's return from furlough on Dec. 31st. And so we came to the end of another busy year in the work of our Lord. Being leaders of our missionary group in South Africa was very different from being at our Bible College. For me it took in more entertaining and, of course, keeping up in correspondence, but we both knew we were in the center of God's will for our lives!

January, 1995

A new year began in January with three missionary couples arriving. As I mentioned at the end of the December the Orai Lehman family came on the last day of 1994. The new year brought two other missionary families, the Robert Bagleys and the Mike Helvies. Needless to say we had a house- full for two days. The Bagleys moved on to their home in Swaziland at EWBC. However, with the Helvies we had a problem. Bob and I had looked at a house in the Port Shepstone area the past November. But what we needed to happen was for the Jim Lo's house located in Pietermaritzburg, to sell so that we could buy this house. The Los were scheduled to leave January 25th. We ask our prayer partners to pray this house would sell soon. We planned a farewell for the Jim and Roxy. It was hard to see them leave. We knew, though, that God was leading them to work in Cambodia.

The Lehmans were with us awhile longer since they had been appointed to Mozambique. There were two things needed for the Lehmans, a place to live in Mozambique and a vehicle that would take the roads in this country. So we went out looking for a trailer and hoped we could find something in which they could live for maybe up to a year. It was hard for Linda when she realized that all the stuff they had packed would not fit into a small caravan (trailer). There were times like this that missionaries really needed prayer.

Later during the month of January, Bob worked on the mission journal. He had to get it all put together. The book contained 60 pages of reports and business stuff and would be given out at our mission council meeting. All the missionaries of the region would be coming for this meeting that was held at the Wesleyan Seminary in Brakpan. At this meeting we took time to say farewell to the Jim and Roxy Lo and their boys Andrea and Matthew.

We had planned to go with Orai and Linda to Mozambique but our plans got changed. On January 16th, Bob, Orai, Linda and I went down town to Johannesburg to the Mozambique Immigration to get our visas. Since our Regional Supt., Rev. Robert Nhlengethwa couldn't go with the Lehmans, we felt we should go to help in searching for the right location. When we went back to the Mozambique Embassy, it was closed. A couple days later I was able to go with Orai and Linda to pick up the visas. Well guess what??? They told us (Bob and me) that our passports were too full to put our visas in them and that we would need to bring in new passports! So Linda and Orai had to go alone.

Here I am going to include what I wrote in my January 27th letter: "We have had a busy week since the Los were here getting ready to fly home. The Marc LaPointes were here too so we had the Los, the Lehmans and LaPointes all staying in our house with us. This made twelve people sleeping in our house and Shepherd sleeping in the ikhaya (worker's quarters). On Monday after breakfast our guests went to visit Gold Reef City. On Tuesday we all went out to eat at "Turn and Tender" in Boksburg. That was very nice for me because I didn't need to cook a big meal that day. On Wednesday the Los left. I cooked a very big breakfast and a big lunch at noon. After they left I didn't know now if I could cook for just two people! I really did enjoy having them around, particularly Di and Marc LaPointe's two little girls, Kristy and Kaley ages 5 and 3. They are so cute and such well-behaved little girls."

Every once in a while Bob would be asked to speak at one of the churches in the area. The Brakpan Wesleyan Church had the Lehmans and Cheneys come for a missions Sunday on January 15th. Orai spoke in the morning and then Bob spoke in the evening. It was at this service that a drunken black man came into the church and caused a real disturbance. Shepherd took the man out. He was so drunk he couldn't talk sense at all. It was so sad because he was a soul who desperately needed God in his life. It reminded me that missions are close to home. We need to witness to those who are around us, those who are hurting and not right with God.

The next day, Monday, we had to prepare for a ministerial fellowship meeting. Since Orai I. Lehman and his wife Orpha were leaving for the States to retire February 15th, we wanted to give them a farewell. However, early in February Orpha Lehman became very ill and had to be taken to the hospital. After spending twelve days in the hospital, she and her husband were able to come and stay with us while she continued her recovery. Consequently, the Lehmans were unable to leave for the States like they had planned. We knew God had touched her and we praised Him and thanked the people who had prayed. Their planned return to the States for their retirement would be after she became stronger.

February events: Orai and Linda had to come back from Mozambique because they went into the country with the wrong kind of visa. They were supposed to apply for a work permit. After looking over their situation in Mozambique, they came back to stay the rest of February projecting to go back sometime in March. During this time in South Africa they were able to buy a caravan (trailer) nearly eight meters long (26 feet) with a tiny bathroom, a big frig and stove and a nicely arranged bedroom. It had a large sofa in the living room that made into a bed. The cost was very reasonable, 26,750.00 Rands or in U.S. Money $7750.00. It would be ready to go in two or three weeks. Then during this time they looked for a four-wheel vehicle that could pull this trailer.

The next week-end we went to Swaziland for the engagement of Dr. Galela to Lindiwe Mtethwa. Doctor was one of our students at EWBC and now pastored a church in the Joburg area. We went down on Saturday morning and stayed at Joy Mission, then after the meeting on Sunday we returned to Brakpan.

The Lehmans (Orai and Linda) finally got off for Mozambique March 1st. They left at about 7:30 a.m. and Linda called me that evening at about 8:00 p.m. They had quite a sizeable load and pulled the trailer with their Toyota 4x4 pickup. They found a house to rent for a year. However, it was nice for them to have the trailer when they went out for services in other parts of the country. I referred to it as "a house on their backs, like a turtle!" So for the year they would figure out if it was best to rent or build a mission house. Orai and Linda were our first Wesleyan Church missionary couple to reside in Mozambique.

About the middle of March, Bob had to participate in a seminar for District Superintendents at Altona Mission. There were ten districts in our Southern Africa region which included the countries of Zimbabwe, Mozambique, South Africa and Swaziland. We definitely needed prayer that the ground work that would be laid for understanding church structure and its responsibilities could be clear to all these church leaders.

One of the highlights of this month of March was the visit of Mrs. Minnie Gray, former missionary to South Africa. She and her daughter shared a meal with us. It was a real joy to reminisce about old times down in the Port Shepstone area when we arrived to take over the Bible College at Methlomnyama. Also during this month we visited Marc and Di LaPointe and their daughters in Petersburg and then traveled to the South Coast to visit Mike and Cindy Helvie and their children Eric and Melody. We went to encourage them in language study and to visit one of our African churches in the area. Our trip to the South Coast was very profitable. We had a few days of wonderful rest and relaxation at the Helvies. They had a lovely guest place to put people when they visited. Both Cindy and Eric celebrated their birthdays in March and so I made birthday cakes and decorated them. It was truly a fun time!

April arrived with Easter to celebrate. At holidays, pretty much every business and mail distribution comes to a standstill. However, we had a houseful again with Di LaPointe and the girls coming and Orai and Linda back from Mozambique.

Then Dr. and Mrs. Storer Emmett returned again for medical reasons.

Bob had to pick them up at the airport as they had flown down from Zambia. So I stated in my letter: "We have a total of eleven people sleeping in our house," a full house for sure!

One of the things we decided to do during Easter Holiday was visit the Easter Rand Show. It is kind of like a great big county or State Fair. It was so big that we didn't even see half the things but it was relaxing and this was what Bob and I needed. There are booths with all sorts of products being advertised and demonstrated. Linda and Orai bought a massager that is really nice and really felt good. Linda said, "Maybe it will put your dad out of business!" I doubted it because we didn't buy one!

By April things were cooling down and frost could come any time. Plans were made for us, along with several Wesleyan Women from Zimbabwe, to travel to Beira, Mozambique for Revival April 19-26. We had visited Beira last in September of 1993 when we held meetings and conducted "College on Wheels". There were many different languages in Mozambique. One of the most used in the Beira area was very much like the Shona language in Zimbabwe. Ladies from Zimbabwe who spoke Shona were a great blessing and help in training and speaking to the ladies in Beira. We were so happy that the Lehmans could be with us in these special meetings. We felt our efforts in this meeting were going to produce many souls for the Kingdom of God.

It was toward the beginning of April that our daughter informed us about a dear friend's passing. Paula had become a real friend to me some eleven years before. She gave us so much support in gifts and prayers. She was living in Omaha with her husband when we first became acquainted. When we last saw Paula she had cancer and it was this dreaded disease that finally took her home to heaven. Our hearts were saddened to hear of her death but we rejoiced that she no longer was suffering.

As May rolled around it was time to do the Regional Prayer calendar and letter. On top of these duties, there was a wedding cake I needed to decorate so we could take it to Swaziland. May was also full of birthdays and anniversaries, Kim's, our daughter-in-law, was May 11th, my mom's May 17, Mom's and Dad's Anniversary was on May 19, Rylan's and Amy's Anniversary May 23rd and, of course, my birthday was May 12th.

My husband truly treated me royally on my birthday. On this day I turned 59 years old. Bob took me out to eat and then we had a big shopping trip to East Rand Mall. Bob was so sweet and it almost seemed like everything I wanted, he told me I could go ahead and buy. One thing he purchased for me was a lovely purse. Looking back on this day, I know God allowed us to have a really special day because Bob would never again be there for my birthday. I'm so thankful I have this wonderful memory.

Another thing I wrote home about in May was our plans for Christmas of 1995. I wrote in my May 23rd letter that we were hoping to have our Mission Council before Dec. 10th and then take our holiday time from Dec. 11-January 11th. This was when our children were planning to be with us. In fact, I wrote that Ron and Karla planned to come December 4th and we would take them with us as we attended the council meeting.

Another missionary from Zambia, Barbara Bennet, was having trouble with her eye. She was with us for over a week and it appeared she would have to have an eye operation. During this time Linda Lehman was staying with us because Orai left to go to northern Mozambique. He planned to go on even farther North of Beira. He and some of the church leaders intended to visit the two young converts who were saved under the ministry of Rev. Budie at Cinderella Mission Church. Orai wouldn't be gone too long because he wanted to be at Dr. Galela and Lindiwe's wedding in Swaziland. Linda would ride down with us for the wedding.

As I have said a number of times it was always so good to receive letters from our family. The problem was I never heard from our children as much as I wanted. They all were so busy. However, with Mom it was a different story. She faithfully filled me in even on what our children were up to. In the latter part of May she wrote how Randal and Candy had visited and how Rylan and Brian our nephew and some other guys came to help them brand their calves.

Ron and Karla called us around the 7th of June. They told us they had taken Randal and Candy to Omaha Airport to fly to the Northwest and that they planned to return around August 14th to do some roofing for Allen and Kim's and Ron and Karla's houses.

My sisters, Esther and Elaine, planned a special celebration for our parent's 60th wedding anniversary. I was very sad that Bob and I couldn't attend. They set the date as June 25th for this celebration. Since Bob and I couldn't attend I wrote a special letter for my parents to be read during the program.

June 29th was Bob's 61st birthday and I wanted to do something special but since we were planning to leave for Casteel District Conference in Eastern Transvaal, his birthday seemed like just another day of work and getting ready to leave for a conference. So, rather than my fixing for guests, for his birthday, Bob and I went out to eat. I did bake an angel food cake with strawberries for him. I said in my letter, "I guess when you get our ages one doesn't care as much for celebrations!"

The Brakpan Wesleyan Church was getting ready to celebrate 45 years. Miss Elliot baked a fruit cake and had asked me to decorate it. Then I learned that the lady who worked for me, Lydia, was also celebrating her birthday on June 26th so I made and decorated a cake for her too. She was all smiles when she saw it!

More visitors came in June which was not unusual for us, The Helvies from Margate and their children and Bill Niemack. Helvies are doing marriage counseling and services here at the Brakpan church. To top this off, I needed to do a birthday cake for Melody. Then I looked after the children while they did the counseling. I planned to serve the Father's Day dinner for Helvies and Bill Neimack.

Later in the month we purchased a new car for Dorcas Croft, a new missionary arriving July 4th. She was assigned to go to Altona Mission that is close to Swaziland. Dorcas was doing leadership training with some of the nationals there. Speaking of cars, we wanted to up-date our mission fleet of cars. We purchased a 1994 Toyota venture costing R52, 000.00 (that's about $14,285.00) plus we had a 1985 car to trade in. Anyway, we were happy to get rid of the old car and upgrade our mission fleet of vehicles. Now we have two 10 seater Hi Aces Toyotas, a 1988 and 1989 and our car is a 1990 and Lehmans is a 1991 and there are two Venture Toyotas a 1992 and 1994. The Ramsays have a 1991. Bob kept a fleet plan for insurance on all these cars as they were owned by the Southern Africa Mission Council. This gave Bob a lot of paper work to keep up!

We went on July 4th to meet Dorcas Croft at the airport. She didn't have a work permit and customs wouldn't let her into the country. So we had to send her on to Swaziland and the Bagleys met her at the Airport in Matsapa. It shouldn't be any problem for her to get a work permit if she applies while in Swaziland. We took her car to her in Swaziland.

Bob is teaching a three week module at the Bible College which started on July 10th. I was hoping to get some much needed rest as well as catch up on my correspondence. Our plans were to return to Brakpan July 28th after Bob had finished his class at EWBC.

The guest rondovel was our place to stay while in Swaziland. I fixed breakfasts and suppers but our main meals we ate down at the school dining hall. There was quite a bit of uncertainty in Swaziland while we were there but we hoped nothing serious would happen in the country. The trade unions and the government were not getting along so they were having a mass stay-away from work. I got food supplies to last a while and we prayed that everything would go smoothly and that they would get their problems ironed out.

Some other things I did while in Swaziland were helping Brenda Bagley while she was teaching a module. I read stories to their little Mary

Beth and visited with some of our friends there in the country. I did make a birthday cake for some of the students who had July birthdays. I also made Bob Bagley and their daughter Tracy birthday cakes and cooked dinner for Brenda so we could all eat together. This was for Bob Bagley's and Tracy's birthday celebration! Also, one week-end we were able to attend Jon Madden and Melanie's wedding at Manaba Beach Wesleyan Church south of Port Shepstone.

When we arrived back in Brakpan we found such a mess!!! While we were gone to Swaziland our hot water pipe in the ceiling froze and broke. When it thawed out, water flooded the two office areas in our house, the back bedroom and bathroom and some of the storage room where we stored books. You can imagine what a mess we had! The bedrooms, bathroom and kitchen areas in main part of the house were alright. I am thankful Shepherd was here in the evenings otherwise, when would it have been found?? We dried it out enough that it didn't smell. The ceiling did have a great big gaping hole where the water came down through it. The ceiling board came off and we could look right up to our roof! And so ends the month of July.

Many of the District Conferences were held in the months of August and September. Of course we could not attend all of them. We did attend the Transki District Conference because their District Superindent had to attend an important funeral. This trip was rather on the spur of the moment as we only found out about two nights before we had to leave. We got up early on Friday morning and left around 6:00 a. m. arriving around 5:00 p.m. so I was really tired. It was a good conference and we had a safe trip. We got to stay with the Helvies at Margate on Sunday evening. As we came back on Monday we were able to eat lunch with Patti (Bransby) Church. We had sort of lost track of Patti but learned later where they lived in Hilton near Pietermaritzburg. Patti was the young girl at Eden Park when we stayed there in 1976-1978. She also came as a rotary exchange student to the U.S.A. She and her husband now had a baby girl born May 22. They called her Eva Louise. I told Patti I felt like I was coming to visit my grandchild. She was such a sweet baby!

Bob wasn't feeling very good at this time. Finally he went to the doctor. They said he had bronchial pneumonia. I knew he didn't feel well and his breathing was very shallow. The doctor had x-rays taken and gave Bob two choices, either to go to hospital on a drip for five days or take high powered antibiotics and rest at home. Of course, Bob chose the home remedy. He did get better but we had called people to pray and had sent headquarters a fax to send out a prayer request for Bob.

The next conference was Swaziland District Conference beginning Aug. 25-27th. We didn't manage to get there for the beginning services but were able to get to the Women's Malihambi service on Saturday. Linda and

Orai were there, too, since Orai was teaching a module on Missions. It was nice to see them again because we hadn't seen them since the first part of July. On the Monday morning we drove back to Brakpan to prepare for the trip to Zimbabwe conference.

Our Last Journey to Zimbabwe

It was the first part of September, 1995. As usual there were a number of district conferences that took place at this time. Bob and I always tried to attend these conferences if possible. We especially wanted to attend the District conference in Zimbabwe. It was being held in the New Wesleyan Church at Victoria Falls so we were quite excited. Seeing all the Christians in Zimbabwe was a high light to us, just being able to see how the church had developed and the spiritual growth taking place in the churches.

We began our journey from Brakpan with two young men riding with us. One of them was Dr. Galela who would do the preaching for a revival being held in Bulawayo. The first day we traveled as far as Bulawayo and the next day made our way on to Victoria Falls. I'm not sure of the dates of this conference but it was around the 1st, 2nd, and 3rd of September. We were so happy to see the new church building and to be able to hold services in it. The meeting was well attended and the presence of the Lord very real. Bob did do preaching for some of the services. We stayed at one of the visitor's camps in town. We also took time to view the great Victoria Falls near the town of Victoria Falls before leaving to go back to Bulawayo. It was late as we came back into the city of Bulawayo. The Obert Gonera's were wonderful friends who took us into their home for the rest of the week. This gave us extra time to visit with many of our Zimbabwe friends in the area. Another reason we were planning to stay for the week was to allow one of the young men to finish a revival he was holding in the Entumbane Church. He would be finishing the following Sunday then ride back to South Africa with us. It was truly a great week seeing friends and visiting some of the churches close around the area.

Bob's Death

Sunday morning arrived and Bob and I decided we would attend the last service of the revival in Entumbane. We had a wonderful breakfast with the Goneras and then started getting our things together to leave. I was still at the dining room table talking with Mr. and Mrs. Gonera but Bob excused himself to put the last few things in our van. I said my goodbye and headed out the door to join my husband. What met my eyes as I came through that door headed for our van, I shall never forget! My husband was lying on the ground and the camera case hanging half way out the door. I'm sure I probably screamed as I ran to where Bob was lying. Kneeling down by his side I tried to see if he was still breathing. I yelled for someone to call an ambulance. Then I quickly decided I needed to do CPR. As I breathed into Bob's mouth he finally made some movement and seemed to be in terrible pain. While all of this was going on, one of the Gonera girls had gotten hold of an ambulance. Before the ambulance arrived, however, Mr. and Mrs. Gonera and I decided we should get Bob out of the sun. As best we could we dragged and carried him into the hallway of their house. I knew Bob was still alive but by his groans I knew he had great pain.

I don't think it was more than seven minutes before an ambulance arrived. This was probably at least 9:30 on Sunday morning, September 10th. Central Hospital wasn't more than six or seven blocks away from the Gonera's house in Parklands Suburb so the ambulance was able to come quite quickly. Mr. Gonera rode in the ambulance with Bob and the medical aids but I felt I should drive our van over to the hospital in order to have transport for myself.

How I went through all this only God knows. When we arrived at the emergency room they rushed in with Bob. I believe God is in control in every situation of our lives. Do you know there happened to be a French Heart Specialist on duty that morning?! Did he just happen to be there? No, I believe God made the connection and that he was there to help Bob. They worked with my dear husband for some time giving special medication and shots. Soon they were able to put him in I.C.U.

The doctor talked with me and really did not give me a lot of hope. He stated that, "It could go either way." Bob could make it or he might not. I felt so alone although I must add, Mr. Gonera never left me alone. And I knew God had not left me alone. While they worked with Bob, Mr. Gonera and I waited in a special room, praying. How I wished I could call someone and ask them to pray. If only I could call some of the churches and ask them to intercede for Bob. But it was Sunday morning and most everyone would be in church services in South Africa. Cell phones were not prevalent in those days as they are now. How I wished that I could reach Orai and Linda who were in South Africa. And I wanted so desperately to get in touch with our children and with headquarters to have an emergency prayer chain going up all over the world.

Finally the doctor came to tell us that Bob had arrived at a stable state and would probably make it. I decided I should take Mr. Gonera home and then try to get hold of Allen. He then could call his sister and brothers and headquarters and a prayer chain could form the world over. The time difference was about eight hours from where my children were, it was early Sunday morning. I was finally able to get in touch with the Lehmans and let some of the churches in South Africa know about our situation. I tried to be with Bob as much as possible. Many friends in the Bulawayo area kept contact with me, too.

I remember my good missionary friend Nancy Shenk went to one of the large Department Stores down town with me. This may sound a bit strange but Bob and I had been looking for a nice set of dishes to buy. While we were at the department store I found exactly what I wanted. I knew Bob would be pleased if I bought them. (I'm using these dishes even today). They were made in Zimbabwe's famous Wills grove pottery. I just loved them. I wanted to bring one of the dishes to show Bob but he said, "No, don't bother to get one out now. I'll see it when we get home."

Bob was in ICU until Wednesday. Then they thought he was over the critical stage and could be put in a regular room. The rest of the week I spent as much time with Bob as possible. A number of friends dropped in as well. We knew our Mission Department in the U. S. had put out an SOS for prayer on Bob's behalf. We were confident that God was healing Bob.

On Sunday afternoon the 17th of September, some of the Kumalo Church folk decided to go to Central Hospital to visit Bob and also to have a little church service with him in the afternoon. I remember that meeting so well. In fact Bob gave a little sermon to us speaking from his bed from James, chapter 4:13-16. As Bob was speaking in a very earnest and emphatic tone, I had the most unusual feeling. It was as though I was hearing the Apostle Paul or Peter speaking. I had never heard Bob speak like this before. I actually don't have words to express how I felt and what I heard that day. To me it was amazing.

Orai and Linda Lehman, Bob's sister and husband had been in contact with us by phone. They had discussed going back to Mozambique before coming back over to Zimbabwe. I believe it was Linda who felt an urgency that they should come to Zimbabwe first. So the decision was made that they would pick up Marc LaPointe in Petersburg on the way to Bulawayo. Marc then would drive our van back to South Africa and Orai and Linda would arrange for Bob and me to take the plane back to Joburg. It seemed that Bob was well on his way to recovery. That afternoon, Sept. 18th, the Lehmans and Marc arrived. They made their way to the hospital. It was a remarkable afternoon with our visitors. Orai and Linda had gotten a room at the Brethren in Christ guest house and would be staying for as long as we needed them. I'm not sure but I think Marc stayed with the pastors of Kumalo Wesleyan Church, the Makushas.

After our evening meals, we all decided to go back and visit. I noticed Bob was not feeling quite as well that evening. Then, a little before 9:00 p.m., we said our goodbyes. I was the last one to leave the room and I gave Bob a good night kiss. Orai and Linda took me back to Gonera's for the night.

What I'm going to write now is probably about the hardest thing I've ever faced in my life. Orai and Linda dropped me off and headed for their sleeping quarters. I had only been in the house maybe five minutes when the phone rang. One of the Goneras answered the phone and said it was for me. I took the phone and said, "Hello". The person on the other end said, "I'm calling from Central Hospital." She continued, "Your husband has just passed away." I could not believe my ears! The nurse questioned, "Would you want to come and see him?" "You mean he has died?" I cried? "Yes." was her answer. In shock, I cried out, "Yes, we will come!"

I went into a real shocked state trying to think what I should do. I knew I should let Orai and Linda come too, but I had a hard time trying to find the phone number for the guest house where they were staying. I was searching all through my purse and phone book. The Goneras were trying to help me. Finally I did get a phone number and got hold of Orai. They came right away to pick me up and we headed for the hospital to the room where Bob was.

When we entered that door I knew Bob was not really there. It was only his earthly body. His spirit and soul were in heaven with Jesus. I cried and mourned along with my sister-in-law and brother-in-law. Why had God taken my dear husband? We thought and really believed God was healing him. I only know that somehow God got me through that night. I didn't sleep much knowing that never again would my husband be sleeping beside me. I prayed a lot and I questioned God, "Why did this happen?"

That night, sometime in the wee hours of the morning, I turned to my Bible and God gave me a very comforting scripture. It was from Psalm 57:1 "Be merciful to me, O God, be merciful to me! For my soul trusts in you; And in the shadow of your wings I will make my refuge, until these calamities have passed by." I realized my only help and refuge was in God. He would help me somehow to get through this.

God was so good to let Orai and Linda be with me. I couldn't have made it without them. Of course, family had to be called. I really depended on my oldest son, Robert Allen, to help get the word out to headquarters and everyone who needed to know. I talked to some of the children, maybe all of them. It was their desire that their daddy's body be shipped back to the U. S. and buried at Ash Hollow cemetery near Lewellen. So then preparations had to be made for this to happen. Before the body was taken to the funeral home we ask for an autopsy. They recorded that Bob had died from a pulmonary embolism. A blood clot in the lungs probably made its way into the heart. Having a body shipped back overseas requires special rules to follow. On

Tuesday Orai and Linda helped me take care of things at the mortuary, picking out a casket or coffin as the English call it, bringing in clothes, and getting his passport that had to be with the container holding his body. There were so many items to take care of. The mortician was very kind.

We wanted to have a memorial service at the Kumalo Church on Wednesday afternoon. Word had to get out to our churches and to our friends. My mind and body were so numbed from shock and lack of rest that I don't remember all that took place. Of course the shortness of time to announce the memorial service made it so not many people could attend. I cannot even remember who gave the message at the service.

The next day, Thursday, Sept 21st, we packed up our things and said goodbye to the Gonera family. Linda and Orai took me in their van to South Africa. Marc LaPointe had gone earlier with our van. As we traveled along I kept talking about memories I had about Bob. Once I said to Orai and Linda, "Oh, I probably am boring you with all of this." And Orai so kindly said, "No, Eva, you just keep on talking." He realized, I'm sure that this was good therapy for me. We traveled all the way back to Brakpan in South Africa. It was late afternoon when we arrived. Walking into our home, knowing never again would Bob walk into our house with me, was hard. I was alone and feeling like I was half there. My other half had been cut off. I was so glad for Orai and Linda staying close to me. They were such a comfort. They will never know what it meant to me. The next morning I remember walking into Bob's office with them. They just put their arms around me as we cried together.

There were so many things that needed to be taken care of. It was Friday. I needed to go through all Bob's clothes. I believe a lot of the clothing was sent to Mozambique via the Lehmans. We got our plane tickets. Orai and Linda flew with me back to the States. Suit cases had to be packed. Linda so kindly said, "Don't worry about your personal household things," "I'll take care of it and ship your barrels later." That was so thoughtful of her!

We decided, or maybe I was the one making the decision, that we needed to have another memorial service for Bob on Monday Sept 25th. There were many people in the Johannesburg area who wanted to show their respects, even in Swaziland and the South Coast. I called Patti Church who lived in Petermartizburg area. It was her little baby that Bob prayed for the healing of her spine. Patti and baby Eva made their way to Brakpan and stayed with me at our mission Director's house. Also Shepherd, the young Zimbabwean man whom we gave a home to while he worked in the area, was there to comfort me. Some fifty people came by bus from Swaziland for the service. People from all over were calling by phone and giving comforting words. One Zimbabwean girl told me that my husband's death helped her to get back to the Lord. How I ever got through the week-end was only by the strength of the Lord. Philippians 4:13 "I can do all things through Christ who strengthens me." And Romans 8:28, "for all things work together for good to those who love God to those who are called according to His purpose." These two verses became so precious and helpful to me as I faced the reality that Bob was no longer with me. The second memorial service was held at the Boksburg Wesleyan Church on Monday Morning.

By late afternoon on Monday, all our suit cases and carry-on bags had been packed and we headed for the Johannesburg airport. That evening after going through customs we made our way to the plane. When would I see my beloved southern Africa again?? It was hard leaving behind nearly twenty-five years of ministry in Wesleyan Missions and not knowing if ever I would see this place again. So now, as we were flying in the dark toward our homeland, I began looking forward to some of my family that would meet us in Tulsa, Oklahoma. I don't remember the airlines we flew on nor what city we flew into before flying into Tulsa. It seems my mind was dulled by overload of the past week. In the evening as we arrived at Tulsa airport, two of my sons and my daughter-in-law, Karla, were there to meet me. I remember so well coming into the area where people were waiting for us. My dear sons Ron and Randal hurried toward me and we threw our arms around each other. It was so comforting to feel my sons' hugs and just cry with two of my children. We had arrived Tuesday evening, September 26th. The Lehman children were also there to greet their parents and a few other friends and family of the Lehmans.

The rest of that week is rather a blur in my mind. Ron and Karla took me to Western Nebraska. At this time Rylan and Amy were living in the Pink House and Rylan was working for Uncle Charles on the farm. Rylan and Amy fixed the basement of their house for me to stay in. Little Annie was about a year and a half old at the time. She truly was a joy to be around. There were lots of family members to see and other contacts to make. We planned another Memorial Service because we knew many people would be coming to celebrate Bob's life. It was so good to be with my parents and with my sisters, Esther from Oregon and Elaine and Steve from Canada.

We planned the service for Sept. 30th at the Lewellen High School Gym. The Gym was filled with 200 or more people. One thing that happened was that Bob's casket was miss-sent to California instead of Denver. Gerald Delatour was the mortician at the time and had to tell us. So the coffin with the body was not at the service. It is hard for me to remember all the people who attended this service but I do remember our General Missions Director, Rev. Don Bray, was there. Also, Esther Phillippe who worked with us in Swaziland came for the service. I felt that I needed to speak on people preparing to meet the Lord because life is so uncertain here on earth. God helped me so much to have the strength to encourage those who had not accepted Christ into their lives to do it right in that service. I ask Reverend

Duane Lauber to give the memorial sermon. Our children sang the special in the Zulu language. I also want to express my thankfulness to Leland Swan for taping this Memorial service. After the service the family and many friends gathered at the Community Wesleyan Church for a meal.

On Oct. 2nd the family gathered at Ash Hollow Cemetery for a grave side service. The casket had arrived at the Oshkosh Funeral home by that time. It was so nice to have all the children and grandchildren around me as we laid Bob's body to rest next to his Grandpa and Grandma George and Annie Cheney. Many of us followed one of the African customs of taking a handful of soil and throwing it on the casket as it rested at the bottom of the hole. We just took our time and recalled many things about their daddy, my husband. 1 Corinthians 15:54-57, "So when this corruptible has put on incorruption, and this mortal has put on immortality then shall be brought to pass the saying that is written: "Death is swallowed up in victory, O Death, where is your sting? O Hades, where is your victory? The sting of Death is sin, and the strength of sin is the law. But thanks be to God, who gives us the victory through our Lord Jesus Christ."

These verses brought us comfort as we laid Bob's body to rest. We knew we would be with our beloved husband and father on the resurrection morning when, "the dead in Christ will rise first. Then we who are alive and remain shall be caught up together with them in the clouds to meet the Lord in the air. And thus we shall always be with the Lord. Therefore comfort one another with these words." 1 Thessalonians 4:16-18

Life Must Go On 1995

After the celebration of Bob's life and his burial in Ash Hollow Cemetery, I found it hard to believe I really had lost my husband. I remember so clearly being at my childhood home with my folks. I was walking across the meadow wearing Bob's red winter coat and just sobbing my heart out. It didn't make sense that God had allowed this to happen. I felt like only half of me was on earth. Bob and I had spent 37 years and almost nine months together and had five grown children, all married, and we were grandparents to eight lovely children. Now these children would grow up not knowing their grandpa, Robert A. Cheney.

At that time I lived with Rylan and Amy Cheney and their little girl Annie. Annie was a real treasure. She and I used to take walks with their golden Retriever, Emma. Sometimes Grandma put Annie on her back like the Africans did. She was only a year and a half but she was a great blessing to me. At that time Rylan was working on the farm for Uncle Charles Cheney.

After the funeral, it was actually a memorial service, we made plans to attend the Homecoming events at Wesleyan Bible College in Bartlesville,

Oklahoma. I got to stay with Randal and Candy and Baby Nathaniel. What a joy little Nathaniel was! He was such an active cute little boy almost one year who loved to play with the ball. He reminded me so much of his daddy when he was that size.

Then, back home we went to Nebraska. I actually felt lost and didn't know where I fit in. I hated being a widow. I was only fifty- nine years old and that was too young to be without a husband. Bob and I had looked forward to celebrating our fortieth wedding anniversary and even a fiftieth but that didn't happen for us.

Our mission headquarters was very kind to me and didn't ask me to go out in Home Ministries until late January. This was a real act of kindness on their part. I received my monthly wages besides a life insurance that I had not realized headquarters carried for us. With this, Rylan helped me get a little blue four-wheel drive pickup that would give me transport to the sandhills where my folks lived. Remember the roads to my childhood home were sandhill trails, not paved highways.

The holidays were hard to face. My children gave a lot of support and this was a great help to me. But, I shed many tears thinking about spending these times without my dear Bob. On December 22nd all my children were present so I decided we should all celebrate what would have been Bob's and my 38th Anniversary. I suggested we all go to a nice Chinese restaurant in Ogallala Nebraska and have dinner together. There were 18 of us. Although we were all feeling the sadness of losing husband, father and grandfather; the Lord was strengthening us.

If I remember correctly Rylan, Amy and Annie decided to make a trip to Idaho to be with Amy's family. I stayed behind to care for Emma, the dog, and to keep the home running smoothly. One day I decided to prepare an evening meal and invite Charles and Linda Cheney and their son, Brian, I included Georgia, Linda's mother who had lost her husband, Evan, in June of 1993. As a thoughtful gesture, I also invited Clinton Reeves. He and Charles often hunted geese together and he, too, had lost his mate. Grace died in 1993. Besides, I just didn't want to sit and mope around by myself.

My mother once told me while Grace had cancer, "Eva, I just don't know what I'm going to do when Grace dies. She has been my best friend." Grace was a wonderful Christian lady and I also loved her very much. In fact while my parents were snowed in for about six or seven weeks, I ask Grace to open my letters to Mom and Dad and read them over the phone so that my parents would hear from us. Then Mother would dictate to Grace what she wanted written to us in Africa and Grace would mail those letters to us. Grace truly was a wonderful friend.

I remember going with Mom and Dad to visit at Clinton's home and really not wanting to be there. I'm not quite sure why I felt this way but maybe it was because I no longer had Bob and Clinton no longer had Grace. So maybe it was just the hurt of remembering the former things and now change had come about for both of us.

With time I began to feel that Clinton really did understand what I was going through and eventually we began communicating over the phone. I missed Bob so much and I missed the companionship. It wasn't that this man was taking Bob's place. No one would ever be able to fill Bob's place but it just helped so much to talk to someone who really understood. Sometimes people say they understand but you know they really don't since they have not experienced the loss of a spouse. Clinton did understand and he helped me a lot. One Sunday in January before I left on my missionary tour, Clinton asked me to sit with him in the morning church service. It may have been a shock to some people but it really felt right to sit beside him.

We got through the holidays and Rylan and Amy came back from their trip. I corresponded with headquarters and learned they had some churches for me to visit. Some missionaries, John and Marge Conner, were going through Lewellen and they made it a point to take me back to headquarters to fetch a mission car. It was great to travel with them and not be on my own.

My first assignment was Heritage Church in Colorado Springs where my dear friend and her husband pastored, Gerald and Elsie Kahre. We had been friends for many years. In fact, Elsie played the piano at Bob's and my wedding back in 1957. After I shared at Heritage Church I left my car with the Kahres. They took me to Denver airport and I flew to Tampa, Florida to speak Sunday morning in Brooksville, Florida. Ed and Wilma, who lived in Brooksville, met me at the Tampa airport. It was so nice to be with my dear sister-in-law and her husband again. I was there for about a week in February. It was during this week I received a letter from Clinton that was sort of like a proposal for marriage. I knew I needed to do a lot of praying because more than anything else, I wanted to be in God's will.

At Brooksville I spoke for the main service. I really wasn't scared but it was a congregation of about 300 people, probably the most I had ever spoken to, but God was with me. I was also able to share with some of the Wesleyan Women on Wednesday. Some of them were new to me and a number of them were former missionaries from our earlier terms. From Tampa I flew to Atlanta, Georgia and then on to Greenville, South Carolina where the Karns met me and took me to their house in Seneca, South Carolina. There I spoke at a Wesleyan ladies gathering at Trinity Wesleyan Church. I met a number of great ladies and some of whom had been prayer partners for us. How good God is to give us praying people to lift up our needs before His throne. I was able to see Central Wesleyan College (Southern Wesleyan University) where our daughter Roxane attended school for two years and where our son Ron attended one year before he was accepted in Med School for Physicians assistant training. This is all happening during the month of February.

In March there were more churches to visit in Ohio and Michigan. In Ohio I was able to connect with Cliff and Naomi Ward in Mulberry, Ohio. They were such fine supporters as were Naomi's sister and husband the Shirleys who lived nearby the Wards. Then I went on to a small church close to Columbus, Ohio. I remember how scary it was going to a place I had never been before. With the help of maps and phone I found my way to this church. Now as I look back, I wonder how I ever did this! I could not have done it without God's help.

In May of 1996 I was ask to speak to the Wesleyan Women of Harvest Christian Wesleyan Church in North Platte. I believe it was a Mother's Day event and it was held at the airport restaurant. Clinton went with me and we drove my blue pickup. He wanted to look for a new car. By this time we had decided it was God's plan for us to get married. Many couples during this these times were just living together without being properly married. We determined that would not happen in our case.

While I was speaking at the mother's day program, Clint hunted for a new car. I learned that when he looked for cars he put the salesmen through a rather tuff times. However, he always came through with a good deal. Sometimes, I was at the point of embarrassment because he was a hard dealer but he knew how, from his point of view, to get the best offer. I don't remember if I went back to the church parsonage with Roxane and was at Lauber's house or if it was while we were still at the restaurant when I got a call from Clint saying he had found a really nice new red Chrysler Concord for a good price with a trade-in of my pickup. So that day we drove back to Lewellen in a new 1996 Chrysler Concord all paid for.

Clint asked me to ride with him as he did his mail route. It really brought back memories of my carrying mail in the sandhills way back in 1955. Of course the route had definitely changed but still it covered some of the same road I had traveled on my route. It was during these times we had many conversations. Clint told me a lot about his home life as a child. He was the third child of 13 children born to Thomas and Ruth Reeves. I always thought it rather amazing that I was attracted to the third born in the family. Bob Cheney was also a third born child.

Clint told me so many things, some so funny we would laugh and laugh and others so sad I wanted to cry. In fact tears did come to my eyes many times. My heart ached for what this family went through. One more thing Clint told me was when his father gave him an old harmonica at age 14. His brother Tom told him he would never learn to play on it. This was all Clint needed to make him determined to play the harmonica. He learned it well and I don't think I've ever heard anyone who could play a harmonica like he did. He just had a very special ear for music. My dad also played a mouth harp. Clint and Dad would play for church sometimes. Clinton not only played the harmonica but he could play the keyboard and the accordion. In fact he played his harmonica and keyboard at the same time. I loved to play with him, either with another accordion or on the piano. Georgia Rittenhouse, played with him a lot too even before I came on the scene. One of the things Clint and I did was to play music at the rest homes and assisted living facilities. The older people loved the kind of music that we played.

Since I'm recording some of Clint's life story I want to tell about his and Grace's amazing conversion to Christ. After he and Grace were married in June of 1960, Clint was called into the army. He took his training at Fort Ord, California and then was transferred to Virginia Beach, Virginia to become a chauffeur for the Army officers who looked after the missile sites on the east coast. Here I must add that Clint was a very careful driver. I suppose that is why he was driver for these officers. Grace also went with him to Virginia. After getting out of the service they moved back to Idaho to be near Grace's family. Clint got work in the forestry department and lumber mills.

One Sunday afternoon or evening, Clint said he and Grace were driving around discussing about getting a divorce. Grace had been divorced before and had twin girls who were grown. She was 15 years older than Clint but young for her age. Clint said when they met at a dance he was so amazed and attracted to Grace because she was such a good dancer. Clint was a very accomplished dancer too so they hit it off well. As they drove around deciding how to divide their belongings they came across this little church with a great big revival sign out front. One of them said, "Do you want to go in?" and the other one said, "We just as well." So they parked and went into the church, sitting at the back. That night the evangelist preached a great salvation message and when the invitation was given Clint and Grace went forward to receive Christ into their hearts. This very night their lives made a complete turn around and they began serving the Lord. I can't help but think that some of my sister's prayers were answered after many years. It seems that my sister had invited Clint to a revival at the Missionary Church north of Lewellen. He told me that he was pretty mad at her when she said she was praying for him. How important prayer is!!! I just marvel at the miracle of salvation in Grace's and Clinton's lives.

Later on they came to the Lewellen area to help Clint's oldest brother finish up some contracts in cement work. Tom was having heart trouble and could not work. At one point Grace and Clint joined the church which at that time was called Pilgrim Holiness. This was in the middle sixties. After the cement contracts were finished, Clint bought his own truck and began hauling hay, ensilage and grain for farmers in the area. In 1976 Clint and Grace placed a bid on a star mail route going into the sandhills. This is when they became better acquainted with my parents because they were on that route. Clint was still carrying mail on that route when he and I married in June of 1996. My folks had him as their mail carrier for twenty-two years.

Ron's Graduation and Gillian's Birth

Ronald Cheney graduated from medical school on May 31st, 1996. I was so excited about this and, of course, I wanted to attend his graduation. From the time Ronald was eight years old he had wanted to be a doctor. While we lived at Ebenezer Mission in Swaziland, when the children played "hospital" it was understood by Roxane, the Ramsay girls, (Susan and Shari) and with his brothers, Allen and Rylan, as well as the cousins, Valarie and Michael Lehman, that, Ron was the doctor.

When we were in the States and Ron was attending high school in Oshkosh, I remember so clearly our conversation in the car one morning when I was taking him to school. We were discussing what Ron wanted to do with his life. He turned to me and said "I'd really like to become a doctor but I wouldn't have money for schooling." I told him, "Ron, if God wants you to become a doctor, He will provide the money." Now, at this graduation he not only had finished Physician's Assistant program but was becoming a surgeon. His dad would be so proud of him, and so is his mom!

Randal, Candice and little Nathaniel were visiting at the farm. Since Amy was pretty close to the birth of their second baby, Candice decided to stay with Rylan and Amy. Randal and Roxane drove with me to DesMoines, Iowa where the graduation took place. The very day Ron graduated, our little Gillian Cheney arrived. Grandma couldn't be two places at once so I was very glad Candice would be with Amy when baby Gill arrived.

Clint and Eva Get Married

Clint and I made plans for a June 22nd wedding because it seemed a good date for all my children to be present. I looked for a simple wedding dress and found one at Herberger's in North Platte. Myrna Houston did all my imitation flowers. I ask Carolyn Miller and Roxane to stand with me and Clint ask my dad and Ron to stand with him. Carolyn came with her daughter Kathy and husband Jim in their motor home from Indiana. Clint told me that before the wedding he was going to try crawling out the window and run away but Ron and Dad wouldn't let him! Of course he was just teasing. He told me that he and Grace went to a judge in Winnemucca, Nevada to be married. When he ask the judge how much he owed him, the judge said, "That will be $10.00." Clint complained to the judge that the price was pretty steep.

Then the judge very solemnly said, "That's only the beginning, son, only the beginning!"

So now ours was a regular church wedding and a little scary to Clint I guess!! Orai Lehman and my son-in-law did the ceremony. Candice Cheney and Janelle Lehman sang and then Clint played the accordion and we sang together, "Each for the Other". After the wedding we had a reception. Joyce French made our wedding cake. Our family then had an evening meal together with grilled hamburgers.

I want to insert here that the week before, June 15, my niece April and Ron Talbot got married. Clint and I had taken Mom and Dad to the Denver airport so they could fly up to Canada for their wedding. We had a new car that made it easy to travel. Mom and Dad did get back for our wedding.

Clint was full of fun and tricks. As we were on our way home from the Denver airport with Mother and Dad they sat in the back seat. Clint would press the button for the back window where Dad sat. The window would go down a ways then he would press it and the window would go back up. My dad was wondering how this was happening and would look with wonder at the window. Clint got a real kick out of this. I guess Daddy wasn't use to automatic windows that could be operated on the driver's side. I don't know if he ever did find out Clint was doing this.

Our wedding took place June 22, 1996 at 2:00 p.m. I became Mrs. Clinton Reeves. We didn't really have much of a honeymoon but I do remember Clint and I went to the Assembly of God Church the Sunday morning after our wedding. They ask Clint to play his harmonica and I played the piano.

July, 1996

When Clint and I were first married, I would sometimes go with him on his mail route. He had actually asked me to be his substitute driver so I had to be passed by the post office department with my identity and record. By riding with him I would learn the route and the people.

One day as we prepared to go I forgot to make Clint's thermos of coffee. He always took a thermos full of strong coffee because if he got a migraine headache it helped if he drank strong coffee. On this certain day I forgot and I felt so bad but he said, "I know Arlene Grace will make me some coffee." They were right close to the road on our route and it was before they moved closer to Lewellen.

I will always be grateful to Arlene for doing this. I didn't actually meet them that day because I was too embarrassed to go into their house. It wasn't too long after this that Merlyn and Arlene moved and bought a house about a mile and a half east of where we lived and then Arlene and I began walking together and became good friends.

She invited me to become a member of their club "The Nimble Finger's Club". With her encouragement I did join. It was a club with members who had lived in the Sandhills in the Racket Community. They did different projects for the Sandhills community and exchanged names as secret sisters. It was fun to meet with these ladies in their different homes and become better acquainted. I learned that Arlene had family who were missionaries in Southern Africa. She even loaned a book to me to read, one written by one of the cousins about their missionary life in Lesotho Africa. It was very interesting.

Then I became acquainted with Cynthia Miller who became another close friend and a prayer partner. We would try to meet once a week and share prayer requests and pray for our families and our church. Cynthia and I still share important and urgent prayer requests although now our schedules have changed. I became more involved with beginning new Bible Studies and reaching out to others in our community. As time went by I became better acquainted with people I had known in my younger years.

The children of the community were on my mind and heart very much. This helped me to see the need of teaching Sunday school in our church and also in teaching about missions. I was delegated to teach WKFM which stands for Wesleyan Kids for Missions both in Oshkosh and Lewellen churches. Many of those children are now grown and in College or working. I'm so glad Clint was willing for me to take part in the spiritual training of children in our community.

My friend Cynthia and I decided we should take part in the Volunteer Hospice Program. She and I took training at the Ogallala Hospital then volunteered to help families who had members in the hospice program. This was a very fulfilling project helping those who had loved ones dying. Our duty was to give relief to the family when they needed to get out of the house. It helped us to know the needs in our community and to know the people in our community better.

Later I became involved with Teammates, a program started by Tom

Osborne. It was a mentoring program wherein one could work with the young children in the primary and secondary schools. We could encourage the young students to get better grades and help them learn and to encourage them in their abilities and talents. It is a great program in which I am still working.

It was the later part of July that we got word that Dad's youngest brother, Bill Thornton, had passed away. I felt my dad should go to his brother's funeral and I wanted to take Mom and Dad. Clint really didn't want me to do this but consented in the end. He had to stay home because of the mail route and, of course, his dog Gretchen needed care. We were not gone for long although we did stop in Iowa at Allen's as a bed and breakfast.

I will say here that our marriage was a great adjustment for both of us. Neither my children nor my mother wanted me to get married so soon. However, I didn't want to stay with my children or my parents for any length of time. It wouldn't be fair to Rylan and Amy and I didn't want to live clear out in the Sandhills, 28 miles from town. I knew what the Bible said in 1 Corinthians 7:39, "A wife is bound by law as long as her husband lives, but if her husband dies, she is at liberty to be married to whom she wishes, only in the Lord." So we both felt we were doing this in the Lord.

However, two different personalities require a lot of give and take. One thing I will say, you must never compare the second husband to your former spouse. I know that if it had not been for God's help and our determination to stay together there might have been another divorce. I must say here everyone needs to learn about each other's Love Languages! It helps in understanding each other. Let me give an illustration of what I learned about my husband's love language. He would ask me every so often, "How much money do you have in your purse?" So I would say, "Oh, I don't know." To me money wasn't really important, just so I had enough when I went shopping. Clint would say, "Check it out." Then I would tell him. If it was $10.00, he would give me $90.00 or if I had $40.00, Clint would give me $60.00. Whatever the amount was that I needed he would always make sure I had $100.00 in my possession. Eventually learned this is one of his ways of showing and saying, "I love you." I am sure his upbringing made him very aware of money since, when he was growing up, his folks never had much even for food.

Clint was a very safe and careful driver so I always felt safe with him. In 2006 or 2007 we bought a brand new 900 Kawasaki motor bike. I had not ridden much with someone on a motor bike so my dear husband, Clint, had to teach me how to balance. He and Grace had motor bikes years before so this was not strange for him. Anyway, I loved riding with him. Many times we would ride around the lake and back to Lewellen on Highway 26.One spring day we took off for Oshkosh and then turned south on Highway 27. It was such a beautiful ride with the green wheat fields, the birds flying and the smell of spring in the air. I just loved it. Now Allen and Kim enjoy these rides on the bike.

In September, 1996 Clint decided he wanted a different car. He learned that we could get a better Chrysler Concord, a 1997, because they had just come out with the new model; so to North Platte we went to McKay Motors. After much dickering we ordered a new Chrysler Concord, just the way we wanted it. When it came in toward the end of September we went down and turned in our 1996.Except for the headlights, we loved this car and drove it until July, 2012. We accumulated about 160 thousand miles before trading it for a 2012 Dodge Avenger.

Ron and Karla's first baby Jessica was born October 7, 1996. On the long Columbus Day weekend, we made the trip to Iowa to see our eleventh granddaughter. Clint had a long weekend because of the holiday.

During the week mail days were Monday, Wednesday, and Fridays. We usually got back from the route around 2:00 p.m. This left some afternoons to hunt or fish and even cutting wood. Clint did a lot of wood cutting and he would sell it in fall time and sometimes even deliver it with his truck. Numbers of times I would go with him to help load the wood in our truck as he cut it up. Usually that would be on Tuesdays, Thursdays, and Saturdays, the days he didn't carry mail.

One thing that Clint and I enjoyed doing together was going fishing. The Cheneys had a sand pit and river land which made it easy for us to find a place to fish. I really enjoyed this past time with Clint. We caught many catfish. But the fish I enjoyed catching most were the Northern Pike. These fish were bigger than any I had ever caught. They put up a good fight. The biggest we ever caught were over 30 inches in length. Clint was good at cleaning and flaying the fish and we were able to put fish in the freezer.

Before my time, Clint would also hunt rattle snakes in prairie dog towns. Then it got too dangerous for him because he couldn't hear them rattle. He had jars of rattles from the snakes he had killed. Later we gave some of them to Ed, my brother-in-law, to make the numbers on clocks. I have a clock that Ed made for us from a saw blade and he used rattle snake rattlers to make some of the numbers on it. It is quite unique!

Another pastime that Clint and I really enjoyed was prairie dog hunting. Clint learned of a farmer out on the south table who wanted to get rid of these pests in the pasture where he kept cattle. Prairie dogs make it dangerous for cattle. They dig holes in the ground and sometimes the cattle step into the holes and break their legs. The farmer told us he hoped to poison these little animals but if we wanted to shoot them we were free to do so. Clint and I took our 22 rifles and went to this farm several times. After several days we had killed over 700 of the little pests.

Clint loved to deal for cars and pickup. As I said before I was almost embarrassed because he really made hard bargains. But he always came up with good deals. We had the 1997 Chrysler Concord and now he had his heart set on a new pick-up. I guess we really did need a new one because the old blue 1984 Chevrolet pick-up had seen better days. However, we still used it to do the mail route in the sandhills. Clint always paid close attention to ads for car and pick-up sales. One day he saw an advertisement for a new 1998 Ford pick-up. He really wasn't a Ford man but he wanted to go to Ogallala and look at it. He decided it was a good deal and bought it. Then Clint got the idea that we should have a slide-in camper so we could go camping. He began watching the ads in the paper and listening to swap shop. It wasn't long until we found the slide-in camper.

One day we learned there were many prairie dog towns in Wyoming so we decided it would be a good chance to try out our new pick-up and the camper. Clint knew some of the Gordons had a ranch close to New Castle Wyoming so we contacted them and we headed there. We didn't kill a lot of prairie dogs. Others had been hunting them so we didn't have much success, but it was fun camping out in the wide open spaces of Wyoming.

Our first trip out west into Montana, Idaho and Washington was after Clint had retired from his mail route in June of 1998. My Mom's sister, Aunt Chrystal, and her husband, Uncle Ken Hut, lived in Whitefish Montana. We stayed overnight with them and then traveled through Idaho to Clarkston Washington where Randal and Candice were living at the time with their family. The children, Nathaniel, Marlena and Olivia, were small but I remember what fun we had with them. We even had a picnic by the Snake River with them.

After this trip Clint decided he didn't like the Ford Pick-up seats. They didn't fit his back quite right and it made his back hurt after driving for some distance. So he started looking for another pick-up after this trip. He figured he could get a pretty good trade-in on a Dodge. Sure enough— Schmidt's Garage and Car sales just happened to have a beautiful black and red 1998 Dodge pick-up on the lot and would give us a good trade in for our Ford. Now we had our second new pick-up to go with our slide-in camper.

My nephew, Paul Lehman, was soon to be married to Jody. Her home was near Rapid City. South Dakota. They had stopped by our house one evening and had supper with us. Paul knew that his Aunt Eva made wedding cakes and he wanted me to have the honor of making theirs. Clint decided this would be a good trip to try out our new '98 black and red Dodge Ram 1500. We traveled to Rapid City and parked at a lady's house who offered her home and especially the kitchen so I could make the special cake. There certainly was not enough room to create a wedding cake in our camper! It was fun to be with family too, who came for the wedding of Paul and Jody.

Gillian's Illness

Now I want to go back to September of 1997. Our little Gillian was only about three weeks old when Clint and I got married. We were very privileged to live close to Rylan and Amy and were able to baby sit our little granddaughters, Annie and Gillian. They grew so quickly and brought a lot of joy to our lives. Then after Gill turned a year old she seemed to have sick spells every so often. One would think of these sick times as teething as she was of that age. I remember going to hear a singing group that came to Lewellen on Labor Day week end. Clint and I went to hear them sing in the open park under the trees. I took Gill and held her close to my chest as she fitfully tried to sleep. I could tell she was a really sick little girl.

Rylan and Amy took Gillian to doctor appointments to be checked, trying to find what was making her so listless. One day shortly after Labor Day I went to their home to see how Gill was doing. They had her lying on a blanket on the floor. She looked so sick. I reached down to feel her little chest and tummy and felt what seemed like a lump. I called Rylan and he palpitated the area. Something was really wrong! They called a nurse who was at Lewellen with a mobile unit. She then had them rush Gillian to Ogallala to the hospital. As soon as the doctor in Ogallala checked her, he sent them on to North Platte to a pediatrician. There they kept Gill in the hospital for the night and did some testing. Ron and Roxane came to the hospital and prayed over Gill. The next morning Rylan called me, "Mom, the doctors here in North Platte are telling us to take Gill directly to Denver Children's Hospital. Can you keep Annie for us?" Of course my answer was, "Sure we can!" Rylan and Amy came by our house later that morning and left Annie with Clint and me.

On September 15, 1997 at Denver Children's Hospital the doctors diagnosed Gill with Neuroblastoma cancer. She had a tumor on top of her kidney which they said would need to be treated with chemotherapy. What a shock this was to everyone but word spread and prayers began rising to the throne of God for this little 15 and 1/2 month old baby. There was prayer going up all over the world for my son and family. We could not understand why this little one should have this dreaded disease of cancer. Many people all over western Nebraska knew about this through the news that spread quickly by newspaper and radio. Even benefit dinners were scheduled and people from all over the communities of Oshkosh and Lewellen came together to help with finances or any way they could.

I've never said much about this incident that happened to me but it still is so clear to me that I want to include it. It was sometime later, I think probably during a lull in her treatments and she was at home for a short time, that I went over to Rylan's and Amy's to see Gill. On the way, I had Christian

Radio on and a song came on about the four friends who carried their sick friend to Jesus so he could be healed. They couldn't get to Jesus because of the crowd but they were determined and decided to go up on the roof of that house and make an opening through which they could let their sick friend on a mat down right in front of Jesus. Jesus saw their faith and healed the man. I was so touched by this song and as I prayed I just felt I was bringing sick little Gill right before Jesus as these men did and Jesus was going to heal her!

It wasn't just my prayer that was going up to God but prayers of people all over the world. God did do a miracle of healing in Gillian's life. Today, as I'm writing, she is a sophomore in college preparing to be a nurse. SHE IS OUR MIRACLE FROM GOD!!!

My Ruptured Appendix

I believe it was October of 1998 or 1999 when Clint and I decided to go to Mom and Dad's ranch for a visit. We always took our pickup and Clint would take his gun just in case he saw a coyote or maybe some ducks. It was duck season in October and, of course, on our way we did see ducks on the little pond by one of the windmills. When we noticed the ducks, Clint drove on by the pond and then circled around to sneak up on them. He shot two of them that day. We decided to take them to Mom at the ranch thinking she would fix them for us to eat at dinner. I loved duck breast sliced thinly and dipped in seasoned flour and fried. Oh, Yumm! We got to the ranch and Mom butchered the ducks. Then I asked her where I could bury the entrails and she told me to take them out into the field east of the house. I took the shovel and the pan with the entrails and feathers to bury them. In digging this hole my shovel slipped and the handle hit me on the lower right side. I didn't think much about it but noticed that it was hurting slightly.

After lunch Clint said, "Our pickup needs to have the battery charged." So Mother and I decided we would drive it seven miles to the mailbox out along the main road. We did this several times even though I noticed that my side was beginning to hurt a little more. After a while we returned to Lewellen. I didn't rest well during that night so Clint thought I should go to the doctor. It was Tuesday morning and we were able to get an appointment for me with my P.A. Carol Packard. Something just was not right. Carol took me in the exam room and I told her about digging the hole and the shovel handle hitting my side as it slipped out of my hand so she wasn't sure if it was my appendix or if just some strained muscles. She called in another doctor and an intern who happened to be present. They all decided I probably had just strained some muscles and sent me home.

I didn't do much the rest of the day and next morning, Wednesday. I just sat in my chair. Suddenly, about 11:00 a.m., I had such a sharp pain in my lower right side I could not even move. The pain was excruciating and I thought to myself, this is worse than having a baby. I could not even go to the door to call Clint. I later realized this pain was probably when my appendix ruptured. After about 20 or 30 minutes the pain subsided and I felt a little better.

It was during the month of October that my son Ron who was doing a rotation in surgery with Dr. Schiefen at Imperial, Nebraska. He decided that since he had the week-end off he would come to visit Rylan and Amy at the farm. I thought I was feeling a little better but Ron pushed around on the tender area and said, "Mom if you aren't feeling a whole lot better by Monday morning I want you to go to the Imperial hospital." On Sunday I went to Church and everyone was asking how I felt. I guess they didn't think I looked very well but I would say, "Oh I think am getting better."

Monday morning Ron came by and told Clint he thought I should have a CAT scan at Imperial. So that morning Clint and I drove down with Ron. I had the exam late morning then was scheduled for a CAT scan right after lunch. After the scan Ron came to me and said, "Mom, your appendix is ruptured and we are preparing to operate right away." As I look back on the whole week before I realized that probably Wednesday when I had that terrible pain was the exact time that my appendix ruptured.

They prepared me for surgery and Ron wheeled me into the operating room where Dr. Schiefen prepared to operate on me. I remember so well how my son reassured me and prayed with me before the operation. He will never know what a great blessing that was to me.

The operation went well and they took me to my hospital room with tubes all over me. I really feel God touched me that day and started the healing process. I was in the hospital for five days before Clint was able to take me home. During those days I had a number of visitors. Since we had lived and pastored at the Wesleyan Church in Imperial back in the 60's, a number of people remembered me. I remember how Pastor Todd Burpo came to pray over me. Even my daughter-in-law, Karla, and my two grandchildren, Jessica and Jared, came to see "uGogo" (Zulu language for Grandma) in the hospital. We truly praised God for His healing touch. I could have died but it seems God wasn't finished with my life here on this earth.

Family Reunions

It was 1999 that we decided to have a French-Mecham-Swan Reunion. The Cheney side of the family also decided to start having reunions every five years. The Cheney Reunion is always held around the 4th of July. So in the year 2000 we made plans for not only the Cheney reunion but also the French-Swan-Mecham Reunion. This was important to do because my mother and her siblings were all getting older. We had the meeting place at our Community Wesleyan Church and Jim French and Kay catered the meals.

One thing that stood out in my mind was how the older ones shared their memories. Ruth MacPherson and her son and wife were present, Rebecca and Wayne and their son and wife. In fact Ken Osborne favored us with his singing bass voice. At our Sunday afternoon meeting we invited the community in to hear him. A number of the Swan family attended: Dorothy Swan and some of her boys, Harold Swan and a number of his family, and Leland Swan family. Family pictures were laid out and memories recalled. I decided to lay out the family tree of the Mecham family on a large sheet. It all started back in England about 1630. Grandma Alice French, Aunt Hazel Swan and Caleb Mecham all came from this Samuel Mecham family.

For the Cheney family Reunion it involved the William Alfred Cheney family. There were ten children in this family. At the 2000 Reunion we remembered four of this family had passed away. Now, Clifford, Carolyn, Ted, Robert and Elaine had passed on. However, the families of Elaine, Robert and Ted were present. The Robert Cheney family included five children and their families, about 29 persons. The Oakes family, the Lark family, the three daughters and families of Elaine, the Charles Cheney family, the Lehman family and the Ted Cheney family. The Charles Cheney family hosted this reunion in 2000 during the 4th of July holidays. There were a lot of interesting events taking place in Oshkosh. The Cheney tribe was present for many of these including the kids races and the outdoor barbeque in the park and the parade. It all made for a fun reunion.

Our Canadian Trip

In the spring of 2000 Clint said to me, "I think we should take your folks and make a trip to Canada to see Steve and Elaine". Our brother-in-law Steve was not at all well and Clint felt we should go see him. Let me explain why Steve was sick. Back in 1989 he was out hunting with a friend when he accidently got shot. He almost died. He was given quarts and quarts of blood. Unknowingly the blood was contaminated and Steve got hepatitis C. This is deadly but one could take the cure. Steve did this cure and during that time we visited them at Cremona, Alberta. We left early part of May taking Mother and Daddy with us. We drove our 1997 Chrysler Concord. It gave us a really comfortable ride to Canada and back. Steve did not feel well at all but was able to visit some. Elaine put us up in the parsonage. Steve was pastoring the Cremona Missionary Church but was soon retiring because of his health issues.

Some friends decided they should put on a benefit sale for Steve and Elaine. This occurred while we were there and we got to see many people. One person I was privileged to meet was Jeanette Oakes who is the author of Canadian Frontier stories. We also got to visit my Uncle Jewel and Aunt Annie French my mother's brother who was living in Canada now. During our stay there we celebrated Mother's Day with our Mom. It also was my birthday so it truly was a double wonderful Day for me. I just wish now that our other sister Esther could have been present.

Then it came time to leave. We decided to go over to Whitefish Montana where mother's sister Chrystal and husband Ken lived. We were here for my Mom's 83rd birthday. My Aunt made her a birthday cake and we celebrated. Sometimes when you look back you wonder and marvel at how God worked. Mother would not have seen her daughter Elaine and husband Steve, nor her sister and
husband if Clint had not felt we should do this Canadian Trip. This trip would be the last one she would make and she thoroughly enjoyed it. On the way home we got a motel in Sheridan Wyoming before our final leg of our journey. In Sheridan I have friends the Welty family. So I called them up and Laura brought her girls and came to see us at the motel. It was good to have a short visit with them. The next day was Mom and Dad's 65th Wedding anniversary. Mom said, "I don't want another celebration. I have had enough celebrations for my life." They had celebrated their 25th, 40th, 50th, and 60th wedding anniversaries with programs and open house. So we made the day special by stopping in Scotts Bluff and buying them a new radio cassette CD player. We arrived safely at home in Lewellen. It truly was a wonderful trip!

Our Neighbor Next Door, December 10, 2000

A nice older man by the name of Mr. Brown lived to the north of our place. Once in a while he would visit with Clint. He had a dog he called Sandy and she really adored her master. Mr. Brown had children in Colorado and one morning we got a call from one of his daughters saying, "We have been ringing our Dad's phone but can't raise anyone. Clint, would you go and check to see if he is alright?" This happened in December. Clint went over to the house and noticed the light was on in the kitchen but when he knocked on the door he couldn't raise anyone. Clint tried to look in at one of the windows. He couldn't see too well but it appeared that Mr. Brown was lying on the kitchen floor. So he came back and called the daughter telling her what he was able to see. The ambulance and police were called. When they got into the house they found Mr. Brown had died. His children came as soon as possible to make arrangements. At that time Clint ask them if they would consider selling their Dad's house since none of the children lived in this area. He said, "If you do sell it would you give us a chance to buy it? We are looking for a place for my wife's parents to move in close to us." They said they would keep us in mind. In early March they offered the place to us and we took their offer after talking it over with my parents.

My mother was thrilled to think they might be moving in next door to us but my Dad not so much! He wanted to stay on his ranch till he died. I really don't think he realized what a struggle it was for my mother. For many years we carried water in from the windmill out by the barn. Mother didn't have an indoor bathroom but in later years my Dad did put down a pump and got running water into the kitchen. He got electric lights powered by a wind charger and batteries and then finally he switched to solar panels. But as a whole Mother did not have a lot of conveniences on the ranch. Buying Mr. Brown's place was exciting for her. She looked forward to making curtains and making this place one she had always hoped for with conveniences she had never had. Mother and Daddy often came to have Sunday dinner with us at our house. I remember how excited Mother was when after dinner she would want to go and do some measuring for curtains. It was her dream home!!!

My sister Elaine and her husband Steve came from Canada to help fix up Mother's dream house. They painted, put down carpet and tiles and fixed up so many things. Toward the end of their stay mother got sick to her stomach. Mother never complained but I think she suffered more pain than we realized. Uncle Jewel, mom's brother had come with Steve and Elaine from Canada and so Mom had a great visit with her brother. Then it was time for Elaine, Steve and Uncle Jewel to leave for Colorado to visit Uncle Jewel's nephew there.

Mother Leaves Us, 2001

It was Monday, April 10th 2001 and Mother and Daddy decided to come down to Lewellen. Daddy went on to Ogallala but Mother stayed to visit with me and to help me clean my cupboards. She was such a help that afternoon. She was right down on the floor cutting out plastic shelving for me while I arranged the cupboards and put down the plastic shelving. We had such a wonderful afternoon. Then it came time for me to go meet with one of the grade school students in a program called the Buddy Program. This program helped students who struggled with some of their classes. I remember saying to Mother, "Make yourself a cup of tea", and she said back to me, "If your Dad come before you get back we will just go on home". I never realized at the time that this would be my last conversation with my mother. When I did return, Mother and Daddy had gone on back to the hills. I wish I had never left that afternoon and would have just spent the time with my Mother. But how can one know???

It was about 8:30 that night when my dad called me and said, "I think your Mom is gone". "Gone", I said. "What do you mean she's gone"? I could hardly believe what my ears were hearing. "Yes, she fainted and I can't wake her". I said, "Oh, Daddy, we will come right now." We grabbed our coats but first made a call to pastor Lynn. They would drive up in the hearse and Clint and I would come in our pickup. On the way up we stopped at Charles and Linda's to tell them the sad news. I was really in shock. I'm so glad I had a good understanding husband.

It was a cold blustery night but we got to my childhood home and soon after that the undertaker and Pastor Lynn came. I can still see so clearly my poor father sitting on the chair with a look of despair and on the floor lay my dead mother. I sobbed and cried out but realized Mother wasn't really there. Her spirit had gone to heaven to be with Jesus. Daddy told us that mother had an arm load of wood and was walking up the sidewalk to the porch. He came up behind her and he heard her say, "Oh, I feel like I'm going to faint". Daddy caught her and let her down slowly. That was the last thing she ever said. Daddy tried to revive her but her dear heart had stopped beating. He managed to get her to the kitchen floor and then called me. In a short time pastor and the mortician arrived and put mother inside the hearse and headed back to Oshkosh. We convinced my Dad to come back to our house and stay with us for the night. It reminds me that none of us know the time nor the hour God will call us home. We must be ready at all times! I know Mother was ready to go.

The next morning April 11th was a snowy and blustery day. Daddy felt he had to go check his chickens and give them food and water. He and Clint took our 4-wheel drive pickup and made their way to the ranch. I did not go because there was phone calling and various things I had to do. I quickly got hold of Steve and Elaine. They were just ready to leave next morning to go to Canada. Instead of heading to Canada they headed for Nebraska in a snow storm. It's a good thing Steve was use to driving in snow with bad roads.

The next few days were filled with funeral arrangements and choosing the things we wanted to have for the funeral. Steve spoke and Pastor Lynn gave the funeral message. Esther, Elaine and I sang. The day of the funeral turned to be quite a nice day. In fact I remember a rain shower came up right after the burial service in Ash Hollow cemetery. Many people attended the funeral especially relatives. Just the day before, however, we had another shock. My Uncle Howard French, my mother's brother, who lived in Lewellen suddenly passed away on Thursday, the day before Mother's funeral.

He had not been well but just the shock of losing Mom and now my uncle was difficult. However, a number of people stayed and this funeral was held on Monday after Mother's funeral on Friday the 13th of April and Uncle Howards held on Monday April 16th.

My children, Roxy and Ron and Rylan and Amy and grandchildren came. Before everyone headed home we went to the Ranch to have one last meal together and many memories were recalled. We convinced Dad to stay with us for a while. Also other arrangements were made to being the chickens down. There was a small chicken house at the Brown place which we fixed up. This would give Dad chores to do feeding and watering the chickens. The weather got more spring like and moving things down from the ranch became easier. Dad stayed six or eight weeks at our house. Then Allen came for a visit and we convinced Dad that he should move into his house next door so that Allen would have a place to stay during his visit. This made Dad's transition a little easier.

As fall came on we suggested Dad sell his cattle and live full time beside us. He was now 88 years old and it wasn't wise for him to stay in the hills during the winter. At this time Tim Barrent helped us get the cattle down here to his place and in November we saw them sold at Ogallala Sale barn. I'm sure this was very difficult for my dad but I'm thankful mother didn't have to go through the stress of all these changes.

After our dad sold his cattle, then came the decision of what do we do with the land? He wanted to rent the pasture land for grazing. Lynn Myers was really interested in doing this. He rented it from the end of May to about end of October or beginning November. Lynn didn't pay as much per animal as was paid by others but he took very good care of the land. He was very careful to not overgraze the land and fenced it off so that he could rotate the grazing. Another reason we didn't mind so much about the lower cost of grazing was because Lynn checked the water and wells from week to week. Lynn was someone we could trust.

Heart Problems for Clint

Clint began having more and more problems with migraines. In May of 1998 one day while he was cutting wood east of the old Cheney farm he seemed to have a really bad migraine. At the time I had gone back to DesMoines, Iowa to help Ron and Karla. Karla was having a lot of trouble carrying their second child so I had ridden the bus back to stay with them. Actually Karla had to be hospitalized and Ron was in medical school doing surgery rotations; so little Jessica needed Grandma to stay with her. One evening my mom called and told me that they had taken Clint to the hospital in Scotts Bluff because he appeared to have a stroke. Clint told me later what happened. He had come home from cutting wood and tried to call our dog Gretchen. He realized then that he could not say a word, couldn't even call the dog's name. About this time my folks drove into the yard. He had to write on paper that he could not talk. Right away they took him to the hospital in Oshkosh and they decided he needed to go to Scottsbluff hospital. They diagnosed it as a light stoke. After learning all of this and talking things over with Ron, he said he would try to get me on the bus the next day. Karla's mom was coming in a few days and they thought they could manage with some of their friends helping out. I did make it to Ogallala by bus and Tom and Clint were there to meet me. It took Clint a few weeks to get his speaking ability back but eventually it came back.

After Mother's death in 2001, Clint began experiencing a lot of weakness. He could hardly walk to the small white garage without losing his wind. He had to stop often to rest and catch his breath. Also, the migraines seemed to increase. Dr. Harold Keenan was his doctor at the time and he wanted Clint to be checked in Fort Collins 'Heart Center of the Rockies'. Clint and I drove out for the scheduled heart catheterization. We got a motel so as to make it easier to keep his appointment time. This exam really gave a lot of insight as to what Clint's problem was. They found that he had only two flaps to his aorta valve instead as the normal three flaps. Clint was born with a birth defect but this wasn't all. The doctor said the valve was scarred so bad that there was only an opening the size of a lead pencil for the blood to pump through. No wonder Clint could hardly go sometimes!

The doctor then suggested that Clint have an aorta valve replacement. There was the choice of a mechanical valve or a cow or pig valve. We were told that a pig or cow valve would last only about seven years whereas a mechanical valve would probably stay with you the rest of your life. But with the mechanical valve one would need to take a blood thinner to keep blood clots from forming in the heart. Clint decided he only wanted to go through this once so chose the mechanical valve. We were told that the surgeon, Dr. Mark Guadagnoli, had done hundreds of these surgeries and was highly recommended. We were given a date for the surgery the middle of September. When that time, Clint had developed a bad cough and after getting him prepared for the surgery they decided they should get him over the cough and cold before doing the operation. They sent us home with antibiotics for him to take and rescheduled the operation two weeks later at the end of September.

In two weeks we went back to Fort Collins for the operation. I remember so clearly how Pastor Lynn Lutz and Leland Swan came out to be with me during the surgery. It was so thoughtful of them. They will never know what this meant to me because the surgery lasted several hours. I'm sure it reminded me of another time I spent in a hospital in Zimbabwe Africa after Bob had heart problems. There I was alone except for our African friend, Mr. Gonera. So I know what it means to have your pastor there and, also, a relative. After about five hours they brought Clint to the recovery room but he had not yet awakened. I needed a few things at Walmart and, since Pastor and

Leland were going, they said I could ride along with them and they would bring me back.

That night a friend Dorothy Fraze ask me to come and stay at her house. This was much nicer than staying at a motel. Clint was terribly sore and coughed more than he wanted to. Having your heart taken totally out of your chest cavity means they have to split you down the middle. Then after getting your heart back into your chest they wire the rib cage shut. So you see it is no small matter and takes a long recovery time. But now we had hopes that Clinton would begin feeling much better and would have a lot more energy. There were several visitors who came to see Clint. Among them were Rev. Kerry Johnson, Ben Miller, Dorothy Fraze and Rev. Dan Dennison. Clint appreciated their visits.

After five days Clint was released from the hospital and I drove us home. Some of the roads were rough and Clint felt every bump. Finally he was home and on his way to recovery. We did have a visiting nurse coming in the check Clint's progress and give suggestions to help him recover. We both were glad that this ordeal was over!

A Good Grandpa for My Grandchildren

There is one really neat thing about my husband Clint that made me so happy. He loved my grandchildren, especially when they were tiny babies. His sister once told me, "Clint always loved tiny babies. When Greg was just a new-born he would take him and just make over him and holding him like it was the natural thing for him to do." Clint seemed to just have a natural ability in holding tiny babies. You could tell he just loved them. When other men were so afraid to even hold a tiny new-born this was never a problem for Clint.

My grandchildren are so important to me—all twenty-five of them— and now seven great grandchildren included. Clint really was so good to let me go visit them and I truly appreciated this. He did not always feel well and it wasn't as easy for him taking trips. However, we did have several trips with our pickup camper and our motor home.

One trip I remember was the time we took a little golden Retriever puppy out to Randal and family. Rylan and Amy's dog Emma had the cutest bunch of puppies and Rylan wanted his brother and family to have one. They chose a beautiful golden brown puppy and it was decided that Randal's family and Rylan's family would meet at a reservoir lake out southwest of Billings Montana. Rylan ask me to go along. They had Annie, Gill and baby Erin, camping equipment, and the puppy so we had a pretty crowded car. It was a fun trip though despite the fact we were pretty packed in! The kids had a fun time playing in the lake and especially in the mud. We slept in tents and cooked on an open fire.

Another trip was when I went in December just after William turned a year old in November. At that time Randal and Candy were living in Clarkston, Washington. I flew into Spokane, Washington and the kids met me there. It was the time my dad flew with me to Portland and I saw that he got on his flight to Medford where my sister Esther was to meet him. He would be staying with her for a few weeks. This is one way my sister shared in the care of Dad for a few weeks. When I got ready to leave from Clarkston the kids all went with us to Spokane. As I mentioned, William was a year old and just learning to walk all over. I had promised to take the family to "Chucky Cheese" to celebrate some 'unbirthdays'. I had just crocheted a little cowboy outfit for William. He looked so cute walking around in it. Later I crocheted another little cowboy outfit for Quinn Cheney in orange and black the school colors of Cody – Kilgore High School. William's outfit was blue and white. Sometimes I wonder how I ever do all this crocheting, making blankets and birthday cakes for all my 25 grandchildren. At this time I have made all 24 grandchildren birthday cakes at least one time. Now that Roxy and Ron have added another little grandson named Adon, I have another birthday cake to make. The Scripture in Psalm 127:3 says: "Behold, children are a legacy from the Lord; the fruit of the womb is his reward." I feel so blessed! It has been so much fun teaching granddaughters and even grandsons to crochet, embroidery, baking cookies and cakes and decorating.

Our Kentucky Trips

It was March of 2004 that we decided to take trip to Falls of Rough, Kentucky to see Clint's brother Steve and his wife Barb. March is not always a good time to travel but this year it was ok. We stopped by Clint's sister Sally's North of Omaha and spent the night. The next day we traveled on to Indiana where my Aunt Virginia and Cousin Dave and family lived. We stayed overnight at Aunt Virginia's farm close to Covington, Indiana. It was so nice to have a visit with my aunt and cousin, Dave. The next day we headed out for Kentucky and arrived at Steve and Barb Reeves late afternoon.

We had such a good time in Kentucky. They took us to visit Abraham Lincoln's home and then we attended one of the singing jamborees. Many people attend these singing programs. Many western singers performed. One little girl, about 10 or 12 years old, sang the song "Rocky Top". I think this was my first time to hear the song and I was quite impressed. We attended the Baptist Church near Barb and Steve's home and also visited and had a meal with Nancy and Rodney Willis, their friends. It was nice to meet Steve and Barb's sons Dave and Stephen and their families.

We decided it would be good for us to go visit Clint's sister, Ruth, in Arkansas and her family. This was my first time to meet Ruth and her son and family. We stayed a couple nights at their country home near London, Arkansas then headed for Oklahoma and Kansas. Orai and Linda Lehman, missionaries to Southern Africa, were home on furlough and we wanted to see them. Linda is my former husband's sister and worked with us on the mission field. We learned that they were not in Bartlesville, Oklahoma but were holding meetings in Kansas at a Wesleyan Church where Dennis and Connie Engles were pastoring. So we headed north through Wichita and Salina Kansas to his country church. It was great for me to get a visit in with missionaries again. Clint, however, was so tired he went to bed after getting our camper parked. We were here a couple nights before heading home to Nebraska. This was one fantastic Trip!

Caring for an Aging Father 2001-2006

It was such a shock to us when my mother died suddenly. I had always hoped she and Daddy would live next door and I would be able to do many things with her. Mother was an expert seamstress. She could make any kind of clothes and did many quilts. It just would have been such fun if we could have sewn, crocheted or embroidered together. But I think my mother was under quite a lot of stress trying to figure how she and daddy would get everything moved. My dad shared some things with Clint that made me think he really didn't want to live down here at Lewellen. It seems his thoughts were they would live in this house north of us on Wednesday nights and the week-ends. That is not what Mother wanted to do. She was tired of traveling over those trail roads. God saw that Mother had gone over those Sandhill trails long enough and He rewarded her by just taking her to her eternal home.

After mother was gone Daddy wasn't anxious to live at the brown house they had bought. He wanted to try living at the ranch for the summer. He still was able to drive and so we agreed he could try it for the summer. I would call him every day by phone to make sure he was ok. But Daddy found it wasn't the same since mother was gone. He had to do everything—cook, find his clothes to wear and many other things that mother did for him. I did do his washing. The first of November Daddy sold his cattle at the Ogallala Sale Barn. We took him to the sale. I know it was so hard for him to see his cattle being sold. Then we encouraged Dad to stay near us for the winter. We moved all the things he would need to set up housekeeping. I helped Daddy by making sure he had his breakfasts, dinners and suppers. Often he would come and eat with Clint and I. I did his washing and house cleaning from November 2001 till March 2005. My Mom used to read to Daddy so I would try to do this in the evenings. One of the books I read to him was "Uncle Tom's Cabin". Of course he could read too and always had plenty of political reading material. Daddy was a staunch Republican and took great interest in his country's government.

I always feared in the morning when I went to get Dad's breakfast and to see that he was awake, that one morning I would find him dead. One morning I really did have a scare because he never answered when I knocked. I went into the house calling "Daddy, Daddy" but he would not answer. As I came into the living room and was able to see into his bedroom. He was still in bed. I thought "Oh my daddy is gone". I kept calling, "Daddy, Daddy." and finally he awoke. I was greatly relieved!

Every Sunday we would pick Daddy up for church. Then one day Daddy complained of a really bad head ache and he was having trouble seeing. We took him to the eye doctor and sure enough he had had a slight stroke. After this he had to spend some time in the Scottsbluff hospital.

It was in the first part of March that Dad just did not have strength. He had a terrible cough so we took him off to the doctor. The doctor put him in the hospital. Daddy had pneumonia. He was in hospital for several days and finally recovered somewhat. One day while visiting with the doctor at the hospital she called me aside and told me she thought I needed a rest and that we should probably put him in the River View Assisted Living. So we arranged to put him in Room #7, a very nice little apartment. We took his things from the house that would make him feel more at home. He seemed to adjust quite well. Now Clint and I felt we could get away for a while because my father was in a safe place and being looked after. This was when we were able to make our trip to Washington to see our kids, Randal, Candice, and grandchildren.

Daddy went to the rest home in August of 2005 so we had to move things out of the assisted Living. I know my Dad never wanted to live in a rest home but he was gracious about it and never made a big fuss. We tried to visit him often and took part in special activities that were held. The staff told me, "Your dad has been so nice to care for." I really appreciated their comments.

We celebrated Dad's 93rd birthday at the nursing home on Sept. 23, 2005. I made his birthday cake, his special favorite German Chocolate. Actually on special holidays we ate with Daddy at the dining room of the nursing home. During this time I had to be on crutches because of my knee hurting. I even had therapy on my knee but it just didn't help that much. So eventually I had arthroscopic surgery on both of my knees. It definitely was a help. Now I could walk much better.

While Dad was in the home he had a number of visitors. Rylan and Amy and children went several times to visit. After all he was a great grandpa to 31 great grandchildren. His sister Grace and husband Homer came in the fall of 2005 and enjoyed some special time as brother and sister.

About the 30th of March, Dad became very sick. They called me from the nursing home to let me know that they felt his pneumonia was very serious and he should be put in the hospital. I agreed with them. He was in the hospital nearly two weeks. I would go in about every day. I spent quite a bit of time with my Daddy. I knew that this was probably his time to go to his home in Heaven for he was not getting any better. It was Easter week again just like it was when Mother died. I always considered this was a great time to go home to heaven because we know Jesus gave us a great hope of a home in heaven by his death and resurrection. During my father's stay in the hospital I took his radio and played a number of Christian CDs for him to listen to. It seemed like his room was so peaceful. I took Daddy's arm and quietly said to him, "Daddy, it's ok to go. Jesus is waiting for you." On April 11th, Daddy was so bad that I decided I needed to stay overnight. They gave me a bed to sleep in next to my Dad's room.

Clint had to take Tom, his brother, to Hot Springs, South Dakota to the VA hospital for an appointment the next day April 12th. I talked with the nurse after fitfully sleeping through the night. I said, "Do you think I'll have time to run home to see my husband before he leaves for Hot Springs?" I continued, "I won't be gone long—maybe eat a bite of breakfast and be right back." Clint was leaving at 6:30 a.m. for South Dakota. So I rushed home and had just a few minutes with Clint. I told him it didn't look like Dad would last much longer. Clint and Tom then left. I decided to eat some breakfast and then head back to Oshkosh hospital. As I was eating the phone rang. I answered it and the nurse from the hospital said, "Eva, your Dad has just passed away." I exclaimed, "Oh no, I wanted to be there with him." Then I continued, "I'll be right there." Why did God let him die while I was gone? I wanted to be right there when Dad went to heaven but it didn't happen that way. As I turned into the hospital parking lot and hurried for the door I knew now that Dad was in a better place but why didn't he wait until I was there by his side? It was kind of like when Bob, my first husband, went. That is when I got a phone call saying your husband has just died just after we had visited in the evening.

I rushed in the door and quickly down the halls to where the nurse's station was. There I saw our faithful pastor Lynn Lutz. He was always there when you needed him. The nurse gave me a hug as well as did Pastor Lynn. I said, "Why didn't he wait until I was here?" Then the head nurse, bless her heart, she was so kind, she came over to me and said, "He was your dad and you know your dad has the last word." Then she told me how she had gone in beside my dad and put her hand on his arm. She said the Lord's Prayer right there close to my dad. Judy said, "As I repeated the prayer his breathing became shallower. Then when I said, 'Amen' your dad just gave one last sigh and that was it. He laid there so peaceful." Pastor Lynn prayed with us then we parted. Now Daddy was in heaven with mother. They both were gone but I would miss them so much. However, never would I wish them back into this world of pain and suffering. Both of them were with Jesus where there is no more earthly pain.

Finally got hold of Clint to let him know Daddy had passed away. He and Tom were on their way home. Then I called my children and my sisters and others to let them know. They all came for the funeral. It was a time of celebration of my dad's life. Both Esther and Elaine were present for the funeral. At the funeral we sang together one of Dad's favorite songs, 'Oh how I Love Jesus'. My brother-in-law and Pastor Lynn spoke at the service. Many friends and relatives attended. It truly was a celebration of our dad's life.

My Trip Back to Africa 2006

One day after Daddy's death, Clint said to me, "I think you better think seriously about making a trip back to Africa. You aren't getting any younger." That truly was music to my ears. I knew when we married that Clint had said he didn't want me going back to Africa. As time went by he realized I had not had closure on Bob's death. Clint did have a real gift of discernment. Now he wanted me to have this closure. His statement took me a little by surprise. I had been praying about going back because I, too, felt that I had left Africa too quickly. Real excitement arose within me. I thought about who could make this trip with me. I knew Clint didn't feel he was well enough to make the trip. My brother-in-law's sister came to mind, Alice Wyatt. She had lost her husband a few months before this. I thought maybe she might like to go with me. When I mentioned this to Clint, he seemed pleased because he definitely didn't want me going alone so I called Alice to present her with the idea. Alice was the daughter of missionaries and actually was born in South Africa. When I called, she seemed really excited about it and from that time we began making our plans. We decided the month of October would be the best time to go. It would be early spring in Southern Africa and yet wouldn't be so cold in the States when we returned first of November.

We got our plane tickets. Alice would meet me in Denver as she would be flying from Tulsa Oklahoma and I would take the shuttle bus from Big Springs to Denver International Airport. We connected with each other and made our way to check our luggage and go through security with our carry-on luggage. Our flight would be direct to London leaving in the evening and arriving early morning in London England. It was a good flight. At Heathrow airport we spent the rest of the day and in the evening boarded our flight to Johannesburg, South Africa. This was an all night flight and so by now we were getting a little tired but the excitement of being back in Africa after eleven years kept me perked up. Then around 9:00 a.m. we arrived at Jan Smutts Airport in South Africa. Orai Lehman (Alice's brother) and Jason Helm met us at the airport. In a way it was like going home for me. Bob and I and our family had spent a lot of our time in this area of the world over a period of about 25 years. Of course I remembered the night I flew out of this airport after Bob's death with my dear sister and brother-in-law on September

25, 1995. That was not a pleasant memory but I knew the Lord was with me and giving me strength.

That night after we arrived we stayed in Brakpan with Liz Anderson who was living at the mission house at that time. The mission house was the one for the mission director. There had been a lot of changes made since Bob and I had lived there. Liz put Alice and I in the bedroom that Bob and I had slept in when we lived there during Bob's time as mission director. Of course this brought many memories flooding back into my mind.

The next morning Orai and Jason met the parents of Jason's wife Rachel at the airport. Then we all headed for Nelspruit where Linda and Rachel were. They were having a vehicle fixed in Nelspruit and so we had to stay over one more night in South Africa. The place we stayed was called Mercy Air. This mission had planes that flew out to various areas in need of help. When the big flood happened in Mozambique in the Chokwe area they flew in supplies and helped people get out for medical supplies and food.

The next day we headed for Mozambique border. Alice and I had to purchase visas at the border costing us $25.00 each. As we crossed over into Mozambique, I could see a tremendous amount of progress had taken place since the time we had been there in1991 the first time. The roads were like nice four lane roads going into Maputo the capitol. Going through Maputo was quite another experience. A lot of building was going on including roads, streets and housing. It was a little hairy getting through this city but eventually we were on our way to Xia Xia about 200 kilometers north of Maputo.

We were definitely a tired bunch when we reached Orai and Linda's home close to Xia Xia. We met the missionaries Jim and Karen Picket and their two children. Linda and Orai had a big mission home with an apartment down stairs. Alice and I each had our own bedrooms. We had to sleep under mosquito nets here. The nets were hung from the ceilings and you could let them down around you each night to keep mosquitoes from attacking you and giving you malaria. I also had my own private bath room. And to top this off they lived just across the street from the ocean. Alice and I enjoyed several trips down to the beach where we walked on the shore of the Indian Ocean and collected sea shells. Needless to say this place was really beautiful with trees and flowers.

Orai and Linda took us to see the Bible College and to meet the Phillip Macaringe family who was now principal of the school. Phillip and his wife had been students at EWBC when Bob and I were there in Swaziland. How exciting it was to see students we had taught now using their abilities in a new Bible College in Mozambique. They were teaching other students to be workers in God's Kingdom. It really gave one a sense of fulfillment seeing how God was using these men.

While being there for two weeks we were able to attend the Bible College graduation. Again, what a blessing this was. One day Orai and Linda took us to the market in XaiXai. Oh my, what a sight with all the little shops and everything imaginable for sale. Rachel Helm took us to a lady who made African dresses from material that you could select. It was quite amazing because the lady just took your measurements then said come back in a few days and you could get your dress. I selected a bright fabric and she made me a skirt and top which fit just right.

We also attended some out station churches. One church we attended was out in the open under a big tree. God is just as real out there in the open under a tree as He is in our big fancy churches here in America.

The two weeks we had in XaiXai passed quickly. There was one thing I felt I must do to help put closure to Bob's and my time spent in Africa. Orai and Linda were such a blessing and a help to me when I lost Bob in Bulalwalyo Zimbabwe. I wanted to take time to thank them in a proper way. So one morning shortly before we were returning to South Africa at morning devotions I ask to speak. I poured out my heartfelt thanks for all they did to help me through the worst experience of my life—having my husband die in a foreign country. They stood by me so faithfully and helped me through this most terrible crisis of my life. God does "Work all things together for good to those who are called according to His purpose." Romans 8:28 I feel with all my heart that God placed Orai and Linda there at just the right time I needed them. I give all the praise to God!

We planned to visit the Kruger National Game Park on our way to Casteel Mission. This mission is where Alice and Orai spent much of their childhood and Alice had not been back after she left for college in the U.S.

Game parks are always so interesting especially Kruger National Game Park. There is no way you will see this entire park in a couple days for it is probably 200 kilometers long. But we saw many animals and birds. Of course one animal people always look for is from the cat family-- the lion, leopard or cheetah. As we drove along I thought I saw a lion. In backing up we realized it was only a big baboon. However as we were stopped a car pulled alongside of us and said, "There is a cheetah kill just up this side road." We thanked the man and drove quickly up the side road. About a kilometer or more over we saw a number of cars parked along the road. Sure enough over in the bushes a cheetah had killed an impala. He was chewing away on the carcass. However, there were many vultures who noticed this kill and decided to come and get their share. It was so funny to watch these birds light on the ground and just edge closer and closer to the cheetah and his food. As they continued getting closer more birds were flying in. The cheetah turned around so he could watch these birds while he was eating his meal. Before long he decided his had had enough of the impala and dashed off into the bush.   Suddenly as the Cheetah dashed off the vultures came rolling in and all you could see was a big ball of dust filled with vultures. In all my times in this game park I had never seen this happen. I guess nature has a way of getting its food!!!

After we left the game park we drove to Palaborwa where a missionary by the name Faith Amos lived. She invited us into her home to stay Saturday night. Her daughter fixed a big feast for us. The next morning we all headed for Casteel Mission. This was a real homecoming for Alice. They gave her gifts and fixed another big feast for us. Later afternoon we headed back to Palaborwa to stay the night with Mrs. Amos. We did side track to another small village on the way. Bob and I had worked with the Naphtali Langas. They were teachers with us at the Bible College in Port Shepstone and moved with us when the schools were merged in Swaziland. After we separated ways Naphtali passed away and his wife and some of the children were living near Palaborwa. It was so good to see them again and to see their grown children.

That Sunday evening Faith made it so very comfortable for Alice and me. The Lehmans stayed with Faith's daughter and husband. Next morning Faith made a delicious breakfast for us of toast and savory mince gravy with fruit and cereal. She also invited Ben and Marti Lubbe who are doing mission work down by Chokwe in Mozambique. We also got to see Faith's son Paul who had just gotten back from a cricket competition. We left the Amoses about 10:00 a.m. And drove to Tszaneen where we had lunch. Then we headed for Petersburg where we found Winston and Annette Callighan. They invited us to spend the night after having a good meal and visit.

On Tuesday about 8:30 a.m. we left Callighans and headed for Durban on the South Coast. We made good time through Pretoria and Joburg and followed the N3 to Durban. This time we headed for Oria and Alice's cousin Elizabeth Cox and her family who lived in Pinetown a suburb of Durban. She fixed a wonderful meal of lasagna and salad for our evening meal. It was rather rainy down here on the south coast. We stayed here at the Coxes until Friday the 3rd of November. It was nice to meet the cousins and spend several days with them before heading for Swaziland. We left Liz and Georges about 8:15 a.m., heading for Durban in a cloudy misty day. Durban had changed so much since Bob and I were in Port Shepstone in 1976-1978. It has grown and roads are much better. We traveled to Mkuzi where we had lunch before coming to the border of Swaziland. It didn't take much time to go through the border and head for Phonjawane. This was my first time to be back in Swaziland after Bob's death. It was hard going through Phonjawane and heading for Joy Mission. I had a few teary moments remembering the times Bob and I had in this area: his teaching at Phonjawane High School while we lived there about two years and the birth of our son Randal having his first home on earth here were great memories. Those memories were from way back in the years 1971 and 1972.

Swaziland had changed so much, people everywhere and buildings going up all along the highway. As we came close to Israel and Victoria Langa's home I ask Orai if we could stop there.

Orai thought it would be a good idea to stop and make a plan with them for a visit. It was so good to see the Langa family again. Victoria invited us for a meal on Sunday evening.

Joy mission looked so different with the big building. I was anxious to see the place again. We did some shopping for food in Manzini before going to Gibela Farms where we were staying for the week-end. Saturday morning I was awakened early by the guinea fowl. After showering and reading my Bible I did some bird watching. There are quite a number of different birds and all so interesting to watch. After breakfast we left for Joy Mission around 10:00 a.m. At Joy they have a small orphanage called "The Fortress". Goodness Twala is the head person of the orphanage and Lady Lindiwe Sihloganeyane, the manager of the home caring for the needs of the children. At my home church we had learned about this project and so it was nice to see it in person. Orai took video of the orphans and the home so we can show it at our churches in Nebraska-Colorado District. We then drove to the Bible College so we could see Esther Phillippe and Dorcas Croft and Mathias. They invited us to have supper with them. In the mean time I got to renew acquaintances with Bill NieMack, Ron Inkosi, Dolly and Bekesisa Maziya, Koliwe Sigwane and her husband and Pinto Langa. Dolly invited me to have tea with them and for the first time I had cassava bread with roibos tea. I don't remember ever having cassava before. Soon Orai came looking for me. They were ready to go back to Gibela Farms. It was a wonderful day renewing old acquaintances. I gave praise to the Lord for allowing me to once again be in Swaziland.

It was always my desire to give out the Robert A. Cheney Memorial Scholarship to one of the students graduating from E. W. B. C. The graduation day was November 5th 2006 on Sunday. I was up early excited because finally this day had arrived. I was able to award the scholarship to Dumisani Sitole, a Swazi Student who had the highest academic score for the year. I also got to meet Elmon Dlodlo and Hlanhla Sibanda two Zimbabwean students. I met with Vuyiswe Mazibuko the Swaziland D. S., Esther Mazibuko, Lena Dlamini and her husband, Bethel Mohale to name a few. Esther Mazibuko was one of the young girls who worked for me at Ebenezer Mission when Randal was a baby. We had a great meal at the school and later that evening had a wonderful meal and visit at Israel and Victoria Langas.

Monday morning we headed for Johannesburg on our way going

back to the States. Alice and I had such a wonderful time on this trip. We truly appreciated her brother Orai and sister-in-law Linda, taking us to see so much. Seeing so many friends from years past and being able to present the Robert A. Cheney Memorial Scholarship was a real blessing from the Lord!

After arriving back in Joburg, in the evening we were able to attend a Pastor's get together with a meal at Wesleyan Evangelical Seminary. This was where Daphne NieMack taught and worked. We got to see the Rev. Stanlelys, the Merricks and Auburn Williams. Auburn even asked about Roxane my daughter as he had remembered her as a teenager.

Tuesday Nov. 7th, was voting day in the U.S. But we didn't hear much about it. I had voted by absentee ballot before I left. In South Africa it is really a beautiful spring day. We did not get up early, then had a late breakfast before going to Orai's cousin Vicky. Victoria is the daughter of Faith and Thomas Sorenson and was born in Nebraska when the Sorensons pastored the church where my mom and dad went as young people. We met a number of Victoria's relatives throughout the day. They invited us for lunch and Dinner. Orai explained about the work in Mozambique being started by his grandfather Isaac Lehman. Even the first Nazarene Churches were started by him. Also about a Mr. Shirley that started a printing press is the Uncle of the Mr. Shirley who supported Bob and me while we were missionaries and now were supporting Orai and Linda. His wife is the sister of Naomi Ward. The Wards also visited us while we were missionaries in Zimbabwe. They were with a tour group visiting different missions in Southern Africa. Orai talked about the history of the churches in Mozambique, South Africa and Swaziland. Vicky talked about a number of people who were in the church I grew up in "The Missionary Church" then called the "Mennonite Brethren in Christ Church". She remembered Lyle Young and some of the ones I remembered. Thank the Lord for the way He works in the lives of people.

November 8th, 2006 Wednesday was another beautiful day. We washed our clothes and prepared for our trip back to the U. S. Orai took Alice around the area seeing where she and Orai grew up and also looking for their Grandpa Lehman's grave at one of the cemeteries. I stayed at the Mission house and read and prayed. There are many memories in this house where Bob and I spent our last times together while he was Mission Director. I believe this was a real time of closure for me and I'm feeling at peace.

Daphne Niemack came over and shared her heart with us. Poor girl, she has had so many sorrows to go through. I gave her a book "Classic Christianity" and Alice gave her the blanket she had received at Casteel Mission.

I was able to get Shepherd Gonera's phone number and so called him to let him know I was in South Africa. Shepherd is a young Zimbabwean that Bob and I tried to help out while we lived here. He and his wife and two little boys, along with his sister Shamiso came over for a short visit on Thursday Nov. 9th in the morning. This was our last day in South Africa. I had "the frosting on the cake" as they say with this visit from Shepherd and his family. He actually goes by the name of Shepherd Mlambo. His wife is Kathy and two little boys are LeRoy age 4 and Kyle age one. What a lovely visit we had together over coffee. It was so nice to meet Shamiso again as well.

In the evening about 5:30 we left for the airport. We said our goodbyes to Orai and Linda and thanked them for all they had done. Alice and I got seats together in middle of the plane. Our plane left at about 10:00 p.m. They gave a good meal and in the morning probably as we were flying over France they gave us breakfast. It is November 10th and Friday—kind of hard to tell yesterday from today when you ride a plane all night. We got to London Heathrow Airport about 6:30 a.m.at terminal one. We then rode the bus to terminal four to catch our flight to Denver. Our plane left from Gate #24 around 1:15 p.m. We were now on the last leg of our journey on a BA777 flight 219. We flew over Ireland and Greenland and headed for Hudson Strait and Hudson Bay then came over North and South Dakota. We had breakfast early on the 747 plane from Joburg, ate lunch before arriving in Denver.

We landed in Denver at 5:15 p.m. With strong winds 50-60 mph. Plane flew at 38,000 feet but we did have a nice trip—Praise the Lord! Alice waited to see that I got my bus to Big Springs. I was a little afraid I would miss the bus because of going through long lines at customs and immigration and waiting for our luggage to come through. Judi Morris was the bus driver and she was late in coming so I had no problem. Alice's Father -in-law, Mr. Wyatt, met her at the airport.

I called Clint as I got into Denver and then about Sterling I gave him another call so he could be in Big Springs when I arrived. There was one other lady on the bus with me. I was getting quite excited anticipating seeing my husband again. When we arrived in Big Springs at the Motel Six sure enough there was our Silver dodge Ram waiting with a funny looking man getting out. I had to laugh as I hugged this long gray curly haired man. I'm not sure what the other ladies thought but my husband wanted to impress upon me that I had been gone too long and he needed a haircut! He actually borrowed this wig from Pastor Lynn. This was what I liked about my husband. You never knew what he would come up with next. He could be full of fun and surprises! Praise the Lord for a most wonderful safe trip and a wonderful husband who agreed to let me go on this trip. It's wonderful to be home again with Clint!

I believe it was in 2007 that Clint and I decided we should go visit Steve and Barb and also take Clint's oldest brother Tom with us. Again it was the month of March. This time we took a different route down through Kansas and Missouri. Clint didn't like driving in the cities and so he let me drive through Kansas City and St. Louis. I took the wrong exit and had to drive right down through the middle of St. Louis. It was a little stressful but we got back on our right freeway, headed for Kentucky.

On this trip we had the great privilege of going to Nashville, Kentucky to visit the Grand Ole Opera. It was St. Patrick's Day and Barb had purchased tickets for us to attend the show. Some of the special singers performing were Connie Smith and Jim Ed Brown and others. This was a real treat for Tom, Clint and me. It was one of those "once in a lifetime" experiences. Before we knew it the time came for us to return to our home in Nebraska. I must add though, we didn't drive through St. Louis like we did going down to Kentucky. This time our journey wasn't stressful!!

Clint and I made two trips to Clarkston—one with our slide in camper and the other with our motor home. It was, in fact, during one of my visits that Clint called me about this motor home and ask what I thought about purchasing it. I said, "Yes, I think it would really be nice." The motor home had a frig, microwave, bathroom, stove and oven, plenty of storage space, and places for about six people to sleep. Sounded like a good deal to me!

This very motor home did make a trip to Clarkston. It was in 2005 while my dad was living at the River View Assisted Living. This was the trip we traveled around to Whitefish, Montana to visit my Aunt Chrystal and Uncle Ken. After leaving there we traveled around through Glacier National Park. We stayed close to St Helena, Montana. We both agreed we were enjoying our trip so much that we didn't want to go home! This trip took us about three weeks. Both Clint and I needed a rest from the grind of home and knowing that Daddy was being looked after gave us peace of mind. Since Randal and Candy lived far from us it was just nice to savor the time we had with them.

My Life after 2006

I am going to shorten some of the events taking place after the year 2006. Although I continued to keep very busy the story won't be as much in detail. It was much different not having my parents alive now. We three sisters (Esther, Elaine and I) did inherit the little ranch that my folks owned, but we continued to rent it out to the same rancher as before. I was very thankful that Lynn Myers took very good care of the pastures and did not overgraze or expect us to look after the cattle when he was grazing them there. Esther and I had organized a time we could start sorting through stuff and getting rid of what was junk. Finally in 2012 we got ready for a sale, but first I want to tell about some of the things that I was doing before this happened.

My desire was to help some of the new Christians in our church to develop in their Christian walk. There were about five or six ladies that I had a study with and we still get together at least at Christmas and sometimes just to eat together. Over the years things do change and now this Bible study is being led by a newer member of our Church, Chris Andrews. I have always felt that the prayer and Bible study at our church was the foundation of our Church and praise God we are reaching out to new people in our community.

My Brother-in-law and His Dog

I believe it was about July of 2007 when my husband's brother, Tom, came to our house with a little six week old Chihuahua puppy. She was the cutest thing and so tiny. He called her his "Little Girl". He and Clint were out doing something so he left her in the rocking chair on top of a towel. When I came into the room, the puppy was all curled up sleeping. I looked at her and said, "Oh, she looks like a little Tootsie Roll", so after this Clint and I called her "Tootsie". Tom took his Little Girl wherever he went most of the time.

One week-end Clint and I took off for Cody Nebraska to visit my son Rylan and family in our motor home. We did go quite a few places in our motor home even when we went to visit the kids. Anyway, the day after we had gotten to Cody and settled for our visit we got a call from Clint's brother, Jim. He told us that Tom had been in a bad accident and that they had taken him to the Scottsbluff hospital. He had Little Girl with him and they had to put her in the animal clinic just off highway 30. After hearing this, Clint and I felt we had to go and see what we could do about the dog and to find out how Tom was doing. This was Saturday when this all happened so we made our way back to Lewellen that evening and on Sunday morning went to pick up the dog. She knew us well and was so happy to see us. Ever after this Clint and I became Tootsies caretaker. Tom had to be in the hospital for some time and then in the Assisted-Living so he was not able to keep the dog. We tried to take her every time we could to see Tom. This made both of them very happy!

An Auction of My Parents' Things

It was during the month of July 2012 that my sisters and I, as well as my children, started rounding up house hold good and furniture from the ranch. We transported it down to two storage garages in Lewellen so we could prepare for a farm sale on August 25th. My, what a job this was! Some of my sisters' family also helped and this was such a blessing. Our dear friend, Butch Dykes, was our auctioneer. The day of the sale was very nice but we were a bit disappointed that not a lot of people came. Actually the fire whistles blew and a number had to go fight fires. But in all most of the stuff sold and we were able to clean out the garages. I was so glad when that was over; however, we still had stuff of Mom and Dad's which we needed to sort through. This was stored at Clint's and my house to be sorted out later.

Clint's Home going October 2012

Clint was having more trouble with eyesight at this time. I did appreciate that when it came to driving he would say, "Today, you better drive because I'm not seeing very well." Often Clint would take his brother Tom to doctor appointments. On October 4th Tom had an appointment in North Platte at the cancer center. This was one of those times Clint said, "You drive." Off we went. While Clint was with Tom at the cancer center I went to Walmart to do our shopping and then came back for the men. We drove to Ogallala and there we stopped at McDonalds for hamburgers then headed on home.

That afternoon the weatherman reported that our weather was going to change. I decided I better get the rest of my garden things taken care of. There were tomatoes to pick and a few other things that needed caring for. I also was doing exercising at the VOA so felt I better do that as well before finishing with the garden. When I came back from the exercise Clint ask me to help him with cleaning the stove pipe to our wood heater, so I said, "Can you wait just a bit till I bring the rest of these tomatoes in?" and he agreed. I got all the tomatoes in the cellar and came into the house.

As I entered the door Clint said to me, "Oh, I don't feel good!" I looked at him and immediately said, "Honey, have you had a stroke?" because he was talking funny and couldn't move very well. I said, "Shall I call the ambulance?" and of course Clint agreed.

It was a few minutes before the ambulance arrived from Oshkosh. The ambulance crew brought in the gurney and finally got him loaded. I had to do a few things first then drove right up to the Oshkosh hospital to their critical care unit at the back of the hospital. Pastor Lynn was already there waiting. They had Clint checked very thoroughly and were connecting with Scottsbluff hospital deciding what to do. They knew he definitely had had a major stroke and informed me that they thought he should be flown to Scottsbluff by helicopter. I was so tired and stressed out that I ask Pastor Lynn if possibly his wife Vonnie could drive my car to Scottsbluff. Pastor drove on ahead so as to be there at the hospital as soon as possible after the helicopter arrived. Vonnie drove me back to my house in Lewellen to get some clothes and personal things because I didn't know how long I would be staying.

They found that Clint had a cerebral hemorrhage on his brain causing the stroke to affect his whole left side, making him paralyzed. They talked of drilling a hole in his skull to drain the blood but decided to wait to see how things went through the night. Pastor Lynn and Vonnie were so good to help me. I will forever thank them for being with me. They helped me get a motel for the night before returning to Oshkosh about 1:30 a.m.

Next morning I went to the hospital to see Clint. Also, I looked into getting a room at the place where families with loved ones in hospital could stay. They reserved a place for me from this time on.

It was hard to see Clint this way. His whole left side paralyzed and not being able to talk very well. This was now Oct. 5th and we had a number of visitors coming in. I especially remember some of the Don Alexander family and Sue and Mike and Callista coming to see Clint, and Carol and Sharon who lived in the area. It was on Friday I believe that my son Rylan came to spend some time with us. He was such a blessing.

On Sunday afternoon, Rylan had to drive back to Cody because of his teaching. On Monday Linda Cheney brought Clint's brother Tom to visit. Clint had been asking to see Tom. It was Tuesday and my daughter, Roxane, arrived to stay with me. I can't tell you how blessed I felt that two of my children were spending time with me. During this time the doctor talked with us about the possibility of whether to do surgery or just to let it go for a while to see how Clint would revive. I didn't want to see him go through more pain with an operation but we weren't even sure the operation would help. I tried with help of family to do what was best for Clint. I pretty well knew what Clint would want.

Then he was developing pneumonia and his lungs were filling up because he couldn't swallow very well. Roxy and I went back to the motel for the night and next morning after some breakfast went back to Clint's room. He was not doing well but they were trying to make him as comfortable as possible. Roxy and I sat by the bedside and started praying for God's will to be done. During that prayer Roxy looked up and said: "Oh, Mom I think He's going!" I went over by his side and the monitor was showing his heart beat leveling out. My dear Clint was on his way to be with Jesus! It was October 10th at about 10:00 a.m. It was such a comfort to have Roxy right there with me. God has our times in His hands!

Clint's Funeral

Clint's funeral was held on October 16th. I sort of wanted it on the 16th so as to remind me that Clint and I had been married over 16 years. My children all came for the funeral and a number of other relatives including my sister Esther and Elaine and Steve. My son Randal had planned a trip to Omaha and Bartlesville, Oklahoma with his son, Nathaniel. He changed his ticket and flew into Denver so he could attend the funeral.

After the funeral, Randal actually was going to take the bus to Iowa but I said, "Randal, you can just take my car. Don't take the bus!" Then his words were to me, "Well, Mom, why don't you go with me to Iowa and Bartlesville?" He had a missions service to do at Allen's church that weekend. This is what we did and I do thank the Lord for the interlude, how he worked this all out. I needed a break and I got to spend time with my son and my grandson. It gave me a chance to see Oklahoma Wesleyan University again and quite a number of people whom I had known some years before. We drove back to Omaha so that Randal and Nathaniel could take their plane back to Portland. Barb Glissman my good friend in Omaha let me stay with her that night. Then I made my way back to Lewellen to carry on.

CLOSING CHAPTER

After losing my second husband Clinton L. Reeves, on October 10, 2012, it became a different way of life for me. It was hard learning to live alone but I had a wonderful church family and was not far from two of my children, Rylan and family at Cody Nebraska and Roxy and family at North Platte.

One of the things I really appreciated was that Clint and I had decided to buy a new red Dodge Avenger car in July before he passed away in October. The 1997 Chrysler Concord was having some issues and it seemed the right time to update to another new car. This truly was a blessing in my travels.

Being involved in different things at church and school was a great blessing too. It kept me from being lonely. I had Bible studies, helped pastor by playing the piano for the Rest Home and Assisted Living. Of course I missed Clint so much, especially when it came to playing at the Rest homes and Assisted Living. I loved it when we played our accordions together or when playing the piano while he played his harmonicas. I can say I never heard anyone else play harmony as well as Clint did. He truly was the best!

Having my brother-in-law's little Chihuahua dog to care for was nice. Tom Reeves, Clint's brother, gave us his Little Girl to care for after he had to go into Assisted Living and then the Rest Home. She is a very loving little dog and a lot of company for me.

My Second Trip to Africa

In October of 2013, I made my second trip to Africa to visit Randal and his family who are missionaries in Swaziland. This trip was made with two of my sister's -in law, Vivian Lark and Sue Cheney. My son and family had returned to Swaziland as full time missionaries to work in our Bible College there.

I had talked with two of my sister's-in-law, Vivian Lark, and Sue Cheney and asked if they would be interested in going to Africa with me. At that time Orai and Linda Lehman were missionaries in Mozambique. Linda and Vivian of course were sisters, and Sue was our sister-in-law. Sue thought that it sounded very exciting and Vivian thought it would be nice to visit her sister in a new country (Mozambique). So we made our plans to leave early October and would return early November. Vivian and I left from Denver and met Sue who flew from Omaha, at the Atlanta airport in Georgia. From there we all three flew together to Johannesburg where my son Randal met us. Vivian and Sue visited in Mozambique where the Lehmans lived but I stayed with my son and family in Swaziland. It was so nice to be with my grandchildren Marlena, Olivia, William and Clark. Of course big brother Nathaniel was in college at Corban University in Salem, Oregon. It was truly a fun trip with my sisters-in-law.

My Third Trip

Picture of Joy Mission Hill   by Annie Cheney

As I near the finish of writing my book, it is 2017 and I am back in Swaziland visiting my son and his family once again. This time I returned to Southern Africa with my sister-in-law, Kathy Oakes, and my granddaughter, Annie Cheney.

Sitting here on this veranda I am looking out over the beautiful green hills dotted with Swazi brick homes rather than grass thatch huts; a gentle rain is falling and cars and other vehicles are speeding along the highway at the foot of the Joy Mountain. It is a most gorgeous sight, really more than one could ever hope to see in this beautiful little country.

The main reason for this third trip back to Southern Africa is coming back to Zimbabwe, 21 ½ years after my husband's death in Bulawayo. On Monday, January 23 we began our journey headed for Zimbabwe via the Kruger National Game Park. Because my sister-in-law was experiencing her first visit to Africa, we wanted to let her see the animals in the wild. We saw many elephants, giraffe, impala, kudu and African buffalo but didn't see any lions or rhino. With the rainy season on, the grass, underbrush and trees were so thick it was hard to see the animals. We did see a cheetah from a distance that had made a kill. That night we stayed in a lovely thatched roof cabin that held all six of us at Skakuza Camp. From the game park we journeyed to Petersburg to stay the night.

It was a privilege to meet old friends again, Annette and Winston

Callaghan. Annette served us a beautiful evening meal as we shared our family news. That night we stayed in Bolvia Lodge before continuing our journey to Zimbabwe. We prayed at the beginning of our day that God would help us get through the busy borders of South Africa and Zimbabwe. Many people pass through these borders at Masina and Beit Bridge, and we wanted to make good time in order to arrive in Bulawayo before it got late. It isn't wise to travel Zimbabwe roads at dark because one shares these roadways with cattle.

January 26th, Thursday, was a day to remember my wonderful husband, Bob Cheney. Randal took us on a tour of the city. Then at 3:00 p.m. we were invited to the Gonera's home, the very place where Bob and I stayed when Bob had his first attack September 10, 1995. The memories came flooding into my mind as we entered the Gonera's yard. Finally my dream of returning to the place where I was last with my husband was fulfilled. Tears came to my eyes as I gave dear Mrs. Gonera a great big long hug and then shook hands and hugged Mr. Gonera. The memory of that day would never be erased from my mind. The place where my husband collapsed is now a beautiful array of flowers and plants. The narrow hallway where we placed him until the ambulance arrived and the phone and stand further in the hallway where I received the message from the hospital nurse that Bob had died, the actual place was right there in front of my eyes. It all brought so much sadness to my heart and tears to my eyes. Mr. and Mrs. Gonera and I will never forget that dark night, September 18, 1995. But now we have a wonderful hope of meeting in heaven and worshiping our Lord and Savior. Death is not the Victor! Remember Corinthians 15:55-57 "O death, where is your sting? O Hades, where is your victory? The sting of death is sin, and the strength of sin is the law. But thanks be to God, who gives us the victory through our Lord Jesus Christ." Look also at 1 Thessalonians 4:13-18.

I had finally experienced what I had wanted to do for years, to return to the place where my dear husband had departed from this earth on his way to heaven. It was my desire to once again say a big THANK YOU to the Goneras for standing by me. Now I have the fulfillment of this desire. All praise goes to my Savior for carrying me through this tragedy. Psalm 57:1 "Be merciful unto me O God, be merciful to me for my soul trusts in you. Yes, in the shadow of your wings will I make my refuge until these calamities are past.

So now I will sign off till my next trip to Africa. God is so Good, ALL THE TIME!!!

MY CONCLUSION

As I am sitting here with Randal, Candice, their family, and with Annie and Kathy, in Swaziland, Africa at Joy Mission and Emmanuel Wesleyan Bible College. We had beautiful rains last night and early this morning. Looking out the picture windows, I see beautiful green rolling hills and what we missionaries called Joy Mission Hill. This beautiful mountain hill covered in green foliage is the main landmark for this Wesleyan Mission and Bible College. Large and small homes of the Swazis dot this beautiful hillside and one can observe a main highway from Manzini to Big Bend running at the lower base of this mountain. The sounds you hear is a mixture of the bleating of goats, the crowing of the chickens and many cars, buses, trucks and taxis speeding up and down this paved road. Also, there are people walking to the bus stop or just walking along the road. We hear the sounds of children playing at the pre-school. It is a much different scene compared to the first time we arrived in Swaziland, December 2, 1970. There definitely are many signs of progress over the past 47 years. Swaziland is called the little Switzerland of Africa accept here we do not see the mountains covered with snow. Instead, we see green grass, bush and houses large and small clinging to those hillsides.

Coming to the close of my book, and just sitting here in a perfect temperature brings back so many memories of Bob's and my time spent here as missionaries. I would like to dedicate my book in memory of my husband, Robert Alfred Cheney who died Sept. 18, 1995 and to our grandson, Andrew L. Lauber whom we lost April 11th, 2015. Then I want to say how much I appreciate our family and all their support. Since I first started writing, our family has grown to include, as of now, 46 people. We have quite a family tree now with 24 grandchildren—four of them married and seven great-grandchildren.

So to each of these grandchildren and great-grandchildren, I want to say how special you are, not only to this Grandma uGogo, but most of all to God. Never ever forget God loves you more than anyone here on earth. John 3:16 "For God so loved the world that He gave His one and only Son that whoever believes in Him should not perish but have eternal life."

Most of all I give praise and Thanksgiving to my God and Savior Jesus Christ for calling out to me as a child with His convicting power and forgiving my sins as I confessed them to Him. Then in my development into youth, how I learned what it meant to have my life totally committed to Christ and to walk in fellowship with Him down through life.

What My Children Are Doing Today

In this concluding chapter of my book I would like to tell what my children are doing at this time and about their families. I'm so delighted and joyful to report that they are all serving the Lord. This pleases me greatly and I know God is very pleased.

Roxane and Ron Lauber and some of their children are now living near Kearney, Nebraska. Two of their daughters, Alicia and Abby are married and serving God. Roxy and Ron have three grandchildren at this time. Alicia and Steve have Ian and Faith. Abby and Ty have little Hudson. Their son Micah and daughter Michelle work and are taking further education. Michaela finished high school, May, 2016, Aimee, Marcus and Adon are in school. Roxy works in the school where their younger children attend and Ron works for the Good Samaritan Society in Kearney. Ron is also the Bible Teaching Pastor for a new outreach church of the Kearney Grace Fellowship Church. God is blessing them in this new ministry as they reach out to the lost and unchurched in that area.

Allen and Kim Cheney live in Guthrie Center Iowa. Both of them have jobs with the Guthrie County Hospital. Allen is Director of the hospital lab and Kim is Director of the Medical Records department. They attend Faith Bible Church in Panora, Iowa where Allen is an Elder. Kassie (Daughter) and Ryan live south of Guthrie Center and Kassie works as a RN for Guthrie County Hospital in the surgery department and Ryan works for the City of Casey. Their son Kyle and wife, Mackenzie, live in Des Moines, Iowa where Kyle works for Pioneer and Mackenzie works as an RN Supervisor for Unity Point Health Care. Allen and Kim have four grandchildren--Kassie and Ryan's Ryder, Kaleb and Karys and Kyle and Mackenzie's little Frankie.

Drs. Ron and Karla Cheney and family live in Carroll, Iowa with their two younger children, Jared and Joelle, who are in High School. Their oldest daughter, Jessica, is in college preparing to be a veterinarian. Ron is a general surgeon and Karla a pediatrician. Ron has also started a Christian Radio station in the area. He is on the Iowa Board of Medicine which does physician's licensure and discipline, and on the advisory board of the Pan Africa Academy of Christian Surgeons.

Rylan and Amy Cheney and their four younger children, Erin, Ry, Quin and Susie, live in Cody, Nebraska. They attend the local Church of the Sandhills and are very involved. Rylan is the High School teacher for the Science Dept. as well as Sport's Administrator and track and cross country coach. Amy is also very involved in the school system and helps with coaching. Their oldest daughter Anlan (Annie) is about to receive her Master's Degree in

Journalism and communication and Gillian   (the daughter who was healed of cancer) is getting her nursing degree.

Randal, our youngest son and his wife, Candice, along with their three youngest children, Olivia, William and Clark are missionaries living in Swaziland in Southern Africa. They have two older children: Nathaniel who is preparing for Christian Ministry and Marlena who is preparing for Social Work. Randal is working with Christian Education for a number of countries in Africa connected with the Wesleyan Church. Candy is a Registered Nurse using her abilities in areas of Swaziland where needed.

I truly praise God for all my family and the work they are doing. Everyone of this family holds a special place in my heart. May God receive all the Honor, Glory and Praise!

ACKNOWLEDGEMENTS

It is hard to know where to begin to thank the ones who have helped me write my book. I feel honored to have had your help in so many ways. I fear I may forget someone. So if anyone reading my story has contributed in any way, please know that I appreciate all you did, even in the smallest way.

First of all I want to give recognition to my dear mother, Beulah Thornton. She was faithful in saving my weekly letters. From those letters, in a period of about 25 years, I was able to write about our work in Africa and about our family. She has long since departed for heaven, April 10, 2001, but I pray God has rewarded her for her part in missions. She saved those letters and I know she prayed over them and, as well, she and Daddy gave faithfully to missions.

Next a very wonderful dear friend, Lois Dunwoody, offered her services in editing. She spent hours in organizing my stories in chronological order and correcting sentence structure. Lois, what would I have done without your help?? I can never thank you enough. May God reward you.

Kim Cheney, my first daughter-in-law, spent hours and hours typing out my handwritten stories from stacks of notebooks I had filled. Thank you, Kim. You were so kind and such a help to me. To my five children, Roxane, Allen, Ron, Rylan, and Randal, my daughters-in-law, Kim, Karla, Amy,

Candice and son-in-law Ron, I say thank you for giving me so much encouragement. Allen said to me, "Mom, you just get your book written and we will see that it gets printed." Thanks, Allen!

Another group that more recently I have appreciated is "The Writer's Club" from Oshkosh area. You so eagerly welcomed me into your group and listened to bits and pieces of my story in various things I wrote. Thanks you for giving me encouraging remarks.

A resounding thank you goes to Linda and Orai Lehman, my husband's sister and her husband, for standing with me during my husband's death. You were such a comfort and help to me in the hardest thing I ever went through in my life.

I want to thank my missionary son, Randal Cheney, and his wife, Candice as well as their children. You made the trip back to Zimbabwe possible the first time, 21 years after Bob's death. Thank you, to three very special granddaughters, Marlena, Olivia, and Annie, for preparing our meals and serving Aunt Kathy and me tea while we were in Bulawayo. You treated us like Queens! May God bless you.

Baby Grace Eva with Mom and Dad

My Dad and I

Grace Eva with baby carriage and turkeys

Dad, Mom, Esther and Myself

First year of school in the sandhills

My favorite teacher Alta Graham

Family picture with Elaine, Esther and Myself

My High School Graduation picture

Grace Eva at Bethel College

Our wedding 1957

At the Denver Airport before leaving for Africa 1970

Missionaries we served with in Swaziland 1971, Alberta Lemley, The Ramsays and The Lehmans

384

On top of Phonjawane Mountain in Swaziland 1971

Family at Rhodes grave 1979

Emmanuel Wesleyan Bible College in Swaziland

Joy Mission in Swaziland

Dedication of Regional Superintendent's house

Building Regional Superintendent's house, Joy Mission

The Sigwanes, National Regional Superintendent of Southern Africa

Graduation at EWBC

Baptism Service in Zimbabwe

Eva teaching a Typing class

Robert Cheney Family June 2017 photo by David Graham

Dee p 222
me p 102

Made in the USA
Columbia, SC
06 August 2017